SIXTH EDITION

GROWING UP WITH LITERATURE

SIXTH EDITION

GROWING UP WITH
LITERATURE

Walter E. Sawyer, EdD
Foreword by Francis P. Hodge
Hodge Podge Books, Albany, NY

 CENGAGE

Australia • Brazil • Mexico • Singapore • United Kingdom • United States

CENGAGE

Growing Up With Literature, **Sixth Edition**

Walter E. Sawyer, EdD

Publisher/Executive Editor: Linda Schreiber-Ganster

Acquisitions Editor: Mark Kerr

Assistant Editor: Rebecca Dashiell

Technology Project Manager: Dennis Fitzgerald

Editorial Assistant: Genevieve Allen

Marketing Assistant/Associate: Dimitri Hagnere

Marketing Manager: Kara Kindstrom-Parsons

Marketing Communications Manager: Tami Strang

Production Manager: Matt Ballantyne

Content Project Management: PreMediaGlobal

Senior Art Director: Jennifer Wahi

Cover Image: Jeff Bane at CMB Design

Cover Designer: Jeff Bane at CMB Design

Production House/Compositor: PreMediaGlobal

For product information and technology assistance, contact us at **Cengage Customer & Sales Support, 1-800-354-9706 or support.cengage.com.**

For permission to use material from this text or product, submit all requests online at **www.cengage.com/permissions.**

Library of Congress Control Number: 2010940903

ISBN-13: 978-1-111-34265-4
ISBN-10: 1-111-34265-2

Cengage
20 Channel Street
Boston, MA 02210
USA

Cengage is a leading provider of customized learning solutions with employees residing in nearly 40 different countries and sales in more than 125 countries around the world. Find your local representative at: **www.cengage.com.**

Cengage products are represented in Canada by Nelson Education, Ltd.

To learn more about Cengage platforms and services, register or access your online learning solution, or purchase materials for your course, visit **www.cengage.com.**

Printed in the United States of America
Print Number: 06   Print Year: 2020

DEDICATION

To Jean C. Sawyer, who truly understands the beauty and power of literature.

W.S.

CONTENTS

CHAPTER 1

CHAPTER 5

MAGIC MOTIVATIONS 151

CHAPTER 6

HOW MANY WAYS CAN A STORY BE TOLD? 177

CHAPTER 8

BIBLIOTHERAPY: USING BOOKS TO HEAL 259

CHAPTER 9

USING COMMERCIAL AND EDUCATIONAL MEDIA 293

CHAPTER 10

INVOLVING THE COMMUNITY 317

FOREWORD

BY FRANCIS P. HODGE

I am delighted to introduce the sixth edition of *Growing Up with Literature*. Many texts are available emphasizing classroom instruction in literature at all grade levels. Many texts also are on the market offering guidance to parents about the importance of books in the development of young children. This text, with 200 newly added children's book titles, takes the best of the aforementioned examples and treats the continuity of one to the other. This feature distinguishes *Growing Up with Literature* from many other contemporary literature-related texts.

Dr. Walter Sawyer is eminently qualified to address this topic. I have known Dr. Sawyer, who is both a father and an educator, for over thirty-five years. He has worked diligently with his own children in their development as literate human beings. He has studied and guided school programs aimed at improving literary facility among school children, particularly at the early childhood level.

Dr. Sawyer's approach is truly grassroots in origin. He starts with the WHYS and carefully leads the early childhood educator and the parent along the road to the WHAT, WHYS, and the HOWS. His approach is a carefully conceived road map of operational ideas and suggestions. His points have been tested and have proven successful in numerous cases. He offers alternatives, suggesting titles that might be utilized; he indicates areas of concern; and, significantly, he advises caution and thoughtful planning by both parents and teachers.

Encouraging a love for literature, developing good readers, and making reading an integral part of everyday life are so important for young readers. Without a foundation from home and early childhood, children often experience difficulty in school, especially in mastery of reading skills. Working through the suggestions and recommendations offered by Dr. Sawyer in *Growing Up with Literature* can instill in young readers a love for and understanding of literature.

PREFACE

TO THE SIXTH EDITION

The sixth edition of *Growing Up with Literature* is a book that celebrates the interaction that can take place when quality literature is shared with children. It is a comprehensive guide for the individual wishing to learn how to use children's books effectively in early childhood programs. Sections are included on selecting appropriate books, motivating children to participate in the experience, integrating literature into a program, and managing the process. Although the primary audience for this text is practitioners in early childhood education programs, parents will find a wealth of information here as well.

Philosophy of the Book

The philosophy of the book is to present literature as a primary focus of an educational program rather than as an isolated feature used only at storytime. This approach is supported by much of the current thinking, theory, and research on language development and emergent literacy. While the foundation of the book rests on firm conceptual ground, the practical aspects of working with children are at the forefront of the presentation. The book is a hands-on tool for both short- and long-range program planning. It explains such concepts as the link between language and thinking, the role of technology, and emerging literacy in easily understood terms that are easily translated into classroom practice.

The text, which focuses exclusively on picture books for young children, makes a valuable contribution to the field of early childhood education. Few practical books on using literature in early childhood programs are based upon the thinking, research, and theory on emerging literacy. *Growing Up with Literature* provides a wealth of practical ideas and strategies that can be implemented in the classroom. The clear, concise explanations describing the process of implementation ensure their transfer. In addition, hundreds of books appropriate for young readers are cited. A wide range of titles is used to familiarize the reader with the variety of books available. The citations range from classics to the latest contemporary publications. The sixth edition includes a listing of two hundred additional children's book citations. They represent the best of children's titles published over the last few years.

Organization and Key Content

Many special features are included. First, and most important, is the approach stressed within the book. The focus is on integrating literature as an integral part of education throughout all areas of the curriculum. This edition also includes expanded sections about nonfiction and multicultural titles for young children. Each chapter includes both references for further reading and a set of questions for thought and discussion. The questions tend not to seek rote types of answers.

Rather, they require a more careful analysis of the material in the chapter in order to give a thoughtful and logical response. The chapters of this book are arranged in an order that provides a logical development to understanding an early childhood literature program. They may, however, be read in any order that suits the needs of the reader. Chapter 1 provides an introduction, while Chapter 2 describes a variety of physical environments for enhancing the sharing of literature. Chapters 3 and 4 focus on literature itself. They describe criteria for selecting quality books and strategies for using various types of literature with children.

Chapters 5 and 6 describe a variety of procedures for the motivational and creative sharing of literature. Chapter 7 explores the critical aspect of integrating literature with all parts of the curriculum. It provides a variety of approaches and suggestions for developing units. Chapter 8 addresses ways of using books to assist children with their emotional understanding of the world through bibliotherapy and a cautionary note on didacticism. Chapter 9 discusses the influence of television, media, and technology on literature and how they can be used effectively with children. Finally, Chapter 10 summarizes the concept of using the community in conjunction with a literature program for children.

New to This Edition

Major changes and updates found throughout the entire book include:

- Two hundred of the best new children's literature titles are suggested for use in activities outlined in the book. These new titles were selected for their relevance, interest, and beauty. Also included are strategies for locating virtually any picture book desired.
- Key terms and phrases within the context of each are identified with boldface type.
- The *Tips for Teachers* sections have been expanded.

Major changes and updates by specific chapters include:

- Chapter 1 updates research on the increased active and background electronic video screen viewing by young children and its effect on literacy.
- Chapter 2 includes an increased emphasis on children's books about the varieties of families and cultural backgrounds that young children experience.
- Chapter 3 presents a new section about children's books that include the concept of sexual orientation as well as how to approach the topic.
- Chapter 4 provides new content on the history of children's literature, accommodating children with special needs, and a new section dealing with controversial topics found in children's books (e.g. same sex marriage, child abuse, incarceration of a family member).
- Chapter 5 includes new material on guidelines for the development of good listening skills, strategies for using formative and summative evaluation of children's learning, and tools for emphasizing positive reinforcement as a classroom management strategy.
- Chapter 6 describes new ways for involving children, parents, and community members in the story telling experience.
- Chapter 7 contains new tools for planning literary units and a revised section on holidays to better meet the needs of children from diverse backgrounds.
- Chapter 8 presents new material addressing the issues of racial bias, traumatic brain injury, the death of a friend or family member, and Internet resources for bibliotherapy.
- Chapter 9 includes revised material on the use of computers, literature-related CDs, DVDs, on-line programs, podcasts, digital imaging, and the Internet, as well as new material on digital literacy.
- Chapter 10 provides new information on websites that provide for digital field trips to story book settings and new strategies for increasing the

involvement of children, parents, and community members in the education of children.

Features

Tips for Teachers

This feature is presented in highlighted boxes in numerous locations throughout the chapters, and is directly related to the content in the surrounding text. Each of the tips found here is a practical idea for using the concepts when working with children.

End of Chapter Resources

- Summary—This section, found at the end of each chapter, serves to remind the readers of the major ideas and concepts presented. It can be a useful tool allowing readers to reflect upon whether they feel comfortable with the degree of their new knowledge.

- Questions for Thought and Discussion—These questions provide an opportunity to demonstrate an understanding of the material presented in the chapter. Rather than focusing on rote recall of information, these questions require readers to demonstrate comprehension, analysis, synthesis, and evaluation of the material they have learned.

- Children's Books Cited—This section includes a listing of every children's book noted or described in the chapter, including publication information.

- Selected References and Resources—This section includes all of the professional literature cited in the text as well as other sources of related information that readers may wish to explore.

  Internet References and Helpful Websites—This section includes all of the websites cited in the text as well as other websites containing related information that readers may wish to explore. The author and Cengage Learning affirm that the Website URLs referenced herein were accurate at the time of printing. However, due to the fluid nature of the Internet, we cannot guarantee their accuracy for the life of the edition.

Appendices

The four appendices at the end of the book which provide readers with a wealth of additional resources. Appendix A provides a listing of major publishers and suppliers of children's literature, including contact information. Appendix B presents a complete listing of all of the Caldecott Medal winning books, authors, and illustrators. Appendix C provides a complete thematic unit outline for preschoolers on the topic of bears, giving readers a practical model for understanding the material presented in the book. Appendix D lists numerous classic and contemporary children's books by subject heading and lists numerous classic and contemporary children's book authors by their cultural background.

Ancillaries

Instructor's Manual

The Instructor's Manual, available online, contains answers to the questions for thought and discussion at the end of each chapter, as well as supplementary activities and projects.

Companion Website

The companion website to accompany the sixth edition of *Growing Up with Literature* contains many features to help focus your understanding of children's literature:

- Author's biography—find out more about the author and his or her motivation for writing this book.
- Checklist with criteria for selecting nonfiction and multicultural children's literature and evaluating a classroom literary environment.
- Web links to homepages of children's book authors.
- Sample evaluations.
- Tables as organizational tools.
- Full-color photos of selected children's book covers.
- Extension Activities corresponding to each chapter; apply what you have learned to your own classroom.

You can find the *Growing Up with Literature* companion website at www.cengage.com/education/sawyer.

ABOUT THE AUTHOR

Walter Sawyer is a graduate of Siena College, Assumption College, and the State University of New York at Albany. He holds B.A., M.A., and EdD degrees. He is certified in and has worked at all levels of education from nursery school through graduate school. Currently an independent consultant and writer, he served for many years as an administrator in the Waterford-Halfmoon School District in upstate New York while teaching graduate courses in the field of literacy at Russell Sage College. He has been an active member at all levels of the International Reading Association, and is past president of a local reading council. He was named "Educator of the Year" in 1994 by the School Administrators Association of New York State. He has a deep personal interest in storytelling and has published over sixty articles, books, papers, and chapters in the field of literacy. He is also author of *The Storm,* a children's picture book (Katonah, NY: Richard C. Owen, 1999).

ACKNOWLEDGMENTS

The author would like to extend an acknowledgment to several key people in this endeavor: To Jean Sawyer who listened to and provided critical feedback on many of the chapters in addition to watching the children. To the authors and storytellers who provided photographs for this book. To the publishers who generously granted permission to reprint covers of their children's books. To Frank Hodge for the Foreword to this book and for guiding us all down the right road. To my editors for their support and encouragement. To the following reviewers whose perceptive feedback and useful comments were both insightful and helpful:

Donna Graham
  Ozarks Technical Community College
  Springfield, MO

Deborah Ann Jensen
  Hunter College—CUNY
  New York, NY

Amy M. McGraw
  Iowa Western Community College
  Council Bluffs, IA

Donna Rafanello
  Long Beach City College
  Long Beach, CA

Claire Batt-Vandenburg
  Lansing Community College
  Lansing, MI

Betty Ann Watson
  Harding University
  Searcy, AR

Bonita Friend Williams
  Columbus State University
  Columbus, GA

WHAT'S SO SPECIAL ABOUT LITERATURE?

Making reading a joyful experience for children lies at the heart of this book. Introduced correctly, **literature** can be seen throughout life as the friend and companion it deserves to be. In order for this to happen, the adults who work with young children must foster this relationship with literature in their own lives. One cannot teach children to love reading and literature without possessing that same love. Children are quite perceptive; they can often quickly spot false enthusiasm. This chapter begins with an exploration about the value of literature in terms of connecting with the world, supporting positive attitudes, and creating connections with others. This is followed by an examination of the concept of literacy and how authors, illustrators, and readers contribute to helping young children learn to read.

Some of the best books written today are written for children. The books available for children are a wonderful place to begin or to extend a love for literature. The success of the strategies suggested in this book will depend on this love.

Literature has a special place in the development of the young child. Stories shared aloud in a warm atmosphere and at an appropriate

A child's world is fresh and new and beautiful, full of wonder and excitement.

—RACHEL CARSON

pace can be the vehicle through which children learn about their world. The technology of television, telecommunications, and computer science sends information at us at an ever increasing speed and in greater abundance than ever before. However, people are not always capable of processing this information in any meaningful way. This is true for adults and it is true for children. When the amount of information is too great and the speed too rapid, the full meaning is lost. The nuances are not noticed. The subtle humor slips past. The message becomes devoid of emotion.

TIPS FOR TEACHERS

Appendix D lists a variety of children's books for reading aloud, theme development, and sharing with young children. The listing is organized by topic, making it a valuable resource for future use.

Each of the books in the listing has been used many times, with children responding enthusiastically to the stories.

There has been an abundance of research over the past quarter of a century that stresses the importance of books and literature as part of a child's development.

When children come to school already reading or with a deep interest in reading, certain critical facts can often be found in their preschool experiences:

- They usually had books in the home.
- They observed adults reading.
- They were read to by adults.
- They had someone to talk to about books, reading, and literature.

While experience is a powerful teacher for a young child, books and literature can have a profound influence as well. Early in life, children strive for meaning.

They try to find out how things work. They attempt to learn how people respond to them and what control they have over their environment. Young children need experiences with print that let them hear, tell, create, and explore the world around themselves as they seek to find meaning (Davis & Williams, 1994). The purpose of literature and education is to help people arrive at this meaning. Given this, a broad exposure to literature is a critical component of child development.

Although families acknowledge the importance of books and reading, and there is an increasing number of children's books published each year, it is still difficult to foster literacy development. Our society seems to raise the value of the celebrity culture while trying to foster a more balanced environment for children. The listing of the top fifty magazines cited by the Magazine Publishers of America is tilted dramatically toward those focused on celebrities seen on television. Research (Nielsen Wire, 2009) has found television viewing by young children is at an all time high. Children aged two to five watch an average of twenty-five hours of TV per week plus another seven hours of DVDs, video games and computers. Children aged six to eleven watch an average of twenty-two hours of TV per week plus another six hours of DVDs, video games, and computers. Added to this is background television, which disrupts children's play. Background television refers to a situation where a television is on in the child's environment, perhaps being viewed by an adult, while the child is not specifically attending to it. These numbers are also increased by one to two hours per day for children who attend home-based daycare centers as opposed to center-based care (Christakis & Garrison, 2009).

Recent research on **brain development** and television viewing provides some important information. Citing research conducted over the past several decades, the National Institute on Media and the Family reports that television's impact can vary depending on the quantity and quality of the viewing. For example, preschoolers who watch some carefully created developmentally appropriate programs such as *Sesame Street* actually improve their literacy skills compared with those who do little or no viewing. Viewers of extended amounts of cartoons and general entertainment do more poorly. The institute also reports on studies that conclude that a large amount of television viewing over an extended period of time can negatively influence the development of brain neural networks as well as decrease the time devoted to other literacy and cognitive development activities. In a separate study, Christakis, Zimmerman, DiGuiseppe, and McCarthy (2004) also concluded that attentional problems are linked to television viewing, particularly when the quality is not controlled by parents and other caregivers. Media and marketing stereotypes of boys as players, superheroes, slackers, and competitors are a constant negative force in the culture according to Brown, Lamb, and Tappan (2009).

Murray (2001) describes the three major **negative social effects** (aggression, desensitization, fear) related to viewing **television violence**, identified as a result of thirty years of research. Increased aggressive behavior occurs due to changes in attitudes that come to accept the use of aggression as a problem-solving strategy. As children increase their exposure to televised violence they become not only less sensitive to violence but also more accepting of it as a part of everyday life. Television and video game violence can also trigger feelings of innate fear as viewers come to believe in an unrealistically high risk of violence to themselves. In his own study using magnetic resonance imaging (MRI) for brain mapping, Murray found that exposure to televised violence activated brain areas involved with arousal, detection of threat, memory encoding/retrieval, and motor programming. He subsequently described his findings as similar to the threat perception and memory storage found in posttraumatic stress disorder in terms of the emotional processing of the televised violence.

Young children should be encouraged to develop interests and attitudes toward reading and literature that will stay with them throughout their lives. Reading is about feelings and relationships. It connects the reader to the author, to the characters, and to those sharing in the reading of the story. Such attributes can help children become competent students and thoughtful adults. Literature will enrich their lives and help them find meaning in their existence.

THE VALUE OF LITERATURE

Literature serves many needs and imparts many values. Literature helps to establish the values of appreciating the world, developing a positive self-image, and understanding the connection between all peoples of the world. The most important value, however, is the love of books and the personal enjoyment they can bring.

Although literature may not appear as spectacular as a computer game or television program, it provides something that neither of them can. Children and adults often need time to reflect on their experiences. Allowing time to think about the content can result in deeper learning and understanding. One can always go back to a book to reread an enjoyable, confusing, or important part. This often cannot be done with other media. For example, a child's first experience with snow and playing in the snow can be thrilling. To make it even more meaningful and memorable, one might share Kim Lewis's touching tale, *First Snow,* set in the snowy whiteness of northern England. Other good choices include *Snow-song Whistling,* a nostalgic look at rural New England by Karen Lotz, and *When Winter Comes* by Robert Maass. A related story based on a German folktale is *Grandmother Winter* by Phyllis Root. This tale tells of a grandmother with her snow white geese preparing for the season of winter, which she truly loves.

TIPS FOR TEACHERS

Encourage children to relate their experiences to the story being read.

- Ask, "Can anyone tell us about a pet cat or dog?"
- Keep the child speaking by responding with, "What happened next?"
- Let children finish their explanations.
- Use open-ended questions.

If a child seems reluctant about playing in the snow, one might read Emily Arnold McCully's *First Snow.* Told entirely in illustrations, it is the story of the smallest member of a mouse family who overcomes a hesitancy to play in the snow. Each of these books can be shared over and over again with a child.

The issue is not a matter of literature being positive and technology being negative. Rather, it is more a problem of balance. Both may be used for helping children develop in appropriate ways. There is certainly a need for children to be aware of the technology of their world. It will be an important part of their lives. However, it is equally important for books and literature to be an integral part of living. Literature can help children comprehend their world, build positive attitudes, and make a connection with their humanity.

Learning about the World

Through books, children can both learn about and **make sense of their world**. They learn about their world when books inform about or explain various parts of it. In so doing, books can also arouse the curiosity of children. After reading

Children should feel comfortable with books.

about something, youngsters will often seek to learn more about it. They may request similar books. They may re-create scenes from the book.

Children can understand their world better through the reinforcement of books. They may have experienced or seen something they do not fully understand. By learning more about it in books, they are often better able to achieve an accurate understanding. When plans are made for children to see or experience something new, books about the topic can be shared prior to the experience. If a trip to the zoo or a fair is planned, one might choose *The Pumpkin Fair* by Eve Bunting. If it is an agricultural fair, *Higgledy-Piggledy Chicks* by Barbara Joose is just the book with its tale of danger, mischievous chicks, and a mother hen who is always there for them. *Peek-A-Zoo* by Marie Cimarusti engages younger children by having them lift flaps for clues to identify the animals by the sounds they make. Books will enable children to have more meaningful experiences. Learning is a process of relating new things to things that are already known. Because the pages of books can be studied, reread, and thought about over time, books are ideal tools for helping children learn and understand. However, do not wait for the right theme to come along to introduce a great book. Books should be chosen and read frequently just because they contain great stories or they contain ideas and values that should be shared on a regular basis.

Building Positive Attitudes

Besides learning about their world, it is critically important that children develop **positive attitudes** about many things. They need to develop positive self-esteem and to see themselves as competent human beings capable of caring and of being loved. They need to develop tolerance for others who may not share their beliefs or who may be different from themselves in various ways. They need to develop a curiosity about learning and life. Books and literature can become primary tools for developing and satisfying that curiosity.

Self-Esteem. Literature can help children develop **positive self-images** in a stressful world. Economic hardships, crime, drugs, and conflicts in the world may be readily apparent even to young children. Family and health problems may be factors children are dealing with as well. Parental love is strong and usually exists even when there is tremendous hardship. The concept of parental love can be reinforced with books such as *The Mouse That Jack Built* by Cyndy Szekere and *Koala Lou* by Mem Fox. In the latter story, Australian author/educator Mem Fox illustrates parental love in its purest form. The patience found in parental love is brought out by Susan Middleton Elya in *Bebe Goes to the Beach*, an English/Spanish-language story about how Mama just wants to relax on the beach, while Bebe keeps things going at a lively pace until she tires herself out. Two children discover the love found in a family in *Kitchen Dance* by Maurice Manning. They wake up at night to discover Mama and Papa happily singing and dancing in the kitchen. The parents eagerly sweep the two children into the act in this wonderful bedtime book. In *Waiting for Gregory,* Kimberly Willis Holt gives voice to the idea that siblings as well as parents are involved in the birth of a new baby. Through books, children can identify with others like themselves. They can see how others deal with similar problems. By sharing a story with an adult, children can be encouraged to talk about some of these issues.

Literature can help children define their feelings and develop a sense of self. Perceptive adults can choose stories that mirror the child's situation or are at least related to the situation. Reading about others who are attempting to make sense of a similar situation can bring hope. Learning that some feelings are normal can enable children to understand that they themselves are normal. They can learn that there is no need for guilt. In *Clumsy Crab,* Ruth Galloway tells how Nipper the crab hates his claws because they always seem to get in his way. Later in the story, Nipper rescues an octopus from the seaweed and learns that everyone has a special gift. In *Adios* by Susan Middleton, Little Piggy has mixed feelings about selling at the family yard sale the tricycle that he has grown too big to use. The rhyming narrative interspersed with Spanish words explores with sensitivity the idea of letting go of parts of childhood.

Many books explore the idea of **self-concept**. Many address this as an issue of developing relationships among siblings and peers. Watty Piper's classic, *The Little Engine That Could,* has long been used in this way. The importance of developing relationships with new friends can be explored in *Baby Duck's New Friend* by Frank Asch and Devin Asch. In this tale, a young duck learns a lesson about relating to others and discovers something new about himself. The problem of childhood obesity can have a negative effect on children's self-concept, and it is important not to add to those feelings by drawing additional attention to it. Nancy Carlson deals with the issue from a positive angle by promoting exercise and a healthy lifestyle in *Get Up and Go!* The lively characters in this story are not depicted as idealistically thin.

Tolerance of Others. Literature can help children understand how they fit in and how important it is to relate to others. Each year sees an increase in the publication of multicultural children's books. By sharing these books, children can grow up appreciating many different people and cultures.

Literature, through its art, imagery, humor, and empathetic characters, provides a teaching tool for developing **tolerance**. By learning how characters in stories develop solutions to social problems, children can begin to assume a role in goal setting and limit setting for their own behavior.

There are wonderful books that explore the nature of differences among people and the acceptance of others. *Watch Out for the Chicken Feet in Your Soup* by Tomie dePaola explores the acceptance by a young boy of his grandmother and her Old World habits. *Jamari's Drum* by Eboni Bynum and Roland Jackson identifies the importance of culture, tradition, and family through a story of African drumming. Two young girls near a temple in Vietnam demonstrate how all cultures value good deeds in *Fly Free* by Roseanne Thong. Karen English brings readers a look at traditional weddings in Pakistan in *Nadia's Hands. Bearsie Bear and the Surprise Sleepover* by Bernard Waber raises the potential for accommodation.

The relationship between parent and child is universal, even when there are bumps in the road. *Hush! A Thai Lullaby* by Minfong Ho shows a mother in Thailand putting her baby to sleep. Using a repeated rhyme, the mother goes to each of the animals in an attempt to quiet them down so that her baby can get to sleep. In the end, it is the mother who falls asleep while the baby stays awake enjoying the night sounds. The strong protective nature in the father/son relationship is shown by Karen Williams in *A Beach Tail.* From Australia, Mem Fox gives us the delightful *Harriet, You'll Drive Me Wild!,* in which a pesky child and her harried mother connect in their special way. Sometimes, two different cultures are found in the same family. This is the case in *Halmoni's Day* by Edna Coe Bercaw. In this story, Jennifer, a Korean American, brings her grandmother

Halmoni to school on grandparent's day. The problem is that Halmoni is visiting from Korea, wears only traditional Korean clothes, and does not speak a word of English. Jennifer fears that she will be embarrassed. With her mother as a translator, Jennifer is surprised by her classmates' positive reaction as Halmoni tells of her childhood in wartime Korea. Set in Mexico, Tony Johnston's *My Abuelita* portrays a flight of fancy involving a child and her grandmother with its universal theme of intergenerational love. Though not specific to a culture, *The Family Book* by Todd Parr explores the love found in all kinds of families.

Adults who are successful in working well with others can provide good **role models**. They tend to know how to have their needs met in society while pleasing others at the same time. Besides providing a role model, adults work to set realistic goals and limits for group interaction. Providing appropriate role models is a powerful instructional tool.

A particularly useful tool in this area is *Multicultural and Multilingual Literacy and Language: Context and Practices,* the publication edited by Boyd, Brock, and Rosendal (2003). It provides information and strategies to help those working with young children to foster self-identity, empathetic interaction, critical thinking skills, and the confidence to advocate for tolerance. The work provides information on creating a positive environment, implementing a sensitive program, and integrating these ideas throughout an early childhood program.

Curiosity about Life. Children possess a **curiosity** about the world around them. They want to know about things and places. They want to know about different people. They are proud of the things they have learned. Keeping this sense of wonder alive through a literacy program that includes a sound read-aloud component will help to encourage success in later schooling and in life. Books keep introducing new and fascinating topics. They encourage children to ask more questions and to seek more answers.

TIPS FOR TEACHERS

Praise children when they demonstrate a skill or ability.

- Say, "You recognized the letter 'S,' Susan, just like in your name."
- Comment, "When you told your story, you made it sound so funny."
- Smile, nod, and respond when children speak to you.
- Acknowledge children's interest and enthusiasm and other intangible responses.

Interest and pleasure in reading are often enhanced by the good feelings shared in reading a book together.

If children are to succeed in later schooling, it is critical that they want to learn and succeed. Although children can be forced to learn bits and pieces of isolated reading skills, no amount of pressure can force children beyond their capability. Exerting this kind of pressure on young children can be destructive to their desire to learn and read. Pressure cannot force them to be curious and enthusiastic about books and literature once they have decided that reading is tedious, dull, and boring. Once the desire to better understand one's self and life is lost, it is difficult to revive it. It is far better for adults to focus on sharing appropriate stories that foster self-esteem, a tolerance for others, and a curiosity about life.

The Human Connection

Reading a book with a child can do many things for child and reader alike. For example, *Feeling Thankful* by Shelley Rotner and Sheila Kelly provides the reader and child with an opportunity to pause and talk about things they are thankful for as they explore the words and photographs in the book. *Twinkle, Star of the Week* by Joan Holub can spark a discussion about what it means to feel good about yourself. *The* sharing that emerges from the relationship creates an important human connection. There is a **personal interaction** between the child and reader. There is time for the reader to react to the child's delight, confusion, anger, or fear. There is a feeling of warmth and safety for the child in the physical presence of the reader. The reader can assure the child that all is well and detect unasked questions. The book can be stopped or reread. Discussion can take place at any point without destroying the overall experience of the story.

The book becomes much more than a set of papers with markings and illustrations. The sound and rhythm of language can be slowed down, speeded up, made louder, or made to express emotions. The beauty of the language and the story can be developed in a manner appropriate to the children. The illustrations and photographs in the book can be touched, studied, discussed, and returned to as the story goes along. All of this is created within the relationship developed by the child and the reader.

EMERGING LITERACY AND LITERATURE

The National Association for the Education of Young Children (2005) identifies three key kinds of information that should always be used when working with young children in order to create developmentally appropriate practices. The first is a knowledge of **child development** and **learning**. This knowledge of age-related characteristics helps adults to develop materials and plan activities that will be healthy, engaging, and challenging to children. The second kind of knowledge is about the **capabilities** and **interests** of individual children, which is necessary in order to adapt and respond to those individuals. The third is a knowledge of the social and **cultural environment** of the lives of children. This information enables adults to develop meaningful learning experiences that are also respectful of the social and cultural environments of the children.

All adults want children to learn to read. However, there has been substantial debate as to when the teaching of reading should begin. Should reading skills be taught to preschool children? Should formal reading instruction be delayed until the child reaches seven years of age? Should the first-grade curriculum be pushed down into the kindergarten? Should children who have not mastered kindergarten readiness skills enter a transitional program between kindergarten and first grade until they have mastered the skills?

The answers to these questions depend on what is actually meant by the word "reading." **Reading is the acquisition of meaning from a written text**. The focus is on meaning. In view of this, children begin the process of learning to read from the moment of birth. They are engaged in learning to read when they first begin to listen for the voice of a parent, the rhythm of a story, or the soothing sounds of a lullaby. Some may argue that the very young child is using only listening skills, but this distinction between listening and reading is an artificial one. The two are inextricably related to each other; each supports the other. In any case, even very young children are learning about books when stories are shared. They learn how to hold them, what to do when you finish a page, that the sentences go from left to right, and that words have meanings.

Frank Smith, an educator who has studied, researched, and described the emergence of literacy for more than half a century, provides a brilliant summary of this concept in *Reading without Nonsense* (2005). He begins with the assumption that although not all children learn to do it at the same time, reading is a natural act much like talking. That is, children do not learn speech through a set of lessons and skills exercises. Children learn to speak by living in a non-threatening environment with others, usually adults and older siblings, whom they observe using oral language to communicate. They see that the oral language has meaning and so they begin to make speech and use language themselves to communicate meaning. Just like oral language, reading should always make sense if it is to be learned effectively. Children learn to read by reading, even if an adult does some or most of the reading for them at the initial stages.

Smith applies this framework of reading in his criticism of the manner in which **letter recognition** and **phonics skills** are frequently taught as a precursor step in the process of learning to read for meaning. He demonstrates the meaninglessness and discouragement that can come from such an approach. First he notes that phonics at the letter level is both complex and unreliable. For example, putting just two letters together (for example, "ho") can result in a wide range of sounds depending on the word in which they are found (for example, hop, hole, honest, hour, hoop, hoof, and so on). The rules and exceptions to the rules quickly become too numerous for a young learner. Secondly, Smith notes that the average adult reader has mastered approximately 50,000 words by sight without ever sounding out most of them. How could this happen? It happens in the same manner that millions of people learn Chinese, a language that has no alphabet, phonics, or sound–symbol correspondence. It happens because the symbols have meaning; when they are learned, they can be used. Smith, however, does not suggest that phonics skill is not useful. Rather, he contends that it is more useful to start with meaning to get at the sounds of letters and meanings of words. In other words, phonics is most useful if the reader has a good idea of what the words are to begin with. That knowledge typically comes from contextual meaning.

Viewing grade levels as distinct is also an inadequate way of thinking about the way children learn to read. The grade levels in schools are for the convenience of adults rather than children. They enable adults to sort children based on age, ability, cultural awareness, and reading level. Children develop at widely varying rates and learn to read at different times in their development. Expecting all children to learn to read at a certain age or grade is hopelessly naive. Children tend to send signals when they are ready for new challenges. It is up to the adults to do a better job of reading these signals and responding appropriately to them.

There is a need to be aware of how literacy emerges long before formal schooling and to understand the role that literature can play in that emergence. To develop this awareness, one must comprehend the basic theory and research underlying the literacy development of young children. Following this, it is necessary to develop a concept of what is contained in a real literacy curriculum and to couple this concept with a realistic understanding of how reading skills emerge. Based on this view, a set of realistic expectations for individual children can be formulated.

Theory and Research on Literacy

The view held in this text concerning how children learn language and how to read and write is based on both the work of educators over the past century and developmentally appropriate practices. It is a view that has been described variously as a holistic approach, whole language approach, and a whole child approach. Contrary to some comments in the popular media, a **holistic approach** is not the opposite of a skills-based, basal reader, or traditional approach. Rather, it is a set of assumptions and beliefs about children, learning, and language that, if understood, can support the literacy development of children.

Assumptions of a Holistic Approach. As a springboard to understanding a holistic approach, four assumptions are identified:

- Although children are engaged in developing literacy from at least the moment of birth, they develop in different ways at different ages. This means that it's inappropriate to do the same things with all children and expect all children to possess certain language skills at the same age.

- Using a single approach or program to foster literacy in children is inappropriate. Whether it is a commercially developed product or a program developed more informally, there is no single road to literacy.

- Caregivers, parents, and others in children's lives are most valuable when they function as participants in literacy development. Instead of being in control of the learning, they interact, relate, share, and provide feedback to support literacy.

- Language, reading, and writing are not subjects to be studied. Rather, they are tools for thinking about and making sense of the environment and of life.

With these assumptions in mind, we can begin to identify those things that are seen and used in a holistic approach to literacy.

Characteristics of a Holistic Approach. A whole is greater than the sum of its parts. Each of the characteristics of a holistic approach can, and has been, studied as an individual concept (Butler, 1987; Hillman, 2002; Robbins, 1990). Including one or two features of a holistic approach in a more traditional approach, however, misses the spirit or essence. It is the combination of the characteristics that follow that guide caregivers in supporting literacy development.

One of the initial characteristics is the use of **whole texts**. This means that whether language is used orally or in written form such as a storybook, it is used in large enough pieces that it makes sense. If children show interest in learning the name of an animal or how to write their first names, for instance, the skill always has a reference to a meaning. If Jill has difficulty remembering which direction to draw the capital letter "J," we do not insist that she master that letter before encouraging her to write the remaining letters of her name.

This leads to another characteristic, the use of **children's literature** as a key component to literacy development. Although children see and hear language in every corner of their environment, storybooks have a special role. Shared reading, guided reading, repeated readings, and re-creating stories in play provide much of the content of literacy. Through storybooks, children see and hear words, rhythms, and concepts of language.

A holistic approach is **child centered**. Language is about relationships and interactions. Through storybooks, connections are made among the author, child, reader, and text. A characteristic closely related to this is that a holistic approach typically includes numerous cooperative activities. These activities usually involve other children and tend to give all children ample opportunities to practice language and become confident users of language.

A final characteristic of a holistic approach is **parent involvement**. Parents are the first teachers children have; they should continue to serve in that role as other caregivers and teachers become involved. Parents deserve thoughtful explanations of what is involved in literacy development. Caregivers and parents can learn much from each other by sharing observations, stories, and activities for the children.

Theory Supporting a Holistic Approach. The theoretical support for a holistic view of language learning comes from both psychology and reading. The influence of two twentieth-century psychologists continues to be significant. Swiss psychologist Jean Piaget provides key understandings on how children view the world. His work revealed that children actively seek information through play and interaction with their environment. Children categorize the world in ways that may be different from adults. It's important to understand this, because children bring these differing worldviews to early childhood programs and situations (Duckworth, 1987).

Russian psychologist Lev Vygotsky connected the relationship of children to their social environments (Vygotsky, 1986). Through his study, Vygotsky noted that in play, children perform beyond the expectations one would have for their ages.

This "zone of proximal development," as he termed it, becomes the primary source for their development (Vygotsky, Cole, John-Steiner, & Scribner, 2006). In other words, that gap between the actual and expected performance represents the space where learning occurs.

Over the past 100 years, teachers and educators have identified and explored key theoretical components of a holistic view. Louise Rosenblatt (1996) was the first to describe the act of reading as a transaction between the reader and the text. That is, children bring their own experiences to the story and this enables them to establish the meaning of the text. Sylvia Ashton Warner (1986), a pioneering educator in New Zealand, questioned the use of a mandated uniform English reading program for Maori children. She discovered that language learning and reading dramatically increased when she made her instruction totally meaningful to the children.

Using this earlier work as a springboard, educators further refined the concepts and eventually developed the "Language Experience Approach (LEA)" and the shared reading experience, two strategies that continue to successfully support the development of literacy in young children. The LEA begins with a shared common experience for children. That may include a field trip, storybook reading, or collecting leaves on a playground. The experience is accompanied and followed by language and discussion that can lead to the construction of stories, lists, and charts related to the experience. After a number of ideas are generated, the caregiver or teacher records the statements of the children as a story, describing the experience on large sheets of paper or poster board. The language of the child is accepted unless it is incomprehensible. In that case, the child can be asked to restate the idea or it might be paraphrased. With younger children the LEA may consist of a few words or a sentence; older children may create a story with several sentences. The recorder must write quickly, use large, legible manuscript letters, include as many children as possible, use the names of the children in the story, and draw quick sketches about each statement. Finally the story is read, reread, and discussed. It can also be copied, displayed on the wall, or collected into a big book (Dorr, 2006; Ivey & Fisher, 2006). LEA stories can help children develop the schema of a story, increase vocabulary, reinforce left–right and top-to-bottom concepts, and provide opportunities for meaningful reading (Roe, Stoodt-Hill, & Burns, 2007).

The shared reading experience, which encourages the use of children's storybooks as the significant material in teaching reading, was pioneered by New Zealand educator Donald Holdaway. A teacher or caregiver using this approach typically uses an easel and what is called a "Big Book," a version of a book with print and illustrations large enough for all children in a group to see. The children are totally immersed in the reading. Prior to reading aloud, the adult reader might explore the relevant background of the children, introduce new vocabulary, and set the purpose for reading. As the story is read, the reader points to each word. At pauses in the reading, children are encouraged to discuss the possibilities presented by the story, **predict events**, and listen to **confirm their ideas**. Following the reading, children are involved in stating personal responses to the story, rereading the story, and recreating the story in art and play (Fisher & Medvic, 2000).

Research Supporting a Holistic Approach. Over the years during which the theory and strategies for a more holistic approach to literacy were being developed, educational researchers were studying these issues. However, since classrooms, centers, children, and teachers/caregivers are so varied, the behavioral model of empirical research is not an appropriate research tool. Goodman (1989a, 1989b, 2005) also notes that while a controlled experiment seeks to control discrete parts of the environment, in a holistic approach the whole environment must be examined, and that environment is greater than the sum of its parts. Therefore, case study research on single children and ethnographic studies on individual classrooms is the appropriate method for studying a holistic approach (Bissex & Bullock, 1987).

In his research on reading miscues (oral reading errors), Kenneth Goodman learned that readers are constantly in the process of predicting while they read and that they use the reading to confirm or refute their predictions. Based on this, it is known that emergent readers find storybooks easy or difficult, both in miscues and comprehension, depending on how predictable they are. This goes a long way in explaining the additional research that demonstrates that children come to understand phonic relationships more effectively when they are learned as part of the reading process rather than as isolated units in workbooks (Goodman, 2005; Goodman & Goodman, 1978).

An important tool for looking at research is the meta-analysis, a study of studies. In this process, researchers analyze a large number of individual research studies in order to identify a consensus of shared findings and conclusions. It is a powerful tool because it establishes ideas and frameworks in common that are supported by multiple investigations. A meta-analysis of studies on early literacy development research conducted over several decades was conducted by Gunn, Simmons, and Kameenui (1998); it yielded several major findings. Several of the findings are related to the social context of the literacy environment. Although a family's socioeconomic status does not directly contribute to literacy development, other family factors such as interest in academics, learning to read, aspirations for the child, reading in the home, and cultural activities are positively related to literacy. Storybook reading and adult-child interactions are powerful positive factors in literacy development. This is related to a finding that children learn to attend to language and to apply this knowledge by interacting with others who model language functions. Further, it was determined that these ongoing experiences with print help children develop an understanding of the purpose, functions, and conventions of print. In regard to letter recognition and phonemic awareness, skills were developed in these child–adult interactions and these associations were stored in memory. That is, the skills were developed through interactions with adult models using print in a meaningful context. This coincides with a later meta-analysis in which it was concluded that there is no unequivocal evidence of a causal link from **phonemic awareness** to reading and speaking acquisition (Castles & Coltheart, 2004).

A Literacy Curriculum

Over the past few decades there has been an abundance of research on how young children develop literacy. Obviously, literacy develops best in a literate environment. Given the view taken in this book, a literate environment possesses certain features. These features are the experiences and materials that will best enhance the ability of children to derive meaning from their environment. Jerome Harste and Virginia Woodward (1989) have studied early literacy programs for many years. Their research identifies three key aspects of a literate environment:

- Supporting the success of the learner;
- Focusing on learning language; and
- Allowing the learner to explore language.

Each of their points must be considered.

Supporting the Success of the Learner. This concept holds that children tend to learn best from firsthand experiences. The environment should be filled with a variety of printed material. Story time should have a prominent role in a program. Many opportunities should be available for children to read, write, and draw. The physical environment might have a variety of age-appropriate centers set up in such areas as housekeeping, art, music, mathematics, poetry, flannel board, puppet stage, magnetic/chalkboard, writing/publishing, and literature. Finally, the program should make use of the community by both exploring it on field trips and by inviting members of the community to visit.

Focusing on Learning Language. Given the assumption that children acquire literacy skills at different points in their development, one must be willing to invite them to read and write on their own level. Literature should be seen as a vehicle for exploring the world rather than as a tool for teaching reading skills. Reading and writing should be seen as playing, learning language, experimenting with words, sharing meaning, and clarifying thought.

Exploring Language. Language is a complex concept, and mastering it can take a lifetime. Sophisticated strategies are required to fully master language and use it effectively. When there is an abundance of language opportunities and experiences, children learn to be strategic in their attempts at reading and writing. Having parents, teachers, and visitors as models encourages children to attempt more complex language skills. By providing extensive opportunities for them to expand their communication through story times, play, pretending, and dramatizing, adults can help children develop a sense of authorship. **Authorship** is the idea of putting one's unique self into a story. Children may begin to do this by listening, creating, interpreting, reenacting, dramatizing, and discussing stories.

Reading Skills

Learning to read is important and necessary for all children. It occurs best after children have developed a love of stories and an interest in reading. A variety of reading skills are needed to be a competent reader. Some say that a phonetic approach in which children focus on learning the sounds of the letters is best. Others contend that a look–say approach that focuses on learning whole words is the superior approach. Advocates from both sides largely ignore the more important issues. They tend to believe that their position represents the focus of reading. They ignore the fact that reading is more than sounding out words or identifying a list of words. Reading has to do with finding meaning in written text.

Children eventually need to develop both phonetic skills and a store of words that they can recognize on sight. However, they also need to understand other features of language such as semantics, syntactics, and pragmatics. **Semantics** refers to the meanings that words possess. Since the purpose of reading is to get meaning, understanding the meanings of words is critical to true reading. **Syntax** refers to the parts of speech. Nouns are different from verbs and verbs are different from adjectives. Each does something different in a sentence. What they do in combination is give a sentence meaning. **Pragmatics** refers to the practical functions of language. Such things as tone of voice, the degree of formality, and idioms might be grouped under this area. Each lends another key to the true meaning of the message.

Although phonemic awareness, phonological awareness, and alphabet principles are important skills for decoding words, there is concern about the methods for learning them (Morrow, 2001). Phonemic awareness refers to the ability to recognize and discriminate individual sounds. Children with this ability can identify the three sounds in the word "cat," and they understand that the three sounds can be blended into "cat." Phonemic awareness does not refer to matching a sound with the letter or letters that make that sound. Phonemic awareness is one aspect of phonological awareness that also includes the identification, rhyming, and matching of larger spoken units such as syllables and rhyming words. Alphabetic principles refer to understanding the relationship between visual letters and oral sounds. Although all of these skills are useful to emergent readers, it is not developmentally appropriate to teach them directly to kindergartners and younger children. Governmental legislation encouraging or requiring such still does not make it developmentally appropriate. When they are taught, it should always be in relation to a meaningful text or story rather than as isolated skills.

The final point on reading skills concerns how and when they are taught to or learned by children. Traditionally, both word attack and comprehension skills have been taught in isolation. That is, the skills are taught through word lists, parts of words, sentences, and brief paragraphs developed to teach a particular skill. They may or may not then be tried out in an assigned piece of text. The belief is that if children are taught all of the little pieces of the "reading puzzle," they will then be able to put the puzzle together.

A contemporary holistic approach to teaching beginning reading uses real words in real books written by real authors. The skills of reading are taught in the context of literature. There are no reading skills that were traditionally taught in isolation that cannot be meaningfully taught in the context of literature. Such an approach provides far more opportunities to also teach the semantics, syntactics, and pragmatics of language. A holistic approach also includes parents in each part of the process: obtaining information about their child's interests, sharing titles of books for follow-up reading, and learning about their values concerning books, learning, and literature.

More appropriate methods for introducing, teaching, and learning would include adult–child interactions using storybooks. For example, the use of phonics to confirm young readers' attempts to read words can be taught and practiced with *When Sheep Sleep* by Laura Numeroff. In this story, rhyme, predictable end words, and picture clues assist the reader in word reading attempts. The semantic skill of understanding word meanings can be developed in a reading of *Don't Be Silly, Mrs. Millie* by Judy Cox. In this tale, kindergarten teacher Mrs. Millie interacts with the children and substitutes words, usually nouns, in delightfully obvious ways. Understanding parts of speech, a syntactic concept, can be developed through a story such as *Joey and Jet* by James Yang. In this story, a boy and his dog play fetch in a field of prepositions. In each situation, the object the dog seeks is found among, between, over, or on some other objects. *Noises at Night* by Beth Raisner Glass and Susan Lubner can be read in a repeating pattern between adult and child to reach an understanding of the pragmatic skill of the use of tone of voice. In this story, the boy tells of the noises he hears at night, thus providing an opportunity to use different tones of voice. An excellent resource on emergent literacy is *Learning to Read and Write: Developmentally Appropriate Practices for Young Children* (2000), developed jointly by the National Association for the Education of Young Children (NAEYC) and the International Reading Association (IRA). It provides a comprehensive summary of reading issues, research, and appropriate practices for preschoolers, kindergartners, and children in the primary grades.

Realistic Expectations

Children need **realistic expectations**. Goals, when they are reached, can provide satisfaction and a sense of self-worth. If they are set too high they can lead to frustration, anger, and a sense of failure. If set too low they can encourage a lack of effort and a tendency to be satisfied with mediocrity.

Who sets the expectations? In education, it is generally the teachers and parents who set expectations. Perhaps this system should be questioned.

Children may need to become more involved in developing expectations. When someone else sets the goals, there is a lack of emotional involvement by those who must strive to attain those goals. This does not mean that children should have total control. They need the security of knowing that adults can be depended on to provide appropriate guidance and to set reasonable limits.

At all governmental levels and in political campaigns, calls are heard for raising standards and greater accountability. Although most would agree that we always want our children to grow and achieve, the main response of government to meet this desire is an ever expanding use of standardized tests. More recently, this approach is beginning to be questioned in regard to all children, but particularly for young children, speakers of other languages, and those from different cultures and backgrounds. Kenneth Wesson (2001) identifies the key problems with the increased use of such tests:

- The tests correlate better with socioeconomic background than with learning.

- It is illogical to demand that all schools perform in the above-average range because statistically one-half must fall below average.

- Test scores for children from multicultural backgrounds tend to be lower but they do not accurately reflect ability.

- The tests only test what can be easily quantified and leave out many important goals of education: ingenuity, problem solving, loyalty, commitment, and so forth.

When expectations are set too uniformly or too high, serious problems can occur. This is already happening in education. It is probably impossible to determine exactly what happens first, but the net effect is often demoralizing to children.

TIPS FOR TEACHERS

Make sure the program is ready for all children.

- Prepare paint, crayon, and clay activities for children who must continue to develop their fine motor skills.
- Remove all physical barriers that would prevent wheelchair access.
- Communicate with parents of children with disabilities to learn about their hopes, needs, and interests.
- Use screening test results to help change a program, not to deny access to a program.
- Make note of a variety of reactions to stories.

Accountability movements in education are an example. As the public demands improved education, legislatures respond with cost-effective devices. They tend to include such things as more rigorous standards for becoming a teacher and increased competency tests in reading, writing, and other basic skills for children. In order for children to be ready for the tests, the curriculum is pushed downward.

Prospective kindergartners are now routinely screened for readiness to enter school. Kindergartners are frequently retained for a second year of kindergarten or placed in transitional first grades. Some school districts have two levels of kindergarten, one for those who are "ready," and one for those who supposedly need more time to become "ready." Various rationales are presented for each of these policies. They usually sound well intentioned, often citing a need to give children more time to prepare. Basically, however, this is a program designed to categorize children on the basis of such factors as intelligence, cultural background, and language skills. By separating more able children, it is likely that the expectations for them will be raised to an even more frustrating level. This separation also deprives them of the opportunity to share their skills with, and to develop an acceptance of, those who are less able. Separating less able children deprives them of a group of good language models and may also crush their sense of self-worth.

A true literacy program can accommodate nearly all children whether they are gifted, average, culturally deprived, or have special needs. This is accomplished by providing a rich language environment, accepting children with the skills they possess, and countering some of the narrow views of literacy that still exist.

© Cengage Learning

A book that is interesting to a child can take on a magical quality for that child.

TIPS FOR TEACHERS

Borrow library DVDs of authors reading their own books.

- Always read the book aloud to children before using a tape.
- Preview the DVD ahead of time.
- Give children something to listen for or discover in the tape, such as how the author reads certain lines of dialogue.
- Have children act out the roles of the characters in the story as the author reads it.

Children can often make their own decisions about when and where to read.

Sketch (left) by Dick Bruna (right). A visit with an author or illustrator can be a most exciting time.

Authors and Illustrators

The people who write and illustrate books for children often rely heavily on their own childhood for ideas. They tend to be careful observers of youngsters they see around them. As such, they are quite in tune with much of childhood. Learning about the personal life and thoughts of an author or illustrator can be a powerful motivation for reading that author's book. The knowledge can be shared with children at various points surrounding the reading of a book. Some books even allow readers to see how authors develop their books. *The Art Lesson* by Tomie dePaola is an autobiographical depiction of a young child who later becomes an author/illustrator of children's books. *How a Book Is Made* by Aliki clearly and accurately depicts the creation of a children's book. Information about authors can be found on book jackets, in reference books in the children's sections of libraries, in the stories themselves, in magazines about children's literature, and by writing to publishers. If resources are available, a day with an author can be a tremendously rewarding experience for children and adults alike. Author visits to bookstores are a low-cost option. Many authors also have Websites.

SUMMARY

Literature should be a joyful experience. It is really about the wonders of life. The basic assumption of this book is that literature has tremendous value for young children. Literature is different from other informational media in that it usually includes another human being with whom the story is being shared. Literature derives its value from three things. First, it informs and excites children about the world in which they live. Second, it contributes to developing a positive self-image and the acceptance of others. Finally, literature serves to help children connect to both the people sharing a story with them and the people within the story.

Literature has a definite place within a literacy program. It serves as the material in which children explore language. Children do this through such things as listening to, reenacting, and interpreting the story. Unlike the passive viewing of television, literature forces children to actively visualize or imagine the story. Within the literacy curriculum one must determine the appropriate place of reading skills and how they will be learned.

Realistic expectations must be formed with each individual child's needs in mind. One of the ways literature can be made more meaningful is to help children make the connection between the people who write and illustrate children's books and themselves.

QUESTIONS FOR THOUGHT AND DISCUSSION

1. How does the transfer of information from a book differ from the transfer of information from a television program?

2. Defend or refute this statement: The United States is a "nation that reads."

3. How can literature help young children learn about their world?

4. How can a child's self-esteem be addressed through literature?

5. Defend or refute this statement: Preschool children who are capable of learning the alphabet and word lists should learn them at that time.

6. What does the term "reading" really mean?

7. How can reading competency tests for elementary school have a negative effect on the preschool or kindergarten child?

8. According to Harste and Woodward, what three key features should be present in a literacy curriculum?

9. Why aren't phonics enough to help a child learn to read?

10. How do traditional and holistic approaches to teaching beginning reading differ?

11. What effect does viewing television violence have on young children?

 For additional resources, access the *Growing Up with Literature* companion website through www.cengagebrain.com <http://www.cengagebrain.com/>.

CHILDREN'S BOOKS CITED

Aliki (Brandenberg). (1986). *How a book is made.* New York: Harper and Row.

Asch, Frank, and Asch, Devin. (2001). *Baby duck's new friend.* Orlando, FL: Harcourt.

Bercaw, Edna Coe. (2000). *Halmoni's day.* New York: Dial.

Bunting, Eve. (1997). *The pumpkin fair.* Boston: Houghton Mifflin.

Bynum, Eboni, and Jackson, Roland. (2004). *Jamari's drum.* Toronto, Ontario, Canada: Groundwood.

Carlson, Nancy. (2006). *Get up and go!* New York: Viking.

Cimarusti, Marie. (2003). *Peek-a-zoo.* New York: Dutton.

Cox, Judy. (2005). *Don't be silly, Mrs. Millie.* Tarrytown, NY: Marshall Cavendish.

dePaola, Tomie. (1974). *Watch out for the chicken feet in your soup.* New York: Simon and Schuster.

dePaola, Tomie. (1989). *The art lesson.* New York: G. P. Putnam's Sons.

Elya, Susan Middleton. (2008). *Bebe goes to the beach.* New York: Harcourt.

English, Karen. (2010). *Nadia's hands.* Honesdale, PA: Boyds Mills Press.

Fox, Mem. (1988). *Koala Lou.* San Diego, CA: Harcourt Brace Jovanovich.

Fox, Mem. (2000). *Harriet, you'll drive me wild!* New York: Harcourt.

Galloway, Ruth. (2005). *Clumsy crab.* Wilton, CT: Tiger Tales.

Glass, Beth Raisner, and Lubner, Susan. (2005). *Noises at night.* New York: Abrams.

Ho, Minfong. (1996). *Hush! A Thai lullaby.* New York: Orchard.

Holt, Kimberly Willis. (2006). *Waiting for Gregory.* New York: Holt.

Holub, Joan. (2010). *Twinkle, star of the week.* Park Ridge, IL: Albert Whitman.

Johnston, Tony. (2009). *My Abuelita.* New York: Harcourt.

Joosse, Barbara. (2010). *Higgledy-Piggledy Chicks.* New York: Greenwillow.

Lewis, Kim. (1996). *First snow.* Cambridge, MA: Candlewick.

Lotz, Karen. (1993). *Snowsong whistling.* New York: Dutton.

Maass, Robert. (1993). *When winter comes.* New York: Holt.

Manning, Maurice. (2008). *Kitchen dance.* New York: Houghton-Mifflin/Clarion.

McCully, Emily A. (1985). *First snow.* New York: Harper and Row.

Middleton, Susan. (2009). *Adios.* New York: Putnam.

Numeroff, Laura. (2006). *When sheep sleep.* New York: Abrams.

Parr, Todd. (2004). *The family book.* Boston: Little Brown.

Piper, Watty. (1930). *The little engine that could.* New York: Piatt and Munk.

Root, Phyllis. (2004). *Grandmother Winter.* Boston: Houghton Mifflin.

Rotner, Shelley, and Kelly, Sheila. (2000). *Feeling thankful.* Brookfield, CT: Millbrook.

Szekere, Cyndy. (1997). *The mouse that Jack built.* New York: Scholastic.

Thong, Roseanne. *Fly free.* (2010). Honesdale, PA: Boyds Mills Press.

Waber, Bernard. (1997). *Bearsie Bear and the surprise sleepover.* Boston: Houghton Mifflin.

Williams, Karen. (2010). *A beach tail.* Honesdale, PA: Boyds Mills Press.

Yang, James. (2004). *Joey and Jet.* New York: Simon and Schuster.

SELECTED REFERENCES AND RESOURCES

Benett-Armstead, V. S., Moses, A. M., and Duke, N. K. (2006). *Literacy and the youngest learner.* New York: Scholastic.

Bissex, G., and Bullock R. (Eds.). (1987). *Seeing for ourselves.* Portsmouth, NH: Heinemann.

Boyd, F. B., Brock, C. H., and Rosendal, M. S. (Eds.). (2003). *Multicultural and multilingual literacy and language: Context and practices.* New York: Guilford.

Brazelton, T. B. (1988). *What every baby knows.* New York: Ballantine.

Brown, L. M., Lamb, S., and Tappan, M. (2009). *Pakaging boyhood: Saving our sons from superheroes, slackers, and other media stereotypes.* New York: St. Martin's Press.

Butler, A. (1987). *The elements of whole language.* Crystal Lake, IL: Rigby.

Castles, A., and Coltheart, M. (2004). Is there a causal link from phonological awareness to success in learning to read? *Cognition, 91,* 77–111.

Christakis, D. A., and Garrison, M. M. (2009). Preschool-aged children's television viewing in child care settings. *Pediatrics*, 124:1627–1632.

Christakis, D. A., Zimmerman, F. J., DiGuiseppe, D. L., and McCarthy, C. A. (2004). Early television exposure and subsequent attentional problems in children. *Pediatrics*, 113 (4), 708–713.

Clay, M. (1991). *Becoming literate: The construction of inner control.* Portsmouth, NH: Heinemann.

Coppola, J., and Primes, E. V. (2009). *One classroom, many learners.* Newark, DE: International Reading Association.

Cooper, D. J., and Kiger, N. D. (2005). *Helping children construct meaning.* Boston: Houghton Mifflin.

Davis, J., and Williams, R. P. (1994). Leading sprightly into spring. *Young Children* 49 (4), 37–41.

Dorr, R. (2006). Something old is new again: Revisiting language experience. *The Reading Teacher.* 60, 138–146.

Duckworth, E. (1987). *The having of wonderful ideas.* New York: Teachers College Press.

Fisher, B. and Medvic, E. F. (2000). *Perspectives on shared reading: Planning and practice.* Portsmouth, NH: Heinemann.

Fox, M. (2001). *Reading magic: Why reading aloud to our children will change their lives forever.* Fort Washington, PA: Harvest Books.

Garand, E. M. (2004). *In defense of our children.* Portsmouth, NH: Heinemann.

Goodman, K. (1989a). Roots of the whole language movement. *Elementary School Journal.* 90, 113–127.

Goodman, K. (1989b). Whole language research: Foundations and development. *Elementary School Journal.* 90, 207–221.

Goodman, K. S. (2005). *What's whole in whole language.* Muskegon, MI: RDR Books.

Goodman, K., and Goodman, Y. (1978). Reading of American children whose language is a stable rural dialect of English or a language other than English (final report). Washington, DC: National Institute of Education.

Gopalakrishnan, A. (2010). *Multicultural children's literature.* Newbury Park, CA: Sage.

Gunn, B. K., Simmons, D. C., and Kameenui, E. J. (1998). *Emergent literacy: Synthesis of research.* Mahwah, NJ: Lawrence Erlbaum.

Harste, J., and Woodward, V. (1989). Fostering needed change in early literacy programs. In Dorothy Strickland and Lesley Morrow (Eds.), *Emerging literacy: Young children learning to read and write* (pp. 147–154). Newark, DE: International Reading Association.

Hillman, J. (2002). *Discovering children's literature.* Upper Saddle River, NJ: Prentice-Hall.

International Reading Association (Opitz, M. F. Ed.). (1998). *Literacy instruction for culturally and linguistically diverse students.* Newark, DE: International Reading Association.

Ivey, G., and Fisher, D. (2006). *Creating literacy-rich schools for adolescents.* Alexandria, VA: Association for Supervision and Curriculum Development.

Machado, Jeanne M. (2010). *Early childhood experiences in language arts:Early literacy.* Florence, KY: Wadsworth/Cengage.

Meier, D., and Wood, G. (2004). *Many children left behind: How the NCLB Act is damaging our children and our schools.* Boston: Beacon.

Morrow, L. M. (2001). *Literacy development in the early years.* Boston: Allyn and Bacon.

Murray, J. P. (2001).TV violence and brainmapping in children. *Psychiatric Times,* 18 (10), 1–8.

National Association for the Education of Young Children (NAEYC) and International Reading Association (IRA). (2000). *Learning to read and write: Developmentally appropriate practices for young children.* Washington, DC: National Association for the Education of Young Children.

National Association for the Education of Young Children. (2005). *Basics of developmentally appropriate practice.* Washington, DC: National Association for the Education of Young Children.

National Institute on Media and the Family site. *Television's effect on reading and academic achievement.* Retrieved November 3, 2006, from http://www.mediafamily. org.

Nielsen Wire, (2009). *TV viewing among kids at an eight year high."* Retrieved October 26, 2009, from http://blog.nielsen.com/nielsenwire/media_entertainment/tv-viewing-among-kids-at-an-eight-year-high/

Peterson, P. E., and West, M. R. (2003). *No child left behind? The politics and practice of school accountability.* Washington, DC: Brookings Institution.

Prescott-Griffin, M.L. (2005). *Reader to reader.* Portsmouth, NH: Heinemann.

Robbins, P. A. (1990). Implementing whole language: Bridging children and books. *Educational Leadership,* 41, 1–34.

Roe, B. D., Stoodt-Hill, B. D., and Burns, P. C. (2004). *Secondary school literacy instruction: The content areas.* Boston: Houghton Mifflin.

Rosenblatt, L. (1996). *Literature as exploration.* New York: Modern Language Association of America.

Smith, F. (2005). *Reading without nonsense.* New York: Teachers College Press.

Trelease, J. (2006). *The read-aloud handbook.* New York: Penguin.

Vasquez, V. M. (2004). *Negotiating critical literacies with young children.* Mahwah, NJ: Lawrence Erlbaum.

Vygotsky, L. (1986). *Thought and language.* Cambridge, MA: MIT Press.

Vygotsky, L. S., Cole, M., John-Steiner, V., and Scribner, S. (2006). *Mind in society: Development of higher psychological processes.* Cambridge, MA: Harvard University Press.

Warner, S. A. (1986). *Teacher.* Austin, TX: Touchstone.

Wells, G. (1986). *The meaning makers: Children making language and using language to learn.* Portsmouth, NH: Heinemann.

Wesson, K. A. (2001). The Volvo effect—questioning standardized tests. *Young Children,* 56 (2), 16–18.

INTERNET REFERENCES AND HELPFUL WEBSITES

Center for Early Literacy site. Retrieved January 4, 2010, from http://www.beginningwithbooks.org/

International Reading Association site. Resources by Topics. Retrieved January 4, 2010, from http://www.reading.org/focus/resources/

National Association for the Education of Young Children site. Retrieved January 4, 2010, from http://www.naeyc.org/positionstatement

National Children's Literacy site. Retrieved January 4, 2010, http://www.child2000.org/lit-tips.htm

Read A Story site. Retrieved January 25, 2010, from http://www.readastory.org

United Through Reading site. Retrieved January 25, 2010, from http://www.unitedthroughreading.org

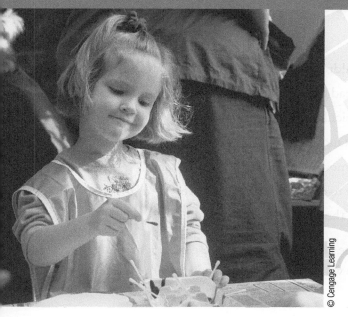
© Cengage Learning

CHAPTER 2

PLANNING FOR SUCCESS

The experience of reading to young children is enhanced by prior planning. This chapter addresses the key components of cognitive development and creating environments that prepare teachers for maximizing the benefits of sharing literature with young children. The sections within this chapter cover the basic knowledge that caregivers should possess for different age groups in terms of language, literacy, and child development. The following chapters expand upon these areas with strategies that can be integrated with plans based upon the components learned in this chapter.

A suitable place for reading is more than just ambiance; it sets the tone for the entire reading experience. The individual who will read to children must develop understandings, patterns, and plans for a successful reading encounter. Each age has different needs, interests, and preferences that can be used to encourage children to interact with the story. Teachers must be able to answer several questions when planning a reading:

- Is the material age appropriate?
- Did I read the story first so that I am familiar with it?

There are no problems— only opportunities to be creative.

—DORYE ROETTGER

- How will I motivate the children to want to be involved with the story?
- Where and when will we read the story?
- Why am I reading this particular story?
- How will I monitor understanding as the reading occurs?
- How can I make this story most meaningful to the children?
- Is the story understandable to children from all cultures?
- How will I determine what the children got from the story?

A great deal of material must be considered before these questions can be answered. Knowing the answers will benefit both the reader and the children each time a story is read.

KEY PRINCIPLES OF CHILD DEVELOPMENT

The field of neuroscience has yielded some fascinating suggestions about how individuals learn, particularly in the early years. Using observations based on magnetic resonance imaging (MRI) and positron emission topography (PET), Sousa (2006) contends that **brain research** demonstrates that language learning and reading are positively related to factors such as emotions, physical environment, and past experiences. These beliefs have been translated into a number of strategies for working with children of various ages (Hardiman, 2003; Lyons, 2003). They agree with Sousa's (2006) conclusion that the role of emotion is one of the most important factors derived from brain research. Tileston (2005) has summarized the research in this area in a set of recommended teaching practices, some of which are particularly useful with young children. Targeting the concept of the emotional, she cites the importance of a climate that is enriched and positive. Further, there should be a moderate level of stress (a complete lack of stress equals boredom), realistic goals for learning, and a sense that each child is important. Other practices cited by Tileston include the use of techniques that involve visual, auditory, and tactile senses, making connections between new learning and a child's existing knowledge/background, and providing opportunities for children to interact in a variety of ways with the new learning. Helping children connect the new to what they already know helps them recognize the relevance and be motivated to acquire and use the new learning.

The findings and beliefs from the field of brain research correspond with and support the most recent contentions in the field of literacy development. Whitehead (2002) states that most of the brain's potential is mapped out in the first year of life. She contends that thousands of significant connections are made in the first year in a loving, stimulating environment and that these are the beginnings of literacy. Morrow and Tracey (2005) cite an abundance of research that cites the importance of a safe and supportive environment in which children are involved with more literate others. The social interaction involved is particularly powerful because it involves societal functions, conventions of language, a link of reading to writing, and a connection of all of these with a sense of pleasure and satisfaction. This leads to a continuing engagement that is self-motivating. Morrow and Tracey also stress how the use of storytelling, shared reading, theater, music, art, and creative movement can extend the learning of language in an emotionally and physically safe climate.

The work of Arthur Applebee over the last few decades has a particular relevance to this area of a child's development. In his early work, he focused on how children view a story and relate it to their own lives (1989). He found that a critical shift in a **child's perception** occurs from age 2 to 9. At the earlier ages, children focus on the objective truth of a story in a bit-by-bit approach. They tend to see stories as true (e.g, Cinderella was a real person). As they develop up to about age 5, children acquire the **conventions** of a story (e.g., they lived happily ever after) and an expectation of what certain characters are like (e.g., lion, witch, fairy). As they continue to grow, they shift their focus to viewing a story as a whole and they are able to respond to whether the story amuses or angers them. It is these responses that provide opportunities for learning and language development. Applebee, Burroughs, and Stevens (2006) contend that literacy develops best in a situation where conversations are a major focus. When they are, the environment is characterized by emotional safety, motivation, relevance, and importance.

It's important to keep in mind several key principles of child development in planning literacy activities. These principles are derived from those identified by the National Association for the Education of Young Children (NAEYC) as particularly relevant for informing developmentally appropriate practices. While all of the NAEYC principles are important, four are especially applicable to planning successful literacy activities for young children.

- The physical, social, emotional, and cognitive domains of child development are closely related. Activities should therefore be planned that foster the **integration** of these domains.
- Development proceeds at different rates from child to child. Children should not be expected to all be interested in or respond to a single activity in the same way.
- Adults must plan activities such that **bridges to understanding** can occur.
- **Play** is an important vehicle for learning. It constitutes an opportunity for practicing new capabilities and allows children to demonstrate their learning in a safe context.

CONDITIONS OF LEARNING

In studying the best practices for acquiring literacy, Australian educator Brian Cambourne observed several characteristics that seemed to appear in the most successful environments. He identified these characteristics as "conditions for literacy learning" (1993). Cambourne's **conditions** are widely used in early childhood education. Consequently, he has been able to study their implementation in additional early childhood settings. This has enabled him to further clarify and explain the eight "conditions for literacy learning" (Cambourne, 2000/2001).

- *Immersion:* This refers to providing multiple opportunities for children to experience the sights and sounds of print and stories. It includes use of words on walls, reading aloud to children, shared reading, and choral reading (e.g., poems, songs).

- *Demonstration:* This refers to adults and caregivers modeling how to read, showing how to go about reading (e.g., explaining how to think about what is read), and sharing different types of texts (e.g., stories, labels). This might include reading aloud and a collaborative development of the meaning of the text, including the spelling and writing of words from the text.

- *Engagement:* This refers to how caregivers provide ongoing and relevant explanations of why it is important to become a good reader. This might include sharing personal stories of how reading has helped the adult as well as demonstrations of how this happens.

- *Expectations:* This refers to communicating to children that they all can become good readers and that it is expected they will do so. This would include regularly changing mixed groups in the class, the avoidance of any negative comments, explanations of effective reading practices, and reminders that by learning to talk they are showing that they are effective language learners.

- *Responsibility:* This refers to encouraging children to begin to make some decisions about what and how they learn and demonstrating how to do it. This might include discussions about books and topics that include open-ended questions. Expect comments and statements to have a supporting explanation.

- *Approximation:* This refers to the expectation and explanation that we must take language risks. That is, in order to grow in literacy it is necessary to try to speak, read, spell, and write new words and ideas even if they are not initially conventional language. This includes modeling this process, using invented spelling, and explaining how it usually takes practice to become proficient in many activities (e.g., spelling, riding a bike).

- *Use:* This refers to providing opportunities for children to apply their literacy learning in authentic and meaningful tasks. This includes multiple opportunities to engage in real reading and writing activities. It should include language use for many different purposes.

- *Response:* This refers to the role of adults to attend to the literacy learning approximations of children, guiding them to strategies and providing them with additional demonstrations that will help them adjust their approximations. Set up situations that will allow children to receive feedback from both caregivers and other children and show them how to use that feedback for further learning.

CREATING A GOOD ENVIRONMENT FOR INFANTS

The most important factor in the language acquisition process is the **interaction of adult with child**. It is the sound of soft, soothing words that helps the infant respond when frightened or upset. These sounds may be a parent's voice, the sounds and rhythm of a lullaby, or the words of a pleasant rhyme. Infants do not need circle time for this sharing; they will not stay in a circle. What they do need is a lap and a reader with whom to share the story.

Emerging Language

During the first few months of life, babies begin to communicate wants and needs through crying and, to some extent, facial expression. Crain and Lillo-Martin (1999) contend that language begins with babbling without meaning, which becomes attached shortly thereafter. From 6 to 10 months, the babbling varies (e.g., ba, bo, be). Crain and Lillo-Martin have found that this occurs in deaf children and in children in all cultures. They suggest that first words (e.g., Mama) are observed at about one year and that two-word combinations (e.g., Mama... up) are noted about six months later. They speculate that the child at this point in life may know more language than can be used. Brain research suggests that the auditory and cognitive processing skills that underlie language development are present as early as one month, according to Newman, Ratner, Jusczyk, Jusczyk, and Dow (2006). They base this on the observation that, although most speech directed at babies is multi-worded, infants as young as seven weeks have been observed responding to single words both in isolation and in fluent speech.

Throughout this period, there is a need for adults to provide language to children through talk and through contact with the environment. Adults should provide encouragement and opportunities for infants to experience their environment. Part of this exploration will be the investigation of language and its uses. Children will explore how it sounds, what it does, and how it can be used.

Linking Language to Literature

Singing songs, reading stories, doing simple fingerplays, and playing games with a high amount of adult-child interaction are the best ways to initiate a connection with literature. Traditional rhymes, Mother Goose stories, and poetry are easy to memorize and recite. Infants enjoy hearing these types of literature whether they are being cuddled, rocked, or just resting in a crib.

Holding an object in front of an infant and telling a story about it is pleasurable for an infant from birth. For example, one might hold a small stuffed kitten up to the child and recite the "Three Little Kittens" rhyme while the child touches or pets the toy. With infants of 8 to 15 months of age, learning the sounds that things make is a great motivation. As they develop, babies enjoy making the sounds of an object. They do this well before they are able to name the object. Familiar objects to use for this activity include a car, truck, airplane, train, animal, and boat. One can further encourage children's language acquisition and understanding of the words by reinforcing and accepting their approximations of the sounds. This lets children know that others understand their developing language patterns.

Reading to Infants

Each month that books are not read to infants is a month that is lost forever. Books can be read to infants from the moment they are born. The books should, of course, be durable if the child will handle them. Hardcover books, board books, and plastic books are good beginning books. The books used should include pictures that are simple and bright, as very young children are not able to focus on busy pictures.

TIPS FOR TEACHERS

Children are never too young to hear a story.

- Read stories aloud at nap time, during feeding, and at snack time.
- Recite rhymes and finger plays as stories for very young children.
- Talk about what you are doing, in the form of a story, to infants.
- Create a spontaneous song-story about what we are doing right now.

Books should be treated as something special. They are not something one eats. The concept of respecting books can be constantly **modeled**. Because they do not hold up well to touching, paperback books are more difficult to use with infants. This does not mean to avoid such books. Rather, the adult must maintain more control over the book. There is nothing wrong with saying that some books will be kept by the caregiver as long as other more durable board books and books created from plastic materials are available for children to choose freely. Nondurable books can always be shared again. This approach allows the use of many books with children.

When reading with infants, include the use of props and toys. Effective utilization of puppets, toy cars, and other objects featured in the story can enhance the reading experience. The object connects the infant with the tale in a positive, hands-on manner.

Reading Areas for Infants

In setting up a reading area for infants, safety must be a primary concern. The caregiver must remember that infants sit on laps, crawl about, and listen in various positions and in various places. Ideally, the reading area should be on the floor. Although too many decorations can become distracting to infants, colorful pillows, quilts, stuffed animals, and mats are inviting and comfortable.

Mobiles, wall hangings, and soft sculptures can be added to enhance the setting. Cardboard boxes can be used to make story-related cars, boats, and trains. This stimulates the children's imaginations by creating a concrete representation of the story. **Re-creating** parts of the story in play is an important part of language development. Through re-creating the story, children are dealing with and making sense of language. In this case, they replicate the language of the author and the reader.

Dorothy Kunhardt's *Pat the Bunny* is great fun to read with infants. As the book progresses, the reader has the opportunity to touch the cottontail of the bunny, smell some flowers, look in a mirror, play peek-a-boo, and engage in other similar activities. Re-create the reading and language experience by using the ideas from the book within the reading area. For example, include in the reading area a peek-a-boo game, a mirror activity, and scented flowers. The book is most interesting for infants, but both older children and adults may enjoy reading it over and over again. Since this book and many other books for infants are designed for touching, it is important to clean them between readings. Two other board books that can be used in a similar manner are *You Push, I Ride* by Abby Levine and *You Go Away* by Dorothy Corey. Enjoyable books should be read as often as infants respond to them.

Children will usually point to their favorites even before they can ask for them verbally. It is important to continuously share the beauty of the language through repeated readings of favorite stories. Language should be shared in a warm, pleasant environment. Books will naturally be a part of children's lives if shared from birth. The very young will enjoy books at bedtime such as *Bright Baby Touch and Feel Bedtime* by Roger Priddy.

CREATING AN ENVIRONMENT FOR TODDLERS

Picture a lovely summer day with an occasional tornado roaring through, touching down to commit mayhem every few miles. This provides some idea of a toddler's day. Ever curious, toddlers seem determined to fit years of exploration and discovery into each day. Toddlers' attention may quickly jump from object to object. On the other hand, they can sustain attention in a particular pursuit if motivated and involved. Most toddlers enjoy completing tasks. However, the tasks must be age appropriate in order for toddlers to achieve success without becoming frustrated.

Toddlers are more able to assert themselves and their independence than younger children. The word "no" is more than a word for many of them; sometimes it seems to be a creed. For this reason, care must be taken when encouraging toddlers to stay on a task, especially when they feel they have completed it. "Me done!" is rarely spoken by a toddler without the exclamation mark at the end.

Motivation is important in planning environments for toddlers. They want to hear stories and look at books if they feel the activity is exciting. The storyteller or reader must provide effective presentations of the tale and show enjoyment in the activity. The closeness and warmth of the reading experience is a major part of the setting. Toddlers like to point to and touch books as they are read. They like to feel they are a part of the experience. Caregivers must plan for this when choosing books. To enhance the environment for toddlers, be patient, provide pictures and language, and create language together through stories and storytelling.

Using Language

Citing the groundbreaking earlier work of Roger Brown (1973), Crain and Lillo-Martin (1999) summarize an alternative to looking at the pace of language development milestones in terms of years and months. Brown viewed the development as one of stages rather than ages. He did this by observing the average length of spontaneous language in children and described it as mean length of utterance (MLU). That is, if in spontaneous speech a child averaged three words, it would be described as an MLU of 3.00. Although the increases in MLU do occur at similar ages in children, there is substantial variation. In any case, a toddler of about 2 years of age is often at stage one with an MLU of 1.75 and with a speaking vocabulary of about 400 words. About five months later, this child would typically move to stage two with an MLU of 2.25 and a remarkably larger speaking vocabulary of about 900 words. Some syntax is noticed at this time (e.g., use of past tense), but it is often over generalized (e.g., I eated cookie). Newman et al. (2006) note that children from a range of linguistic communities reach similar stages at comparable points in time.

The beginning stages of writing emerge at this stage. From the first time a child touches a crayon to paper, or even thinks about doing it, writing has begun. It will take several years to develop, but all of the pictures and **attempts** to put something meaningful in a visual form are part of the child's **developing writing ability**.

During this period of life, adults must provide time, opportunities, models, encouragement, and acceptance. Children are drawn to whatever language is available. They like its sounds and rhythm. Language models and a wide variety of experiences should be provided. On the other hand, this is not the time for correction of faulty language structures. The same is true for drawing and writing attempts. Children need acceptance of their honest attempts to create meaning. They need someone to listen to them communicate about their drawings.

Toddler Humor

During this time, children develop a sense of humor. This humor begins with simple substitution in which the toddler is aware that the substitution has been made. For example, a child knows that "Mama" is the sound for mother and "Dada" is the sound for daddy. In the name game, Mother asks "Who am I?" The child responds with "Dada" and then bursts out laughing. The child has made a joke. More jokes will be attempted, especially if they are encouraged by laughter from the child's audience.

Toddlers love zany humor, and there are many books to satisfy this craving. In the big book *One Duck Stuck*, Phyllis Root creates a sloppy, hilarious story in which Mucky Ducky is helped by a variety of animal friends when he is stuck in the mud. Toddlers will see humor in the silly attempts of Titus the dog to be like the children and the other animals on the farm in *No, No, Titus* by Claire Masurel, a Spanish/English bilingual story.

Stories in which animals act out of character are sure to get a response. Good choices in this area include Daniel Pinkwater's *Bad Bears in the City*,

Cover from *One Duck Stuck Big Boo: A Mucky Ducky Counting Book* by Phyllis Root. Jacket art copyright ©2008 by Jane Chapman. Reprinted by Permission of Candlewick Press. All rights reserved.

Reprinted by permission of Neil Morris

Author/illustrator Dave Ross. Reprinted by permission of Dave Ross.

Tad Hills' *Duck and Goose,* and Tony and Jan Payne's *The Hippo-Not-Amus.* The zany antics of frogs jumping in the mud and riding skateboards provides fun on every page in *Bad Frogs* by Thacher Hurd.

More subtle forms of humor for toddlers are available as well. Good beginning choices include *Baby Rock, Baby Roll* by Stella Blackstone, *Where's the Bear?* by Byron Barton, and Dave Ross's two books, *A Book of Hugs* and *More Hugs.* Mem Fox creates a tale that allows the reader to make full use of voice to create a mental picture in *Night Noises.* Two fanciful choices for more able children include *Dear Mr. Blueberry* by Simon James and *Animal Lullabies* by Slovenian writer Lila Prap.

Many nursery rhymes also provide humor. For example, have you ever really seen a dish run away with a spoon? Have you ever seen kittens washing mittens? Do people really live in pumpkins? Picturing the absurdity is half the fun of listening to or reciting these rhymes. Nursery rhymes also lend themselves to wonderful art activities and dramatic presentations that toddlers can easily enjoy. For example, children can engage in dramatizing dishes running away with spoons and creating such items as bags of wool, golden eggs, and spiders on tuffets. Barbara Reid has selected, and illustrated with clay relief, a number of Mother Goose nursery rhymes in *Sing a Song of Mother Goose.* Another good choice, Zena Sutherland's *The Orchard Book of Nursery Rhymes,* combines Mother Goose with familiar short verses, tongue twisters, and nonsense poems. The illustrations are effective and the books are sturdy. The repetitive parts of stories are easy for toddlers to repeat. They can often join in reciting some of the repeated lines.

Careful selection of nursery rhymes will help to eliminate those that are violent or sexist. Many of the Dr. Seuss books with their **repeating sound patterns** provide a reinforcement for phonological awareness.

Toddler Interests

Toddlers have an interest in the objects and events around them. They want to know the sounds, the "whats," and the "whys" of everything. They want to know who everyone is and what they do.

One way to respond to this need is to provide appropriate books for children to explore. Toddlers are also drawn to books about the everyday events that make up their lives. Board books and other smaller books are just right for toddlers. They often provide basic terms and ideas that toddlers see and do each day. Examples of such books include *It's Quacking Time* by Martin Waddell and *I'm Sorry* by Jennifer Eachus. *Here a Chick, Where a Chick?* by Suse MacDonald will be popular with its sturdy lift-the-flap introduction to farm animals and their sounds.

British author Neil Morris.

Book cover from *Jump Along: A Fun Book of Movement* by Neil Morris, illustrated by Peter Stevenson, copyright ©1991. Reprinted by permission of Carolrhoda Books.

Cover from *Me and You* by Janet A. Holmes. Jacket art copyright ©2009 by Judith Rossell. Reprinted by permission of North-South Books. All rights reserved.

Toddlers can explore their emerging vocabularies in books such as the multilingual number book *Come Out and Play* by Diane Law and John Scieszka's *Truckery Rhymes,* which uses Mother Goose rhymes to create verses about trucks with distinctive personalities. In *All Kinds of Families* by Mary Ann Haberman, toddlers discover the likenesses that children throughout the world share through common objects such as bottle caps, button, and marbles. The activities and accomplishments of toddlers are presented in *Jump Along* by *Neil Morris, Busy Day* by Sonali Fry, and *Let's Help* by Catherine Lukas. They will feel a real sense of accomplishment as they quickly grasp the concept of counting in *Olly and Me 1 2 3* by Shirley Hughes. As toddlers begin to reflect on their own existence as individuals, they can begin to appreciate stories such as *A Long Way* by Katherine Ayers, international best-seller *The Rainbow Fish* by Marcus Pfister, and from Germany, *Gloria the Cow* by Paul Maar. Youngsters will also relate to the idea of friendship between themselves and others as they discover the joy of sharing and fun along with the two rabbits in *Me and You* by Janet A. Holmes.

Other books and authors have specifically addressed the interests, lives, and environments of toddlers. The family and home is the world of the toddler. They often join or are joined by siblings in a growing family. In *Not Yet Rose* by Susan Leonard Hill, a young hamster eagerly awaits the arrival of a new baby with a mixture of emotions. Through parental love and her own increasing self confidence, she grows into the important role of big sister. *When We're Together* by Claire Freedman extends the good feelings of loved ones in a great read aloud book. Toilet training is an area of interest that can be paired with *Danny Is Done with Diapers: A Potty ABC* by Rebecca O'Connell and *Underwear!* By Mary Monsell. Finally, the toddler can be introduced to the concept of changing seasons in the ridiculously humorous *Sleep, Big Bear, Sleep!* By Maureen Wright.

Eric Carle's writing is exceptional for toddlers. The illustrations are excitingly colorful. They possess a visual texture not often found elsewhere. Each book has a special attraction. For example, *The Very Hungry Caterpillar* shows caterpillars and what they might eat. In fact, the caterpillar eats right through the illustrations. This book is always a favorite.

Reading Areas for Toddlers

A reading area for toddlers must be engaging, interesting, and safe. Although circle time is not a necessity for all children in each group, some toddlers can enjoy a brief group reading, particularly if there are enough laps to sit on. The area should be on the floor, but a low loft-type structure might also be used. Toddlers love to climb. To add comfort and fun, place large pillows and stuffed toys in the area.

© Cengage Learning

Reading is special anywhere. If the story is captivating, any place can be the right place for reading.

Book cover from *Rainbow Fish*, written and illustrated by Marcus Pfister, copyright ©1992. Reprinted by permission of North-South Books.

A large stuffed toy for the toddlers to sit on can be a creative addition. Rocking chairs are a nice touch in any reading area. The motion is soothing, and a rocker is usually large enough for a reader and a couple of toddlers to sit together to share a story. Carpeting should be used with any wooden loft or stairway loft.

Decorated walls and mobiles are an easy accent that can be changed often. They keep the interest level high. Visibility is important with toddlers. Objects and furniture should not interfere with the adult's ability to maintain eye contact with the children.

Boxes and large climbing structures with pillow centers also make a reading area a special place. If large boxes are used, they should have many windows. The boxes can be decorated with white paint to make an igloo. Windows can be cut to suggest a spaceship. Boxes can be painted brown to make a jungle hut. Books that represent the topic can be placed inside the box. The children's interest is heightened when they participate in creating and changing the reading area and its props.

CREATING AN ENVIRONMENT FOR PRESCHOOLERS

Children of 3 to 4 years of age never seem to stop asking "why." Their questions are both the bane and the bonus of parents and caregivers. Preschool children are interested in themselves and their families. They are fascinated by the world around them, and are beginning to realize that it includes others outside their immediate environment. It is a time of incredible stretching and growth of knowledge. Preschoolers seem to be sponges for information, always wanting to know how, why, and where.

Using Language

At the preschool level, children continue their rapid development of language skills and **vocabulary growth**. They are now able to use **language as a tool for understanding** themselves and their surroundings. During the first half of their third year, children typically reach the third stage of language development with an MLU of 2.75 and they increase their speaking vocabulary to about 1,200 words. They continue to expand their use of syntax, use multiple clauses, and form questions. As they grow toward the age of 4, they move into stage four, increasing their MLU to 3.50 and their speaking vocabulary to about 1,500 words. They also begin to incorporate multiple clauses in their speech and engage in telling stories (Brown, 1973; Crain & Lillo-Martin, 1999).

TIPS FOR TEACHERS

Use books that contain new and interesting words.

- Tell children the meaning of the new words they will be hearing in the story.
- Use new words from a story in your own speech after the story.
- Provide or create an illustration depicting the new word or concept.
- Respond positively to children attempting to use new words they have learned in a story.

The writings of preschoolers consist of drawings, attempts at writing, and dictated stories. Whether or not adults can tell what the child has drawn, the artwork does have definite meanings to the child. The role of the adult is to interact with the child in the form of listening, answering questions, asking questions, providing language models, and sharing experiences.

Preschool Humor

The child's sense of humor is beyond simple word substitutions. Preschoolers are more sophisticated than toddlers and don't laugh as readily at dishes running away with spoons. They can begin to appreciate the more subtle forms of humor

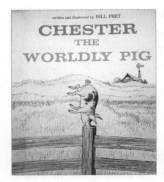

Cover from CHESTER THE WORLDY PIG by Bill Peet. Copyright © 1966 by William Peet, renewed 1993 by William B. Peet. Reprinted by permission of Houghton Mifflin Harcourt Publishing Company. All rights reserved.

in books such as the classic *Chester the Worldly Pig* by Bill Peet. The preschool child's humor sometimes requires a semblance of possibility. *Curious George* by H. A. Rey appeals to this more sophisticated humor. George, a well-loved character, gets into all sorts of mischief by circumstances rather than by design. The humorous aspects of the plot are possible, yet highly improbable. Therein lies the humor. For example, when George plays with the telephone, he mistakenly rings the fire department. This causes a hilarious chain of events. In *Pouch!* By David Ezra Stein, Little Joey the kangaroo repeatedly ventures outside Mama Kangaroo's pouch. Each time he encounters another animal he yells "Pouch!" and dives back into safety. When he eventually meets another young kangaroo, they both yell "Pouch!", burst into laughter, and then play together.

Although 3-year-olds and 4-year-olds still laugh at certain words, they are more likely to substitute a possible rather than an impossible term. Fantasy and **dramatic play** are still important for these children. Preschoolers love to "play house" and act out roles as well. At this age, "Little Red Riding Hood" is no longer just a story. It is an event that can be acted out both seriously and humorously with only a few props. Steven Kellogg's retelling of the English fairy tale *The Three Sillies*, which includes his hilarious illustrations, will have everyone giggling. The situation for all of the silliness is ridiculous, which is where all the fun comes in.

Preschooler Interests

Values are often included in the stories intended for preschoolers. Children at this age are concerned with themselves and their feelings. Don Freeman's *Corduroy* tells of a teddy bear that is rejected by children because it is missing a button. Eventually it is acquired by a little girl who loves it anyway. The story is reassuring to preschoolers because it demonstrates the value of love over perfection. In *That's Mine Horace* by Holly Keller, Horace the leopard struggles with his conscience when he finds a toy he really wants for his own. He tells a fib when he claims it belongs to him. Unable to live with his decision, Horace does the right thing and returns it to its owner. This is a book that can lead to discussions about honesty and doing what is right.

Dr. Seuss's books often reinforce values while providing great fun through illustrations and language. Horton the elephant makes difficult decisions that, in the end, reinforce the correctness of the honest choices made. The Grinch shows how love can change people. The Lorax challenges children to think about the environment. Each book has a special style. In *Horton Hatches the Egg,* Horton sits on a bird's egg through terrible trials and tribulations. The egg hatches eventually, and the reader is treated to an amazing conclusion. Children will sit through this lengthy book over and over again. They do so because they can empathize with the story from beginning to end. In *Barn Savers* by Linda High, young children can understand the concept of valuing both older people and old things using barns as a metaphor. In this nonfiction book, a father and son learn valuable lessons about both sharing a task and appreciating the value of the old barn they dismantle.

Preschoolers are fascinated with **differences**. They notice differences of gender, size, disability, houses, and so forth. As might be expected, they want to know why these differences exist. Todd Paar's *The Family Book,* Jonathan Emmett's *Ruby in Her Own Time*, Lisa McCue's *Quiet Bunny*, Keiko Kasza's *Ready for Anything*, and Stan and Jan Berenstain's *He Bear, She Bear* address some of these differences in positive and reassuring ways. Their tone is quite appropriate for preschoolers.

The concept of differences can be explored in fiction and in nonfiction. In *Unbeatable Beaks* by Stephen Swinburne, birds from around the world are presented through their beaks and what those beaks are used for. Soyung Pak explores how a young child and his grandmother, who lives in Korea and speaks no English, shed their language differences by communicating in pictures in *Dear Juno. No Mirrors in My Nana's House* by Ysaye Barnwell is a special book that delves into the concept of inner beauty and the things that people have in common. A CD accompanies the book; it includes both a regular reading and a reading with musical accompaniment.

Preschoolers also have **fears** that should not be ignored. Realizing that others have similar fears can alleviate much of the stress created by these fears. Children fear being alone, dealing with an older sibling, anger, frustration, the darkness, and so on. Some titles that address these topics are Bernard Waber's *Ira Sleeps Over,* Judith Viorst's *Alexander and the Terrible, Horrible, No Good, Very Bad Day,* Maurice Sendak's *Where the Wild Things Are,* and Allen Say's *Allison.* In Say's book, a young girl comes to an awareness and acceptance of her adoption by befriending a stray cat. Fear of the dark is the topic of the classic *There's a Nightmare in My Closet* by Mercer Mayer. A more humorous book on the same topic is *A Beasty Story* by Bill Martin, Jr. The oversized rhyming text and the fine illustrations by Steven Kellogg tell the lighthearted story of the four mice as they walk through a candlelit spooky house. The subject of night-mares is addressed by Kate Klise in *Little Rabbit and the Night Mare.* In this story, Little Rabbit tries everything to make the scary creatures in his dreams go away. At last, he dreams up a clever way to face his fears. Finally, *Black Cat* by Christopher Myers puts an urban twist on the haunted house atmosphere. With a hip-hop beat, the pulsating rhyme of the text follows the cat through subway tunnels and dark streets.

Reading Areas for Preschoolers

The reading area should be more adventurous for preschoolers than for toddlers. Lofts, mattress tents, and truck tires with pillows are good choices. Lighting is important with this age group because the children will be looking more closely at the words, and some may be beginning to read. Daylight should be used when possible. Locating the reading area near a window is recommended.

In creating a reading area it's important to recognize the need of this age group to understand the "why" of things. Include mobiles of seasons, planets, and stars. A good choice would be posters that are realistic rather than cartoon style, illustrating the inside of such things as bodies, mountains, and Earth. Locating real animals near the reading area is a fine idea, particularly when focusing on animal stories.

TIPS FOR TEACHERS

Encourage children to respond to each other's questions.

- Reinforce children's responses to each other.
- When children don't respond to each other, help them do so by repeating or rephrasing the question raised.
- Model a response and ask children for additional responses.

Obviously, these ideas take careful planning. However, including them as part of the lesson helps motivate the children. The availability of props after the book is read will encourage the children to recreate the story through talk and play. For example, after reading Jimmy Kennedy's *The Teddy Bear Picnic*, place a teddy bear and the book in the reading area on a rocking chair. In most cases, children will soon be in the chair, leafing through the book and hugging the teddy bear. Making the reading area easy to change will help the adult and the children continue to have creative interactions with books.

CREATING AN ENVIRONMENT FOR KINDERGARTEN

Kindergarten children are successful in many tasks. Their skills often show a good deal of self-reliance. Supervision by adults need not be as direct as it is for the earlier age groups. Kindergarten children are active and enjoy outdoor play. They show more **cooperative play** both at home and in school. On the other hand, the mix of 5-year-olds and 6-year-olds can present a wide range of skills and abilities, and children this age take note of what their friends say and do. The result can be a concern for what others think that may lead to reluctance to join in activities unless others are involved first. Adults must sometimes initiate the involvement of children in activities. The activities and stories must be chosen to engage the active interests of these children.

The Power of Language

From the age of 4 to 5, children move to stage five of language development. They expand their speaking vocabulary to about 1,900 words and demonstrate an MLU of 4.00. They use more complex sentences, tell longer stories, and begin to acquire metalinguistic skills as they correct themselves. They have learned the basic rules of language, but not all the exceptions to those rules (Brown, 1973; Crain & Lillo-Martin, 1999). During the ages of 5 and 6, children experience the power of language. They come to understand how language can express ideas and emotions, create stories and meanings, and share life experiences. For some time now, they have been aware that they are surrounded by print. They read some words, and attempt to use words in their drawings.

The role of adults at this stage of a child's language development is to take advantage of the many opportunities that arise for helping the child experiment with and enjoy language. One can encourage children to understand that the printed word can represent all of the meanings and feelings that oral language can contain. The focus should be on meaning rather than on the correct form. A child's **invented spellings** (e.g., "I lik mi kat." for "I like my cat.") should be accepted without negative comment. The child will come in contact with correct spellings over and over again. The discovery of the correct forms will occur naturally and be incorporated into the child's original writing.

It is important for those working with and caring for young children to understand invented spelling and the role that it plays in literacy development. Just as children seek to communicate orally through speech, they also seek to do so visually through their pictures and written language. In fact, drawing pictures or simply making marks on a paper with a crayon can be viewed as an early stage of writing.

As children grow, they typically add language to their pictures. Invented spelling refers to the attempt of children to use what they do know about spelling in order to write their thoughts. Linguists such as Charles Read and Carol Chomsky were among the first to recognize and study invented spelling. Research has shown that invented spelling, supported and guided by teachers and informed parents, is an effective tool in learning to spell and important to foster academic achievement and individual empowerment (Kolodziel & Columba, 2005). A systematic classification of the stages of invented spelling was developed and refined by Richard Gentry. In looking at Gentry's levels of invented spelling, it is important to note that there is a wide age range in which each level can be observed.

Therefore, it is not the ages that are important but rather the characteristics of each stage leading to the next and ultimately to conventional spelling. An abbreviated description of Gentry's (2000) five stages of invented spelling includes:

- *Precommunicative:* At this stage, the child uses some alphabetic letters but does not understand sound–symbol correspondence. The child may not distinguish between uppercase and lowercase letters, and may not write from left to right. An example might look like "KDJEWOPHGG."

- *Semiphonetic:* The child begins to understand sound–symbol correspondence and that writing goes from left to right. Single letters and abbreviated groups of letters are sometimes used to represent entire words. An example might be "IMHAB" (I am happy).

- *Phonetic:* The child uses a letter or letters for each speech sound heard in a word. The letters might not be correct, but they are logical and more easily understood. Word segmentation is frequently seen. An example would be "I lik my mare gornd" (I like my merry-go-round).

- *Transitional:* At this stage, the child begins to use some conventional spellings. Instead of relying on sounds, the child begins to use visual and word structure knowledge. The child may reverse some letter pairs, but tends to use more learned words in writing. An example of this stage is "Mercry is the nerist plaent in the soler systome" (Mercry is the nerist planet in the solar system).

- *Conventional:* At this stage, the child has basically mastered the orthographic language system, understands word structure (e.g., prefix, suffix), can use generalizations, and spells most words correctly from memory. A spelling sense emerges and the writer recognizes when something does not look right.

Kindergarten Interests

The powerful and the mystical are of great interest to kindergarten children. New editions of the classic stories of "Cinderella," "Sleeping Beauty," and "Rapunzel" are wonderful for reading aloud to 5-year-olds and 6-year-olds. They respond to epic adventures where, through enchantment and strength, the hero overcomes evil. The more overwhelming the odds, the better the story is for them. There are many lesser-known fairy tales and stories that can be used to both keep children's interest and to compare with more popular versions.

Cover from *Thumbelina* retold by Hans Christian Anderson (retold by Brian Anderson). Jacket art copyright ©2009 by Bagram Ibatoulline. Reprinted by permission of Candlewick Press. All rights reserved.

For example, children can discover that Snow White had a sister named Rose Red in older tales. Reading several versions of the same story can help children compare stories. Kindergarten children enjoy giving their opinions.

Fairy Tales from Hans Christian Andersen, by the author of the same name, and *Tales from the Brothers Grimm: A Classic Illustrated Edition,* compiled by Edens Cooper, are good sources for classic tales. The texts, however, may be challenging for some young readers. Many classic tales are also told in single books with wonderful illustrations. A favorite is *Beauty and the Beast* illustrated by Karen Milone. The jealous sisters in this book are so ugly that the beast is not so scary in comparison. The ending is pure fairy tale. *Thumbelina*, retold by Brian Anderson, presents the classic story about tiny Thumbelina in an approachable format. The dreamy illustrations by Bagram Ibatoulline reinforce the message of happiness being achieved through kindness to others. Some fairy tales are quite violent and would be inappropriate for reading with young children. Always read stories in advance to check. Traditional and contemporary folktales are useful as well. *Fiddlin' Sam* by Marianna Dengler is a tale that takes place in the Ozarks. In it, Sam searches high and low for someone to pass his music on to before he plays his last. The important message the book shares is that talent is not a gift for one to keep. Talent should be shared and passed on to others.

Kindergarten children are very involved with learning about their bodies and **social interactions**. At times they may find it difficult to play and interact because of the increased need to fit in with their peers. It is healthy for them to discover that these mixed feelings occur with other children as well. *Never Say Boo* by Robin Pulver provides a beautifully constructed message about not making judgments about others based on appearances alone. In this story Gordon, a young ghost, looks frightful and has no friends. When an emergency occurs and Gordon saves the day, others are forced to examine their attitudes.

Troubling issues greatly affect the kindergarten child. The same issues that cause conflict for adults can be agonizing to a child. When the adults in a child's life are going through the **emotional stress** of death, divorce, separation, unemployment, or other personal difficulties, they often seek to protect the children from the hurt. Unfortunately, this seldom works. Children feel the pain anyway; when adults try to protect them from it, they may feel excluded. Being isolated or feeling isolated rarely helps anyone through a difficult time. Reading books on the topic that is causing distress can help the child understand what is happening.

Other issues that kindergarten children are concerned with include adoption and disabilities. Youngsters can be cruel to other children who are different. Yet most children will act kindly and supportively to such children when given the opportunity to learn about the differences. **Fear and ignorance provoke unkind behaviors**. In *Weslandia,* Paul Fleischman shares a story about Wesley, a boy who was rejected by others and who invents his own highly creative

Cover from *Never Say Boo* by Robin Pulver. Jacket art copyright ©2009 by Deb Lucke. Reprinted by permission of Holiday House. All rights reserved.

imaginary world. When those who had rejected him discover what he created, it becomes clear that Wesley is the most fascinating one of the group. Adoption is presented in a reassuringly perceptive manner in *McDuff Moves In* by Rosemary Wells. A similar approach is used by Maggie Glen in *Ruby,* the story of a teddy bear with physical disabilities. Readers will cheer for Ruby right through to her triumphant victory over the prejudice and ignorance of others. Additional books that present disabilities with clarity and sensitivity include *One for All, All for One* by Brigitte Weninger, *Just Teenie* by Susan Meddaugh, *Helen Keller* by David Adler, and *Jooka Saves the Day* by Giles Eduar. Such books put to rest fears and beliefs such as, "I'll get adopted if I misbehave . . . This is catching . . . He's just trying to get attention." Dealing with these concepts honestly through literature can replace ignorance with truth and understanding. Understanding often leads to caring and acceptance.

TIPS FOR TEACHERS

Invite many different people to share a book at story time. Orient them on childhood development, how to read to a group, and how to hold the book.

- A nurse or doctor could read a book about a sick child.
- A social worker could read a book involving adoption.
- A grocer could read a book in which food plays a role.
- Make it an official event yearly, quarterly, or monthly.

Our world is undergoing an **information explosion**, and kindergarten children are involved in this phenomenon. They can acquire knowledge, concepts, and ideas from both fiction and nonfiction titles that address things such as calendars, dinosaurs, tsunamis, and aboriginal life in the Australian outback. Titles worth reading include *The Shape of Things* by Doyle Ann Dodds, *Big City Song* by Debora Pearson, *A Picture Book of Thurgood Marshall* by David A. Adler, *Gulls . . . Gulls . . . Gulls* by Gail Gibbons, *Ten in the Bed* by Jane Cabrera, *What Is Science?* By Rebecca Dotlich, and *Selvakumar Knew Better* by Xiaojun Li. Li's book is the story of escaping the danger of a tsunami and could be used to explore the concept of global warming. Books about winter and the changing of seasons include *Winter Eyes* by Douglas Florian, *Snow Bear* by Jean Craighead George, and *In for Winter, Out for Spring* by Arnold Adoff. Adoff's book features Jerry Pinkney's wonderful illustrations of an African American family enjoying the changing seasons. Content books can provide much information for children who thirst to know the what, why, and how of things.

Children can enjoy picture books even if they are not able to read all of the words.

Interest in reading grows for kindergarten children. ABC books, counting books, and I Can Read books have an increasing attraction as the year progresses. Whether one is a proponent of early reading instructional programs or not, ABC books can be delightful. There are a great many available, each different, with a variety of illustration styles. Norman Bridwell's *Clifford's ABC,* Steven Kellogg's *Aster Aardvark's Alphabet Adventures,* Brad Herzog's *R Is for Race: A Stock Car Alphabet,* Bill Martin, Jr., and John Archambault's *Chicka Chicka Boom Boom,* Woody Jackson's *A Cow's Alfalfa-bet,* and Richard Scarry's *Find Your ABC's* are just a few of the favorites. The counting book *One Duck Stuck* by Phyllis Root uses a bouncing story with repetition. Keith Baker's *Quack and Count* also uses rhythm to introduce simple addition. His earth-tone collages provide the background for the white text. Joan Graham uses poetry to explore shapes in *Flicker Flash.*

Reading Areas for Kindergarten Children

Setting up a reading area for kindergarten children should be a group project. Involve the children in the planning, constructing, and changing of the area. Start the year with just the space set aside in the room. Bring in materials, and discuss how the reading area can be created. The more children are involved in the planning, the greater their emotional commitment will be to the reading area and to reading. Most ideas, even if they initially seem impossible, can become a reality to some extent. With some imagination, one can create gardens, planets, caves, jungles, or tree houses for a classroom reading area.

Practical Considerations for Reading Areas

The reading area is for reading, sharing, and interacting with books. It may also be referred to as the reading corner, reading nook, or reading center. The reading area and the time spent there with children should reflect the caregiver's attitude toward books, reading, literacy, and children. The best attitude is a relaxed one toward all four. Children will experience, listen to, interact with, and enjoy the ideas in books and children's magazines. A reading area should give the feeling that books are an open invitation. They are to be enjoyed. The size of the space set aside for the reading area is not particularly important as long as it can comfortably contain the people using it at one time. What is important is the effective use of the space by the children. The visual and aesthetic appeal of the reading area promotes its effective use. This is achieved by making the space warmly inviting and appropriate for the age of the children.

Where to Put a Reading Area. Every room is set up differently. Any room arrangement has both strengths and weaknesses. A reading area may be in a corner, along a wall, or in a loft. When initially planning an area, keep in mind traffic patterns and lighting.

Traffic patterns are important in a classroom. Move tables and screens to create large and small spaces within the room. Large spaces encourage movement. They can be distracting and chaotic. Small spaces are useful for separating children into interest areas for smaller projects. However, small spaces used to channel children through a room can be busy and noisy. The reading area, therefore, is best located off the beaten path, away from both large and small traffic areas. One may locate a reading area near a dress-up or music area. In this way, books and ideas can spill over into play in these other areas. Try a variety of arrangements to see which works best with a particular class and program. A guiding principle is that there is seldom a wrong area to place books.

Because inappropriate lighting can cause problems that are easily avoided, lighting is an important consideration for a reading area. Natural lighting is preferred. This means that the reading area should be near a window if possible. A location near the window allows for such reading-related activities as daydreaming, bird watching, and cloud gazing.

Because it is not always possible to use natural lighting, there should be a backup plan for cloudy days, dark mornings, and late afternoon hours. Although many schools have fluorescent lighting for the whole room, some situations might call for a darkened room with only a small lamp for reading. Incandescent lamps are preferred for the softer glow they emit. Some find fluorescent light hard on the eyes. This is especially true when it creates a glare on glossy pages and chalkboards. Lamp bulbs should be a minimum of 100 watts when used for reading. Soft white bulbs are superior to regular lamp bulbs as they reduce the glare. The new energy-saving fluorescent bulbs can replace incandescent bulbs to save energy and money while providing the same soft lighting.

What kind of lamps should be used? Heavy lamps sitting on tables can tip over too easily, resulting in injury to children. Hanging lamps, wall lamps, and under-counter lamps avoid these tipping dangers. Cords are a hazard in areas that encourage lounging, crawling, and snuggling. They can be chewed on and tripped over. Lamps that are securely attached to walls or ceilings are not in the way. They cannot be knocked over, and their cords can be covered or discreetly tucked out of the way.

For those difficult spots such as lofts, cubby areas, and cloakrooms, under-counter lights are inexpensive, safe, and easily installed. They offer a good source of light. Any lamp used should be properly installed, carry the Underwriters Laboratory stamp of approval, and have no frayed or uncovered wires.

After space and lighting have been selected, consider the furnishings of the reading area. Will a couch or carpeting be used? Will it be a theme space? A loft? These decisions are determined by size, creativity, and available materials. The possibilities are endless.

Costs of a Reading Area. Cost is a factor in any planning. For child care centers and schools, a reading area is a necessity. Although most schools and centers include the cost of reading areas in their budgets, it's a good idea to also consider alternative funding and sources of supplies. Stores, families, friends, yard sales, and social service agencies are good sources of free materials. Once the reading area is planned, a list of needed materials can be shared with potential donors. Thank-you notes set up a friendly contact for future classroom endeavors. Both the school and the donor enjoy positive public relations when the school or town newspaper publishes a story about the donations.

Kinds of Materials Needed

The most important need is for many, many books. A reading area also needs places to shelve books and places for people. It needs dividers, props, and decorations.

Audiovisual equipment such as tape players, personal electronic devices, VCRs, CD/DVD players and recorders, and computers may be used in the reading area but kept elsewhere. These audiovisual items are generally shared with other areas within the school or center, and are borrowed or loaned only for specific activities.

Places to Display Books. Display books on wire racks or front-facing bookcases that allow the book covers to be seen. These are generally constructed of sturdy metal or hardwood. They are long-term investments that will give many years of use. The two sizes ordinarily used are shorter tabletop models and taller floor models. Both types can be costly, however. Someone with basic carpentry skills may be able to provide a comparable display at a more reasonable cost.

Secondhand bookcases are also a source for book storage and display furniture. Stores that are refurbishing or going out of business may be able to provide display units that are appropriate for books. One center used this approach to purchase a sturdy case with four lower drawers and a peg-board on the back. The inexpensive five-foot unit now serves as a peg-board, room divider, storage unit, and shelving area for children's books and other materials.

Retail stores and grocery markets can also provide displays made of heavy cardboard. Most often these displays are discarded after they are used for a limited amount of time. When stores are finished using displays, they are often willing to give them away. They work fine for most children's books. One such display, a display turkey from a liquor store, was used for several years in a center for a variety of purposes. Think creatively to see the possibilities in these store displays.

Other unconventional items may also be used for book storage and display. These include plastic dishpans, apple baskets, laundry baskets, milk crates, wicker baskets, metal laundry tubs, kitchen cabinets, and plastic wastebaskets. With some construction skills, one can create inexpensive and sturdy shelving with pine boards and concrete blocks from a lumberyard.

Whatever material is used, it should showcase the books. The books should be placed in such a way that they almost ask to be picked up and read.

Places for People. "A gentle rain pattering on the window . . . a warm quilt wrapped around you . . . nestled in a lap for a story." This is an image of a great place to be for a story. It is cozy, warm, and comfortable. Comfort is essential for a reading area. Keep in mind the age and size of the children when planning a safe space. Children love to snuggle into reading. They move around. They wriggle. They sometimes sit perfectly still. The seating in a reading area should be on the floor or a mattress for the greatest protection against falls.

Small beanbag chairs as well as regular-size stuffed chairs might be used. Care should be taken when using furniture with hard wooden armrests. Furniture legs can be cut off or removed to make the size more appropriate for children. Sofa cushions and mattresses can be used on the floor as seating areas. Tent covers for a mattress can turn the area into a boat, automobile, or cave. A child's swimming pool can be filled with pillows and stuffed toys as a seating area. Small chairs, rocking chairs, and stools might also be used.

A low loft makes a wonderful reading area for young children. Have a knowledgeable person construct or prepare the loft. It should be carpeted, no

Reading can be done almost anywhere.

higher than four feet from the floor, and sturdily built. Protective railings should be made with slats spaced no farther apart than two inches so children will not become stuck. Avoid pillows and other items that could cause a fall from the loft. When using carpeting as a seating surface, inspect the best carpets before making a decision on which to use. Wool carpets can be hot and itchy. Indoor-outdoor carpet is very durable. Nylon carpet cleans easily. Remnants from carpet distributors can be bound for a minimal price, eliminating any ragged edges. With large needles and upholstery thread, create a patchwork carpet out of carpet samples. The finished rug will contain various patterns, textures, and types of carpeting. It can become a tactile masterpiece and define each child's space. Be aware, however, that carpeting might be a poor choice of material for children with allergies.

Wall Dividers. A reading area should be apart from the flow of traffic. Room dividers can help create a space where there seems to be none available. Dividers that allow for maximum flexibility include wide bookcases, bulletin boards, peg-boards, stand-up flannel boards, and chalkboards. Furniture can form part of the boundary of the reading area. The back of a sofa, a row of chairs, and a row of cushions can all serve as dividers. One can purchase room dividers and supports from commercial supply companies, and they can be constructed from large cardboard boxes or four-foot-by-eight-foot sheets of plywood. Dividers need be only three feet in height to provide reading privacy. This height allows the adult to retain visibility of all of the room.

Creating a Reading Area

It is the extras that often make a difference in almost anything. Attention to details can make a good thing better. So it is with reading areas. Think of the reading area as an expressive part of the room. It should include items that reflect children's work and creativity. Part of the wall can include a bulletin board that changes as the seasons pass. Various themes can be reflected. Puppets or stuffed toys can reflect favorite stories.

During "Dinosaur Week," books such as Martin Waddell's *The Super Hungry Dinosaur*, Andrew Plant's ABC book *Could a Dinosaur Play Tennis?*, and Bob Kolar's *Stomp, Stomp* could be read. A mobile of children's renderings of favorite dinosaurs could be hung up.

A stuffed dinosaur or an inflatable dinosaur could be added to the other animals in the reading area. A dinosaur chart might be placed on the wall. Place red vinyl balls in the area as dinosaur eggs. Sources for these items include educational supply companies, yard sales, relatives, and friends. In addition, bookstores increasingly stock stuffed characters from books.

Holidays are an important part of any program for young children. The topic can be used throughout the year and should include a good deal of parental involvement through surveys, messages back and forth to the home, and parent meetings. Holidays should be inclusive. Different cultures celebrate different holidays; sometimes they celebrate the same holiday in different ways. Research parents' attitudes about how many holidays to celebrate, which to include and which not to include, and how best to recognize them. In some situations, you might decide not to celebrate a holiday or not to focus on some aspects of it (e.g., the commercialization of Christmas).

TIPS FOR TEACHERS

Invite parental participation in the creation of reading environments.

- Ask a team of parents to create a themed area for holidays or seasons.
- Ask parents to suggest titles of children's books.
- Plan a unit with parental input, including ideas for extension at home.

Other innovative ideas for decorating include using large boxes to create special environments from telephone booths to ships. Add a branch of a tree for an aesthetically pleasing feature in a reading area. It can be decorated for the season using crepe paper leaves, cotton balls, or cutout snowflakes. The children can add these to reflect the seasonal change. Nontoxic live plants are always pleasing and popular in reading areas. They should be kept out of reach of small infants and toddlers.

Children can and should contribute to the aesthetic surroundings of the reading area. Constructing books and posters is personally rewarding to children. When displayed, these items surround the area with an aura of positive self-esteem. The children become aware that their contributions are as important as the books and other materials in the reading area.

PUTTING IT ALL TOGETHER

In order to see the "big picture" of a reading area, sketch out all of the parts of the area on paper. Seeing all the components together gives a feel for the total package.

The photographs in this section illustrate actual classroom reading areas. Keep in mind that the more involved children are in the design and makeup of the area, the more comfortable they will be in the exciting world of books and stories.

Although reading areas can vary in size, shape, and furnishings, they should always provide a feeling of closeness and welcome.

A successful reading area is one in which children feel comfortable and safe.

HOLDING A BOOK FOR STORY TIME

Note the significance of the small details in successfully reading a story to children. Reading to children is more than picking up a book and reading it aloud. The setting is important. The choice of materials is important. The way the book is held is important—the children will see much better if the reader tilts the book directly to the children's eye level. The book should be firmly grasped by the reader and held at eye level for the children.

After or during the reading of each page, the book should be moved from side to side. This will ensure that all children see the pictures and the text. If the children cannot see the illustrations, they may become bored or frustrated. If this happens, they will likely lose interest in the story.

If the adult is familiar with the story, holding the book in this fashion will cause no problems in the flow of the narrative. If the children are seated, the easiest way to hold the book is to keep the thumb in the center of the pages and the book open in front of the group. One need not move the book, as the children should be able to see quite well from their seated position.

Choosing a Place

The place chosen for reading a book depends on the size of the group and the space used to accommodate the group. With larger groups of children, the reader will generally select a circle time area. With smaller groups, the reading area of

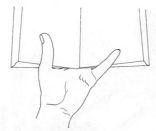

Holding a book so that children can see the words and pictures may take a little practice, but it is an important skill for story sharing.

Everyone can see the book being shared.

a small corner will work well. Nap time is a good opportunity for reading aloud. A story at that time provides a soothing listening experience for the children as they begin their quiet time.

Several factors contribute to a **positive reading experience**. Always select a comfortable spot where the lighting is adequate but not in anyone's eyes. Make certain there is plenty of room for wriggling so the children will not be bumping into each other.

Choose a place without immediate distractions. The housekeeping corner of the room or a spot next to the class gerbil may be too busy for a reading spot. When reading outside, check for anthills, damp ground, and insects that could turn reading time into first-aid time. Children warm up for the story with a related fingerplay or song. This will provide both motivation and personal involvement in the story. Make sure all children will be able to see the illustrations. Finally, always know the story before attempting to read or share it with others.

Discovering Great Books

Books are a key part of any classroom's inventory. Adding to the classroom library within a budget can be a difficult problem. Once the teacher has decided which books are needed for the classroom library, the challenge becomes one of finding the books.

a.

b.

c.

d.

e.

Successful seating patterns can take a variety of formats. Shown clockwise from upper left are (a) single line, (b) children on lap, (c) semicircle for a small group, (d) floor and chair combination for larger groups, and (e) risers for larger groups.

Libraries. If the room is housed in a public or private school, the school library is the first source for borrowing needed books. Most librarians welcome suggestions concerning book selections for the school library. Librarians are terrific at finding the right books to complement themes, units, and special classroom projects. The public library is an additional source of books. Every classroom should have its own permanent collection as well. To find these books, search in yard sales, bookstores, catalogs, book clubs, library discard sales, book fairs, estate sales, and moving sales.

A question to be addressed is whether paperback books should be part of the classroom library. For reading aloud, a paperback offers the same story as a hardcover edition, but at a lower cost. Some disagree over whether paperback books are viable for classroom use. There are valid points to each side of the argument. The use of electronic books, or books presented through any kind of video screen, is not encouraged due to the growing amount of screen time young children are exposed to as described in the first chapter.

Paperback Books. There are many excellent editions of both classic and contemporary award-winning books available in paperback. Technology has improved the quality and durability of many paperbacks.

For the price of one hardcover book, one can purchase several paperback books. With the cost so much lower, a teacher can buy more books now rather than buying only a few copies each year. Book fairs put on by book distributors are an inexpensive source of paperback books. Book clubs are now found mostly on line. However, these clubs have greatly increased their non-book merchandising of toys, games, and clothing.

Teaching children to care for books is an important literacy lesson. It is a good idea to have a "First-Aid Kit for Books" handy in order to patch and repair damage as soon as possible. The kit should include scissors, invisible clear tape, white glue, and a glue stick. Children can help with the repairs and develop a sense of respect for books.

Hardcover Books. Hardcover books are more expensive, but they stand up better to the wear and tear of everyday use. Although the initial cost is higher, the books need not be replaced as often. Since most books are printed initially in hardcover, a wider variety of titles is usually available.

The answer to the paperback versus hardcover argument is probably that both have a legitimate place. The caregiver can take advantage of both kinds by buying some paperbacks to increase the variety and some hardcover books to enhance the durability of the collection. If necessary, paperback books can be limited to short-term use so that their life can be lengthened.

Children need access to a wide range of books.

Since infants and toddlers need a hands-on experience with books, one might wish to limit their paperback book use. On the other hand, literacy development demands that books get into the hands of children as soon as it can be done meaningfully. Plastic books with rounded edges and poster board books are best for babies and very young children.

Big books are large-size editions that enable children to more easily share the reading experience. Some big books are trade book stories reprinted in a larger format. Others are stories made specifically for a big book. These latter stories tend to be predictable in terms of repeated phrases and sentences throughout. This predictability allows children to recognize some of the text and join in the actual reading. Publishers that distribute big book editions include Scholastic, Harcourt, Raintree/Heinemann, and The Wright Group (see Appendix A). When writing to publishers, it is usually helpful to indicate the age or grade level you are interested in. Popular big books include:

A Cake for Barney, Joyce Dunbar, Harcourt, 1998
A is for Africa, Ifeoma Onyefulu, Raintree/Heinemann, 2003
Crazy Hair Day, Barney Saltzberg, Candlewick, 2008
Farmer Duck Big Book, Martin Waddell and Helen Oxenbury, Raintree/Heinemann, 1997
Five Little Monkeys Jumping on the Bed, Eileen Christelow, Sandpiper, 2006

Flower Garden, Eve Bunting, Harcourt Brace, 1999
Goodnight Moon, Margaret Wise Brown, Harper Festival, 2007
If You Give a Pig a Pancake, Laura Numeroff, Harper Collins, 2000
One Duck Stuck Big Book: A Mucky Ducky Counting Book, Phyllis Root, Candlewick, 2008.
Mrs. Wishy Washy, Joy Cowley, Wright Group, 1997
The Snowy Day, Ezra Jack Keats, Scholastic, 1993

Adults and Children as Storytellers

Clara Thompson, a turn-of-the-century educator, said that nothing in human nature had changed in education since she first taught in a one-room schoolhouse. Education is only as good as the individuals working within it. Children learn when one is able to reach them and bring them into the process of education. This is still true.

TIPS FOR TEACHERS

Show children how to use their faces and body language to help tell a story.

- Create a "copy me" game to show children how it feels when they make a happy, sad, surprised, or scared face.
- Use a mirror to help children create facial and body movements relevant to a story.
- Have children strike poses in response to a series of words and phrases (e.g. bat a ball, pick an apple).

Adults must remember that **body language** and **preparation** impart nuances that young children perceive. When one is prepared to share a story or teach a lesson, there is an air of confidence. Children notice this and respond to it. The enthusiasm is increased when the reader feels confident and at ease. One becomes natural and less inhibited in the telling of the tale when this confidence is present. The chapters following this describe the range of aspects that should form the preparation of the reader or story teller. Children can build on this modeling, using their terrific imaginations to do some storytelling of their own.

Communicating a Message. Telling a story involves more than reading it. **Share the message** and the emotion that exists between the lines and within the illustrations.

In planning a reading, know the story well. It is impossible to plan a story experience if the plot and the story are unknown to the teller.

When reading or retelling, don't start until the children are listening. Use a transition activity and a motivation to bring the children into a story mood.

The reader must speak clearly and maintain eye contact. It helps to speak a little slower and more distinctly than when using a normal speaking voice. This helps everyone to understand the words.

Use of Voice. Use the **voice** effectively. A powerful and adaptive tool in storytelling, the reader's voice can be soft, loud, teasing, brash, or soothing. Different voices for different characters and varied pitches and tones of voice all help create and maintain interest in the story.

Maintain the rhythm of the story. This means reading louder and faster for some parts of the story. Other parts might require a slow or whispering voice.

Body Language. Body language is a part of storytelling. To eliminate the need to shift and move, get into a comfortable position before beginning the tale. With just a bit of exaggeration, one's face can be used as a mirror of the story's action. Subtlety is necessary here. Maintaining **eye contact** is important for keeping the children's attention on the story. Pausing before plot shifts adds to the excitement. One might even **pause** at a suspenseful point and ask an **open-ended question** about what might happen next. Finally, **demonstrate enjoyment** in the telling of the story. Choose a wide variety of books that both the teacher and children will enjoy. Be discriminating. Never use a book just because it's available or because it was used last year. Make each book a special memory.

Accommodation of Special Needs

All children have equal rights and worth. Federal and state laws recognize this and require any program receiving public funding to include children with special needs to the fullest extent possible. It is important that programs strive to **accommodate** children with disabilities to the fullest extent possible. Modifications in the physical environment, staff training, equipment, and materials may be needed.

Some disabilities are less evident than others, so it is important that all individuals working with children have training to recognize and respond to different needs. Full legal definitions of disabilities are found in law, but those most commonly found in children in early childhood programs are briefly described here. **Autism**, including **Asperger's Syndrome**, is a developmental disability affecting verbal communication, nonverbal communication, and social interaction. A communication impairment is one where the individual has difficulty using expressive and/or receptive language. Developmental delay refers to learning capacity difficulty related to language, cognitive, emotional, physical, social, adaptive, and/or self-help skills. An **emotional disability** is identified when significant difficulty is observed in an individual in the area of peer relations, emotions, and/or inappropriate behaviors. **Health impairments** refer to chronic or acute health problems that affect learning (e.g., diabetes, leukemia, attention deficit hyperactivity disorder). Specific **learning disability** is a disorder causing learning delays in reading, writing, or mathematics that are not primarily a result of another disability. Finally, there are **intellectual, physical, neurological, and sensory (i.e., deaf, blind) disabilities**.

The most important factor in accommodating children with disabilities is the teacher or staff member. Attitudes toward disabilities must be reflected upon. It is more than the development of tolerance. There is a critical need to be proactive. A good place to start is to learn as much information about the child as possible from parents, specialists, and other staff members. Every child has strengths, interests, and abilities. It's important to note these, for they will help to make the connections to others and to the environment. Depending on the needs and strengths of the child, many common sense accommodations might be considered. These include removing clutter and barriers, making conscious efforts to include all children, and using a variety of language stimuli such as videos, tapes, DVDs, and computer programs.

Some disabilities might need more specific common sense accommodations when sharing language and literature. For children who are visually impaired or blind, it is helpful to explain the illustrations, use tactile puppet characters, use the other senses in the telling, provide high-powered magnifiers and/or large-print books, and use the child's name when talking. For children who are hard of hearing or deaf, get the child's attention with a light touch on the arm when talking, maintain eye contact, make sure your hands and face are visible, speak normally and clearly, use natural gestures and facial expressions, use writing and illustration to make a point, use well-illustrated books, incorporate American Sign Language signs with all of the children, and speak directly to the child even when an interpreter is present. For children with physical disabilities, be aware that a wheelchair is part of the child's body space. Give time to allow the child to move into the circle independently and bring yourself and the key aspects of the room (e.g., book display, manipulatives) to the appropriate eye level for the child. Depending on the disability, other accommodations might include slant top desks, beanbag chairs, foam rolls and wedges, adaptive keyboards, a large-size computer mouse, and multiple coding signage (i.e., visual and tactile).

SUMMARY

In this chapter, it was found that the environment in which literature is shared with children is critical. Planning the setting for storytelling and sharing books is an important part of any early education program. Children respond to setting. They also respond to the opportunity to be involved in the planning of the setting. Attending to the conditions for literacy learning can help to develop appropriate environments.

The reading environment should be carefully designed to reflect age-appropriate approaches to the children. Therefore, it is necessary to have an understanding of literacy development in infants, toddlers, preschoolers, and kindergarten-age children. These include the interests of children and the role of invented spelling. This information will assist in designing reading areas.

The reading area sends many messages to children about the importance of reading, the joy of reading, and the role of the child in reading and literature. Children come to understand that they are active participants rather than passive recipients.

The adult is the primary tool needed to transfer the information from the book to the child. Storytelling skills may not be natural to everyone, but they can be developed with practice and forethought. The effective use of body language and voice can greatly enhance the reading process. Planning is an essential part of sharing a story with children.

QUESTIONS FOR THOUGHT AND DISCUSSION

1. What concerns should one have when planning to read a story?
2. When do infants begin to associate sounds with meaning?
3. Describe a possible reading area for children.
4. What are some characteristics of a toddler that a story reader might want to take into consideration?
5. What should one look for in an illustration designed for infants and toddlers?
6. How does humor seem to manifest itself in a preschooler?
7. What changes might one make in converting a toddler reading area into one suitable for preschoolers?
8. What social changes seem to occur as children go from the preschool stage to the kindergarten years?
9. Defend or refute this statement: Kindergarten children are too young to be involved in contemporary social issues.
10. How might one change a preschool reading area into one that is suitable for kindergarten children?

11. What should one consider when choosing a site for a reading area?

12. Discuss various ways to display books so that children will be encouraged to use them.

13. Describe various ways of seating children for reading, and identify the circumstances under which each would be used.

14. According to brain-based and language development research, what type of environment best enhances literacy acquisition in young children?

15. How can children with special-needs be accommodated in the sharing of a story?

 For additional resources, access the *Growing Up with Literature* companion website through www.cengagebrain.com <http://www.cengagebrain.com/>.

CHILDREN'S BOOKS CITED

Adler, David A. (1997). *A picture book of Thurgood Marshall*. New York: Holiday House.

Adler, David A. (2003). *Helen Keller*. New York: Holiday House.

Adoff, Arnold. (1997). *In for winter, out for spring*. New York: Harcourt Brace.

Andersen, Hans Christian. (1993). *Fairy tales from Hans Christian Andersen*. New York: Chronicle.

Anderson, Hans Christian. (2009). *Thumbelina* (retold by Brian Anderson). Somerville, MA: Candlewick.

Ayers, Katherine. (2003). *A long way*. New York: Puffin.

Baker, Keith. (1999). *Quack and count*. San Diego, CA: Harcourt Brace Jovanovich.

Barnwell, Ysaye. (1998). *No mirrors in my Nana's house*. San Diego, CA: Harcourt Brace.

Barton, Byron. (1997). *Where's the bear?* New York: Mulberry.

Berenstain, Stan, & Berenstain, Jan. (1974). *He bear, she bear*. New York: Random House.

Blackstone, Stella. (1997). *Baby rock, baby roll*. New York: Holiday House.

Bridwell, Norman. (1986). *Clifford's ABC*. New York: Scholastic.

Cabrera, Jane. (2006). *Ten in the bed*. New York: Holiday House.

Carle, Eric. (1981). *The very hungry caterpillar*. New York: Philomel.

Cooper, Edens (compiler). (2007). *Tales from the brothers Grimm*. New York: Chronicle Books.

Corey, Dorothy. (2010). *You go away*. Park Ridge, IL: Albert Whitman.

Dengler, Marianna. (1999). *Fiddlin' Sam*. Flagstaff, AZ: Silver Moon.

Dodds, Doyle Ann. (1994). *The shape of things*. Cambridge, MA: Candlewick.

Dotlich, Rebecca. (2006). *What is science?* New York: Henry Holt.

Eachus, Jennifer. (2006). *I'm sorry*. New York: Harper Trophy.

Eduar, Giles. (1997). *Jooka saves the day*. New York: Orchard.

Emmett, Jonathan. (2003). *Ruby in her own time*. New York: Scholastic.

Fleischman, Paul. (1999). *Weslandia*. Cambridge, MA: Candlewick.

Florian, Douglas. (1999). *Winter eyes*. New York: Greenwillow.

Fox, Mem. (1989). *Night noises*. San Diego, CA: Harcourt Brace Jovanovich.

Freedman, Claire. (2009). *When we're together*. Intercourse, PA: Good Books.

Freeman, Don. (1968). *Corduroy*. New York: Viking.

Fry, Sonali. (2006). *My busy day*. New York: Simon & Schuster.

George, Jean Craighead. (1999). *Snow bear*. Boston: Houghton Mifflin.

Gibbons, Gail. (1997). *Gulls . . . gulls . . . gulls*. New York: Holiday House.

Glen, Maggie. (1991). *Ruby*. New York: G. P. Putnam's Sons.

Graham, Joan. (1999). *Flicker flash*. Boston: Houghton Mifflin.

Haberman, Mary Ann. (2009). *All kinds of families*. Boston, MA: Little Brown.

Hearn, Diane Dawson. (1993). *Dad's dinosaur day*. New York: Macmillan.

Herzog, Brad. (2006). *R is for race: A stock car alphabet*. Chelsea, MI: Sleeping Bear Press.

High, Linda. (1999). *Barn savers*. Honesdale, PA: Boyds Mills Press.

Hill, Susanna. (2009). *Not yet Rose*. Grand Rapids, MI: Eerdmans.

Hills, Tad. (2006). *Duck and goose*. New York: Schwartz Wade.

Holmes, Janet. (2009). *Me and you*. New York: North South.

Hughes, Shirley. (2009). *Olly and me 1 2 3*. Somerville, MA: Candlewick.

Hurd, Thacheer. (2009). *Bad frogs*. Somerville, MA: Candlewick.

Jackson, Woody. (2003). *A cow's alfalfa-bet*. New York: Houghton Mifflin.

James, Simon. (1991). *Dear Mr. Blueberry*. New York: Macmillan.

Kasza, Keiko. (2009). *Ready for anything*. New York: Putnam.

Klise, Kate. (2008). *Little rabbit and the night mare*. Orlando, FL: Harcourt.

Keller, Holly. (2000). *That's mine Horace*. New York: Greenwillow.

Kellogg, Steven. (1997). *Aster Aardvark's alphabet adventures*. New York: Mulberry.

Kellogg, Steven. (1999). *The three sillies*. Cambridge, MA: Candlewick.

Kennedy, Jimmy. (1983). *The teddy bear picnic*. La Jolla, CA: Green Tiger.

Kolar, Bob. (1997). *Stomp, stomp*. New York: North-South.

Kunhardt, Dorothy. (1962). *Pat the bunny*. Racine, WI: Western.

Law, Diane. (2006). *Come out and play*. New York: Chronicle.

Levine, Abby. (2010) *You push, I ride*. Park Ridge, IL: Albert Whitman.

Li, Xiaojun. (2006). *Selvakumar knew better*. Fremont, CA: Shen's Books.

Lucas, Catherine. (2005). *Let's help.* New York: Simon & Schuster.

Maar, Paul. (2006). *Gloria the cow.* New York: Chronicle.

MacDonald, Suse. (2004). *Here a chick, where a chick?* New York: Scholastic.

Martin, Bill, Jr. (1999). *A beasty story.* San Diego, CA: Harcourt Brace.

Martin, Bill, Jr., & Archambault, John. (1989). *Chicka chicka boom boom.* New York: Simon and Schuster.

Masurel, Claire. (2006). *No, no, Titus.* New York: Chronicle.

Mayer, Mercer. (1992). *There's a nightmare in my closet.* New York: Dutton.

McCue, Lisa. (2009). *Quiet bunny.* New York: Sterling.

Meddaugh, Susan. (2006). *Just Teenie.* New York: Houghton Mifflin.

Milone, Karen (Illus.). (1981). *Beauty and the beast.* Mahwah, NJ: Troll.

Monsell, Mary. (2010). *Underwear!* Park Ridge, IL: Albert Whitman.

Morris, Neil. (1991). *Jump along.* Minneapolis, MN: Carolrhoda.

Myers, Christopher. (1999). *Black cat.* New York: Scholastic.

O'Connell, Rebecca. (2010). *Danny is done with diapers: A potty ABC.* Park Ridge, IL: Albert Whitman.

Paar, Todd. (2003). *The family book.* Boston: Little Brown.

Pak, Soyung. (1999). *Dear Juno.* New York: Viking.

Payne, Tony & Payne, Jan. (2003). *The Hippo-not-amus.* New York: Orchard.

Pearson, Debora. (2006). *Big city songs.* New York: Holiday House.

Pfister, Marcus. (1992). *The rainbow fish.* New York: North-South.

Pinkwater, Daniel. (2006). *Bad bears in the city.* New York: Houghton Mifflin.

Plant, Andrew. (2006). *Could a dinosaur play tennis?* LaJolla, CA: Kane/Miller.

Prap, Lila. (2006). *Animal lullabies.* New York: Chronicle.

Priddy, Roger. (2010). *Bright baby touch and feel bedtime.* New York: Macmillan/Priddy Books.

Pulver, Robin. (2009). *Never say boo.* New York: Holiday House.

Reid, Barbara. (1994). *Sing a song of Mother Goose.* New York: Scholastic.

Rey, H. A. (1963). *Curious George.* Boston: Houghton Mifflin.

Root, Phyllis. (1998). *One duck stuck.* Cambridge, MA: Candlewick.

Root, Phyllis. (2008). *One duck stuck big book: A Mucky Ducky counting book.* Somerville, MA: Candlewick.

Ross, Dave. (1980). *A book of hugs.* New York: Crowell.

Ross, Dave. (1983). *More hugs.* New York: Crowell.

Say, Allen. (1997). *Allison.* Boston: Houghton Mifflin.

Scarry, Richard. (1973). *Find your ABC's.* New York: Random House.

Scieszka, John. (2009). *Truckery rhymes.* New York: Simon and Schuster.

Sendak, Maurice. (1963). *Where the wild things are.* New York: Harper and Row.

Seuss, Dr. (pseud. for Theodor Geisel) (1940). *Horton hatches the egg.* New York: Random House.

Stein, David. (2009). *Pouch!* New York: Putnam.

Sutherland, Zena. (1990). *The Orchard book of nursery rhymes.* New York: Orchard.

Swinburne, Stephen. (1999). *Unbeatable beaks.* New York: Henry Holt.

Viorst, Judith. (1972). *Alexander and the terrible, horrible, no good, very bad day.* New York: Atheneum.

Waber, Bernard. (1972). *Ira sleeps over.* Boston: Houghton Mifflin.

Waddell, Martin. (2005). *It's quacking time.* Cambridge, MA: Candlewick.

Waddell, Martin. (2009). *The super hungry dinosaur.* New York: Dial.

Wells, Rosemary. (2005). *McDuff moves in.* New York: Hyperion.

Weninger, Brigitte. (2005). *One for all, all for one.* New York: Penguin.

Wright, Maureen. (2009). *Sleep, big bear, sleep!* Tarrytown, NY: Marshall Cavendish.

SELECTED REFERENCES AND RESOURCES

Applebee, A. N. (1989). *The child's concept of story.* Chicago, IL: University of Chicago Press.

Applebee, A. N., Burroughs, R., and Stevens, A. (2006). *Creating continuity and coherence in high school literature curricula.* Center on English Learning & Achievement site. Retrieved November 28, 2006, from http://cela.albany.edu/publication/article/creating.htm.

Brown, R. (1973). *A first language: The early stages.* Cambridge, MA: Harvard University Press.

Bullard, J. (2010). *Creating environments for learning: Birth to age eight.* Upper Saddle River, NJ: Merrill.

Cambourne, B. (1993). *The whole story: Natural learning and the acquisition of literacy in the classroom.* New York: Scholastic.

Cambourne, B. (December 2000/January 2001). Conditions for literacy learning. *The Reading Teacher, 54,* 414–417.

Cooper, P. M. (2009). *The classrooms all children need.* Chicago, IL: University of Chicago Press.

Crain, S., and Lillo-Martin, D. (1999). *An introduction to linguistic theory and language acquisition.* Malden, MA: Blackwell.

Dowling, M. (2009). *Young children's personal, emotional, and social development.* Newbury Park, CA: Sage.

Galotti, K. M. (2010). *Cognitive development.* Newbury Park, CA: Sage.

Gargiulo, R., and Kilgo, J. L. (2011). *An introduction to young children with special needs: Birth through age eight.* Florence, KY: Cengage/Wadsworth.

Gentry, J. R. (2000). A retrospective on invented spelling and a look forward. *The Reading Teacher, 54*, 318–332.

Gonzalez, V. (2009). *Young learners, diverse children.* Thousand Oaks, CA: Corwin.

Hardiman, M. M. (2003). *Connecting brain research with effective teaching: The brain-targeted teaching model.* Lanham, MD: Scarecrow.

Kolodziel, N. J., & Columba, L. (2005). Invented spelling: Guidelines for parents. *Reading Improvement, 42*, 212–223.

Lyons, C. A. (2003). *Teaching struggling readers: How to use brain-based research to maximize learning.* Portsmouth, NH: Heinemann.

Morrow, L. M., and Tracey, D. H. (2005). Instructional environments for language and learning: Considerations for young children. In James Flood, Shirley Heath, & Diane Lapp (Eds.), *Handbook of research on teaching literacy through the communicative and visual arts.* Mahwah, NJ: Erlbaum.

National Association for the Education of Young Children. (2005). *Basics of developmentally appropriate practice in early childhood programs serving children from birth through age eight.* Washington, DC: Author

Newman, R., Ratner, N. B., Jusczyk, A. M., Jusczyk, P. W., and Dow, K. A. (2006). Infants early ability to segment the conversational speech signal predicts later language development: A retrospective analysis. *Developmental Psychology, 42*, 643–655.

Sousa, D. A. (2006). *How the brain learns.* Thousand Oaks, CA: Corwin.

Tileston, D. W. (2005). *Ten best teaching practices: How brain research, learning styles, and standards define teaching competencies.* Thousand Oaks, CA: Corwin.

Whitehead, M. (2002). *Developing language and literacy with young children.* London: Chapman SAGE.

Wooten, D. A., and Cullinan, B. (2009). *Children's literature in the reading program.* Newark, DE: International Reading Association.

INTERNET REFERENCES AND HELPFUL WEBSITES

Bookhive. Public Library of Charlotte and Mecklenburg County site. Retrieved January 25, 2010, from http://www.plcmc.org

Booklist. American Library Association site. Retrieved January 25, 2010, from http://www.ala.org/booklist/

Current research on language development. Child Development Institute site. Retrieved January 25, 2010, from http://www.childdevelopmentinfo.com

Literacy Center Educational Network site. Retrieved January 25, 2010, from http://www.literacycenter.net

Literacy resources for parents and early childhood educators. National Child Care Information site. Retrieved January 25, 2010, from http://www.nccic.hhs.gov/

National Institute for Literacy site. Retrieved January 25, 2010, from http://www.nifl.gov

Speech and language development. American Speech-Language-Hearing Association site. Retrieved January 25, 2010, from http://www.asha.org

CHAPTER 3

CHOOSING THE BEST LITERATURE

This is an age of tremendous choice for consumers. Nearly everything purchased or selected requires decisions about the model, color, style, or type. This is true for cars, jewelry, food, stereos, and even the tools used to write this sentence. Choosing books for young children is no different. Every year more than 4,000 new books for children are published. A kindergarten teacher who might use two books per day over a 180-day school year would need 360 books per year. This chapter provides an understanding of the **aspects of literature** to be examined in a book, background of various **presentation styles** found in books for young children, and information concerning the detection of **bias** in the stories.

Making a selection from the tens of thousands of books available is not a simple task. The right choices require sensitivity and thought. The teacher must consider both the curriculum and the needs of the children and then match those considerations to the books available. A book of great quality might not be right for a particular group. A book of poor quality, even if it fits the curriculum perfectly, is of little value to the teacher or the children.

"Two roads diverged in a wood, and I- I took the one less traveled by, And that has made all the difference."

—ROBERT FROST

In addition, one must consider the purpose of using a particular book with children. Is it for the sake of the illustrations and photographs? Is it to help children understand the topic being studied? Younger children might be fascinated with topics such as favorite foods, exploring their surroundings, toilet training, birthdays, and developmental milestones such as walking. Board books for babies and toddlers are great for sharing on a one-to-one basis. If other children are motivated to learn more about a specific topic, such as knights, dragons, or dinosaurs, the high interest these topics generate will help children maintain attention while a longer piece is read. For this reason, it is not unusual for young children to have an amazing knowledge of the names and characteristics of several different dinosaurs.

This chapter examines the way to begin by discussing aspects of good literature and the manner in which books are presented or put together. A summary is included of the various types of literature and some of the honors awarded to them.

HOW TO BEGIN

The best way to get started is to become an expert observer of children. This is not meant in the psychological sense of coding children's activities on a chart or checklist. Rather, the teacher must actively attend to the actions, language, and social interactions of children. One must always wonder what a child means by saying or doing a particular thing, as well as why the child says it or does it in that way. By becoming a child watcher, the teacher will enter the world of children and learn what has meaning for them. This is critical because the most important characteristic about language is that it carries meaning. A book by a famous author, full of dazzling illustrations and gorgeous print, is useless unless or until it has meaning to the child.

By understanding individual children, the teacher can select books that are meaningful to most children in general. This is more difficult than it may seem. It is important for the teacher to consider books that go beyond his or her personal interests and preferences. Although everyone has such preferences, it is important to not act on this personal bias in selecting children's books. Books that reflect the interests of the children will help both the teacher and the children to grow.

The interests of children cross gender lines.

Children enjoy the independence of choosing their own books.

TIPS FOR TEACHERS

Always read a book by yourself before reading it to children.

- Write notes to yourself as cues to use a different tone of voice or make a specific movement during the story.
- Make sure the book does not contain content that would greatly upset children.
- Note places to pause and talk with the children about the story.
- Identify places to stop and ask: "What do you think might happen next?" or Why do you think the character did that?

When listening, children will often understand books they cannot read by themselves. Lists of books grouped according to developmental levels are often distributed by libraries. These lists may provide a starting point for the new teacher or supply additional titles for the experienced teacher.

Mother Goose stories and **fairy tales**, when chosen with care, can be used with very young children along with a variety of other materials. Books with large text, colorful print, simple subjects, touchable surfaces, and rhythmic language are quite pleasing. Young children are also interested in books about themselves, self-help skills, their families, and objects from their surroundings. The teacher should be sensitive to individual problems and concerns within the class. Some characters and topics can be frightening to some children. On the other hand, a child who has experienced the death of a pet might find consolation in a book on that topic.

Betsy Hearne (2000) has stated, "Children's books are the place for powerful emotions, powerful language, powerful art. If the book you're reading seems boring, toss it. The book probably is boring, and there are thousands that aren't." As drastic as this approach may seem, it does have validity. Children should not be bored by the books and stories read to them. The teacher's role is to instill a desire to know, to imagine, and to read. A child who is wiggling and bored by the third page of a 32-page book is not inspired to do anything but escape.

The teacher must take into account the interests of the class when making a selection. Even if the book meets all selection criteria, it may not capture the attention of a specific group of children. If this happens, it should be put aside, or perhaps presented again at a later time.

After getting to know the children, teachers can turn their attention to the books themselves. With bookstores, libraries, and children's book clubs available in most communities, access to books is not usually a major problem.

Talking to librarians, educators, and others associated with children is a good way to gather information on a list of potential books. They may also suggest additional sources such as *School Library Journal, The Horn Book Magazine,* and its parent newsletter *Why Children's Books?*

Hundreds of recent titles are cited in this book, but they may not all be readily available in your area. Books can and do go out of print. Moreover, bookstores and libraries can carry only a fraction of the thousands of books that are available. If you can't find a title cited in this text, ask your librarian to acquire a copy through the interlibrary loan process. If you want to purchase a copy of a certain book, most bookstores will obtain the book for you from their book service company. Purchasing books online has become a very effective way of acquiring a wide range of books, particularly those published by small presses that not all bookstores stock. It is important to keep reading and reviewing as many books as you can.

ASPECTS OF GOOD CHILDREN'S LITERATURE

Are the things that make a book good for children different from the things that make a book a good piece of literature for adults? Probably not. Of course authors who write for adults can write longer pieces with more complex topics, but these are differences in quantity. The quality of literature can and should be similar for both children and adults. Those who spend time reading literature written for children will soon discover that people who write successfully for children possess much talent. They are every bit as competent as those who write for adults. This does not mean that all children's books are good. There are both good and poor books written for children just as there are good and poor books written for adults.

The aspects of literature that make a book good, for children or for adults, include **characterization**, **setting**, **plot**, and **theme**. The adequate development of these elements is found in nearly all high-quality literature. Depending on the piece, one element might be emphasized more than the others, but all are important.

Literature for young children is typically published in a picture book format. **Picture books** are those in which the ideas or stories are related through a combination of text and illustration.

In some cases books may be totally **wordless**, leaving the entire telling of the story to just the pictures. With **concept books**, there may only be a single letter, number, or word on each page. More basic picture books might tell the story primarily through the illustrations, using the narrative to reinforce the pictures. As children age, the balance of narration and illustration changes in books that are written for them. First, the narrative is equally balanced with the illustrations in telling the story. Then, the text carries the story, and the illustrations serve to reinforce it. Eventually fewer illustrations are used to illustrate events in the story. Finally, stories and novels are published with little or no illustration at all. This does not mean that picture books are only for the young. Most of us, young and old, treasure the joy, freshness, and excitement that can only be found in children's picture books.

Characterization

Every story has at least one character, and usually there are more. Characters may be animals, people, objects, or imaginary beings. There should not be more characters than are necessary to tell the story. Above all, they must be real to children. The characters from literature that stand the test of time are those that act realistically and have real emotions. They give a glimpse of the reader's own self. The reader has a sense of "Yes, I know that feeling or that situation." In short, the reader cares about the character because of an emotional bond. Because this is so, it's important to keep in mind a gender issue that sometimes arises. Societal forces tend to foster little boys' preference for male characters. Care should be used in selecting stories in which the child can identify with the character, whether it is male or female. Skilled authors know how to create characters that cause the reader to say "I'm like that." When that occurs, gender becomes less of an issue.

Characters Must Be Credible. Characters must talk and act true to their role or nature. A good author will let the reader know the personality and motivations of the character through the character's thoughts, words, actions, language, and expressions. The author must be accurate with each of these in order for the reader to believe in the character. Babies will enjoy the familiar antics of the baby exploring the world in Helen Oxenbury's board book *I Can.* Toddlers will show smiles of recognition with Ian Falconer's *Olivia* and its sequel, *Olivia Saves the Circus.* In the first book, Olivia goes through a busy day dressing, singing, napping, painting, and dancing. In the second book, when the regular circus performers become ill, Olivia's imagination takes flight as she sees herself saving the circus through her performances in juggling, unicycling, and bouncing on the trampoline. Every toddler and preschooler who has ever had a birthday will recognize the excitement that fills the entire day in *Happy to You!* by Caron Lee Cohen. Barbara Bottner is an author who creates substantial depth in her characters. In *Wallace's Lists,* cautious Wallace and spontaneous Albert arrive at a wonderful place in their developing relationship in which they both thrive.

In *You Have to Be Nice to Someone on Their Birthday* and *Charlene Loves to Make Noise,* Bottner delves into the manners, disappointments, and anxiety that growing up can involve. In *My Great Aunt Arizona,* Gloria Houston masterfully presents a character portrait that possesses believability and depth. Based on a real-life individual from Houston's family in early twentieth-century Appalachia, Aunt Arizona comes across as a credible character because the author helps the reader to believe in what Aunt Arizona does and who she is. Going back still further in history, Lisa Moser creates a sense of the stress and separation families experienced during the period of westward expansion in *Kisses in the Wind.* In this story, a young pioneer girl is sad to be leaving her grandmother behind as her family plans to move to Oregon. Grandma writes all of the stories she has told the young girl in a little book, reminding her that as long as she has the book they will always be together. Returning to Revolutionary War days, Jennifer Thermes uses a historical house as a character narrating history in *When I Was Built.*

In their series of books about the Stupid family (*The Stupids Die, The Stupids Step Out*), the writer/illustrator team of Harry Allard and James Marshall creates characters who are credible in spite of their incredibleness. The Stupids are a family who do everything . . . well, stupidly. The children mow the rug with a lawn mower and water the houseplants with a garden sprinkler. Mrs. Stupid makes a dress out of live chickens, while Mr. Stupid eats eggs in the shower. Only the cat and dog seem to have any common sense. It is the fact that these characters are accurate to themselves that endears them to readers. Also, readers relate to the Stupids because everybody has done something foolish, though perhaps not quite as foolish as what the Stupids do.

Characters Must Be Consistent. The character may change and grow, but the basic portrayal must remain intact. That is, the character should not become a totally different character as a result of the experience in the story. In Munro Leaf's *The Story of Ferdinand,* circumstances change about the famous bull, but Ferdinand remains a pacifist. In *Curious George,* H. A. and Margaret Rey's monkey character learns from his mistakes but doesn't lose his personality or monkey qualities. Sometimes characters don't grow or learn from their mistakes. In Norman Bridwell's books about *Clifford,* the big red dog, the dog is always consistent in his ability to cause problems with his size. Readers can count on that.

Characters can grow in several ways at once while remaining consistent. Such is the case of the main character in Robert Munsch's *Love You Forever.* In this touching story, a newborn baby and his mother grow through the years until the boy becomes a young man with a child of his and the mother becomes old and frail. The reader follows the child as he grows both physically and emotionally

Author/illustrator Norman Bridwell, creator of the much loved *Clifford* books. Courtesy Norman Bridwell.

Author Tom Birdseye.
Courtesy Tom Birdseye.

through childhood, adolescence, and adulthood. The underlying goodness and love that the two share triumph at the end, showing the consistency of the love the generations share. Continuing with this topic, several related books present wonderfully consistent portrayals of babies and children to share with toddlers and preschoolers. These include *Waiting for Baby* by Tom Birdseye, *I Used to Be a Baby* by Robin Ballard, and *Froggy's Baby Sister* by Jonathan London.

Memorable characters from literature possess personalities that render them unique. Their personalities need not be overpowering. Rather, they are based on real aspects of humanity that make them special. Perhaps the character acts or speaks in a way that reminds readers of themselves. Perhaps the character does these things in a way readers wish they could. Few children are unaware of Dr. Seuss and Mercer Mayer characters, even though most don't know exactly what the characters are. The strong interaction between the reader and the character is based on the character's strength of personality and believability. Virginia Lee Burton draws the reader into the personality and emotional feelings of a building in *The Little House*, while Shel Silverstein does the same thing in *The Giving Tree*. Silverstein brings readers into the heart of the tree, feeling the changing seasons and the sensitivity of the relationship between the tree and the boy.

Child characters who are not **stereotypical** are frequently found in books for young children. In *William's Doll* by Charlotte Zolotow, readers meet a boy who, more than anything else in the world, wants a doll of his own. Others in the story don't understand why a boy would want a doll until his grandmother skillfully shows how a doll can be a natural toy for any child. In Tomie dePaola's autobiographical story, *The Art Lesson*, the main character's personality and creativity shine through as he struggles with the rigid requirements of the school art curriculum.

TIPS FOR TEACHERS

Ask children to tell why they like certain storybook characters.

- Validate children's attempts to identify with a character.
- Ask "why" and "how" questions in response to children's statements about the characters.

Ludwig Bemelmans' Madeline, Judith Viorst's Alexander, Rosemary Wells' Max, and Arnold Lobel's Frog and Toad stay with the reader for a lifetime. These characters touch the reader personally with whimsy, humor, empathy, and the stirrings of the need for independence.

Sister Bear and Brother Bear. Reprinted by permission of SSL/Sterling Lord Literistic, Inc. Copyright by Berenstain Enterprises Inc.

Cover from *Not Last Night but the Night Before* by Colin McNaughton. Jacket art copyright © 2007 Emma Clark. Reprinted by permission of Candlewick Press. All rights reserved.

Animal Characters. Animal characterizations are an important part of children's literature. Beatrix Potter gave her animals personality but kept them in their delightful animal roles. She allowed them to continue to follow their natural instincts. Her drawings depicted them with clothing and human aspects as they went about stealing vegetables from a garden and living in a mouse hole. Each character is believable, yet retains the charm of its animal nature. Else Holmelund Minarik accomplishes the same thing with her Little Bear books, as do Jan and Stan Berenstain in their Berenstain Bears series. In the latter series, the actions, emotions, and situations are all human, and the bears do not appear to have just stepped out of the woods. Instead, they have a humanlike home in the form of a tailored tree house.

Stories combining human and animal characters provide a unique bridge between the two types. Colin McNaughton brings this idea to life in a wonderful rhyming tale, *Not Last Night but the Night Before*. In a celebration of a birthday, a child's night comes alive with a wave of visitors from beloved fairy tales. This story can provide a springboard to those fairy tales. Animals behaving like people is referred to as **anthropomorphism.** It is wonderfully portrayed in James Howe's *Houndsley and Catina and the Quiet Time*. Houndsley loves the quiet that the first snow brings. Catina does not care for the quiet and is anxious that their plans for the day will be cancelled. Houndsley is creative, however, and shows how they can still be happy after a disappointment. Other examples of this include *Little Bear's Big Sweater* by David Bedford, *Bears Fly High* by Michael Rosen, *When You Meet a Bear on Broadway* by Amy Hest, and *Tucker Took It* by Bruce VanPatten. A totally realistic view of animals is found in the non-fiction book *Bears, Bears, and More Bears* by Jackie Morris.

Portraying animals in a variety of character roles is quite valid and can be a positive and enjoyable experience for the reader. Approaching difficult topics through animal characters causes less-traumatic reactions from children who may see themselves living or feeling the situation in the book. Topics such as new babies, moving, hospitals, divorce, and death are distanced through the use of animal characters. The safety that such an approach affords can help a child deal with the stressful topic. Toddlers may recognize the anxiety of being lost in *Where Is Maisy?* by Lucy Cousins. Preschoolers and kindergartners will relate to the desire to be bigger in Joyce Dunbar's *Tell Me What It's Like to Be Big*.

Children often learn about animals and their habits from animal characters in books. They will sometimes correct or question a story when an animal character is not true to its animal roots, but this does not lessen enjoyment of fantasy or humanlike animals. It demonstrates the great interest in animals that most children have during their early years. The best authors demonstrate a skillful blending of true animal characteristics and human behaviors in their animal characters.

Cover from *Houndsley and Catina and the Quiet Time* by James Howe. Jacket art copyright ©2009 by Marie-Louise Gay. Reprinted by permission of Candlewick Press. All rights reserved.

Setting

The term "setting" usually makes the reader think about where and when a story takes place. This is partly correct, but a setting is often much more. In addition to the actual location and time period of the story, the setting may include the way the characters live and the cultural aspects of the environment. Suppose a story takes place in a small town at the time of the Civil War; it would make a difference if the town were located in the North or the South. The geography might not have much of an effect, but the moral tone would be quite different. A story is also affected by whether the characters are living in poverty or wealth.

The possibilities of setting are numerous, and each possibility has the potential to change the moral, ethical, and social tone of the story. This is true because the characters are closely connected to the setting. Characters do not act in a vacuum; they act in a specific place, time, and social environment. Just as people in real life do, characters in stories act in certain ways depending on their setting. For example, people who are very hungry will behave differently depending on whether they are in a classroom, church, or restaurant. That is the expectation. Of course, in stories and in real life, individuals who don't quite conform to expectations can create interest and excitement.

The settings in children's books vary widely. Eileen Christelow's hilarious mystery story *The Great Pig Search* is set in sunny, contemporary Florida. The setting for ever-popular *We're Going on a Bear Hunt* by Michael Rosen is simply outdoors. In the first story, readers follow the misadventures of farmer Bert as he searches for the pigs through Florida's busy streets and murky swamps. Of course, the cleverly disguised pigs are right under his nose all along, much to the delight of readers. Robert McCloskey's *Make Way for Ducklings* is set in Boston Gardens a half century ago. The setting can also be real as in the nonfiction book *Child of the Civil Rights Movement* by Paula Shelton. This book takes a poignant, moving, and hopeful look at the Civil Rights movement in the United States.

Japan is the setting for *Three Samurai Cats: A Story from Japan* by Eric A. Kimmel. This is a tale that demonstrates a nonviolent approach to problem solving. Another example of a book presenting different settings is Barbara Cooney's *Miss Rumphius*. In this touching story, also illustrated by the author, a young girl begins and ends her life on the coast of Maine. In the middle of the story, however, the setting shifts as she travels around the world. Cooney uses the reason for the girl's travels to neatly tie the various settings into a unified tale.

A setting can be implied rather than specifically described in the text or depicted in the illustrations. Jungle animals and descriptions of their homes would enable the reader to detect that the setting is a jungle or zoo.

Setting can reinforce the underlying theme of a story. In *Goodnight Moon* by Margaret Wise Brown, the bunny's moonlit bedroom reinforces the theme of warmth, safety, and security that a child finds when settling down for a good night's sleep. In another story that takes place in a child's bedroom, *Where the Wild Things Are* by Maurice Sendak, the author cleverly confines the entire action to the room. Through the child's imagination and the reader's, the setting changes to the sea and, finally, to a faraway island where the wild things live. The reader is carried along with the dream. The child's anger at being sent to his room in the first place is balanced by the love symbolized by the hot dinner found upon returning from the imaginary, anger-filled journey. The dinner, left there by his mother, demonstrates that he is cherished. The changing setting enhances the character's feelings as the story proceeds.

Home Settings. The setting of a home can be used to create a sense of anxiety, humor, or sadness when the unexpected happens. Bedtime can be fun, as shown in the bouncy rhyming text of Bob Shea's *Race You to Bed*. The fuzzy bunny characters will motivate even reluctant young ones to get to bed. In Tomie dePaola's *Nana Upstairs and Nana Downstairs,* a child's familiar world is made bewildering and sad when he experiences the death of a grandparent. It is only through the interaction of the child's creative character and the setting that the problem of the story is resolved. The arrival of a new member of the household and the feelings of displacement are the subject of *Za-Za's Baby Brother* by Lucy Cousins. Another book by Lucy Cousins is set in the backyard garden of a home. *Garden Animals* is a hands-on board book depicting robins, moles, bees, and so forth that make up this familiar place.

School Settings. Stories set in schools are popular because children easily relate to them. Herman Parish creates a fun-filled school story in *Amelia Bedelia's First Day of School*. Here a literal-minded little girl's first day is filled with confusing adventures, all to her delight. The fun continues in *Monster Goes to School* by Virginia Mueller and in *Fish School* by Nancy Poydar, where Charlie tries to educate his pet goldfish by taking him to school.

A more thoughtful tone is set in Marisabina Russo's *A Very Big Bunny*. In this story, Amelia feels sad because she is so big that she is always last in line and none of the others will play with her. Through a new friend, she comes to realize that size is not always the most important thing. The school setting can be an avenue for learning, as depicted in the non-fiction *My School in the Rain Forest* by Margriet Ruurs.

Nature Settings. Romantic settings such as the mountains and the ocean are popular as well. *Whales Passing* by Eve Bunting uses a shifting setting. It begins with a boy and his father on a cliff observing the orcas in the ocean below. Then the setting shifts and the focus is on the whales' observations. Brilliant paintings by Lambert Davis portray the settings in a remarkable manner. Another book with a natural setting is *My Friend Whale* by Simon James. In this book, James addresses the danger of extinction of the blue whale. The outdoors in general can be the setting. as in *First Rain* by Charlotte Herman and *This Tree Counts* by Alison Formento. The plains of the Old West form the setting for *Till the Cows Come Home* by Jody Icenoggle. A beautiful book about living near the ocean is Alvin Tresselt's classic *Hide and Seek Fog*. While the fog creates problems for the adults, the children make superb use of this change in their usual setting. Roger Duvoisin's illustrations of the fog-enshrouded town are so vivid the reader almost feels the moisture hanging in the air.

Plot

The plot is a kind of road map to a story. An author plans a plot to help the reader make sense out of the story. Usually the plot unfolds in chronological order, but not always. Plot is an artificial rather than a natural element; its purpose is to simplify life. The author does this by selecting some events, some characters, and some emotions. There are a limited number of episodes, and only those that are necessary to the story are included. By presenting the action, excitement, and suspense that allows conflict to develop, a good plot allows children to become personally involved in the story (Norton & Norton 2006). When this happens in conjunction with effective character development, children become hooked on the tale simply because they care about the characters as the situations unfold.

A plot is created with characters and settings in mind. The author asks, given the characters in a certain setting, what would tend to occur naturally? Holman and Harmon (2008) contend that from this viewpoint, the function of plot is to translate character into action. In Aliki's *We Are Best Friends,* Peter and Robert are pals who are suddenly faced with the fact that Peter must move away. The reader is taken with wit and humor through a range of emotions and adjustments from anger, loneliness, and boredom to happiness and new friendships.

Good plots contain a beginning, a middle, and an end. The beginning should quickly engage the reader's interest. Younger children have shorter attention spans, so this point is even more important for them. Interest is established by using characters and a conflict that the reader can relate to and care about. The conflict should grab the attention of the reader and create a desire to find out what happens. In *Prudy's Problem and How She Solved It* by Carey A. Ellis, Prudy collects everything. As many readers will understand, the collections have gotten out of hand. The reader wants to see how the problem is solved. The concept of a child wanting a dog while a parent is less than excited about the idea is portrayed in *The Best Pet of All* by David LaRochelle. Though the story involves the improbable adoption of a pet dragon, the problem is solved in a satisfying manner in the end. In *Ira Sleeps Over* by Bernard Waber, Ira's happiness at being invited to sleep over at a friend's house is shaken when his big sister asks him if he will be bringing his teddy bear along. He must then deal with the contrasting problems of wanting to be more grown up yet still desiring the security of childhood comfort objects. Finally, Robert Munsch's witty book, *I Have to Go,* begins on page one with the parents and child involved in the problems of toilet training.

In the middle of the plot, the **conflict** or problem may become more defined. The **rising action** created by the interaction of the characters helps the reader become more emotionally involved with the plot. The **resolution** of the conflict and the recognition of *who* or *what* is the cause of the conflict should not be too obvious at this point. If the reader knows what happens now, there is little point to finishing the story. Rather, the reader should feel more and more drawn into the story. The quickening pace and the building of tension should continue as the reader approaches the ending. By creating twists in the plot through new problems and by suggesting **false endings**, the author intrigues and motivates the reader to continue. Lisa Peters uses this technique in *Frankie Works the Night Shift*. In this story, Frankie is a cat who supposedly stays up all night working. However, there is some question about whether he is really working or just goofing off.

The ending contains the **climax** and the resolution of the plot. The climax is the highest point in dramatic tension, the point at which listeners are quiet and sitting on the edges of their seats. The resolution is the final outcome of the problem or conflict. Even if the ending is happy, it can have an unexpected twist. In Dr. Seuss's *Horton Hatches the Egg,* children delight in the elephant-bird who hatches for the faithful Horton. In Dr. Seuss's *The Lorax,* children are given an unexpected last-minute reprieve from the pollution mess.

When the plot includes a child attempting to resolve a conflict, it is most appropriate if the child solves the problem without interference from adults in the story. In *Kangaroo Christine* by Guido van Genechten, Christine's mother has tried without success to get the little one to come out of her pouch. Finally, another little kangaroo asks Christine to come out and play. On her own, Christine makes the choice to come out of her mother's pouch, thus solving the problem.

The plot should be clear and believable even if the author asks the reader to travel into a world of fantasy. It should move from part to part with ease and consistency in order to maintain understanding and interest. Plots that are transparent or confusing will be boring to young children. If the teacher can tell the final outcome on page one, chances are good that the children will be able to do this as well. If children are confused, it will be difficult to maintain their interest. Books with believable, understandable, and creative plots should be selected.

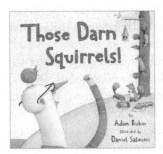

Theme

The theme of a story is an abstract concept the author has embedded in the story. The theme may include such ideas as the strength of friendship, the fragility of life, family life, or becoming independent. It is made concrete through other parts of the story such as characterization, setting, and plot. The theme often teaches a lesson or persuades the reader of something.

Illustrations can enhance the theme. In *The Polar Express*, Chris Van Allsburg establishes the theme with the bleak, gray snow scenes of the home and the child. The full-color illustrations fit perfectly with the theme of Verna Aardema's *Why Mosquitoes Buzz in People's Ears*, illustrated by Leo and Diane Dillon. Good illustrators find a way to reflect the theme in their illustrations.

Identifying Themes. The theme can be an overview or an underlying part of the book. A story can have one or several themes or subthemes. The theme often reveals the author's purpose in writing the book; for example, the author may use the story to help children understand or develop sensitivity to some issue or event. Even simple books for toddlers have underlying themes, such as pride in self and independence in a book about getting dressed. The concept of humans versus nature is an integral theme in *Those Darn Squirrels* by Adam Rubin. In this tale, Old Man Foolwire tries to keep the birds from migrating south by putting up bird feeders. A rollicking man-versus-squirrel conflict ensues, with a surprise ending that makes everyone happy. The themes of fear and not knowing are brought to life in *Wolf's Coming* by Joe Kulka. In a slightly scary suspenseful story, concern is raised by the howl of a wolf in the distance. With each page, the howl of the wolf comes closer until the surprise ending is revealed.

The theme of siblings, with all the joys and difficulties those relationships may entail, is frequently found in children's literature. In *Ballerina Nate* by Kimberly Bradley, five-year-old Nate, portrayed as a dog character, wants to be a dancer. His brother taunts him with the proclamation that boys can't dance. Nate persists with family support, and everybody learns and grows. The joys of lifelong sibling relationships are celebrated in *The Lemon Sisters* by Andrea Cheng. In this story, the three elderly Lemon sisters join three sisters from the neighborhood playing in the snow to celebrate an eightieth birthday.

A theme should unfold for the reader and it should not be too obvious. Most well-written stories have layers of reasons or themes that add depth and dimension to the plot. *Mufaro's Beautiful Daughters* by John Steptoe is an African tale that can be read as a simple story in which the virtuous daughter is rewarded. It can also be read for its themes of kindness, bravery, jealousy, and consequences for one's actions. Many lessons can be learned from this one story about life and human nature. The illustrations, which won the Caldecott

Wolf's Coming by Joe Kulka.
Illustrations copyright
©2007 by Joe Kulka.
Reprinted with the permission of Carolrhoda Books,
a division of Lerner Publishing Group, Inc. All
rights reserved. No part of
this excerpt may be used or
reproduced in any manner
whatsoever without the prior
written permission of Lerner
Publishing Group, Inc.

Self-portrait of author/
illustrator Joe Kulka.
Courtesy of Joe Kulka.

Honor Medal, provide a refreshing complement to the story. In *Perfect Puppy*, Stephanie Calmenson explores perfection, only to discover that it's not necessary to be perfect. Almost everyone has wished to change something about themselves at one time or another. This is a common theme in traditional tales, where those doing the wishing often discover that they were better off before their wishes were granted. A contemporary tale with this theme is found in *Ord Makes a Wish* by Margaret Snyder. Ord, a young dragon, comes to realize that he likes himself just as he is. Finally, an offbeat story that includes some powerful themes is *Click, Clack, Moo, Cows That Type* by Doreen Cronin. The silly antics of literate cows that leave typed messages for Farmer Brown are great fun all by themselves. However, a discussion of what is happening in the story can easily lead to understanding the ideas of social action, labor unrest, negotiation, and compromise on a preschooler level.

The four areas of character, plot, setting, and theme are integrated in a successful story. Keeping a file of books that meet the criteria for each characteristic is an effective organizational tool. A one-page or half-page summary could be developed for each book, including the following items:

- Title
- Author concepts in the book
- Short narrative of the story
- Does it meet the criteria for characterization?
- Does it meet the criteria for setting?
- Does it meet the criteria for plot?
- Does it meet the criteria for theme?

The file of books can grow over the years as new titles are published, increasing its value with each passing year.

Censorship. The American Library Association and its Office for Intellectual Freedom have noted an increase in **censorship** and **challenges** to books over the past few decades. Books written for young children, some of them winners of prestigious awards, are not immune to this problem. Censorship and challenge occur when individuals or groups object to material their children are being exposed to in school. Parents do have a right to hold and discuss their views about materials. Teachers should make every attempt to accommodate those concerns by providing alternative materials for their children. *Challenge* occurs when there is an attempt to restrict the use of a book with some readers. *Censorship* occurs when there is an attempt to restrict the rights of all others by banning the use of a book through removal. The major themes related to censorship include language, violence, parental depictions, religion, sexuality, homosexuality, and low self-esteem. While teachers should be able to use

---

Frequently Banned and Challenged Children's Books

And Tango Makes Three by Justin Richardson and Peter Parnell

Scary Stories (Series) by Alvin Schwartz

Uncle Bobby's Wedding by Sarah Brannen

Olive's Ocean by Kevin Henkes

It's Perfectly Normal by Robie Harris

Captain Underpants by Dav Pilkey

Daddy's Roommate by Michael Willhoite

Heather Has Two Mommies by Leslea Newman

In the Night Kitchen, by Maurice Sendak

The Stupids (Series) by Harry Allard

The Witches by Roald Dahl

Anastasia Krupnik (Series) by Lois Lowry

Halloween ABC by Eve Merriam

Bumps in the Night by Harry Allard

A Light in the Attic by Shel Silverstein

Guess What? by Mem Fox

Banned books. Frequently banned and challenged children's books. Adapted from listings of most frequently banned and challenged books of 2000–2009. Chicago, IL: American Library Association, 2010.

whatever materials they feel best meet the needs of the program, they must be ready to address censorship attempts as they arise.

Educator Rick Traw (1996) describes a South Dakota censorship incident that received national attention and in which he was involved. The schools in Sioux Falls had adopted an anthology of children's literature containing traditional folktales, holiday stories, and multicultural stories. Most of the literature had previously been published in the form of single-volume picture books. According to Traw, within the first month of use of the literature, a group of Christian fundamentalist activists launched a censorship campaign to have the material removed on the grounds that stories involving Halloween, mythology, and non-Christian multicultural settings were teaching the children Satanism and witchcraft. The superintendent of schools appointed a citizens' committee to review the literature and make recommendations for its use. After a year of hearings and discussions, it was decided that the literature was quite innocent and its use should be continued. Traw notes that although the censorship battle was won in Sioux Falls, the censors may have ultimately won the war. The same censorship arguments were repeated across the land, and the book's publisher eventually withdrew it from the U.S. market.

PRESENTATION

The presentation of the story involves those factors that relate to plot, setting, characterization, and theme. It is difficult to separate the aspects of presentation since a good book will integrate them into a whole work that is greater than the sum of the individual parts. They are separated here for discussion purposes only.

The four parts of the presentation discussed include:

- Text style used in the printing
- Narrative style
- The illustrations or photographs used
- Anti-bias factors within the book

Text Style

The type style used in a book can affect the story. Type style also contributes to unity between the text and the illustrations. Hundreds of fonts are available. The style, size, color, and location of the text must fit the purpose of and feeling created by the narrative.

TIPS FOR TEACHERS

Anticipate the visual impact an illustration will have on children.

- Introduce the cover, author, and illustrator before reading.
- Build up suspense by saying, "Wait until you see the picture on the next page."
- Invite children to tell how they feel when looking at an illustration.
- Ask: "Why do we laugh when looking at this picture?"

Print Size. Roger Duvoisin's *Veronica* uses tiny standard text set against humorously huge illustrations of the hippopotamus, making her look even more gigantic. Jean de Brunhoffs *Babar and the King* is set with a script font that appears similar to a child's early cursive penmanship. The illustrations are either at the bottom of the page, or they fill the entire page. Sometimes the text

Once upon a time....

Once upon a time....

Once upon a time....

ONCE UPON A TIME....

ONCE UPON A TIME....

Once upon a time....

Once upon a time....

Once upon a time....

Samples of the types of print available for storybooks.

is placed between the boxed-off illustrations where it fits the story best. The simple, expressive illustrations blend with the cursive font without conflict.

Dr. Seuss's *Hop on Pop* is meant to help beginning readers. He has chosen a standard script font found in many reading books, but the size is much larger. Standard text is about one-quarter of a centimeter tall. In Dr. Seuss's book, emphasized words are a full centimeter tall, while the words in the rest of the sentence are three-quarters of a centimeter tall. This print fits the purpose and style of the book and is a good contrast with the zany pictures.

Dorothy Kunhardt's *Pat the Bunny* has very little text. What text there is, however, is a half centimeter tall and done in a child's script. In *Yo! Yes"?* author/illustrator Chris Raschka, using only thirty-four words, provides a multicultural look at friendship. Each huge charcoal word with its accompanying illustration jumps off the page to tell a story.

In *The Grouchy Ladybug* by Eric Carle, the font starts as one size and grows with the story. Carle's use of small pages building to larger and larger pages as the ladybug encounters ever bigger animals is enhanced by the effective use of font size. The font reaches whale size at the conclusion of the book. Virginia Lee Burton also uses this change of font size in her book, *Choo Choo: The Story of a Little Engine Who Ran Away*. Throughout the story, every time the train's name appears, it does so in larger font, standing out clearly within the text. The frequency of the large printed name grows along with the rising action of the story. The concept of size and shape reinforcing the story can also be applied to characters as in *Come Along, Daisy!* by Jane Simmons. In this story, a young duckling drifts away from her mother to a part of the pond that is considerably scarier until she is reunited with her mother. When she feels brave, Daisy is big; when she feels scared, she is small.

Print Color. Color is another key choice for print. Pamela Edwards uses a large white typeface on dark backgrounds to tell the story of *Four Famished Foxes and Fosdyke*. In this story, the young foxes get a lesson in using their heads during a series of nighttime raids on a nearby henhouse. Robert McCloskey chooses a standard typeface in the same sepia color as the illustrations in *Make Way for Ducklings*. In Ross MacDonald's *Achoo! Bang! Crash! The Noisy Alphabet*, nineteenth-century-style wood type illustrations are printed in blazing color using a hand press in an eye-popping alphabet book. Other books have used color in additional creative ways depending on the needs and purpose of the story.

Text Location. Text can be placed in various locations on the page. It may be spaced as in poetry. Although words are usually arranged in paragraphs, variations can be used. In summary, the choice of typeface and placement of text can

Cover from *Trick or Treat* written and illustrated by Melanie Walsh. Jacket art copyright ©2009 by Melanie Walsh. Reprinted by permission of Candlewick Press. All rights reserved.

enhance or diminish the effect of the narrative and its illustrations. In a quality book, the choice of typeface is always a consideration that shows.

Narrative Style

A good narrative style has several ingredients. First, the flow of language should be appropriate to the story. The use of words should enhance the story and the understanding it is attempting to convey. The narrative style should hold the reader's interest and contain a bit of intrigue, mystery, or surprise. The conflicts and conflict resolutions should make sense and feel right to the reader. They should draw the reader into the story and make the reader care about both. Finally, the typeface choices should mesh with the author's purposes.

Each author has an individual style for telling his or her tale. This style is reflected in the choice of words, the figures of speech, the rhythmic pattern of the language, the structure of sentences, and the use of rhetorical devices. Style differences create a wide diversity in children's books. Melanie Walsh creates a unique style of presentation in *Trick or Treat*. Using a board book format, she adds a lift-the-flap element with some slightly scary surprises to create the rituals of Halloween.

Poetic Style. A. A. Milne uses poetry in the Christopher Robin stories to bring the reader into the world of Christopher and Pooh. The rhythm is bouncy and fun, hinting to the reader that the stories will be likewise. The Brothers Grimm alternate narrative with poetry in a character's dialogue for a special effect that is well remembered: "Queen, you are full fair, 'tis true, But Snow White fairer is than you," from "Snow White and the Seven Dwarfs"; and, "Little tree, little tree, shake over me, That silver and gold may come down and cover me," from "Aschenputtel."

The Night before Christmas by Clement Moore is a classic poetic tale that has enchanted generations of young children. This new edition, with charming watercolor illustrations by Tasha Tudor, is a feast for the eyes and the ears.

Book cover from *The Storm* by Walter Sawyer, illustrations by Kathleen O'Malley. Text and illustrations copyright ©1999. Reprinted by permission of Richard C. Owen Publishers, Inc, NY.

Repetition. Repeating words, phrases, and sentences in stories provides a sense of poetic rhythm, creates a chronological continuity to the plot, and helps young listeners and readers to predict what might come next in a story. In *The Storm* by Walter Sawyer, each page of the quietly scary narrative begins with a "when" statement. The narrative allows the reader to pause in mid-sentence and ask what might happen. This technique encourages children to participate in the development of the story and to verify their guesses. Repetition is used to create a delightful tale in *Millions of Cats* by Wanda Gag. By the time the reader gets to "trillions of cats," children are eagerly anticipating and joining in the repetition.

Ludwig Bemelmans's short, rhyming narrative fits well with the stories of the twelve little girls in the ever popular *Madeline*. The adventures in the Madeline series always begin with the same opening lines that, for hundreds of children, have come to mean that enjoyment will surely follow. Margaret Wise Brown has a natural touch with her books for children. *Goodnight Moon* is one of the most popular bedtime stories with preschoolers because the simple story reflects a reassuring ritual played out in almost every child's house each night.

Judith Viorst uses a running narrative with a repetition that exposes the thoughts and the focus in *Alexander and the Terrible, Horrible, No Good, Very Bad Day*. The title itself is the repetition line. The illustrations aptly show just how the events of the narrative are making Alexander feel. This book causes laughter because all readers can empathize with the story. The descriptive language includes words such as "scrunched," "smushed," and the therapeutic "I'm going to Australia." Many adults love this book as much as children do.

Point of View. No matter what the style, good literary narratives include all the components of good fiction. In addition to such technical aspects as plot and setting, point of view is involved as well. Today's stories, more so than those of yesterday, are frequently told from the child's perspective rather than from the perspective of an adult. Think of how a child might describe a kitchen. In the past, the adult perspective would have determined the words, even though they might be ascribed to a child. For example, "My kitchen has four big chairs with shiny red seats. The cookie jar looks like a big fat doll and it's always full of yummy things to eat." Contemporary literature, using a more realistic child's point of view, might describe the same kitchen as, "The kitchen has lots of legs and a blue floor with crumbs and a sticky Kool-Aid patch that the cat licked almost clean." The latter description was by a four-year-old girl who described the kitchen not as an adult would see it but as she actually did see it. The difference is important. The perceptive writer of children's books has the ability to see life or events from the child's perspective. It is this special ability that creates a child-loved classic. These are the books children want to read again and again.

Topics and themes in children's literature have greatly expanded over the past several years, but the artistry of a good storyteller is still the cornerstone of a memorable book. The narrative style is a major part of the story that will be remembered, repeated, and enjoyed even when the book has long been misplaced or lost. A good narrative is real, touching the child and the child still hiding in every adult.

Good children's literature is good literature. It is difficult to resist its beauty, simplicity, and comedy. A good children's story gives adults the chance to remember, to dream again, and to find joy in the sense of wonder that was once theirs.

Illustrations and Photographs

The illustrations and photographs used in children's literature are as important for young children as the narrative. In picture books, the illustrations play a key role in conveying the message of the story. In *Blueberries for Sal* by Robert McCloskey, Sal and her mother go off to the blueberry patch, not realizing that a bear is bringing her cub to the same patch. Children can follow the story, including the plot twists, using only the pictures. Children should be provided with high-quality artwork that builds an appreciation and love for art. Children have an openness of mind and imagination to appreciate a wide variety of artistic styles. They are not opinionated or biased about one type of art or another.

TIPS FOR TEACHERS

Take children on short field trips to museums and galleries to develop an appreciation for art.

- Create an art show and reception for parents and siblings, and display art created by the children.
- When several children are drawing pictures (e.g., pets), have some use crayons, others use colored pencils, and still others use pastel markers.
- Seek donations of photo equipment to include photographs by children as part of an art display.
- Briefly introduce the life of an artist.

A major resource for those interested in children's book illustration is the Eric Carle Museum of Picture Book Art located in Amherst, Massachusetts. The museum's aim is to present, preserve, and interpret picture book art from around the world. The museum has a fine collection of original picture book art. It also provides opportunities for education and research in children's book illustration.

When judging illustrations and photographs in children's books, use integration with the story, attention to detail, texture, and color as criteria.

Artistic Modes. The criteria used for judging the quality of illustrations can be applied to a variety of artistic modes. In using color, artists may choose crayons, oil pastels, chalk, water crayons, and so forth. Shading, detailing, and smudging techniques give expression to an illustration. These techniques are used to create a soft feeling, a bold expression, or any other emotion. Feodor Rojankovsky,

Raymond Briggs, Thomas Locker, and Nancy Ekhorn Burkert are artists who display exceptional talent with the use of color.

Pen and ink is a traditional medium used quite often in children's books. Illustrators use pen and ink to outline or to enhance detail. Shel Silverstein, Nonny Hogrogian, E. H. Shepard, Robert Lawson, and Leonard Weisgard are masters of this technique.

Woodcuts and **linocuts** are used by several illustrators to create a broad range of finished products. They can yield detailed results or bold and dramatic images. Artists use brown, black, or other darker colors with or without a lighter wash. Ink is applied to the surface of the woodcut or linocut, and then that is pressed against the paper to offset the illustration. Superb examples of the technique can be seen in the works of Wanda Gag, Evaline Ness, Marcia Brown, Don Freeman, Antonio Frasconi, Ed Emberley, and Marie Hall Ets.

Colored pencils or **charcoal** yield a different texture and feel than crayon or paint. This is a painstaking process to use for an entire book, but it can create an effect that other techniques cannot duplicate. Artists Susan Jeffers, Taro Yashima, and Chris Van Allsburg (conte pen) have produced outstanding examples of this process.

Photographers for children's literature are special people. They must be able to visualize as a child, and they must possess the technical skill to capture the picture that precisely meets the needs of the narrative. Tana Hoban, Roger Bester, Bruce McMillan, and Thomas Mattieson provide dazzling examples of this type of photography.

Artists who choose **collage** must have a bit of the collector in them. Ezra Jack Keats pinned fabric bits on his wall to keep them visible. The textures and feelings that collage can offer are limitless. Materials can come from anywhere and anything. Eric Carle used tissue paper and Keats used fabric and wallpaper, the most common materials. Striking collage illustrations by Holly Meade are beautifully integrated with Tom Brenner's lyrical language to create *An Then Comes Halloween*. As the story unfolds, pumpkins are carved, costumes are created, and trick or treating ensues.

Painted Illustrations. Paint is by far the most common medium for artwork in children's books. It is often used with other media to give a contrasting texture and color. Paint can be the thin, soft wash of tempera or watercolor, the bold, brash reds and purples of oil, or the thick, textured look of acrylics. This diversity and richness of color and texture make it a popular medium. Maurice Sendak, Mitsamasa Anno, Gyo Fujikawa, Chris Soentpiet, Stephen Gammell, James Ransome, Susan Jeffers, Brian Wildsmith, Dick Bruna, Tasha Tudor, Tomie dePaola, Steven Kellogg, Arnold Lobel, and Donald Carrick are but a few of the fine painters whose illustrations appear in children's literature.

Cover from *And Then Comes Halloween* by Tom Brenner. Jacket art copyright ©2009 by Holly Meade. Reprinted by permission of Candlewick Press. All rights reserved.

Illustration by Gyo Fujikawa from *Faraway Friends*. Illustrations copyright ©1981 by Gyo Fujikawa. Reprinted by permission of Grosset and Dunlap. All rights reserved.

Artist's illustration of a cat in three media: charcoal (top), colored markers (middle), and pastel (bottom). Courtesy of Emily Sawyer.

The most difficult part of the painter's job is to create a series of illustrations that satisfy the painter as well as his or her audience. Some artists prefer to work in one medium and perfect their craft while others prefer to use several media. Marcia Brown is a multitalented illustrator who has successfully tried almost every medium. In *Dick Whittington and His Cat* she used woodcut in black and white. For *Cinderella,* a Caldecott Medal winner, she used subtle pastels.

Several artists use historical, master, and contemporary styles in their work. Leo and Diane Dillon, in *Ashanti to Zulu* by Margaret Musgrove, use tribal motifs. A sense of sadness about the displacement of native peoples is portrayed amidst Native American motifs in *Broken Feather* by Verla Kay. Paul Goble uses beautifully expressive Native American symbols in *The Girl Who Loved Wild Horses.* Cheryl Harness combines elements of romanticism, impressionism, and the Hudson River school of painting in *The Amazing Impossible Erie Canal.* In this gorgeous nonfiction book, the watercolor, gouache, and colored pencil illustrations can be used to tell the story with or without the text.

Barbara Cooney uses an old master style in *Ox-Cart Man* by Donald Hall. This book is reminiscent of a visit to an art museum's Americana collection. In *Going Home, Coming Home* by Truong Tran, a young girl named Ami Chi makes her first trip with her parents back to their home country of Vietnam. The heat, the smallness of the houses, and the local culture are strikingly portrayed in the illustrations. This book is a bilingual edition printed in both English and Vietnamese. The old master style requires much research and attention to detail.

Effective use of light and dark is another tool of the skilled artist. Chris Van Allsburg paints with dramatic use of light in *The Polar Express* and *Jumanji. Owl Moon* by Jane Yolen incorporates a powerful use of light as the story line progresses through the owl hunt. John Schoenherr's expansive style makes readers feel as though they are walking through the woods themselves.

Rosemary Wells uses type and illustration in a humorous style all her own. For example, when she uses the word "between" in the text, it is actually placed between two objects in the illustrations. When Morris, in *Morris's Disappearing Bag,* hides in a bag, children identify with him. They see themselves hiding in the bag as well.

All of these artists, and new artists such as Mark Teague, Robin Ballard, Chris Raschka, Thor Wickstrom, and Timothy Bush, will keep children's literature exciting for years to come. They follow the path of Randolph Caldecott, William Mulready, Kate Greenaway, Sir John Tenniel, and Leslie Brooke of the nineteenth century. New artists, like new writers, are emerging each year to both continue tradition and explore new possibilities.

When selecting books, ask whether the choices you are making will stand the test of time and love. Every book used with children must reflect quality

Talking about covers and illustrations found in books is an important part of the picture book experience.

in both narrative and illustration. As described earlier, both the text and the illustrations tell the story. Picture books for younger children rely almost totally on the illustrations for meaning, while those for older children increasingly rely more on the text. Additional information about picture book and children's book illustration can be found in sources cited at the end of this chapter. The following are particularly recommended:

- *A Caldecott Celebration: Six Artists Share Their Paths to the Caldecott Medal* by Leonard S. Marcus
- *Artist to Artist: 23 Major Illustrators Talk to Children About Their Art* by Eric Carle and others
- *Children's Book Illustration: Step by Step Techniques: A Complete Guide from the Masters* by Jill Bossert
- *Illustrating Children's Books: Creating Picture Books for Publication* by Martin Salisbury
- *Under the Spell of the Moon: Art for Children from the World's Greatest Illustrators* by Patricia Aldana
- *Wings of an Artist: Children's Book Illustrators Talk about Their Art* by Julie Cummins

Integration with Text. The **integration** of illustrations and photographs with the text refers to whether they fit all aspects of the narrative. One reason that Leo and Diane Dillon are so successful is their ability to transport the reader to Africa. The Dillons received the Caldecott Medal for their illustrations in *Why Mosquitoes Buzz in People's Ears: A West African Tale* by Verna Aardema and *Ashanti to Zulu: African Traditions* by Margaret Musgrove. They do so with the effective use and integration of color, design, and text.

Illustrations must be integrated with each other as well as with the text. Leo Lionni is a master of illustration-to-illustration unity. In *Swimmy,* he creates the feeling of enormity by allowing the reader to see the fish swimming in the entire ocean. The detail even includes a fish swimming off the page. Donald Crews shares this talent for integration. In *Freight Train,* the reader sees the train move from page to page at increasing speed.

An example of good integration of text and illustrations is Pamela Duncan Edwards's *Four Famished Foxes and Fosdyke,* in which the dark background reinforces the bold white lettering. In Aliki's *We Are Best Friends,* the typeface is similar to a primer font. Text is located throughout the book at the page bottoms, apart from the illustrations. The dramatic sadness of the tale is increased tenfold when the typeface changes to a child's beginning handwriting. The heart-wrenching letter that is part of the story is expertly integrated into the narrative. Dr. Seuss is also most adept at effective and creative integration of text

From OWL Moon by Jane Yolen, illustrated by John Schoenherr, copyright © 1987 by John Schoenherr, illustrations. Used by permission of Philomel Books, A Division of Penguin Young Readers Group, A Member of Penguin Group (USA) Inc., 345 Hudson Street, New York, NY 10014. All rights reserved.

and illustration. In *The Shape of Me and Other Stuff,* he successfully integrates bright colors, large bold type, and shadow shapes. The words are clearly and enjoyably emphasized without distracting from the game of guessing the shadows.

Works of lesser quality do not include this thoughtful integration. They often use gimmicks that attempt to be clever. In actuality, such gimmicks detract from and disrupt the story flow. In previewing children's books, look at the typeface to see whether it is appropriate for the type of book and age level of the children. Are the words clear and easy to find, or are they hidden throughout the page? The typeface should not be crowded, preventing the child's eye from picking up on the spacing between the words.

Attention to Detail. Quality illustrations and photographs stand out from mediocre art because of attention to detail. Illustrations must accurately reflect the narrative. For example, if a story calls for a monkey to wear a red hat, it must be the same shade of red and the same hat throughout the story. Poor-quality books may vary these details. Children demand truth from their stories. They will count every object on a page to be certain that the twenty cats are there, just as the story said they would be.

Owl Moon, the 1988 Caldecott winner written by Jane Yolen and illustrated by John Schoenherr, demonstrates a keen attention to detail. The owl seems to lift off the page and stand eye-to-eye with the reader. The illustrations in this book provide a breathless moment and are unencumbered by text except for a few words on the following page. Good illustration such as this draws the reader into the page. It offers something to be discovered. As is the case with good paintings, more is found each time one looks at the pictures.

TIPS FOR TEACHERS

Encourage children to respond to stories through their artwork.

- Tell children about a character or activity that you liked in the book. Have them draw one that they liked.
- Provide clay to make sculptures of storybook characters.
- Involve children in the creation of a mural or diorama of a book's setting using leaves, paper, crayons, glue, and other relevant materials.
- Add art books and posters to the creative center as a jumping-off point.

The exemplary photographer does not merely provide a picture of a boat. Rather, the photographer captures a moment or a time of day so that the photograph of the boat is something special. The backdrop of the shot is carefully chosen. The type of film and the speed of the film are considered. The photographer may take hundreds of shots in order to achieve the one best photograph. These details are reflected in the final outcome and account for the quality difference found in better pictures.

Texture. Distinctive illustration provides a sense of texture that is three-dimensional. Some artists use paint, some use collage, and some use woodcuts. In each case, the best work joins the picture, the text, and the reader. The skillful use of space and art should expand the text. An artist may outline figures in black to clarify shape or use colors to define boundaries or special words. Whatever techniques are used, they should tie the art to the text and further the purpose of the story.

Eric Carle and Ezra Jack Keats are illustrators who work with collage. The appearance of textures in their work effectively invites children to touch the pages. Indeed, some of Carle's books have a three-dimensional component that provides an actual texture to the touch. The illustrations and text blend so well that they seem to be one.

Author/illustrator Ezra Jack Keats. Courtesy of Beverly Hall.

Color. Color can lend a dramatic effect to good artwork and can add beauty, but many books without color, or with limited use of color, are equally memorable. Just as some movies are meant to be seen in black and white, some books are successful because they use color sparingly. *Harold and the Purple Crayon* by Crockett Johnson is illustrated entirely with a purple crayon line drawing. The book is a favorite of young children and inspires them to create their own purple drawings. They readily respond to the humor and novelty of the book. *Little Bear's Friend,* written by Else Holmelund Minarik and illustrated by Maurice Sendak, is another superb example. It is wistfully and delicately illustrated in black line sketching with a soft wash of browns and greens. The effect visually enhances the text narration and is appealing to children. Alvin Tresselt's *I Saw the Sea Come In* is deftly illustrated by Roger Duvoisin. The pages of black ink sketches, washed with blues and touched with black shading, emphasize the lonely beach scenes. When he uses full color as a contrast, the effect is riveting. These illustrations are visually dramatic in terms of the story narrative. In *Bedtime in the Jungle,* author/illustrator John Butler presents spectacular illustrations as each page fades a little bit more into the night while the animal mothers put their babies to bed. The beat of the verses that form the captivating text is inspired by the song "Over in the Meadow." An artistic adventure awaits the reader in *Crazy Hair* by Neil Gaiman. In this story, Bonnie meets an odd fellow with totally crazy hair. A dreamlike, surrealistic adventure ensues, and she is drawn into the hairdo. Through Gaiman's rhyming text and the transforming designs of her outfit created by illustrator Dave McKean, she eventually finds her way to safety.

On the other hand, *Make Way for Ducklings* by Robert McCloskey, still one of the most popular books for youngsters, is etched in soft brown sepia. The detailed, realistic illustrations make the pages come alive without the use of color.

The illustrations and photographs used in children's literature should be integrated with a pleasing design, careful color usage, and a suggestion of texture where appropriate. The reader should find the illustrations interesting and involving. These criteria are demanding, which is one of the reasons one must search for quality among the large number of books published each year.

Many talented artists contribute to high-quality children's books. Young people everywhere, and adults as well, applaud their efforts.

If the artist awakens in the developing child an awareness and love of art, this love will remain long after the child has become an adult. The artist will have opened a world of aesthetic joy forever. Children often attempt to re-create images from the story in a variety of ways.

Responding to literature through art. Young children used art to respond to the book *Four Famished Foxes and Fosdyke* by Pamela Edwards, illustrated by Henry Cole. The illustrations depict: (a) the foxes on their way to raid the henhouse; (b) covered with eggs thrown at them by the chickens; (c) returning to their fox den in failure; and (d) eating the meal prepared for them by Fosdyke. Courtesy Walter E. Sawyer.

Anti-bias Factors

Respectable companies publishing children's books today do not accept works with open bias toward race, gender, religion, age, or disability. However, many older books in libraries and school collections contain both subtle and overt negative bias. It's important to pay attention when selecting books. Anyone planning to use literature with children should preview the books for signs of bias and stereotyping.

Many young adults do not remember the Dick and Jane reading books. In these stories, Jane wore a dress and passively watched as Dick did all the exciting childhood activities. One might wish to share books of this type to appreciate the changes that have occurred in both our society and in children's literature. This activity can help to raise the consciousness of all against such bias.

Multicultural Awareness. Another less obvious prejudice is the absence of multicultural characters. This is bias by omission and is still prevalent in some classroom collections. Sensitivity to bias by those who care for children ensures that book collections reflect a realistic picture of society. Multicultural books should be included whether or not the student group includes children from other than the mainstream culture. Multicultural literature includes characters from other cultures or stories set in another culture. Freeman and Lehman (2001) have identified many benefits for children immersed in multicultural literature. First, because young children tend to be open and curious about the world around them, learning about new and different things is a natural benefit for their cognitive development. Also, children's rapid acquisition of language and vocabulary can be made richer with the sounds and rhythms of words from other cultures and with the visual representations of other cultures. On a social and emotional level, literature based on other cultures can help young children come to the understanding that our common humanity binds all people together, that our differences can be cherished for making the world richer, and that concepts such as right, wrong, laughter, crying, loving, family, and sharing are not bound by ethnicity or culture.

A valuable resource for multicultural stories is Judy Sierra's *Silly and Sillier: Read-Aloud Tales from around the World.* This book contains a treasury of twenty stories from twenty different countries including Bangladesh, Iran, and Argentina. They are all appropriate for preschool and kindergarten children. There are also many fine multicultural books to share with preschoolers and kindergartners. The concept of immigration is addressed by Rene Colato Lainez in *My Shoes and I,* which begins with Mario putting on the new shoes his mother has sent him for the long journey he takes with his father from El Salvador to the United States to reunite their family. The worldwide connection of the world's

Cover from *The Amazing Tree* written and illustrated by John Kilaka. Jacket art copyright © 2009 by John Kilaka. Reprinted by permission of North-South Books. All rights reserved.

people is celebrated beautifully by Mem Fox in *Ten Little Fingers and Ten Little Toes*. This book is a poetic telling about pairs of babies from all over the world, clearly showing all the ways they are alike. Respect for the gifts of all is the message of *The Amazing Tree* by John Kilaka. This story from the Fipa tribe in Tanzania is about cooperation and respect for others. It is illustrated in the author/illustrator's original Kilaka style.

Multicultural books can also add support to social and emotional development. Teachers and parents are always encouraging children to use their words instead of their hands. Books can foster language development that will support the ability of children to deal with conflicts and emotions more effectively. They can also be used as a springboard for learning how to avoid various situations. Finally, the use of multicultural books in this way will show children that people all over the world have the common bonds of emotions and problems as well as those of food, family, and friends.

Sexual Orientation. As our societies move further into the new century, the evolution of human rights continues. Civil unions are becoming increasingly more common, and some political entities have begun to establish same-sex marriage as a legal right. Some individuals and institutions have opposed this for a variety of reasons. Although care must be taken in how this issue is addressed in early childhood programs, it must be clearly understood that very young children are most likely well aware of same sex couples through their engagement with friends, family, and neighbors.

An increasing number of books for children are published each year addressing the issue of sexual orientation. *King and King* by Linda de Haan is one of the best known, primarily because it is a frequent target for challenge and banning. It is a simple boy-meets-boy story. A more nuanced book is *Jack and Jim* by Kitty Crowther. In this tale, Jack (a blackbird) falls for Jim (a seagull). The other birds react in various ways, allowing the reader to explore not only same-sex romance but the issues of race and immigration as well. Earning the top spot in the American Library Association's list of the most challenged children's books is *And Tango Makes Three* by Justin Richardson and Peter Parnell. The story, which is really about loving fathers, involves two male penguins caring for an orphaned egg through the birth of the baby penguin. It is based on an actual scientifically recorded event.

Identifying Bias. It is not difficult to determine whether a book collection is biased by omission. First, count the number of books in the collection. Next, determine how many of the books contain animal characters, white children as characters, Hispanic children as characters, African American children as

Author George Ella Lyon. Used by permission of Orchard Books, New York.

Cover illustration copyright © by Peter Catalanatto from MAMA IS A MINER by George Ella Lyon. Scholastic Inc./Orchard Books. Reprinted by permission.

Author Carol Carrick. Courtesy of Carol Carrick. Photo credit: Jules Worthington.

characters, and other minority children as characters. Finally, look at the numbers and make your own decision. If the percentages surprise you, it may be necessary to take action.

A good collection should have a representative number of minority-based and multicultural books. The stories should appeal to all children; they should not be in the collection simply because they include characters of a certain race, gender, or age and not because they include a character with a disability. Characters must fit into the story without artificial dynamics. The story should be the main element, and all characters should mesh with the story. The fit should be so good that children are left feeling that it is a great story, rather than that it is a great African American story or great Hispanic story. *Abuela's Weave* by Omar Castaneda is a wonderful story from a Hispanic culture; it is wonderful primarily because of its warm characters and important themes, not because it is about Hispanics. *Peeny Butter Fudge* by Toni Morrison and Slade Gordon is a joyful, spirited tale about an African American family in which Mom leaves her three children with Nana for the day. The high point of intergenerational love comes when Nana shares the secret family fudge recipe, admonishing the children to always remember it and to pass it down in the family when they become adults. Many tales from Africa or the inner city have themes that touch all children. Many ethnic fairy tales or farm stories make all children share a common response and feeling. These are the books to add to a collection, books that broaden the sensitivity and understanding of all children.

This same basic idea holds true for sexism in books. Characters such as Ramona Quimby in Beverly Cleary's books, Emily Elizabeth in Norman Bridwell's books, and Maisy in the books of Lucy Cousins are strong female models. They are not perfect children, but they share a common humanity that is appreciated by all children. Bring the subject of sexism out into the open and discuss it with children using books such as *Old Turtle* by Douglas Wood. It is the story of a wise old female turtle who helps those around her understand that everything on earth must be in harmony. Cheng-Khee Chee's watercolor illustrations lend a majestic and finely detailed sense of authority to the story. The issue of boy-jobs and girl-jobs can be effectively dealt with through stories such as *Mama Is a Miner* by George Ella Lyon. The child in the story is both proud and fearful of her mother's hard and dangerous occupation. Peter Catalanotto's large, luminous watercolors of mother and daughter shimmer with energy. Subtle sexism is prejudice that often dissipates when teachers and parents become aware of its existence.

Other biases exist against individuals with disabilities and those with religious or regional class differences. Inclusion of books such as Sharlee Glenn's *Keeping Up with Roo* and Carol Carrick's *Stay Away from Simon* can help teachers and students become sensitive to such realities of our world. One book addresses mental disabilities in adults, the other in children. Each of these books portrays interesting characters who come to a better understanding of themselves and others.

SUMMARY

Choosing the best books available for use with young children is critically important. Because children are forming their thoughts and opinions about almost everything, one must help and encourage them with useful, sensitive, and thought-provoking ideas. Exposure to the best possible stories and illustrations will help them in this area while giving them an appreciation for quality literature as well.

The criteria for choosing literature may seem involved. However, once a teacher or parent gains these critical skills, it becomes second nature to apply them. The criteria combine judging aspects of literature and assessing how stories are presented. Good literature will motivate children to want to hear stories and to learn to read. The illustrations will help children comprehend the story while encouraging them to develop an appreciation for line, shape, and color. Teacher sensitivity allows children to learn to be careful, thoughtful readers who have already started to develop critical thinking skills.

QUESTIONS FOR THOUGHT AND DISCUSSION

1. How should a teacher approach the task of choosing good literature?
2. Why can an understanding of the aspects of literature and knowledge of presentation be helpful in choosing quality literature?
3. How can a list of Caldecott Medal winners be helpful in selecting books?
4. What are the limitations of using only books that have won Caldecott Medals?
5. How can one determine whether the illustrations in a book are appropriate?
6. What are some general goals for using literature with children?
7. Why is it important to consider plot, character, setting, and theme when selecting books?
8. Why is it important to look for bias in children's books?
9. What are some of the different media used in book illustration?
10. When, why, and how should a topic such as sexual orientation be addressed with regard to children's books?

For additional resources, access the *Growing Up with Literature* companion website through www.cengagebrain.com <http://www.cengagebrain.com/>.

CHILDREN'S BOOKS CITED

Aardema, Verna. (1985). *Why mosquitoes buzz in people's ears.* New York: Scholastic.

Aliki (Brandenberg). (1982). *We are best friends.* New York: Greenwillow.

Allard, Harry. (1974). *The Stupids step out.* Boston: Houghton Mifflin.

Allard, Harry. (1981). *The Stupids die.* Boston: Houghton Mifflin.

Ballard, Robin. (2002). *J used to be a baby.* New York: Greenwillow.

Bedfored, David. (2009). *Little Bear's big sweater.* Intercourse, PA: Good Books.

Bemelmans, Ludwig. (1939). *Madeline.* New York: Viking.

Birdseye, Tom. (1991). *Waiting for baby.* New York: Holiday House.

Bottner, Barbara. (2004). *Charlene loves to make noise.* Philadelphia, PA: Running Kids.

Bottner, Barbara. (2004). *Wallace's lists.* New York: Katherine Tegin.

Bottner, Barbara. (2007). *You have to be nice to someone on their birthday.* New York: Putnam.

Bradley, Kimberly. (2006). *Ballerina Nate.* New York: Dial.

Brennan, Tom. (2009). *And then comes Halloween.* Somerville, MA: Candlewick.

Brown, Marcia. (1939). *Cinderella.* New York: Scribner.

Brown, Marcia. (1950). *Dick Whittington and his cat.* New York: Scribner.

Brown, Margaret Wise. (1947). *Goodnight moon.* New York: Harper and Row.

Bunting, Eve. (2003). *Whales passing.* New York: Blue Sky/Scholastic.

Burton, Virginia Lee. (1937). *Choo Choo: The story of a little engine who ran away.* Boston: Houghton Mifflin.

Burton, Virginia Lee. (1937). *The little house.* Boston: Houghton Mifflin.

Butler, John. (2009). *Bedtime in the jungle.* Atlanta, GA: Peachtree.

Calmenson, Stephanie. (2001). *Perfect puppy.* Boston: Houghton Mifflin.

Carle, Eric. (1977). *The grouchy ladybug.* New York: Crowell.

Carrick, Carol. (1985). *Stay away from Simon.* New York: Clarion.

Castaneda, Omar. (1993). *Abuela's weave.* New York: Lee and Low.

Cheng, Andrea. (2006). *The Lemon sisters.* New York: Putnam.

Christelow, Eileen. (2001). *The great pig search.* Boston: Houghton Mifflin.

Cohen, Caron Lee. (2001). *Happy to you!* Boston: Houghton Mifflin.

Cooney, Barbara. (1982). *Miss Rumphius.* New York: Viking Penguin.

Cousins, Lucy. (1999). *Where is Maisy?* Cambridge, MA: Candlewick.

Cousins, Lucy. (2004). *Garden animals.* Cambridge, MA: Candlewick.

Cousins, Lucy. (2005). *Za-Za's baby brother.* Cambridge, MA: Candlewick.

Crews, Donald. (1978). *Freight train.* New York: Greenwillow.

Cronin, Doreen. (2000). *Click, clack, moo, cows that type*. New York: Simon and Schuster.

Crowther, Kitty. (2000). *Jack and Jim*. New York: Hyperion.

De Brunhoff, Jean. (1963). *Babar and the king*. New York: Random House.

deHaan, Linda. (2004). *King and King*. New York: Tricycle.

dePaola, Tomie. (1973). *Nana upstairs and Nana downstairs*. New York: Putnam.

dePaola, Tomie. (1989). *The art lesson*. New York: Putnam.

Dunbar, Joyce. (2001). *Tell me what it's like to be big*. Orlando, FL: Harcourt.

Duvoisin, Roger. (1969). *Veronica*. New York: Knopf.

Edwards, Pamela Duncan. (1997). *Four famished foxes and Fosdyke*. New York: Harper Collins.

Ellis, Carey. (2002). *Prudy's problem and how she solved it*. New York: Abrams.

Falconer, Ian. (2000). *Olivia*. New York: Simon and Schuster.

Falconer, Ian. (2001). *Olivia saves the circus*. New York: Simon and Schuster.

Formento, Alison. (2010). *This tree counts*. Park Ridge, IL: Albert Whitman.

Fox, Mem (2008). *Ten little fingers and ten little toes*. New York: Harcourt.

Gag, Wanda. (1928). *Millions of cats*. New York: Coward McCann.

Gaiman, Neil. (2009). *Crazy hair*. New York: Harper Collins.

Glenn, Sharlee. (2004). *Keeping up with Roo*. New York: Putnam.

Goble, Paul. (1978). *The girl who loved wild horses*. New York: Macmillan.

Hall, Donald. (1979). *Ox-cart man*. New York: Viking Penguin.

Harness, Cheryl. (1995). *The amazing impossible Erie Canal*. New York: Macmillan.

Herman, Charlotte. (2010). *First rain*. Park Ridge, IL: Albert Whitman.

Hest, Amy. (2009). *When you meet a bear on Broadway*. New York: Farrar, Straus and Giroux.

Houston, Gloria. (1992). *My Great Aunt Arizona*. New York: Harper Collins.

Howe, James. (2009). *Houndsley and Catina and the quiet time*. Somerville, MA: Candlewick.

Icenoggle, Jody. (2010). *Till the cows come home*. Honesdale, PA: Boyds Mills Press.

James, Simon. (2004). *My friend whale*. Cambridge, MA: Candlewick.

Johnson, Crockett. (1955). *Harold and the purple crayon*. New York: Harper and Row.

Kay, Verla. (2002). *Broken feather*. New York: Putnam.

Kilaka, John. (2009). *The amazing tree*. New York: North South.

Kimmel, Eric. (2004). *Three samurai cats: A story from Japan*. New York: Holiday House.

Kulka, Joe. (2007). *Wolf's coming*. Minneapolis, MN: Carolrhoda/Lerner.

Kunhardt, Dorothy. (1962). *Pat the bunny*. Racine, WI: Western.

LaRochelle, David. (2004). *The best pet of all.* New York: Dutton.

Lainez, Rene. (2010). *My shoes and I.* Honesdale, PA: Boyds Mills Press.

Leaf, Munro. (1936). *The story of Ferdinand.* New York: Viking.

Lionni, Leo. (1963). *Swimmy.* New York: Pantheon.

London, Jonathan. (2005). *Froggy's baby sister.* New York: Puffin.

Lyon, George Ella. (1994). *Mama is a miner.* New York: Orchard.

MacDonald, Ross. (2003). *Achoo! Bang! Crash! The noisy alphabet.* New York: Roaring Brook.

McCloskey, Robert. (1941). *Make way for ducklings.* New York: Viking.

McCloskey, Robert. (1987). *Blueberries for Sal.* New York: Viking.

McNaughton, Colin. (2009). *Not last night but the night before.* Somerville, MA: Candlewick.

Minarik, Else Holmelund. (1960). *Little Bear's friend.* New York: Harper and Row.

Moore, Clement. (1997). *The night before Christmas.* New York: Simon and Schuster.

Morris, Jackie. (1995). *Bears, bears, and more bears.* Hauppauge, NY: Barron's.

Morrison, Toni, & Morrison, Slade. (2009). *Peeny Butter* Fudge. New York: Simon Schuster/Paula Wiseman.

Moser, Lisa. (2009). *Kisses on the wind.* Somerville, MA: Candlewick.

Mueller, Virginia. (2010). *Monster goes to school.* Park Ridge, IL: Albert Whitman.

Munsch, Robert. (1986). *Love you forever.* Scarborough, Ontario, Canada: Firefly.

Munsch, Robert. (1987). *I have to go.* Toronto, Ontario, Canada: Annick.

Musgrove, Margaret. (1977). *Ashanti to Zulu: African traditions.* New York: Dial.

Oxenbury, Helen. (1995). *I can.* Cambridge, MA: Candlewick.

Parish, Herman. (2009). *Amelia Bedelia's first day of school.* New York: Greenwillow.

Peters, Lisa. (2010). *Frankie works the night* shift. New York: Greenwillow.

Poydar, Nancy. (2009). *Fish school.* New York: Holiday House.

Raschka, Chris. (1993). *Yo! Yes?* New York: Orchard.

Rey, Hans Augusto, & Rey, Margaret. (1941). Curious *George.* New York: Houghton Mifflin.

Richardson, Justin, and Parnell, Peter. (2005). *And Tango makes three.* New York: Simon and Schuster.

Rosen, Michael. (2009). *Bears fly high.* New York: Bloomsbury.

Rosen, Michael. (2009). *We're going on a bear hunt.* New York: Margaret K. McElderry.

Rubin, Adam. (2008). *Those darn squirrels.* New York: Houghton Mifflin/Clarion.

Russo, Marisabina. (2010). *A very big bunny*. New York: Wade and Schwartz.

Ruurs, Margriet. (2009). *My school in the rain forest*. Honesdale, PA: Boyds Mill Press.

Sawyer, Walter. (1999). *The storm*. Katonah, NY: Richard C. Owen.

Sendak, Maurice. (1963). *Where the wild things are*. New York: Harper and Row.

Seuss, Dr. (pseud, for Theodor Geisel) (1940). *Horton hatches the egg*. New York: Random House.

Seuss, Dr. (1963). *Hop on Pop*. New York: Random House.

Seuss, Dr. (1971). *The lorax*. New York: Random House.

Seuss, Dr. (1973). *The shape of me and other stuff*. New York: Random House.

Shea, Bob. (2010). *Race you to bed*. New York: Katherine Tegen.

Shelton, Paula. (2009). *Child of the civil rights movement*. New York: Schwartz and Wade.

Sierra, Judy. (2002). *Silly and sillier: Read-aloud tales from around the world*. New York: Knopf.

Silverstein, Shel. (1964). *The giving tree*. New York: Harper and Row.

Simmons, Jane. (2001). *Come along, Daisy!* Boston: Little, Brown.

Snyder, Margaret. (2001). *Ord makes a wish*. New York: Random House.

Steptoe, John. (1987). *Mufaro's beautiful daughters*. New York: Lothrop, Lee and Shepard.

Thermes, Jennifer. (2001). *When I was built*. New York: Henry Holt.

Tran, Truong. (2003). *Going home, coming home*. San Francisco, CA: Children's Book Press.

Tresselt, Alvin. (1954). *I saw the sea come in*. New York: Lothrop, Lee and Shepard.

Tresselt, Alvin. (1965). *Hide and seek fog*. New York: Mulberry.

Van Allsburg, Chris. (1982). *Jumanji*. Boston: Houghton Mifflin.

Van Allsburg, Chris. (1985). *The Polar express*. Boston: Houghton Mifflin.

vanGenechten, Guido. (2006). *Kangaroo Christine*. Wilton, CT: Tiger Tales.

Van Patten, Bruce. (2010). *Tucker took it*. Honesdale, PA: Boyds Mills Press.

Viorst, Judith. (1972). *Alexander and the terrible, horrible, no good, very bad day*. New York: Atheneum.

Waber, Bernard. (1972). *Ira sleeps over*. Boston: Houghton Mifflin.

Walsh, Melanie. (2009). *Trick or treat*. Somerville, MA: Candlewick.

Wells, Rosemary. (1975). *Morris's disappearing bag*. New York: Dutton.

Wood, Douglas. (1992). *Old turtle*. Duluth, MN: Pfeifer-Hamilton.

Yolen, Jane. (1987). *Owl moon*. New York: Philomel.

Zolotow, Charlotte. (1982). *William's doll*. New York: Harper and Row.

SELECTED REFERENCES AND RESOURCES

Aldana, P. (Ed.) (2004). *Under the spell of the moon: Art for children from the world's greatest illustrators.* Toronto, Ontario, Canada: Groundwood.

Bruce, T. (2010). *Early childhood.* Newbury Park, CA: Sage.

Butler, D. (1997). *Babies need books.* Portsmouth, NH: Heinemann.

Carle, Eric, et al. (2007). *Artist to artist: 23 major illustrators talk to children about their art.* New York: Philomel.

Copple, C., and Bredekamp, S. (Eds.). (2009). *Developmentally appropriate practices in early childhood education programs serving children from birth to age 8.* Washington, DC: NAEYC.

Cullinan, B. (2000). *Read to me: Raising kids who love to read.* New York: Scholastic.

Cummins, J. (2000). *Wings of an artist: Children's book illustrators talk about their art.* New York: Harry N. Abrams.

Deiner, P. L. (2010). *Inclusive early childhood education: Development, resources and practice.* Florence, KY: Wadsworth/Cengage.

deMelendez, W. R., and Beck, V. O. (2010). *Teaching young children in multicultural classrooms: Issues, concepts and strategies.* Florence, KY: Wadsworth/Cengage.

Freeman, E. B., and Lehman, B. A. (2001). *Global perspectives in children's literature.* Boston: Allyn & Bacon.

Galda, L. and Cullinan, B. (2005). *Literature and the child.* San Diego, CA: Harcourt Brace Jovanovich.

Hearne, B., and Stevens, D. (2000). *Choosing books for children: A common sense guide.* Champaign, IL: University of Illinois Press.

Holman, C. H., and Harmon, W. (2008). *A handbook to literature.* Englewood Cliffs, NJ: Prentice Hall.

Hyland, A. (2006). *The picture book: Contemporary illustration.* San Francisco, CA: Laurence King/Chronicle.

Jacobson, T. (2003). *Confronting our discomfort: Clearing the way for anti-bias in early childhood.* Portsmouth, NH: Heinemann.

Marcus, L. S. (2008). *A Caldecott celebration: Six artists share their paths to the Caldecott Medal.* New York: Walker.

Norton, D. E., and Norton, S. (2006). *Through the eyes of a child: An introduction to children's literature.* Englewood Cliffs, NJ: Prentice-Hall.

Salisbury, M. (2004). *Illustrating children's books: Creating children's books for publication.* Hauppauge, NY: Barrons.

Toussaint, P. (1999). *Great books for African-American children.* New York: Plume/Penguin.

Traw, R. (1996). Beware! Here there be beasties: Responding to fundamentalist censors. *The New Advocate, 9* (1), 35–56.

Trelease, J. (2006). *The read-aloud handbook* (5th ed.). New York: Penguin.

Williams, H. E. (1991). *Books by African-American authors and illustrators for children and young adults.* Chicago: American Library Association.

INTERNET REFERENCES AND HELPFUL WEBSITES

Children's Literature Comprehensive Database Site. *Children's Literature.* Retrieved February 1, 2010, from http://www.childrenslit.com

Eric Carle Museum of Picture Book Art site. Retrieved February 1, 2010, from http://www.picturebookart.org

Weber County Library site. *Historical fiction picture* books. Retrieved February 1, 2010, from http://www.weberpl.lib.ut.us/content/booklists/sort/t/36

Lisa R. Bartle site. *Database of Award-Winning Children's Literature.* Retrieved February 1, 2010, from http://www.dawcl.com

New York Public Library site. Retrieved February 1, 2010, from http://www. nypl.org

Ubbes, V. *Children's picture book database.* Miami University of Ohio site. Retrieved February 1, 2010, from http://www.lib.muohio.edu/pictbks/index.php

CHAPTER 4

USING VARIOUS TYPES OF LITERATURE

In addition to having books on the children's level, it is also important to surround children with books at several levels to motivate and inspire them to want to read "all by themselves." In this chapter, a wide range of literature genres for children will be explored, including folk tales, fairy tales, fables, rhymes, fiction, nonfiction, concept books, and poetry. Special attention is given to selecting and using various pieces of literature, to literary devices, and to the awards given to the best books each year.

Books used in traditional elementary school beginning reading programs are known as **basal readers**. These books are part of an integrated set of textbooks, workbooks, teachers' manuals, and related materials used to provide **developmental reading instruction**. Basal readers usually contain a selection of short pieces written for that particular book. The vocabulary of the selections is usually carefully controlled to use only certain words at each level. Basals might be included in programs for young children, but they are not necessary. They tend to neither contain sufficient quality literature nor take advantage of a child's natural curiosity and language.

"I touch the future—I teach."

—CHRISTA MCAULIFFE

In recent years, educational publishers have used more children's literature pieces in their reading texts. The selections range from exact reprintings to abridged versions. Some versions have eliminated some of the illustrations and changed some of the wording to control the difficulty of the vocabulary and coordinate with the program's teaching activities, workbooks, and assignments. Although the quality of the literature in these books is better, it is used for a purpose for which it was never intended—classroom reading instruction. As a result, many authors of children's storybooks refuse to have their works appear in reading textbooks. In any case, such an approach is not developmentally appropriate for preschool children. In fact, those using a holistic approach raise serious questions about the developmental appropriateness of many aspects of commercial elementary school reading program materials and methods.

Because of all that must be considered, much time is needed to make the right choices. Since time is not something most early childhood educators possess in large quantities, it is imperative that the teacher use time effectively. If good matches are to be made between children and books, caregivers need a deep understanding of the children, a solid knowledge of how to select appropriate books, and a broad knowledge of the children's books available. The purpose of this chapter is to expand the reader's knowledge of traditional and current children's literature. Accordingly, summaries are offered of the wide range of literature available for young people.

The categories used here to classify books are broad. They could easily be broken down into further subcategories. The depth of knowledge of each category can be increased by studying book reviews or, better yet, reading and discussing the actual books.

HISTORY OF CHILDREN'S LITERATURE

Contemporary books for children are so numerous and varied that it's hard to believe that there was ever a time when there was no genre called children's literature. Yet such a time did exist, and it was not that long ago. Ancient myths, legends, and folktales that were originally created as attempts to explain the universe and the human condition are now classified as children's literature. William Caxton's 1484 translation of *Aesop's Fables,* the 1760 publication of *Mother Goose's*

Melody, and the early nineteenth-century fairy tales of Hans Christian Andersen are usually identified as early examples of children's literature as well. However, they were not intended for children at all. Most of these pieces were intended to teach adults moral and ethical lessons. They became identified as children's literature for a number of reasons. Because they taught moral lessons, adults began to use them with children. The stories contained within them are appealing in their simplicity and fantasy, and children tended to like them. An early American work that was specifically written for children was John Cotton's 1641 *Spiritual Milk for Children,* a volume created to teach the Bible and moral values.

The idea that literature for children should contain more of an emphasis on entertainment and enjoyment was evidenced in the mid-nineteenth century through works such as Edward Lear's 1846 *A Book of Nonsense,* Lewis Carroll's 1865 *Alice in Wonderland,* Joel Chandler Harris' 1880 *Uncle Remus* stories, Carlo Collodi's 1880 *Pinocchio,* Robert Louis Stephenson's 1880 *A Children's Garden of Verses,* and Rudyard Kipling's *The Jungle Book.* In many of these books, however, an underlying desire to teach a lesson is plainly evident.

The first half of the twentieth century was a time of transition, with changing emphasis on the balance between **moral lessons** and **entertainment**. Authors began to create works clearly intended for children, not just works intended for adults that were then used with children. Nevertheless, authors seemed to be aware that the buying audience for children's books was adults. It was necessary that stories be appealing to adults as well. In 1900, L. Frank Baum published *The Wonderful Wizard of Oz,* a classic volume for children that went on to become a major motion picture and an inspiration for Broadway productions. Elements of traditional stories continued with two notable 1902 works, Rudyard Kipling's *Just So Stories* and Beatrix Potter's *The Tale of Peter Rabbit.*

The late 1920s and the 1930s saw increasing numbers of books written specifically for children on both sides of the Atlantic. These books emphasized entertainment from the child's point of view. These included A. A. Milne's 1926 *Winnie the Pooh,* Wanda Gag's 1928 *Millions of Cats,* Munro Leaf's 1936 *Ferdinand,* Dr. Seuss's 1937 *And to Think I Saw It on Mulberry Street,* and Ludwig Bemelmans' 1939 *Madeleine.* The trend continued and in 1967 Maurice Sendak's *Where the Wild Things Are* introduced the imaginative antics of a child **anti-hero**. This brings us to the explosion of books written as contemporary children's literature as described in this book.

FINGERPLAYS/CHANTS/RHYMES

Young children benefit from the rhythm and sounds of language. Through adult modeling of **fingerplays,** **chants,** and **action rhymes,** children can learn these rhythms and sounds. Perhaps this is why such literary forms are found in almost every culture, country, and language. The songlike quality of these language forms makes them easy to listen to, respond to, and learn. Because these forms are often short, they are easily remembered after several repetitions. **Repetition** can help children learn to speak words as they are needed. Fingerplays allow children to coordinate hand motions with words in a manner that facilitates small muscle development and eye-hand coordination.

Adults should always support children's development of self-esteem. The fact that these literary forms enable children to experience success is an important reason to use them. The successful acquisition of fingerplays and rhymes makes children feel competent about their learning ability while providing a language skill achievement that will enhance their literacy development.

Fingerplays and Chants

A fingerplay is a short poem put to rhyme or beat. A fingerplay has hand motions; a chant does not. Any fingerplay can be chanted in a singsong fashion, and many chants can be made into fingerplays. A teacher can make up and sing a chant such as, "It's clean-up time, it's clean-up time. Let's all cooperate," to help children with the transition from free play to circle time. Chants and fingerplays are positive ways to help children learn about social expectations and concept development in an informal manner. An example of a rectangle concept fingerplay is, "Long-short, long-short. The rectangle is long-short, long-short." As the fingerplay is sung, children trace the rectangle shape in the air. As the word "rectangle" is reached, the children might be encouraged to shout it out. This fingerplay can be used when tracing the shape or drawing it and can be used to help differentiate between the square and the rectangle.

Fingerplays and chants can be invented by adapting favorite short poems and can include motion or action. The teacher can invent fingerplays or have children help to invent some. For example, after sighting a helicopter, this easy, concrete fingerplay was invented:

WORDS	**ACTIONS**
Up and down, Up and down.	Children move up and down with the words, arms out to the
Round and round, Round and round.	sides, then spin in a circle.
The helicopter ... Goes off to town.	Children run off to a corner of the room.

Every caregiver of young children has a varied repertoire of fingerplays and chants. They may be recorded on file cards that are easy to use and store. Fingerplays for transitions, basic concepts, holidays, and even commonplace concepts such as nap time can simplify the daily routine and enhance a program. Some great sources for fingerplays are *Finger Rhymes* (2008) by Lily Erlic, *101 Content Building Fingerplays, Action Rhymes and Songs* (2009) by Pamela Chanko, and *1000 Fingerplays and Action Rhymes* (2010) by Barbara Scott.

Rhymes

Rhymes can be simple poems and chants. They can be used as one would use the fingerplay or chant. Silly rhymes are particularly enjoyable even for young toddlers and are easily created. Children love rhymes that use their names or the names of friends and family members.

Rhymes have been passed down from generation to generation. There are rhymes for jumping rope, learning colors, and just about anything else children find important, frightening, or silly.

"One, two, buckle my shoe"; "Blue, blue, God loves you"; "One potato, two potato, three potato, four"; "Lizzy Borden took an axe . . ." are all rhymes that most remember from childhood. Horrendous rhymes were often created as a way of helping children express and cope with fear. "Ring around the Rosie" was originally an expression of children's fears about death and the terrible processing of bodies during the plague in England. "Ashes to ashes, we all fall down" was playacting the deaths that the children feared. Ridicule is one way that children diminish and process fears. New rhymes are forever adding to the heritage that one group of children passes to the next as a ritual part of childhood.

MOTHER GOOSE TALES/NURSERY RHYMES

Who was **Mother Goose**? There are various versions of the origin of Mother Goose. Some credit the term to the French author Charles Perrault, who in 1697 referred to the rhymes as those told by an old woman tending geese. Others attribute Mother Goose to the English author John Newbury, who first used the term in a book he published in 1765. Still others claim that Mother Goose was a Boston woman by the name of Elizabeth Goose. She was the mother-in-law of a publisher of a slim volume titled *Mother Goose Melodies for Children* published in Boston in 1719. Though the proof is lost in the archives of the Antiquarian Society Collection in Worcester, Massachusetts, it is unimportant who first used the term. Mother Goose is known by children all over the world as a symbol of rhymes and the enjoyment gained from their use.

Mother Goose Activities

Mother Goose stories are easily used to stimulate language acquisition and teach social behavior rules. They can be used for their humor as simple flannel-board stories or as dramatic productions with props and costumes. They can be adapted for art activities as well. An additional benefit of using Mother Goose rhymes is that they lend themselves to movement. The reader can model facial expressions, hand gestures, or body movement to accompany and dramatize the rhymes.

Many of the Mother Goose tales are found in collections. A large collection will offer many rhymes that the teacher may never have seen or heard. They can be used at story time, circle time, or even for transitions. "Jack be nimble, Jack be quick . . ." can be a transition rhyme for leaving the room. Children can say the rhyme as they jump over a paper candlestick while leaving the room one by one. Several Mother Goose tales have been made into picture books with beautiful illustrations. Two good choices of Mother Goose stories are *Sing a Song of Mother Goose* by Barbara Reid and *The Orchard Book of Nursery Rhymes* by Zena Sutherland.

In addition to Mother Goose, rhymes from other countries or collections such as *Gregory Griggs and Other Nursery Rhyme People* by Arnold Lobel are also useful. For example, "The Farmer of Leeds" is a wonderful spring rhyme about the grass growing. It can lead into a grass-growing activity using sponges. The sponges can be cut into the shape of a person, then grass seeds added where a person's hair would grow. When they are placed upright in a dish of water, grass hair will sprout. Such an activity adds much to the enjoyment of the rhymes.

Nursery Rhymes

Collections of Mother Goose and other **nursery rhymes** have always been passed around, added to, changed, and revised. Some were originally written as political satires poking fun at the king or government from the safety of street songs and children's rhymes. These changes explain why rhymes vary from country to country and from region to region within a country.

"Mary Had a Little Lamb" is an example of a Mother Goose rhyme that was added to the collection well after many of the original rhymes were written. The tale was originally written by Sarah Josepha Hale and was first published in 1830. Contemporary writers such as Ruth I. Dowell continue to add to the Mother Goose collection with such tantalizing titles as "I'm Rather Short, Larry Bird," "Pennsylvania Pete," "Mama's Poppin' Popcorn," and "Myrtle Was a Turtle." The traditions and wording of rhymes are important

"Book cover" from POTATO JOE Copyright © 2008 by Keith Baker, reproduced by permission of Houghton Mifflin Harcourt Publishing Company.

to children. The tongue twisters and secret words found in so many rhymes are like echoes of ancient fireside rituals. They provide children with reassurance and control over the mysteries of the adult world. Such carefully followed advice as "Step on a crack, break your mother's back" or "See a pin and pick it up, all the day you'll have good luck" are part of our treasured childhood memories.

Contemporary authors sometimes use a nursery rhyme as a jumping off point in creating a new story. In *Potato Joe* by author illustrator Keith Baker, the familiar "One-potato, two-potato" rhyme is used to create a hilarious counting book. As the story unfolds, Joe and his spud friends meet more and more garden pals as they wander about the farmyard.

FABLES/FOLKTALES/FAIRY TALES

For young children, **fables**, **folktales**, and **fairy tales** constitute a treat that teaches and inspires. Many convey a society's value system; others are simply entertainment. Handed down through oral tradition, they were told to each new generation by storytellers, people revered by earlier cultures, until they were eventually preserved in written form.

Fables

A fable is a story used to teach a moral. Most use animals as characters, but this is not always the case. Other fables use people or inanimate objects as characters. Fables with animal characters are called *beast fables*. Fables are found in every culture throughout the world. In the West, people are most familiar with the fables credited to Aesop. Many other fables have also become part of the English speaking tradition. These include Uncle Remus stories by Joel Chandler Harris and Rudyard Kipling's *Jungle Book*. Phrases from the fables often find their way into common language: "That's just sour grapes" and "No use crying over spilt milk."

Fables can be used for both enjoyment and discussion of the morals they contain. An attractive source of fables is *Anno's Aesop* by Mitsumasa Anno. Related classroom activities include creating fables about school rules or table manners, illustrating the fables, and acting out the fables.

Cover from *Heidi* by Johanna Spyri. Jacket illustration copyright ©2009 by Maja Ducikova. Reprinted by permission of North-South Books. All rights reserved.

Folktales

Folktales are the common man's fairy tale. They are unadorned stories. As with fairy tales and legends, folktales share common plots in which good overcomes

Book cover from Ashpet: An Appalachian Tale, retold by Joanne Compton, illustrated by Kenn Compton copyright © 1994.

evil and justice is served. Every culture possesses these tales. They serve to explain society, history, and natural phenomena and offer a sense of security while sometimes poking fun at things people wish to change.

Folktales have existed since well before recorded history. Because few people could read at the time most folktales were authored, they developed through an oral tradition. Folktales have served to teach, to entertain, and to explain the world to each new generation of listeners. Children's literature today encompasses a marvelous variety of such tales from throughout the world. The classic story of *Heidi* is presented in a new picture book format by Johanna Spyri. Although the original story was first published in 1880, this new version for Spyri makes this well-loved tale accessible to much younger children. A special bonus is the inclusion of Maja Dusikova's gorgeous illustrations. Joanne Compton presents a more modern version of "Cinderella" to create a distinctly American story in *Ashpet: An Appalachian Tale.*

The authors of traditional folktales are unknown. New versions are written, often with humorous twists; these are known as fractured fairy tales. Recently published versions of traditional folktales keep the genre very much alive with contemporary language and appealing illustrations. Jon Scieszka presents a folktale from a different perspective in *The True Story of the Three Little Pigs.* This version, told from the wolf's point of view, has the beast pleading that he was framed. The tale would be a great accompaniment to a telling of the traditional story. Tina Matthews approaches the story of the Little Red Hen in a new way in *Out of the Egg*. With her gorgeous Japanese woodblock prints and lyrical text, she uses the traditional tale to create a bridge to the related nonfiction issues of environmental protection, mindless consumerism, sloth, industrial waste, sharing, and friendship. This story will serve as a starting point to serious discussions. Although not technically a folktale, *You're Lovable to Me* by Kat Yeh would be a good choice to introduce the genre to toddlers and preschoolers. It is an old fashioned story of unconditional love that has a classic feel to it much like a traditional folk tale.

Most cultures cherish their folktales. Such stories make for good reading while helping children to broaden their understanding of the cultures of the world. Many of the tales use animal characters, a familiar device to most young readers. Native American cultures have plenty of tales to share. In *Raven: A Trickster Tale from the Pacific Northwest,* Gerald McDermott uses a clever bird with some all-too-human qualities to present a story about the birth of the sun. The mixed media illustration makes the Native American symbols and motifs come alive. Janet Stevens retells a Ute tale in *Coyote Steals the Blanket: A Ute Tale.* In this story, Coyote ignores Hummingbird's warning and steals a beautiful blanket. The miscreant finds himself pursued by a magic boulder from which only Hummingbird can save him.

Cover from *Out of the Egg* by Tina Matthews. Jacket art copyright © by Tina Matthews. Reprinted by permission of Houghton Mifflin Harcourt Publishing Company. All rights reserved.

Coyote appears as a rascally character in many American cultures. In *The Tale of Rabbit and Coyote,* Tony Johnston draws a story from the culture of Oaxaca, Mexico, where the two antagonists crash from adventure to adventure in an extended saga. In a surprising but pleasant departure from his typical style, Tomie dePaola's illustrations of the blue coyote and purple rabbit will evoke howls of laughter from young listeners. Tales from a number of Native American cultures are included in *Thirteen Moons on Turtle's Back* by Joseph Bruchac and Jonathan London. The collection is symbolic of the thirteen cycles of the moon during the calendar year and the thirteen scales on the back of a turtle. The stories reflect a culture that is close to the rhythms of nature. Rich illustrations by Thomas Locker set wonderful moods for the tales.

The continent of Africa is another rich source of folktales at their best. Baba Diakite retells a clever and humorous story of how a hat maker outwits a band of trickster monkeys in *The Hatseller and the Monkeys.* In another tale, also by Baba Diakite, a deeper message about the importance of living in harmony with nature is portrayed in *The Hunterman and the Crocodile.* Bobby Norfolk retells the classical African folktale about why spiders have no hair in *Anansi and the Pot of Beans.* Using a trickster tale format, Gerald McDermott tells the West African story of *Zomo the Rabbit.* Zomo is not big and strong, but he is clever as he attempts to accomplish the three impossible tasks set before him. The rhythmic language and dazzling illustrations enhance this tale, which is a forerunner of rabbit trickster tales from the Caribbean and the American South. In the latter, the rabbit is known as Br'er Rabbit.

Fairy Tales

Fairy tales are folk stories or legends in which an author incorporates additional aspects of literature. They tend to be more involved and more polished than folktales and legends. Fairy tales such as *The Wild Swans* by Hans Christian

Author Eric Kimmel.
Courtesy/photo credit:
Doris Kimmel.

Book cover from *The Three Princes* retold by Eric Kimmel, illustrated by Leonard Fisher, copyright © 1994. Reprinted by permission of Holiday House.

Anderson have been retold for decades, often accompanied by stunning illustrations such as those created by Karen Milone.

Concern has been expressed by some about the impact of these tales on young children. They sometimes include violence and can be frightening. The justice served in the tales can be swift and bloody, and some of the tales are grim and graphic. Someone who knows the children is the best judge of whether these stories should be used. However, one should consider the fact that childhood is full of frightening monsters and unknown fears. Adults sometimes fail to realize that children will invent these fearsome characters as part of developing coping skills. Using the tales may help children by providing positive role models. Listening to stories about the devotion of the good characters and the destruction of evil forces can reassure children that their own inner conflicts and fears will likewise be settled and resolved positively.

Various types of fairy tales are found in literature. Some are humorous, while some use beasts to represent ideas or traits. Some answer "why" questions, while others are filled with magic and wonder. Frequently recurring themes and ideas in fairy tales include the number three, characters who are all good or all bad, long journeys, and distant times and places. Fairy tales provide heroes who at times use their might. Unlike television characters, however, the hero of a fairy tale will more often use wit, cleverness, and intelligence to defeat a foe. These are admirable traits for a child to aspire to.

Some tales contain excessive violence. Versions that include less violence might be more suitable for young listeners. Children do find the tales both enjoyable and reassuring. The endings always seem to reaffirm that the world is right again and that order has been restored.

The traditional fairy tale continues to be published in new versions. Eric Kimmel presents a fitting example in *The Three Princes*, a story in which a princess determines which of her suitors she will marry. Sending the three princes out in search of the greatest wonder they can find, she proves herself wise indeed in selecting her husband. A clever twist on the classic Cinderella story is presented by Marianne Mitchell in *Joe Cinders*. In this Cinderella story Joe is a poor cowboy mistreated by his mean stepbrothers. A new fairy tale can be created, as has been done by William Steig in *Shrek*. The story is given a unique twist by turning the traditional elements upside down. Everything turns out fine in the end, though, because Shrek and his princess are pleased to live horribly ever after. Another variation of the Cinderella story is found in *The Rough-Face Girl*, an Algonquin tale retold by Rafe Martin. The tale deals with the theme of real beauty. A new version of *Goldilocks and the Three Bears* is retold by Valeri Gorbachev. The story itself is true to the original, but Gorbachev's new illustrations will be welcomed by preschoolers. Big, bright, and colorful, they are completely updated. The bears wear modern clothing and baby bear is always accompanied by his own teddy bear. The age-old story of how gold and riches cannot buy happiness is told against Peter Sis's beautiful illustrations in *The Happy Troll* by Max Bollinger. New fairy tales are sometimes created to deal with age-old issues. In *Aurelie* by Heather Tomlinson, the issue of breaking a promise to a friend sets the stage for a story about three children and their friend, a little river dragon.

Different Versions

Reading contrasting versions of the same story is a way to help children explore the content and respond to the stories. Children can be encouraged to discuss how they feel about the stories and the varied resolutions of the plot. Take, for example, the story of Hansel and Gretel. It is a scary story that can reaffirm the importance of parental care and the danger of going off alone and help children resolve their fear of being alone. The story addresses the themes of stepmother and stranger. In one version retold by Linda Hayward, the wicked stepmother leaves and the children find their way home by their own devices. In another version retold by Barbara Shook Hazen, the children cleverly escape from the witch, leave with a bag of jewels, and return home to find a reformed and repentant stepmother with whom they live happily ever after. After reading the two versions, one might discuss with the children which version they liked best and their reasons for choosing that version. There are also kinder, gentler versions of classic tales. Such is the case with Hans Christian Anderson's *The Ugly Duckling*. In a recent version illustrated with lovely subdued watercolors by Pirkko Vainio, the young child will enjoy the features of the classic story with a substantial de-emphasis on the disturbing aspects of the tale.

In *Rufferella* by Vanessa Gill-Brown, the character Diamante, seeing herself as Cinderella's fairy godmother, turns her dog into "Rufferella" a girl with a beautiful singing voice. Rufferella rises to fame and is invited to the queen's court, where she is found out when she jumps onto the table to eat the sausages. It is ridiculous fun. A modern adaptation of *The Princess and the Pea* by Alain Vaes features an offbeat tow truck-driving princess who wears greasy overalls. An absolutely hilarious version of *The Three Pigs* is presented by David Wiesner. The characters go in and out of the illustrations in totally silly ways. At one point, a cat and a fiddle from a Mother Goose rhyme emerge in this book filled with wit and humor. Another variation of the same technique is found in Bruce Whatley's *Wait! No Paint*. It turns out that it is the illustrator of the story who is behind the silliness because he has run out of the correct color to paint the pigs. As a result, the pigs go from green to polka dots before winding up in the wrong story at the end. Three fairy tales collide in riotous fashion in *The Three Silly Billies* by Margie Palatini. In this book the "Three Billy Goats Gruff,"

"Goldilocks and the Three Bears," and "Little Red Riding Hood" intersect in a tale that will have everyone laughing.

Encouraging responses to the literature allows children to bring up hidden fears and issues. Verbalizing can help children understand that others share and understand their feelings. It is important to validate children's rights to their feelings. One should not allow ridicule or negative attitudes to impede these discussions.

Legends

Ethnic tales, **myths**, and **legends** lend themselves to the preschool program. For example, when teaching about the earth traveling around the sun, discuss the Greek myth about Apollo and his chariot. When teaching about safety and the need to avoid yelling in the pool or yard, use the story of "The Boy Who Cried Wolf to illustrate the dangers of pretending to need help. When teaching about sharing, use "The Fisherman and His Wife" to illustrate what happens when greed gets out of control.

Folktales and legends can encourage language acquisition with their effective use of repetition of words and word sounds such as "Fee, fie, foe, fum"; "All the better to see you with my dear"; and "Who is the fairest of them all?" Children naturally join in with the words of the story. Local tales, ethnic legends, and ethnic tales can also be helpful in integrating multicultural children into the mainstream within the classroom. Sharing one's cultural heritage is a strengthening and unifying way to build understanding among children while helping each child's ego development. Parents, churches, and libraries can often supply tapes or stories that would meet the needs of the class. It's often possible to invite cultural storytellers to tell tales to the children.

Because legends typically involve a kernel of truth that builds over time with retelling, addition, and exaggeration, children can use their imaginations to create their own local legends. A model for this is found in *The Bears We Know* by Brenda Silsbe. This charming picture book is about the bears who live down the road in a big brown house. Although the narrator admits to never having seen them, the legend of the bears grows with each retelling.

PICTURE BOOKS/WORDLESS PICTURE BOOKS

A picture book is a special kind of book for a special audience. Unlike the child who can read many words, younger children gain much of their understanding from the illustrations and through listening to the story. A picture book must possess a well-developed plot, theme, setting, and characterization. It should also use an appropriate style, print dimension, and page size. In addition, a picture book must have a special unity between text and illustration. The two must provide an understandable telling of the story for those who are not yet fluent readers. In most picture books the words printed on the page are not always necessary to comprehend the action, flow, and intent of the story. The author, illustrator, and reader of a good picture book enjoy a communal experience that transcends the written language.

In some picture books, words have been completely eliminated. *Home* by Jeannie Baker is an illustrated **wordless picture book** with a message of hope. In the story, a baby's view of the world, seen from her bedroom window, changes as she grows up. The wonderful collage illustrations will make this a favorite for repeat viewing. In *Four Hungry Kittens,* Emily Arnold McCully creates a wordless story that also brings out the mood of the setting and the personalities of the characters. It is a great choice for one-on-one sessions with preschoolers. A bit more sophisticated for a wordless picture book is *Finding Kate's Shoes* by Erica Dornbusch. In this story, Kate and her mother frantically look for a pair of red sneakers, which are visible to the reader throughout. In his Caldecott Award-winning wordless picture book *Flotsam,* David Wiesner takes the character of a young boy on a fantasy adventure following the discovery of an odd-looking camera that has washed up on the beach. The watercolor illustrations, depicting smaller and smaller images from the camera's photos, are mesmerizing.

CONCEPT BOOKS

Concept books, which include **counting** and **alphabet or ABC books,** are an area of children's literature that has seen tremendous growth and some interesting developments over the past few years. They may be pop-up books, pop-out books, poke-through-the-hole books, puppet books, books cut into shapes, books cut into puzzles, big books, mini books, and textured books. With such talented artists as Peter Seymour, Bruce McMillan, Tana Hoban, Eric Carle, Richard Scarry, and Dr. Seuss involved, it is not a problem to find a good concept book. Rather, the problem is deciding which is most appropriate for a particular purpose. Concept books are fun to use, and they help motivate children to learn about spatial concepts, numbers, and colors.

In selecting concept books, keep some general guidelines in mind. First, the concept should be clearly described and illustrated in the book. The facts included should have validity. If the book is about magnetism, the illustrations shouldn't show a magnet picking up pennies because magnets do not attract copper. The illustrations should possess numerical accuracy as well. If a counting book indicates that there are five objects on a page, there should be five objects on the page. The presentation of the concept should be interesting. If the teacher has to struggle to keep the children focused, the book is probably boring. A good concept book motivates children to use it. They will want to listen to the story and look at the pictures. All these books should be constructed sturdily so that children can use them after the teacher has presented them. Finally, the book should have a sustaining factor. The children should be drawn back to the book after the initial reading by an adult. If this does not occur, perhaps the book wasn't an appropriate choice in the first place. These guidelines assume, of course, that other criteria including age appropriateness were followed as well.

One of the most popular types of concept books is devoted to colors. Children will return to Petr Horacek's *Strawberries Are Red* and *What Is Black and White?* and Byron Barton's *My Car.* Children will love the visual images in *Warthogs Paint: A Messy Color Book* by Pamela Edwards. Emma Dodd combines the concepts of colors, counting, and sounds in *Dog's Colorful Day: A Messy Story about Colors and Counting;* Lorinda Cauley combines colors, shapes, opposites, and animal sounds in *What Do You Know!* Jan Carr presents a rhyming look at spring in *Splish, Splash, Spring,* while Marc Harshman and Cheryl Ryan look at the colors of autumn in *Red Are the Apples.* Eve Bunting takes a look at pirates through the imagination of a child in *Little Badger, Terror of the Seven Seas.* Concept books for toddlers include *Whose Shoes?* by Anna Grossnickle Hines and *Good Night* by Debbie Bailey.

Counting Books

Many teachers will use several different books for each concept they teach. If the concept is counting, for example, it could be introduced with Eric Carle's *1,2,3 to the Zoo.* At story time, the teacher could share Michael Bond's *Paddington's 123.* John Lobban's endearing illustrations are always welcome. The day could end with a reading of Ezra Jack Keats's *Over in the Meadow* and a homework mission for children to check their own yards for things read about in the story. Several additional books might be useful to enrich and expand the concept of counting and numbers. A counting book with an emotional element to it is *One Dragon's Dream, A Counting Book* written and illustrated by Peter Pavez. In the story, a dragon dreams of being teased by two turkeys, three tigers, four frogs and so on. While he is eventually rescued by ten turtles, readers will enjoy the frenetic illustrations as they search for and count the many objects on each page. A wonderful book that combines counting with farm animals, rhyming text, and folk art illustration is *Driving My Tractor* by Jan Dobbins. *Willy Can Count* by Anne Rockwell is based on a little boy's walk down a country lane accompanied by his mother. It is sure to be read over and over.

A counting book that combines science and lyrical four-line stanzas is *Count Down to Fall* by Frank Hawk. Mother Bear counts the ways she loves her baby

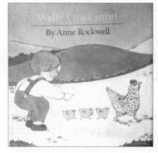

Cover from Willy Can Count, written and illustrated by Anne Rockwell, copyright © 1989. Reprinted by permission of the Illustrator.

in Jonathan London's *Count the Ways, Little Brown Bear.* Counting the numbers 1 to 10 with a wise old owl becomes a game of finding the hidden number shapes among the animals in Suse MacDonald's *Look Whooo's Counting.* Using farm animals, Mary Rayner introduces counting in Ten Little Piglets: Garth Pigs Wall Song. In *Counting in the Garden,* textile designer Kim Parker presents a visual treat brimming with insects, animals, and flowers. Another counting book with an environmental theme is *Turtle Splash: Countdown at the Pond* by Cathryn Falwell. Using a familiar reverse counting rhyme from 10 to 1, the story unfolds with leaf-print and bark-print illustrations. The book includes information about the turtles and easy directions for making leaf prints as an extension of the story.

The books can always be left out for the children to use independently in the classroom. They will often discover that it is more fun to share counting with a friend using books and blocks than to use a workbook page or a photocopied worksheet to learn the same concept. Using these books to develop social skills used is beneficial for children. Additional activities that can be coordinated include creating concept books with real objects and magazine pictures, creating concept posters centered around a book, and acting out a concept with blocks, pillows, or other props.

Alphabet (ABC) Books

The alphabet comprises most of the symbols used in our written language. The more comfortable children become with the letters and their sounds, the less confusing written language will be for them. Because it should not be expected that children will learn the letters and sounds until the elementary school grades, there should be no pressure on them to repeat, write, or memorize the letters. If children learn the letters on their own, that is fine, but it should not be an expectation. The goal is to develop **phonological awareness**, familiarity, and confidence with language and meaning.

TIPS FOR TEACHERS

Create an alphabet book written and illustrated by the children.

- Assign a letter to each child, collect the illustrations, and create an alphabet book. Or have each child create a complete alphabet book.
- Have a group of children create poster-size pages of each letter to create a class ABC Big Book.
- Have children bring in pictures of favorite things and match them to the appropriate alphabet letter.
- Invite parents to participate by coming in to help with the letters.

Alphabet books have a long history. Many illustrators of both children's and adult books have designed ABC books in their careers. In fact, there are literally hundreds of alphabet books from which to choose. They are found in every imaginable illustration technique from woodcut prints to etching to photography.

Selecting Alphabet Books

In selecting ABC books, certain general criteria may be helpful. The objects depicting the letters should be an appropriate size and readily identifiable. A limited number of objects should be used, perhaps one or two per letter. The lettering choice should be particularly legible. Ordinarily, the letter is best placed on the page with the illustrations. The objects should be clearly representative of the sound of the letter and they should portray something with which children are familiar. The design of the book should be colorful and attractive.

It is important that these criteria be considered. It is especially important that the page be designed so that most children will be able to successfully find the letter and objects. The letter sounds should be heard clearly in the name of the objects used. For example, the letter "T" should use objects such as a tiger, top, or teacup for its illustration, rather than objects in which the "T" sound is blended, such as three, tree, or throat. Other letters to examine in ABC books include "S," "W," and "D." The letters "C" and "G" should be illustrated with objects representing the hard sound of the letter (e.g., cat for "C"; girl for "G"). The concept of hard and soft sounds for the same letter is often confusing to young children.

Humor is often found in many successful ABC books. Children will be delighted as they proceed through the alphabet with Miss Spider as she makes plans for a birthday party in *Miss Spider's ABC* by David Kirk. A gentle walk through an imaginary park filled with wildlife is the basis for R. M. Smith's *An A to Z Walk in the Park*. Author/illustrator Mick Inkpen provides another fascinating presentation of the alphabet in *Kipper's A to Z*. Large-type text is combined with bright illustrations and humor that will appeal to children.

One of the purposes of an alphabet book is to provide children with the knowledge to learn to read. Just when you think you have seen everything in an alphabet book, along comes *Q is for Duck: An Alphabet Guessing Game* by Michael Folsom and Mary Elting. Using the game format, the clever presentation helps children begin to use alphabet knowledge to move to the next step in reading. A related title is *Aster Aardvark's Alphabet Adventures* by author/illustrator Steven Kellogg. He uses zany illustrations and witty language to delight readers of all ages. Children will easily identify with *Max's ABC* by Rosemary Wells and *The Alphabet Tree* by Leo Lionni. Jenny Williams uses objects from daily routines to introduce very young children to the alphabet in her book, *Everyday ABC*.

Many activities can spring from ABC books.

Alphabet Activities

As with numbers, a set of coordinated activities to go along with alphabet books may be developed. After reading an animal alphabet book, children can draw or paint an animal for a particular letter. After reading an object ABC book, a letter hunt can be organized to search the room for objects beginning with the same letter. Preparing a food item beginning with a certain letter can be combined with other concepts. If the letter is "S," one could make strawberry sundaes. The letter "N" could be reinforced by having each child draw nine objects of their choice. The group could construct its own tactile alphabet book, alphabet sock puppets, or language-experience story. A **language-experience story** is a story dictated by the children and recorded by the teacher on the chalkboard or a poster-size book. The story is ordinarily about an experience all the children understand or have shared. If a language-experience story is used, perhaps based on words beginning with a particular letter, the focus should be on meaning rather than on recognizing a letter. The main function of learning about letters is to arrive at the meaning of the printed words. A similar caveat applies to the "letter of the week" approach in which the focus of the activities becomes trite rather than meaningful. Barbara Wasik and Carol Seefeldt (2005) have developed a set of guidelines for teaching alphabet knowledge and skills to young children at the preschool and kindergarten level in a developmentally appropriate manner. Their focus is on creating meaningful experiences that provide success rather than failure and playful exposure rather than mastery. The components of their guidelines include:

- Start with the familiar and move toward the unfamiliar. Begin with a common experience such as the first letter of a child's name and encourage the child to move toward familiar words that begin with the same letter. Point out objects in the environment that begin with the same letter.
- Use common experiences. Use storybook reading as an opportunity to point out letters to key words. Introduce such ideas as letters are seen in groups and letters have different shapes and names.
- If a "letter of the week" is used, it should be meaningfully related to what is happening in the program that week. It should not be the focus of the entire program.
- Writing is an effective way to extend knowledge of the alphabet. Children can be encouraged to use single letters, groups of letters, or attempted letters as part of their drawings.
- Direct teaching should only be done briefly and in a context that is meaningful to the children.

FICTION: REALISTIC FICTION/ FANTASY FICTION

The main purpose of **fiction** is to entertain the reader. However, its purpose is often to inform and persuade as well. Fiction is a narrative that comes from the imagination of the author rather than from history or factual information. Fiction gives the reader the author's vision of reality in concrete terms.

Realistic Fiction

Realistic fiction is a story that could have happened, and some parts of it may be from the author's own experiences. The author of realistic fiction is often trying to help children deal with a situation or problem. The world is presented as the author perceives it. The reader is not asked to believe in purple cows or singing dogs. Yet this is fiction, because the scenes, characters, and dialogues spring from the author's imagination. Nevertheless, the imaginary content is based on truth as the author sees it. Robert Cormier, in explaining his purpose in writing realistic fiction, stated, "I was trying to write realistically even though I knew it would upset some people. The fact is the good guys don't always win in real life . . . I also wanted to indict those who don't try to help, who remain

Author Angela Johnson.
Used by permission of
Penguin Books, New York.

indifferent in the face of evil or wrongdoing. They are as bad as or probably worse than the villains themselves" (Hearne & Kaye, 1987).

Realities of Life. Realistic fiction helps children confront the good and bad human feelings within all of us. It allows readers to recognize that all people share these same human emotions and thoughts. Readers are able to explore their own feelings from a safe distance through the characters. Jane Yolen tells a tale of birth, growth, love, loss, and intergenerational kinship in *Honkers*. Leslie Baker's realistic watercolors have a hazy, comfortable feeling. The concept of moving away from a familiar setting, featuring an African American family, is portrayed in *The Leaving Morning* by Angela Johnson. Eve Bunting explores the concepts of law, human dignity, and the ability to get along with others in *Smoky Night*. *The Tenth Good Thing about Barney* by Judith Viorst helps children learn to cope with death, in this case the death of a pet cat. Other topics that realistic fiction may help young children understand include school social situations, old age, illness, and sibling rivalry.

Controversial Topics. Some of the topics addressed in children's literature can be controversial, particularly for the families of children who may have experience, religious concerns, or political beliefs in regard to the subject matter of the book. On the other hand, it is naïve to think that young children are ignorant of these issues, which are often discussed on television or around the kitchen table. It is best to approach the use of books concerning some topics within a context of education and support from families of the children, as well as by having a clear purpose and plan for sharing the stories. Consultation with other knowledgeable professionals may be advised.

The issue of same-sex marriage is addressed in *Uncle Bobby's Wedding* by Sarah Brannen. In this story, presented with guinea pigs in human clothes, Bobby is marrying his boyfriend Jamie. In sweet watercolor and graphite illustrations accompanying the gentle text we meet Chloe, who is mostly worried that her Uncle Bobby won't have time for her anymore. Although it is high on the list of banned and challenged books, it is mostly about the love found in an extended family.

Tragically, the sexual abuse of the very young seems to be an increasingly common phenomenon in our world. *Some Secrets Hurt: A Story of Healing* by Linda Garner confronts this troubling issue with a story that feels all too real. As the story unfolds, the reader learns that Maggie has a secret that makes her stomach hurt and makes her want to cry. She knows all about the danger of strangers, but strangers are not the only ones to fear. The story has a definite tension to it as it reinforces the need to tell someone.

The United States is at or near the top of western countries in regard to the percentage and number of incarcerated adults. Minority group members are vastly over-represented in this group. In addition, stories appear regularly in the media about prisoners released years after conviction when DNA evidence is used to prove that they were innocent of the charges. Because many prisoners are parents, this can be a topic for children whose parents are incarcerated and for the friends of those children. Such parents love their children, and a sensitive book to use in such a situation is *My Momma Loves Me from Afar* by Pat Brisson. The first-person account focuses solely on love, with no mention of the reason for the imprisonment.

Historical Fiction

Realistic fiction also includes historical fiction, which provides an imaginary story based on a historical event or person. The author goes beyond the facts to create a fictional piece. An increasing number of books are becoming available in this area. Brinton Turkle's books about Obadiah are a series of historical but fictional accounts of Nantucket Island in colonial times. *Harriet Tubman* by Dana Rau chronicles the life and accomplishments of the woman who led slaves to freedom on the Underground Railroad. This very readable book conveys the quiet dignity of an extraordinary woman. In an adaptation of the Pied Piper folk tale, Colin Bootman combines history, music, politics, and the themes of honesty and anxiety in *The Steel Pan Man of Harlem*. Set during the Harlem Renaissance, the story provides a springboard to other issues such as cultural identity and human dignity. A darker side of westward expansion, specifically the treatment of Chinese workers, is presented in *Coolies* by Yin Soentpiet. Chris Soentpiet's powerful illustrations, making dramatic use of light, accompany this story about the dangerous work done by immigrants building the first transcontinental railroad. *Summerbath, Winterbath* by Eileen Spinelli depicts everyday life, *The Year at Maple Hill Farm* by Alice and Martin Provensen provides an explanation of the agricultural cycle, and *Curious George Goes to a Chocolate Factory* by H. A. and Margaret Rey can be used as a starting point for a discussion about factories and industrialization.

Americans of Japanese descent suffered during World War II. Rick Noguchi and Deneen Jenks address the difficult topic of their plight of in *Flowers from Mariko*. In this story, Mariko plants a garden to cheer up her parents as they struggle to make the difficult transition back to normal life after their release from a Japanese internment camp. Many of these books provide an added bonus of including women and minorities in nontraditional roles. Historical fiction written at a higher reading level can be read aloud.

The Steel Pan Man of Harlem by Colin Bootman. Illustrations copyright ©2009 by Colin Bootman. Reprinted with the permission of Carolrhoda Books, Inc., a division of Lerner Publishing Group, Inc. All rights reserved. No part of this excerpt may be used or reproduced in any manner whatsoever without the prior written permission of Lerner Publishing Group, Inc.

Fantasy Fiction

Many of the stories written for children are fantasy stories. An author of a fantasy asks the reader to suspend the rules of reality. A fantasy takes place in a nonexistent world and may include unreal characters. The use of physical or scientific principles unknown to the reader's experience is also found in fantasies. David Wiesner presents a "what if" concept in his Caldecott Medal-winning book *Tuesday*. "What if frogs could fly?" is answered in this light-hearted flight of fantasy.

TIPS FOR TEACHERS

Have children respond to fantasy by creating a picture related to the tale.

- Provide children with a variety of materials (e.g., wallpaper samples, paint, glue, fun fur, feathers, fabric) with which to create a scene from the fantasy world.
- Read a folktale from another country and ask children to draw a picture showing what they think a scene might look like.
- Give children clay and pipe cleaners to create sculptures of a fantasy character from a tale.

In fantasy, imagination is stretched and brought into an art form. The author, illustrator, and reader all share the new experience. Fantasy is accepted readily by children because their imaginations allow the belief that anything is possible. Magic, imaginary worlds, and marvelous creatures are real to children. What they can imagine can exist. Paula Fox explains, "Imagination is random and elusive. We deduce its presence by its effects, just as we deduce that a breeze has sprung up, a breeze we can't see, because we hear and see the rustling of the leaves in a tree. It is the guardian spirit that we sense in all great stories; we feel its rustling" (Hearne & Kaye, 1987).

A sense of humor is a powerful and positive coping mechanism, not only for children but for adults as well. It helps one to deal with the stress of modern life. The humor often found in fantasy fiction is contagious and healing. Few children can resist the silliness in *One Potato, Two Potato* by Cynthia DeFelice. Poor old Mr. and Mrs. O'Grady share everything. Down to their last potato, they cook it in a big black pot that they discover is special. Whatever goes in comes out double. Their troubles seem to be over, but when Mrs. O'Grady falls in, the humorous excitement erupts. Using collages and double-sided lift flaps, Eric Carle creates a fantasy world of secret tunnels and passageways in *Watch Out! A Giant*. The antics of the city-dwelling Lyle the crocodile,

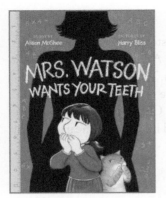

"Book Cover" from
MRS. WATSON WANTS
YOUR TEETH by Alison
McGhee, illustrations
copyright © 2004 by
Harry Bliss, reproduced by
permission of Harcourt, Inc.,
renewed by permission of
Houghton Mifflin Harcourt
Publishing Company.

a character in several of Bernard Waber's books, amuse and delight young readers. *Mrs. Watson Wants Your Teeth* by Alison McGhee is a somewhat scary story about a 300-year-old alien who is a snatcher of baby teeth. The presentation makes it more appropriate for five to eight year olds. In *Dumpy La Rue*, Elizabeth Winthrop tells a tale that is both fanciful and carries an important social message. Dumpy is a pig who marches to his own drummer. He rejects the typical pig role. Instead, he just wants to dance. In the end, he is successful and happy even though he didn't fall into the role society expected him to fill.

Fantasy fiction may have absurd characters, imaginary characters, or animals who behave as people. Fantasy fiction can be based on real-world settings or it can call for reality to be totally suspended and substitute almost anything in its place. Yet all fiction must still provide the basic components of a clearly defined plot, believable characters, an appropriate setting, and relevant themes. Without these skillfully woven into the story, the book fails to move the reader. Using the child-versus-nightmare scenario sometimes the basis for fantasy stories, Barbara Hicks provides an amusing twist with a happy ending in her book *Jitterbug Jam*. In this tale Little Bobo, a monster, is teased by an older brother who tells him that a human is hiding under his bed. In the end, Little Bobo finds comfort in the reassuring bedtime story told by Grandfather Bobo.

INFORMATIONAL BOOKS: FICTION AND NONFICTION

Nonfiction books are written for the purpose of providing factual information. Such books for young readers use either a text or a narrative format. The latter is often used because of its familiarity to children. The author of such books has an obligation to impart only accurate information. Misinformation, misleading information, and outdated information can be found in older books. If new information has been discovered since the book was published, it's important to explain the reason for the inaccuracies. Accurate information should be supplied.

On the other hand, sometimes fictional storybooks are the best way to present information to young children. Good stories are compelling and children can often relate to them better than to nonfiction. Use fiction to present information so long as it is clear and accurate information.

Presenting Information

Antiquated books can be useful for showing children how people used to think about a topic, but the teacher should ensure that children understand the correct information. It is good for children to become aware of the fact that information is not absolute, especially in the area of science. The teacher should always preface science information presentations with such phrases as, "At this time, this is the information that we believe to be true about . . ." Children will gain from the understanding that information changes with more research. For example, it's not necessary to discard a book about animals that states that giraffes make no sound. The photographs of the giraffe and perhaps much of the text can still be used. The teacher can simply add the correct information. Although it was once thought that giraffes made no sound, it is now known that they do make throaty sounds of communication.

Learning that information changes can foster the beginnings of **critical thinking**, the mental process of making a judgment about the information received. A child with a specific interest may have more current information than either the book or the teacher. Children should be encouraged to question information they feel is wrong. Also, resource books and telephone calls to verify information teach children, through example, an important lesson: A primary reason for learning to read is to find answers to questions.

Subtle misconceptions can trickle into a curriculum through a lack of knowledge. The same teacher who would never knowingly bring prejudice into the classroom by reading offensive material might perpetuate misconceptions about Native Americans and Pilgrims at Thanksgiving. Will the children learn that Native Americans no longer live the way they did during colonial times? Will the teacher update the class on current Native American lifestyles? If not, then an inaccurate portrayal of an entire cultural group is being given to every child in the class. The sensitive teacher will provide the whole truth.

In choosing factual books, it may be helpful to consider certain guidelines:

- The book should be checked for accuracy of information. Note the copyright date to ensure that the material is as up-to-date as possible.
- When charts or pictures are used, they should be simple, clear, and easy to read.
- The readability of the material should be appropriate for the children's age group.

Selecting Books

When selecting informational books for young children, it is important to include both fiction and nonfiction titles because a great amount of carefully researched and accurate information is provided by some fiction authors. Young children are particularly open to learning things through narrative stories. A good example of an informative narrative story is Karla Kuskin's

The Philharmonic Gets Dressed. Through the story, children learn about the different sections of an orchestra.

Opportunities exist for correlating different content areas. The concepts of geography, islands, colors, evolution, and animal adaptation can be discussed while enjoying two eye-arresting books by Joy Crowley with photographs by Nic Bishop. *Chameleon, Chameleon* explores the life of the Madagascar panther chameleon, while *Red Eyed Tree Frog* presents this frog in its Central American environment. Over the past decade, a rapidly growing number of books have been published dealing with social studies and science for young children. In each of these areas, nonfiction books can be combined with fiction books to present an abundance of factual information.

Social Studies

The study of community and the development of one's place in the world are addressed in most early childhood programs. A good beginning place is Cynthia Rylant's *Everyday Town,* a board book that identifies the vehicles, parades, lights, pigeons, and buildings that comprise a town. Two children, one from a city and one from a faraway island, forge a unique friendship through the travel and discovery created by a magical wordless picture book, the Caldecott Honor Medal-winning *The Red Book* by Barbara Lehman.

Books that present the multiculturalism found in society abound. Many are wonderful stories that happen to provide accurate information on the cultures that make up our international society. *One World, One Day* by Barbara Kerley shows one day in the lives of children in various regions of the world. The text asks readers to focus on details in the accompanying photographs, but the actual locations are not identified until the end. All readers will readily identify with the African American family on a train trip in *Rattle and Rap* by Susan Steggall. The rattles, whistles, whines, and jolts of the train become the basis for the repeated phrases of the text. The striking torn-paper collage illustrations tell the story of the ride, the landscapes, and the diversity of the passengers. A different kind of noise forms the basis of the problem faced by Agatha, who is unhappy about where she lives in Mara Rockliff's *The Busiest Street in Town.* The concept of connection between the generations of an interracial family is explored in Norman Juster's Caldecott Medal-winning *The Hello, Goodbye Window.*

Hispanic and Asian cultures are increasingly featured in books for young people. *The Beckoning Cat* by Koko Nishizuka is based on a Japanese folk tale that features an iconic white cat, the symbol of good luck often featured in Asian stories and restaurants. The story is similar to the kindness and remembrance found in the mythical tale of Androcles and the Lion. Bilingual nursery rhymes

Cover from *The Beckoning Cat* by Koko Nishizuka. Jacket art copyright © 2009 by Rosanne Litzinger. Reprinted by permission of Holiday House. All rights reserved.

Author/illustrator Yumi Heo. Used by permission of Orchard Books, New York.

Cover from ONE AFTERNOON by Yumi Heo. Scholastic Inc./Orchard Books. Copyright © 1994 by Yumi Heo. Reprinted by permission.

and catchy fingerplays reflect the diversity of the Latino experience in Lulu Delacre's *Arrorro Mi Nino: Lullabies and Gentle Games.* Finally, Minho and his mother provide a universal look at the obvious similarities of all people as they experience the sights and sounds of the city during an afternoon of errands in *One Afternoon* by Yumi Heo.

A beautiful book by Angela Johnson is a good place to begin exploring African American culture. It presents a genuine picture of a culture rather than a stereotyped view of a people. *Joshua by the Sea* is a poetic story of a family's love that all children will easily respond to. Rhonda Mitchell's glowing water-color illustrations are an added bonus. In *A Million Fish . . . More or Less* by Patricia McKissack, the reader is transported to the African American culture of the Bayou Clapateaux in Louisiana. While fishing one day, Hugh Thomas catches both fish and a penchant for creating and sharing hilarious tall tales. This story answers the question of why the oral tradition is so important. *Rosa*, a biography of Rosa Parks by Nikki Giovanni, speaks to young people about an important milestone in the Civil Rights movement.

The family is a long-cherished facet of African American culture. Another story by Angela Johnson is *When I Am Old with You,* in which readers share the warm bond between a child and grandfather. The two are both individuals and universal characters. Maya, a young African American girl, and the huge Alaskan pig that her grandfather brings her as a pet learn from each other in *Julius* by Angela Johnson. Dav Pilkey creates the riotous multimedia illustrations in this book.

World cultures and the universality of humankind are represented in many books for young readers. Mem Fox brings a similar but more personal message in *Whoever You Are.* Three siblings learn a new way of viewing the world and life through the stories of their new panda neighbor in John Muth's Caldecott Honor Book *Zen Shorts.*

Science

Young children are fascinated with nature, the world around them, and the way things work. A great book to introduce the world of penguins is *Without You* by Sarah Weeks, in which a father penguin cares for baby while Mom is away getting food. Bob Barner's *Dinosaur Bones* provides a bouncing rhythmic narrative about prehistoric animals. One of the best ways to introduce nonfiction is with books such as David Macaulay's *The Way Things Work* or Beck Baines' *The Bones You Own: A Book About the Human Body.* The powerful forces of nature are clearly explained in *Flood* by Catherine Chambers, which includes information about flood damage and prevention and other natural disasters.

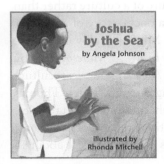

Cover illustration © 1994 by Rhonda Mitchell from JOSHUA BY THE SEA by Angela Johnson. Scholastic Inc./Orchard Books. Reprinted by permission.

Cover from THE WAY THINGS WORK by David Macaulay. Compilation copyright © 1988 by Dorling Kindersley, Ltd. Illustrations copyright © 1988 by David Macaulay. Reprinted by permission of Houghton Mifflin Harcourt Publishing Company. All rights reserved.

Physical science topics are presented in books about the sun, stars, space, seasons, and elements. In a warm, tender story of attachment from Japan, Komako Sakai provides a jumping-off point for discussion about the scientific concepts of helium, air, mass, and weight in *Emily's Balloon. Can I See My House from Space?* by Mark Darling answers many astronomical questions. A family learns about the mythical shapes in the night sky in Natalie Kinsey-Warnock's *On a Starry Night.* David McPhail's illustrations provide a deep, rich, velvety black background for the text. Other books that introduce a discussion of stars and the night sky include *A Book of Sleep* by Il Sung Na and *Night Lights* by Susan Gal.

The element of water is explored in books dealing with winter, rain, and the seashore. A woman explains the solstice to her granddaughter in Jean Craighead George's *Dear Rebecca, Winter Is Here.* Summer, sand, sun, sky, skin protection, ocean, waves, and clouds are all possible topics to explore while reading *Beach* by Elisha Cooper. *Mother Osprey: Nursery Rhymes for Buoys and Gulls* by Lucy Nolan follows up with scientific concepts in a Mother Goose rhyme format. The lighthearted verses present familiar rhymes with new content and the book includes a map showing the location for the content related to each verse.

Gardens, animals, life cycles, and seasonal changes are addressed in *Chick* by Ed Vere, *Bugs and Bugcycles* by Amy Hansen, *Who's Awake in the Springtime?* by Phyllis Gershator, *The Garden That We Grew* by Joan Holub, *The Wind's Garden* by Bethany Roberts, *Bear in Sunshine* by Stella Blackstone, and *Birdhouse for Rent* by Harriet Ziefert. In *Groundhog Weather School* by Joan Holub, Professor Groundhog opens a school to teach groundhogs to forecast the weather correctly instead of looking for a shadow. The tongue-in-cheek pop-up book presents fun facts and information. Within this context of weather, *Tornadoes* by Gail Gibbons presents clear, simple images and text and an explanation of the Fujita Tornado Scale. Jane Dyer uses bird migration and mammal hibernation

Author/illustrator Mike Thaler. Courtesy Mike Thaler, "America's Riddle King."

as elements in her fictional story *Little Brown Bear Won't Take a Nap.* Using a mystery story format, Ellen Stoll Walsh addresses the natural phenomenon of seed migration in *Dot & Jabber and the Great Acorn Mystery.* Water is explored as both a freshwater and saltwater phenomenon in Mike Thaler's *In the Middle of the Puddle* and Charlotte Zolotow's *The Seashore Book.* The latter book is also a good transition from physical science to life science. Wendell Manor's breathtaking paintings let the reader almost feel and smell the salt air and smooth shells.

Life science exploration can emerge from the ocean theme through *The Magic School Bus on the Ocean Floor* by Joanna Cole and Bruce Degen. Children will enjoy thoroughly the character of Ms. Frizzle and her wacky, ever-changing outfits in the "magic school bus" series. Continuing with ocean life, young readers will feel right at home with the multicultural tour group in Rebecca Gold's *A Visit to the Sesame Street Aquarium.*

In *Look at the Animals,* Peter Linenthal presents a wide assortment of animals to babies and young children. The life cycle of a turtle is depicted in an aquatic adventure story format by Paul Geraghty in *Tortuga.* Lucy Cousins explores agricultural animals in Farm Animals. April Sayre takes the reader to the desert for a look at toads in *Dig, Wait, Listen: A Desert Toad's Tale.* Hummingbirds and art are combined in Keith Baker's story *Little Green,* while hummingbirds, moles, hawks, and fawns are found in A *Fawn in the Grass* by Joanne Ryder. In *The Busy Tree* by Jennifer Ward, readers are introduced to all the wildlife that lives in, on, and under an old oak tree. The rhyming couplets of text include information about the circles of life and the seasons. The concept that humans are part of the animal kingdom and that they have both similarities and differences with other mammals is playfully explored by Marion Bauer in *If You Had a Nose like an Elephant's Trunk.* The concept of good nutrition for boys and girls can be introduced in a humorous manner using *Monsters Don't Eat Broccoli* by Barbara Hicks. An investigation of the entire human body is presented in *The Magic School Bus Inside the Human Body* by Joanna Cole and Bruce Degen.

POETRY

Poetry is not stuffy! It is not boring! It is not just for greeting cards! A poem is a song without notes. It is the form used for the most intense and imaginative writing about our world and ourselves. Poetry is lyrical, succinct, heart-touching, and also great fun. The poet selects each word carefully so the impact of what is said and meant is startling to the reader or listener. No matter the rhyme patterns, the rhythm and the cadence of a good poem attract children in much the same way as a song or a jingle. The descriptive use of language conjures up visions in the heads of the listeners so that they almost feel they have witnessed the action of the poem. Winnie-the-Pooh is a favorite poetic character, yet few children are consciously aware that the story of Christopher Robin is written in poetry. They just know that the story is a favorite.

Poetic Devices

Formal poetry has metered verse. It uses syllables, line length, and special structures to create the differences in **haiku, tanka, cinquain, sonnet, limerick,** and **two-word poetry.** Frequently used devices in poetry written for children are **onomatopoeia, personification, simile, metaphor,** and **alliteration.** *Onomatopoeia* is the use of specific words because their sound suggests what is happening in the poem (e.g., pop, sizzle, hiss, bang). *Personification* occurs when human characteristics or emotions are given to animals or inanimate objects (e.g., Pop, pop, pop! I'm inside out and warm and hot! Do not fail to put butter and salt on my top!). A *simile* is used to compare two things that are different, using words such as "like" and "as" (e.g., the puddle was as wet as a puppy's nose, or her hair was as soft as a fire's glow). A *metaphor* is an analogy that gives some of the characteristics of one object to a second object (e.g., my crumb of bread is the giant feasty for all the little ants and buglike beasties). *Alliteration* is the repetition of the initial consonant of a word several times in a line (e.g., Little Lyle laughed loudly).

Using Poetry

With young children, it's possible to use poetry written beyond their reading level. It should be read with expression and tied to the children's level of understanding. Although poetry can be shared simply as a type of literature, another fine use is to integrate it with other thematically related forms of literature. For example, if the unit theme is animals, poems to be read might include "The Hippopotamus" by Jack Prelutsky, "Roger the Dog" by Ted Hughes, and "The Crocodile" by Lewis Carroll.

Poetry weaves itself into children's thinking in a number of different ways. Lee Bennett Hopkins collects and presents theme-related poetry. In his book *April Bubbles Chocolate,* twenty-six poets present diverse moods and subjects as they wander through the alphabet with the reader. It's great fun trying to guess what the subject of each letter will be. Seasons and nature seem to serve as good backgrounds for poetry for the young. Joyce Sidman uses the seasons to set the stage for her verses in *Song of the Water Boatman and Other Pond Poems.* The natural surroundings of a meadow are used as a background for *Butterfly Eyes and Other Secrets of the Meadow* also by Joyce Sidman. In some books, the entire narrative is told in poetic form. In *One Little Spoonful,* Aliki shares the wonder of poetry with toddlers who will relate to both the bright illustrations and the mealtime experience. Preschoolers will laugh to the rhyming text of *There's a Cow in the Cabbage Patch* by Clare Beaton or *Mirror Mirror: A Book of Reversible Verse* by Marilyn Singer. They will also respond to the exuberant, delicate, and messy aspects of spring in Douglas Florian's poems in *Handsprings.* Loris Lesynski's book of poems, *Nothing Beats a Pizza,* is meant to be shared aloud. Young and old will appreciate the reissue of Eve Merriam's classic poems in *Low Song.* Good choices for sharing this type of poetry include *When Crocodiles Clean Up* by Roni Schotter, illustrated by Thor Wickstrom.

Dorothy Aldis and Leland B. Jacobs also write simple, self-explanatory poems. They write about everyday things such as curbstones and the circus. "Hush-a-bye Baby" is a simple poem inspired by the Native American custom of hanging cradles from birch trees. It was written by a Pilgrim who was impressed by the custom (Panati, 2009). It has been called the first poem of rhyme written in the New World, a lullaby rhyme:

> Hush-a-bye baby, on the treetop,
> When the wind blows, the cradle will rock.
> When the bough breaks, the cradle will fall,
> And down will come baby, cradle and all.

This Boston-area version of the lullabye first appeared in print in 1765 in *Mother Goose's Melody.* Children have no problem understanding the meaning of the piece, but adding this other information makes it more interesting. Shel Silverstein is one of the best-known children's poets. He captures children's imaginations with topics from spaghetti to trees. His black-and-white line illustrations add much to his fine words.

Robert Louis Stevenson and Henry Wadsworth Longfellow are traditional favorites. Many little girls, especially on off days, feel a kindred spirit with Longfellow's daughter who inspired the poem that begins, "There was a little girl, who had a little curl right in the middle of her forehead . . ." If a child is sick in bed, Stevenson's "The Land of Counterpane" is *must* reading. It is especially comforting when the child can use toy soldiers to act out the sheet battles. Stevenson's language is always vivid. From the poem "My Shadow," note the expressive lines:

> For he sometimes shoots up taller like an India rubber ball,
> And he sometimes gets so little that there's none of him at all.

Stevenson's lines show how timeless and universal good poetry can be for children. Many fine poets have written verses for children:

- Langston Hughes
- Edward Lear
- Walter de la Mare
- Lewis Carroll

- John Ciardi
- Ogden Nash
- Carl Sandburg
- William Blake
- Eve Merriam

Poet Jack Prelutsky.
Courtesy Jack Prelutsky.

Finally, no discussion of poetry for children would be complete without considering the work of Jack Prelutsky. A prolific writer, his books address most of the major holidays with such well-known titles as *It's Valentine's Day* and *It's Thanksgiving.* Other titles such as *Rainy, Rainy Saturday* and *Rolling Harvey Down the Hill* address themes of loneliness, friendship, and family relationships. In *What a Day It Was at School,* laughter will abound at the appealing animal characters, interesting words, and energetic, bouncy rhythms. Children will relate to the imaginary adventures found in *My Parents Think I'm Sleeping.* Hilarious poems about people, animals, and far-flung places such as Minneapolis, Tuscaloosa, Tucumcari, and Winnemucca are found in *The Frogs Wore Red Suspenders.* Still other titles with lots of fun by Jack Prelutsky include *It's Raining Pigs and Noodles, Awful Ogre Running Wild, Be Glad Your Nose is on Your Face, Good Sports: Rhymes About Running, Jumping, Throwing, and More* and *Behold the Bold Umbrellaphant.* In recognition of his accomplishments, the Poetry Foundation has appointed Jack Prelutsky its first Children's Poet Laureate.

Fostering Creativity with Poetry

Because of its powerful images, poetry naturally lends itself to visual creativity in such books as *Riddle-icious* by Patrick Lewis. Each page of this book contains a rhyming riddle with plenty of clues to the solution right on the page. Debbie Tilley's playful artwork provides the hints. Powerful feelings are played out in the rhymed narrative of *The Upstairs Cat* by award-winning poet Karla Kuskin. Her tale about two antagonistic cats who must share the same house is heightened by Howard Fine's dramatic oil painting illustrations.

Two-word poetry is an easy way to involve young children in creating nonsense verse. The two words, one a noun and one an adjective, can rhyme or not. They can be silly or not. They can be added to other two-word verses to create larger nonsense poems. Illustrations are always a pleasant follow-up to a poem such as:

Sleeping farmer rubbed his purple eyes.
A polka-dot pig with a talking dog.
Wow cow and golly gee, what a sight to see.

It may not be memorable poetry, but it is fun and demonstrates the sense of creativity and excitement that surrounds poetry.

Selecting Poetry

Criteria for selecting poetry to use with children should focus on content rather than the technical aspects of meter and rhyme scheme. The poetry should be melodic, with the rhythm and beat alive and clear. It should have vivid language. Although poetry can be about any thought-provoking topic, it should be interesting and relevant to the audience. A variety of classic, contemporary, and nonsense poetry and poetry written by the teacher should be included to give children a broad exposure. This will allow children to appreciate all types of poetry and to develop individual preferences. One should always remember that poetry is meant to be read aloud. Decide how the poem ought to be read before reading it to an audience. Then, read it with feeling.

TIPS FOR TEACHERS

Create a file-card library of poems to use throughout the year on topics to be explored. Start one day of each week with a poem.

- Seasonal poems
- Poems children bring in
- Activity-related poems
- Theme or content-related poems

When introducing a poem, it is important to set the mood for what is to come. Take care not to over explain the poem prior to the reading. Because poetry touches us in different ways, children should be allowed to experience the poem with their own imaginations. Never make children memorize a poem. Reread it often if the children enjoy it, but don't require memorization. Use an abundance of humorous poetry. Start writing poetry for the children as soon as the reading of poetry is introduced. The two are partners in developing a full appreciation and enjoyment of poetry.

AWARDS AND PRIZES IN CHILDREN'S LITERATURE

Outstanding works by children's authors and illustrators are recognized through a variety of awards and honors. These include formal awards and medals, magazine awards, and library awards. The most famous award for picture books is the **Caldecott Medal**. This American award is given each year to an illustrator by the Association for Library Service to Children. The Caldecott Medal is named for the British illustrator of children's books, Randolph Caldecott (1846–1886). It was first given in 1937 when Frederic G. Melcher established it, as he had the **Newbery Award** in 1922. The Caldecott Medal is limited to a resident or citizen of the United States. It is ironic that this "Americans only"award is named after a British subject. Although not every well-known children's book illustrator has received this award, many have, and many others have been honored as runners-up. A Caldecott Medal-winning book has a gold seal with the award on the cover. Caldecott Honor Award-winning books (the runners-up) have a silver seal on their covers.

A list of winning books provides a good starting point for a search for quality books. (Winners of the Caldecott Medal are listed in Appendix B.) However, it is important to remember that an award does not necessarily mean that a book is appropriate for a given class or for a teacher's purpose. One should keep in mind that it is adults who give the award, based on criteria developed by adults. The genuine award for a quality book is the enthusiastic response of generations of children to a particular work. Today's award winners await the test of time.

Other awards for excellence in children's poetry, illustrations, and writing are given in the United States and in other countries. The Kate Greenaway Medal is given by the British Library Association for distinguished work in the illustration of children's books. The Amelia Frances Howard-Gibbon Medal is a similar award given to a Canadian citizen by the Canada Library Association. The Laura Ingalls Wilder Award is given every three years by the Association for Library Service to Children to an author or illustrator whose books, published in the United States, have made a substantial contribution to children's literature. The Coretta Scott King Award is awarded yearly by the American Library Association to children's book authors and illustrators of African descent for works promoting understanding and appreciation for the American dream. The Newbery Medal is given annually by the same organization to a U.S. author for the most distinguished contribution to children's literature during the past year. Any time authors, poets, or illustrators win one of these prestigious awards, their work has been chosen from more than 4,500 books printed annually.

To learn about new works by favorite illustrators or authors, refer to *Books in Print,* published annually by R. R. Bowker. The three-volume set includes an index by author's name, an index by title, and a volume with publishers' updated information. The four-volume annual *Subject Guide to Books in Print* publishes information about specific subjects. It is also published by R. R. Bowker. *Something about the Author,* published by Gale Research in Detroit, Michigan, is an invaluable source of information about writers and illustrators of children's books. It has been published for more than 20 years, with new volumes added annually. All of these resources are found in the library.

SUMMARY

Expose children to a wide variety of quality literature. This will foster a love of stories, sharing, literature, and wonder. It will encourage them to connect to people and their environment by enjoying their world and gradually including more ideas into that world. By encouraging this desire to learn, you will help children come to see reading as an enjoyable path to understanding the world. This is an important step on the road to literacy. A tremendous range of literature is available to young children. Even if children are not yet reading, they can benefit from listening to stories written several years above their reading level. The literature can be used to reinforce other activities, or it can serve as a starting point for an activity. Basic to all of this is the fact that literature should help create meaning. It should serve as a means of deepening our enjoyment of life and helping us to make sense of our world.

QUESTIONS FOR THOUGHT AND DISCUSSION

1. What is a fingerplay?
2. What is a chant?
3. What is a rhyme?
4. What is the difference between fantasy and realistic fiction? Why should a teacher use each type?
5. Why should a teacher use Mother Goose tales?
6. How can fingerplays be used in the classroom?
7. What are the differences between fable, folktale, and fairy tale?
8. What are the dangers of using fairy tales with young children? How can these dangers be avoided?
9. How should one select nonfiction books?
10. Why are picture books important in an early childhood classroom?
11. Why is it permissible to use poems that are written above a child's reading level?
12. How should one select poetry?
13. How should one use poetry with children?
14. What are some things that have changed in children's literature over the past century?
15. When, why, and how should controversial topics be addressed with regard to children's books?

For additional resources, access the *Growing Up with Literature* companion website through www.cengagebrain.com <http://www.cengagebrain.com/>.

CHILDREN'S BOOKS CITED

Aliki. (2001). *One little spoonful.* New York: Harper.

Anderson, Hans Christian. (1981). *The wild swans.* Mahwah, NJ: Troll Associates.

Anderson, Hans Christian. (2009). *The ugly duckling.* New York: North-South.

Anno, Mitsumasa. (1989). *Anno's Aesop.* New York: Orchard.

Bailey, Debbie. (2001). *Good night.* Toronto, Ontario, Canada: Annick.

Baines, Beck. (2009). *The bones you own: A book about the human body.* Washington, DC: National Geographic.

Baker, Jeannie. (2004). *Home.* New York: Greenwillow.

Baker, Keith. (2001). *Little green.* San Diego, CA: Harcourt.

Baker, Keith. (2008). *Potato Joe.* Orlando, FL: Harcourt.

Barner, Bob. (2001). *Dinosaur bones.* New York: Chronicle.

Barton, Byron. (2001). *My car.* New York: Greenwillow.

Bauer, Marion. (2001). *If you had a nose like an elephant's trunk.* New York: Holiday House.

Beaton, Clare. (2001). *There's a cow in the cabbage patch.* New York: Barefoot.

Blackstone, Stella. (2001). *Bear in sunshine.* New York: Barefoot.

Bollinger, Max. (2005). *The happy troll.* New York: Henry Holt.

Bond, Michael. (1996). *Paddington's 123.* New York: Puffin.

Bootman, Colin. (2008). *The steel pan man of Harlem.* Minneapolis, MN: Carolrhoda/Lerner.

Brannen, Sarah. (2008). *Uncle Bobby's wedding.* New York: Putnam.

Brisson, Pat. (2004). *My Momma loves me from afar.* Honesdale, PA: Boyds Mills Press.

Bruchac, Joseph & London, Jonathan. (1992). *Thirteen moons on turtle's back.* New York: Philomel.

Bunting, Eve. (1994). *Smoky night.* San Diego, CA: Harcourt Brace Jovanovich.

Bunting, Eve. (2001). *Little Badger, terror of the seven seas.* San Diego, CA: Harcourt.

Carle, Eric. (1969). *1, 2, 3 to the zoo.* New York: Collins World.

Carle, Eric. (2002). *Watch out! A giant.* New York: Little Simon.

Carr, Jan. (2001). *Splish, splash, spring.* New York: Holiday House.

Cauley, Lorinda. (2001). *What do you know!* New York: Putnam.

Chambers, Catherine. (2002). *Flood.* Portsmouth, NH: Heineman.

Cole, Johanna, and Degen, Bruce. (1990). *The magic school bus inside the human body.* New York: Scholastic.

Cole, Johanna, and Degen, Bruce. (1992). *The magic school bus on the ocean floor.* New York: Scholastic.

Compton, Joanne. (1994). *Ashpet: An Appalachian tale.* New York: Holiday House.

Cooper, Elisha. (2006). *Beach.* New York: Orchard.

Cousins, Lucy. (2004). *Farm animals.* Cambridge, MA: Candlewick.

Crowley, Joy. (2005). *Chameleon, chameleon.* New York: Scholastic.

Crowley, Joy. (2006). *Red eyed tree frog.* New York: Scholastic.

Darling, Mark (Ed.) (2004). *Can I see my house from space?* Nashville, TN: Southwestern.

DeFelice, Cynthia. (2006). *One potato, two potato.* New York: Farrar, Strauss & Giroux.

Delacre, Lulu. (2004). *Arrorro mi nino: Lullabies and gentle games.* New York: Lee & Low.

Diakite, Baba. (2000). *The hatseller and the monkeys.* New York: Scholastic.

Diakite, Baba. (2005). *The hunterman and the crocodile.* New York: Scholastic.

Dobbins, Jan. (2009). *Driving my Tractor.* Cambridge, MA: Barefoot.

Dodd, Emma. (2001). *Dog's colorful day: A messy story about colors and counting.* New York: Dutton.

Dornbusch, Erica. (2001). *Finding Kate's shoes.* Toronto, Ontario, Canada: Annick.

Dyer, Jane. (2003). *Little brown bear won't take a nap.* Boston: Little Brown.

Edwards, Pamela Duncan. (2001). *Warthogs paint: A messy color book.* New York: Hyperion.

Falwell, Cathryn. (2001). *Turtle splash: Countdown at the pond.* New York: Greenwillow.

Florian, Douglas. (2006). *Handsprings.* New York: Greenwillow.

Folsom, Michael, and Elting, Mary. (2005). *Q is for duck*: An alphabet guessing game New York: Houghton Mifflin/Sandpiper.

Fox, Mem. (2001). *Whoever you are.* New York: Voyager/HarperCollins.

Gal, Susan. (2009). *Night Lights.* New York: Alfred A. Knopf.

Garner, Linda. (2009). *Some secrets hurt: A story of healing.* Salt Lake City, UT: Shadow Mountain.

George, Jean Craighead. (1993). Dear Rebeca, Winter is here. New York: Harper-Collins.

Geraghty, Paul. (2001). *Tortuga.* North Pomfret, VT: Trafalgar Square.

Gershator, Phyllis. (2010). *Who's awake in the springtime?* New York: Henry Holt.

Gibbons, Gail. (2009). *Tornadoes.* New York: Holiday House.

Gill-Brown, Vanessa. (2001). *Rufferella.* New York: Scholastic.

Giovanni, Nikki. (2005). *Rosa.* New York: Henry Holt.

Gold, Rebecca. (1998). *A visit to the Sesame Street aquarium.* New York: Random House.

Gorbachev, Valeri. (2001). *Goldilocks and the three bears.* New York: North-South.

Hansen, Amy. (2010). *Bugs and bugcycles.* Honesdale, PA: Boyds Mills Press.

Harshman, Marc, and Ryan, Cheryl. (2001). *Red are the apples.* San Diego, CA: Harcourt.

Hawk, Fran. (2009). *Count down to fall.* Mount Pleasant, SC: Sylvan Dell.

Heo, Yumi. (1994). *One afternoon.* New York: Orchard.

Hicks, Barbara. (2005). *Jitterbug jam.* New York: Farrar, Strauss & Giroux.

Hicks, Barbara. (2009). *Monsters don't eat broccoli.* New York: Alfred A. Knopf.

Hines, Anna Grossnickle. (2001). *Whose shoes?* San Diego, CA: Harcourt.

Holub, Joan. (2010). *Groundhog weather school.* New York: Putnam.

Holub, Joan. (2001). *The garden that we grew.* New York: Viking.

Hopkins, Lee Bennett. (1994). *April bubbles chocolate.* New York: Simon and Schuster.

Horacek, Petr. (2001). *Strawberries are red.* Cambridge, MA: Candlewick.

Horacek, Petr. (2001). *What is black and white?* Cambridge, MA: Candlewick.

Inkpen, Mick. (2001). *Kipper's A to Z.* San Diego, CA: Harcourt.

Johnson, Angela. (1990). *When I am old with you.* New York: Orchard.

Johnson, Angela. (1992). *The leaving morning.* New York: Orchard.

Johnson, Angela. (1994). *Joshua by the sea.* New York: Orchard.

Johnson, Angela. (1998). *Julius.* New York: Orchard.

Johnston, Tony. (1994). *The tale of Rabbit and Coyote.* New York: Putnam.

Juster, Norman. (2005). *The hello, goodbye window.* New York: Michael Di Capua/ Hyperion.

Keats, Ezra Jack. (1972). *Over in the meadow.* New York: Four Winds.

Kellogg, Steven. (1992). *Aster Aardvark's alphabet adventures.* New York: William Morrow.

Kerley, Barbara. (2009). *One world, one day.* Washington, DC: National Geographic.

Kimmel, Eric. (1994). *The three princes.* New York: Holiday House.

Kinsey-Warnock, Natalie. (1994). *On a starry night.* New York: Orchard.

Kipling, Rudyard. (1996). *Jungle book.* New York: Viking.

Kirk, David. (2001). *Miss Spider's ABC.* New York: Scholastic.

Kuskin, Karla. (1982). *The philharmonic gets dressed.* New York: Harper.

Kuskin, Karla. (1997). *The upstairs cat.* New York: Clarion.

Lehman, Barbara. (2004). *The red book.* Boston: Houghton Mifflin.

Lesynski, Loris. (2001). *Nothing beats a pizza.* New York: Lee and Low.

Lewis, Patrick. (1997). *Riddle-icious.* New York: Alfred A. Knopf.

Linenthal, Peter. (2006). *Look at the animals.* New York: Dutton.

Lionni, Leo. (2004). *The alphabet tree.* New York: Knopf.

Lobel, Arnold. (1978). *Gregory Griggs and other nursery rhyme people.* New York: Greenwillow.

London, Jonathan. (2002). *Count the ways, little brown bear.* New York: Dutton.

Macaulay, David. (1988). *The way things work.* Boston: Houghton Mifflin.

MacDonald, Suse. (2000). *Look whooo's counting?* New York: Scholastic.

Martin, Rafe. (1992). *The rough-face girl.* New York: G. P. Putnam's Sons.

Matthews, Tina. (2007). *Out of the egg.* New York: Houghton Mifflin.

McCully, Emily Arnold. (2001). *Four hungry kittens.* New York: Dial.

McDermott, Gerald. (1996). *Zomo the rabbit.* New York: Scholastic.

McDermott, Gerald. (2001). *Raven: A trickster tale from the Pacific Northwest.* New York: Harcourt.

McGhee, Alison. (2008). *Mrs. Watson wants your teeth.* Orlando, FL: Harcourt.

McKissack, Patricia. (1992). *A million fish . . . more or less.* New York: Knopf.

Merriam, Eve. (2001). *Low song.* New York: Simon and Schuster.

Mitchell, Marianne. (2002). *Joe Cinders.* New York: Henry Holt.

Muth, John. (2005). *Zen shorts.* New York: Scholastic.

Na, Il Sung. (2009). *A book of sleep.* New York: Golden Books.

Nishizuka, Koko. (2009). *The beckoning cat.* New York: Holiday House.

Noguchi, Rick, and Jenks, Deneen. (2001). *Flowers from Mariko.* New York: Lee and Low.

Nolan, Lucy. (2009). *Mother Osprey: Nursery rhymes for buoys and gulls.* Mount Pleasant, SC: Sylvan Dell.

Norfolk, Bobby. (2006). *Anansi and the pot of beans.* Atlanta, GA: August House.

Palatini, Margie. (2005). *The three silly billies.* New York: Simon & Schuster.

Parker, Kim. (2005). *Counting in the garden.* New York: Scholastic.

Pavey, Peter. (2009). *One dragon's dream: A counting book.* Somersville, MA: Candlewick.

Prelutsky, Jack. (2005). *Awful Ogre running wild.* New York: Greenwillow.

Prelutsky, Jack. (2008). *Be glad your nose is on your face.* New York: Greenwillow.

Prelutsky, Jack. (2006). *Behold the bold umbrellaphant.* New York: Greenwillow.

Prelutsky, Jack. (2007). *Good sports: Rhymes about running jumping, throwing and more.* New York: Alfred A. Knopf.

Prelutsky, Jack. (2005). *It's raining pigs and noodles.* New York: Harper Trophy.

Prelutsky, Jack. (1982). *It's Thanksgiving.* New York: Greenwillow.

Prelutsky, Jack. (1983). *It's Valentine's Day.* New York: Greenwillow.

Prelutsky, Jack. (2007). *My parents think I'm sleeping.* New York: Greenwillow.

Prelutsky, Jack. (1980). *Rainy, rainy Saturday.* New York: Greenwillow.

Prelutsky, Jack. (1980). *Rolling Harvey down the hill.* New York: Greenwillow.

Prelutsky, Jack. (2002). *The frogs wore red suspenders.* New York: Greenwillow.

Prelutsky, Jack. (2006). *What a day it was at school.* New York: Greenwillow.

Provensen, Alice, and Provensen, Martin. (2001). *The year at Maple Hill Farm*. New York: Aladdin.

Rau, Dana. (2001). *Harriet Tubman*. Minneapolis, MN: Compass Point.

Rayner, Mary. (1994). *Ten pink piglets: Garth Pig's wall song*. New York: Dutton.

Reid, Barbara. (1994). *Sing a song of Mother Goose*. New York, Scholastic.

Rey, Margaret & H. A. (2002). *Curious George goes to a chocolate factory*. Boston, MA: Houghton Mifflin.

Roberts, Bethany. (2001). *The wind's garden*. New York: Holt.

Rockliff, Mara. (2009). *The busiest street in town*. New York: Alfred A. Knopf.

Rockwell, Anne. (1989). *Willy can count*. Boston: Little, Brown.

Ryder, Joanne. (2001). *A fawn in the grass*. New York: Holt.

Rylant, Cynthia. (1993). *Everyday town*. New York: Bradbury.

Sakai, Komako. (2006). *Emily's Balloon*. New York: Chronicle.

Sayre, April. (2001). *Dig, wait, listen: A desert toad's tale*. New York: Greenwillow. Schuster.

Schotter, Roni. (1993). *When crocodiles clean up*. New York: Macmillan.

Scieszka, Jon. (1989). *The true story of the three little pigs*. New York: Puffin.

Sidman, Joyce. (2005). *Song of the water boatman and other pond poems*. Boston: Houghton Mifflin.

Sidman, Joyce. (2006). *Butterfly eyes and other secrets of the meadow*. Boston: Houghton Mifflin.

Silsbe, Brenda. (2009). *The bears we know*. Toronto, Ontario, Canada: Annick.

Singer, Marilyn. (2010). *Mirror mirror: A book of reversible verse*. New York: Dutton Children's.

Smith, R. M. (2008). *An A to Z walk in the park (animal alphabet book)*. Alexandria, VA: Clarence Henry.

Soentpiet, Yin. (2003). *Coolies*. New York: Puffin.

Spinelli, Eileen. (2001). *Summerbath, winterbath*. Grand Rapids, MI: Eerdmans.

Spyri, Johanna. (2009). *Heidi*. New York: North-South.

Steggall, Susan. (2000). *Rattle and rap*. London: Frances Lincoln.

Steig, William. (1990). *Shrek*. New York: Farrar, Straus, Giroux.

Stevens, Janet. (1993). Coyote steals a blanket: A Ute tale. New York: Holiday House.

Sutherland, Zena. (1990). *The Orchard book of nursery rhymes*. New York: Orchard.

Thaler, Mike. (1988). *In the middle of the puddle*. New York: Harper.

Tomlinson, Heather. (2010). *Aurelie*. New York: Macmillan/Square Fish.

Vaes, Alain. (2001). *The princess and the pea*. Boston: Little, Brown.

Vere, Ed. (2010). *Chick*. New York: Henry Holt.

Viorst, Judith. (1971). *The tenth good thing about Barney*. New York: Atheneum.

Walsh, Ellen Stoll. (2001). *Dot & Jabber and the great acorn mystery.* San Diego, CA: Harcourt.

Ward, Jennifer. (2009). *The busy tree.* Tarrytown, NY: Marshall Cavendish.

Weeks, Sarah. (2003). *Without you.* New York: Laura Geringer.

Wells, Rosemary. (2006). *Max's ABC.* New York: Viking.

Whatley, Bruce. (2001). *Wait! No paint!* New York: HarperCollins.

Wiesner, David. (1997). *Tuesday.* New York: Clarion.

Wiesner, David. (2001). *The three pigs.* New York: Clarion.

Wiesner, David. (2006). *Flotsam.* New York: Clarion.

Williams, Jenny. (1992). Everyday ABC. New York: Dial.

Winthrop, Elizabeth. (2001). *Dumpy La Rue.* New York: Holt.

Yeh, Kat. (2009). *You're lovable to me.* New York: Random House.

Yolen, Jane. (1993). *Honkers.* Boston: Little, Brown.

Ziefert, Harriet. (2001). *Birdhouse for rent.* Boston: Houghton Mifflin.

Zolotow, Charlotte. (1992). *The seashore book.* New York: HarperCollins.

SELECTED REFERENCES AND RESOURCES

Allen, K. E., and Marotz, L. R. (2010). *Developmental profiles: Prebirth through twelve.* Belmont, CA: Wadsworth/Cengage.

Bowie, C. W., and Wellingham, F. S. (2004). *Busy fingers, growing minds.* Watertown, MA: Charlesbridge.

Chanko, P. (2009). *101 content building fingerplays, action rhymes and songs.* New York: Scholastic.

Cummings, P. (1999). *Talking with artists.* Boston: Houghton Mifflin.

Erlic, L. (2008) *Finger Rhymes.* Dayton, OH: Teaching and Learning/Milliken.

Freeman, J. (2006). *Books kids will sit still for.* Westport, CT: Libraries Unlimited.

Gilbert, A. G. (2002). *Teaching the three R's: Through movement experiences.* Bethesda, MD: National Dance Education Organization.

Haynes, J., and Murris, K. (2010). *Picturebooks and pedagogy.* New York: Routledge.

Hearne, B., and Kaye, M. (1987). *Celebrating children's books.* New York: William Morrow.

Hodges, S., and Barnes, P. (1997). *Songs and games for babies.* Everett, WA: Totline.

Panati, C. (2009). *Extraordinary origins of everyday things.* Pleasantville, NY: Reader's Digest.

Scott, B. (2010). *1000 Fingerplays and action rhymes.* New York: Neal-Schuman.

Trelease, J. (2006). *The read-aloud handbook.* New York: Viking Penguin.

Ward, R. A. (2009). *Literature-based activities for integrating mathematics and other content areas K-2.* Boston: Allyn & Bacon.

Wasik, B. A., and Seefeldt, C. (2005). *Early education: Three, four, and five year olds go to school.* Englewood Cliffs, NJ: Prentice-Hall.

Wilkins, E. (2001). *Eloise Wilkins poems to read to the very young.* New York: Random House.

York, S. (2009). *Booktalking authentic multicultural literature: Fiction and history for young readers.* Chicago, IL: American Library Association.

INTERNET REFERENCES AND HELPFUL WEBSITES

Center for Children's Books. Bulletin of the Center for Children's Books. Retrieved February 1, 2010, from http://bccb.lis.uiuc.edu *Children's Choices.*

Choosing Children's Books. News for Parents site. Retrieved February 1, 2010, from www.newsforparents.org/expert_choosing_childrens_books.html

How to Choose a Children's Book. Family Reading Partnership site. Retrieved February 1, 2010, from www.familyreading.org/i-choosebooks.htm

Overview of the Children's Choices booklist. Retrieved February 1, 2010, from http://www.reading.org/Libraries/Choices/cc_Bookmark

Poetry Foundation site. Retrieved February 1, 2010, from http://www.poetry foundation.org/features/children.html

The Children's Poetry Archive. Poetry Archive site. Retrieved February 1, 2010, from www.poetryarchive.org/childrensarchive/home.do

University of Calgary. Children's Literature Web guide. Retrieved February 1, 2010, from http://people.ucalgary.ca/~dkbrown/

CHAPTER 5

MAGIC MOTIVATIONS

"You gotta shake, shake, shake your sillies out" is the start of a wonderful song by Raffi, the popular singer of children's music. Raffi knows, as does every teacher, that young children must wriggle. Even when they try to be still, they seem to shake, shimmy, and move about. Part of being young is to move, to explore, to learn, and to try new things. The best approach is presenting a story of real interest to the children and engaging them in an enthusiastic sharing of the storytelling experience. This chapter provides techniques for doing this by discussing how to capture the attention of children, identify potential problems, plan smooth transitions, and create a healthy environment. The strategies described in this section are generally appropriate for children who are four years and older. At times they may not be appropriate, and at other times they may be used with younger children on a one-to-one or small group basis. The larger the group, the more likely it is that attention will wander. A reader must think about the match between the motivation technique, the story being shared, and the characteristics of the children in terms of development, interest, and personality. The focus should always be on experiencing the delight of the story in a comfortable setting, not on using certain teaching methods. Using great books that captivate children is still the most powerful motivation.

"Adventure is worthwhile in itself."

—AMELIA EARHART

CAPTURING THE ATTENTION OF CHILDREN

Cover from *Sir Lofty and Sir Tubb*, written and illustrated by Binette Schroeder. Jacket art copyright © 2009 by Binette Schroeder. Reprinted by permission of North-South Books. All rights reserved.

Totally eliminating unacceptable peer behaviors may not be possible. However, much can be done to decrease them. Children often engage in inappropriate behaviors when they do not perceive any acceptable behaviors that are of interest to them. Many poor behaviors can be avoided or minimized by using a combination of planning, common sense, and creativity in the presentation of stories. Nevertheless, the teacher who attempts to have perfectly still and quiet children during any activity, including a story reading, is destined to fail. This does not mean that children cannot sit reasonably still or that they should not be expected to listen. But success will depend on realistic expectations of children's behavior as well as the ability to engage, motivate, and plan for the children. Planning to work with the normal wriggles and giggles makes more sense than trying to eliminate them. A good story to approach the topic of behavior and its affect on friendship is *Sir Lofty and Sir Tubb* by Binette Schroeder. Lofty and Tubb were best friends until they wanted the same thing. It is a parable about greed and a wonderful introduction to how conflict starts and why it's important to resolve it.

Transitions are important for all young children. Don't expect children to leave free play or an outdoor activity and immediately sit still for a story. Without some type of transition activity, a smooth change from active play to passive sitting is nearly impossible for many children. Once settled with a transition song or fingerplay, children want to listen to the story. And children will listen if the teacher has set the stage for the story in a way that motivates them.

Listening is a crucial language skill as well as an important socialization life skill. Telling and reading stories to children can help them increase their listening attention span in a natural and enjoyable manner. Assuming that the book choice is appropriate and that the setting for telling the story is comfortable, one can consider other factors that affect the story reading.

Planning the Sharing of a Story

Planning a story is an interesting and challenging activity for anyone who understands how the teacher, child, and story must interact. Keep in mind that sharing is a two-way street between teacher and child. Too often, reading a story appears to be so simple a process that a plan is forgotten or not developed. A good **lesson plan** stretches the teacher's thinking to include planning for disaster. Planning for potential problems within a story-sharing session can help prevent them. The teacher must plan for wriggles, giggles, and other possible disruptions. This can be done by analyzing not only the choice of books, but the method of presentation as well. A lesson plan is an organized way to look at the components of a lesson. It allows one to see how the various pieces fit together, what is missing, and what can be changed. It can also provide a record of the title, author, and publisher of the book, and most important, the children's response to the story. This record will assist the teacher in revising the plan for the next time the book is shared with children. A lesson plan form makes the recording and planning easier. For each book, objectives, motivation, sharing procedures, and evaluation are recorded. The companion website contains a form that can be used for compiling this information.

TIPS FOR TEACHERS

Maintain an awareness of the interests of the children.

- Follow the children's lead by listening to the topics they are discussing and acting out during play and other times.
- Have alternate books and activities ready in case a different direction in the activity is appropriate.
- Know what is important to individual children by communicating regularly with families and being aware of relevant news, trends, and community activities (e.g. sports, Olympics, theater programs, art clubs, local teams).

Objectives. **Objectives** refer to the changes seen in a child as a result of interacting with a story. Many of these changes relate to feelings, attitudes, discovery of self, and new understandings of the world. Objectives focused primarily on remembering factual information from a story are misguided when using literature with young children. Literature should help the child grow spiritually, emotionally, and mentally. Take, for example, the reading of a story in which one of the characters is blind. It is far better for a child to learn about the common humanity of all people regardless of their disability than for the child to learn a definition for the word "blind." In most cases, recalling something such as the specific disability isn't nearly as important as the message of understanding and accepting human differences. Therefore, it is important to think carefully about what a book should accomplish. The teacher must consider the curriculum, the book's purpose, and the development of the children in deciding upon the objectives of the lesson.

Motivation. **Motivation** is a critical key to successful story times. Simply stated, motivation is the process of leading children into a desire to listen to and interact with the story. It is the way children come to see the story as having interest and meaning for themselves. Story motivations can include the use of

Involving children in the telling of the story is a motivational tool.

objects, sounds, fingerplays, games, and personal recollections. Objects such as mystery boxes, silk scarves, and large feathers can bring fun to the activity. Motivations are usually brief but can be lengthy if necessary. A good motivation is one that works!

Consider the possibilities for sharing *The Berenstain Bears and the Spooky Old Tree* by Stan and Jan Berenstain. Before the story, one might place a stick, a piece of rope, and a flashlight into a box or bag. Ask the children to feel the objects and guess what they are. By suggesting how these relate to the story, you can give the children a reason to be interested and involved. Approaching the same story from a different direction, one might display a large picture of a bear and ask the children how they might feel if they met such a bear. With just a bit of acting, the teacher might portray a fearful shaking and with a frightened voice ask the children what kinds of things scare them. This particular story is just a bit scary, but great fun even for older infants and toddlers. The excitement mounts as readers follow the bear children through the spooky old tree. All ends well. The adult should remember to wink at the children from time to time while pretending to be scared. This subtle clue will assure children that it is all in fun while still maintaining the feeling of being scared.

Children seem to love the sense of gentle scariness, the mild pretend fear that comes with knowing there is really nothing to be scared about. Readers can use the mention of a scary animal or feeling to create a mood for this or other books of this type. Though misunderstood, wolves continue to be scary animals. A book making use of this fear *Little Oops!* by Colin McNaughton. The simple

A song related to the story is a useful motivational activity.

phrases and large, humorous illustrations make the stories, in which Preston Pig and Mr. Wolf try to outwit each other, appropriate for toddlers and up. *The Perfect Little Monster* by Judy Hindley uses a rhythmic text and vivid language. A scary book that works as a jumping-off point for discussions about thunderstorms and other natural events is *One Dark Night* by Hazel Hutchins.

Consider the *The Sissy Duckling* by Broadway actor Harvey Fierstein. In the story, Elmer wants to do activities that are nontraditional for a boy. Instead of building forts and playing football, Elmer would like to bake and put on shows. Others bully him and his father is displeased with him. He withdraws from them, but the story has a wonderful and heroic ending with messages about the importance of being yourself, building self-esteem, and having tolerance for others. Children can be motivated with lead-in questions such as, "Has anyone ever told you that you can't do something that you really wanted to do? How did that make you feel? What did you do about it? What do you think Elmer likes to do?" [Show the cover to the children.] For slightly older children, use *Peter Pan: The Adventure Begins* by Namrata Tripathi. Tinkerbelle, fairy dust, Captain Hook, pirates, and buried treasure can be made a real part of the storytelling, with simple props such as foil-covered cardboard swords, glitter, play money, and handkerchiefs. The message of making a decision about who you are remains. Continuing with the pirate theme, a reading of *Tough Boris* by Mem Fox can be followed with a treasure hunt activity using hand-drawn treasure maps

© Cengage Learning

Movement can be used to involve children in the telling of the story.

with picture clues. Finally, in *What About Bear?* Suzanne Bloom raises the issue of feeling left out when friends enlarge their circle of acquaintances.

If the book used is *Heart of a Snowman* by Eugene Yelchin, the teacher could motivate the children by hiding a real snowman behind his or her back. After guessing what is being hidden, the children could be shown the snowman. This activity might be followed by asking them if they would like to have a real live snowman to play with. An alternate activity might include a pantomime of the making of a snowman. Still another idea might be to place a scarf, hat, and pieces of coal in a box or bag and ask the children to think of something that could be made using these items. Books that include the participation of children in the telling are quite motivating.

Such books allow for the involvement of everybody in the reading. Stories that lend themselves to this include *Circus Caps for Sale* by Esphyr Slobodkina, *Anansi and the Magic Stick* by Eric Kimmel, *I'm Walking, I'm Running, I'm Jumping, I'm Hopping* by Richard Harris, and *Millions of Cats* by Wanda Gag. The ideas and objects used to engage children are limited only by the teacher's imagination. Children can hold some motivational objects during the story. If a particular child has difficulty attending to a story, that child might be asked to hold the stuffed animal or to wear the firefighter's hat. Some use a rotating list of students for sharing the story motivation objects. A clever teacher keeps an eye open at yard sales and flea markets for stuffed toys and props to be used as future motivation tools. Post holiday sales are good sources for materials related to holiday stories.

Sharing. The plan for sharing a story includes ideas for making the story interesting and meaningful to children. Jim Trelease's *The Read-Aloud Handbook* (2006) contains an excellent chapter on reading a book to children. Jim Trelease's summary suggests questions to consider when developing the plan for the actual reading of picture books: How will I make sure that everyone can see the pictures? Will I read every word, or will I summarize some parts? What pace or speed of reading will I use? What can I tell the children about the author? Will I have the children draw a picture of the story during or after the reading? Where are the suspenseful parts where I can pause for questions and discussion?

Illustrations are critically important both for understanding the story and for helping children integrate new information with knowledge they already possess. A reader can use the illustrations to teach concepts such as shape, size and color. Readers can model a response to the illustrations. Do they like the pictures and the feelings they inspire? Do the pictures go well with the story and its characters? Are they accurate and true?

Keep in mind some additional factors. First, make sure there is enough time to finish the book. Second, try to use a variety of unfamiliar books. It is more difficult to create interest in a book when children already know what will happen. If some children know the story, let them help tell it. Finally, be prepared to involve the children. Prompt them to ask questions at appropriate times. Discuss the story with them. Accept interpretations of the story that differ from your own.

All of these points are possible if the children understand how to listen. Listening skills are built over time by introducing guidelines one at a time and by positively reinforcing them when they are demonstrated. Simple guidelines can include:

- Listening is not the same as hearing. Listening means using your ears *and* your mind.
- Look at the person who is talking.
- Wait for someone to finish speaking before you speak.
- Don't do anything else while listening.
- Ask questions if you need more information.
- Be aware that good listening builds friendships.

The end of the sharing should include a **closure**. Closure may include recalling all of the important points of the story. At this level, however, enjoyment and language growth will be the most common objectives. These are best assessed by observing the children's attention to the story and by listening to their discussion about the story. Children will enjoy retelling the story at this point, a most worthwhile activity.

Evaluation. The **evaluation** is the final part of the plan but it must be addressed throughout the planning process. Evaluation is more than an assessment at the end of the process to see what was learned. **Formative evaluation** involves on-going assessment throughout the planning and sharing of a story. The reader must determine whether the necessary learning and understanding is occurring at key intermediate points in the sharing of a story if children are to benefit from the overall experience. With practice, this process becomes a natural part of the story sharing. **Summative evaluation** involves the overall intent of the story. That is developed by asking the question "What do I want children to get from this story sharing experience?" With the answer to this question, learning objectives can be developed that might include an idea to be acquired and the criteria for determining the extent of the learning. From this, a judgment can be made in regard to whether the total experience was successful.

For example, if one is sharing the counting book *Hippos Go Berserk* by Author/illustrator Sandra Boynton, the enjoyment of the humorous story of a house full of hippos is the obvious and ultimate goal. However, it may also be used as a vehicle to help children learn or expand their counting skills from one to ten (forward and backward). It may also be used as an introduction to the additive principle (if I have two of something and get one more, than I have three of something). If these additional learning possibilities are part of the intent for the reading, a formative evaluation must be planned and implemented. It will assess how well children are learning and understanding and inform the reader about that learning. Following the reading, a summative evaluation will be used to determine how well the objectives were attained. Much learning occurs by simply experiencing the reading. It is not necessary to structure every story sharing as a content learning lesson. Formative and summative evaluation plans for *Hippos Go Berserk* can be found in the "Sample Evaluations" section of the companion website. At this point one needs to determine whether the objectives were met. This is when the teacher attempts to honestly evaluate what worked, what did not, and what could be changed to improve the story presentation the next time it is used. The sharing of the story can lead into a retelling or discussion. The accuracy of the retelling can reveal the child's understanding of the original story. It might be an activity that relates to the story. For example, in *Listen Buddy* by Helen Lester the theme of following directions plays an important role. Children can show an understanding of the concept by creating and playing a game that requires following directions. A book on following directions that is also appropriate for toddlers is *Good Dog, Daisy!* by Lisa Kopper.

More Motivation Ideas

The best motivation for listening to a story is a great story. *The Tale of Peter Rabbit* by Beatrix Potter is a great story that will engage most children's interest without much help. However, one might use stuffed toys or puppets to introduce the book. The teacher might also hold up a small jacket with a rip in it and ask the children how they think it could have been torn. Still another approach might be to show the children a small watering can. After explaining how it might be a good hiding place for a small animal, the teacher could pull a small stuffed rabbit out of the can. Each of these items is a prop, and many objects with visual appeal can be used as props to capture attention and introduce stories.

Mr. Bear Says Peek-a-boo by Debi Gliori is a fun book for toddlers. Creating story motivation might begin by placing a blanket over the teacher's head. The teacher should say nothing until one of the curious toddlers pulled the blanket off. This action would lead right into the story. A similar procedure can be used for *The Most Beautiful Kid in the World* by Jennifer Ericsson, in which Annie changes outfits to look just right for Grandmother's visit. The storyteller might begin by bundling up in a wild array of outlandish clothes topped off with a huge coat or cape. Inviting children to pull off some of the pieces of clothing before the story begins will bring about both giggles and interest in the story.

TIPS FOR TEACHERS

Collect a box of old clothes and props to be used during the transition to a story.

- Have teacher or child dress in a snowsuit to tell a winter or snow-related story.
- Wear a big straw beach hat for a summer story.
- Put on a football jersey and oversized sneakers to share a story about a sport.
- Collect hats that can be used to portray a sailor, police officer, baseball player, firefighter, chef, king, or queen.
- Make costumes and props available to children following the story.

There are a variety of ways to motivate children to listen to *Farm Animals: Watch Me Grow* by Dorling Kindersley. One might stir interest for each animal story by making the sound of the animal or by pantomiming the animal's movements. A bag mask or stick puppet may be useful for a book such as this. Also, the storyteller could hide a stuffed or real animal in a box or cage. The children can be asked to find or guess what the animal is.

Dav Pilkey's *The Dumb Bunnies* can provide the storyteller with the opportunity for a comedy routine motivation activity. The reader would come into the reading area with an armload of winter outdoor clothes and begin to explain how to prepare for the outdoors in winter. This would be followed by a running commentary accompanied and a demonstration of how to do everything wrong (e.g., zipping up a coat and putting it on a leg, sticking feet into a hat and a mitten, wrapping a scarf around an elbow). From here the reader can read the story in which the bunnies eat lunch in a car wash, go bowling in the library, and perform other activities in the wrong places.

Teachers can create a humorous motivational routine for Esphyr Slobodkina's *Circus Caps for Sale.* Here, the teacher could walk slowly and carefully to the reading area while wearing a huge stack of hats. An alternative to this might include the use of a stuffed or puppet monkey. The toy monkey whispers only to the teacher, who then translates the message to the class. The monkey begins by whispering that it has a great story about other monkeys and hats. Hats can be placed on the monkey as the story is told. Staying with the concept of hats, a reader could use a set of dolls and a "magic hat" that changes the dolls into animals when the hat lands upon them. This will be just the right start for Mem Fox's *The Magic Hat.* In this story, the same thing happens; each time it does, the listeners can join in on a catchy repeating refrain. Because it is magic, a wizard comes to town and sets everything right again.

Hey, Al by Arthur Yorinks can be introduced by having the teacher rush into the reading area. Wearing a baseball cap and pushing a broom, the teacher rapidly pantomimes the activities of a janitor at work. Using the broom and a dust rag to clean under and around the children will create much fun and interest. A quieter approach to the same story would entail the teacher placing a janitor's cap, a fern, and a small broom into a box or bag. The children can be asked to identify each item and explain what they have in common.

Using *The Wretched Stone* by Chris Van Allsburg with kindergartners, the teacher can begin by having each of the children find a small rock outside. After washing and drying the stones, children can show, talk about, and feel their stones. The teacher could then explain that in many cultures stones are thought to have certain powers. Children could close their eyes and think of the special powers that their stones might have. This is just the right time to begin the reading of the story. Another story to create interest and excitement about an object such as a rock is William Steig's *Sylvester and the Magic Pebble.* The teacher might begin by having the children guess what is concealed in a hand. After revealing a brightly colored pebble, the children could be told that the pebble contains magic just like the one in today's story. Another way of gaining each child's involvement is to give each child a magic pebble to hold for the story reading. The pebbles can help the children picture their own wishes. Children

Used with permission
Houghton Mifflin Harcourt.

can paint them, weigh them, and create new stories about them. They can then draw their wishes and take their special pebbles home.

Children are usually quite aware of their own health and familiar with doctors and nurses. *Next Please* by Ernst Jandl is a book on this topic to which children will be able to relate. The teacher might begin by entering the reading area wearing medical garb, either real or homemade. Using medical tools from a box, the teacher would pantomime a medical exam with a doll or puppet. An alternative to this might be to use a doll, animal, or puppet in place of the teacher. Having an alligator doctor do a medical exam on an elephant would surely create interest.

IDENTIFYING POSSIBLE PROBLEMS

It is important that the storyteller be familiar with the story being presented in order to anticipate problems. Even if a book is age-appropriate, it may be uninteresting or confusing for the children. One should be ready to add some excitement to the reading by involving the children in the story. There are a variety of ways to do this. One may pause to ask the children what they think will happen next. Other aspects of the presentation may be changed as well.

The effective use of voice will often help children focus on what is being said. Dr. Seuss keeps younger children involved in the rather lengthy book *Green Eggs and Ham* by periodically asking them, "Will he eat the green eggs and ham this time?" When the children respond with a "No," the teacher should quickly read the ever-growing list of negative responses from the character in the book. Older children thoroughly enjoy this story and have little trouble staying with it. Even though the book is written as an early reader, younger children can follow it if the storyteller provides the rhyming words for the repeating phrases. Follow up the reading by cooking scrambled eggs and using green food coloring in them or serve regular scrambled eggs with green ketchup on the side. This will re-create the experience.

When conducting a lesson involving science or social studies, it is quite valid to use the pictures in books geared for older children when the subject cannot be found in age-appropriate books. If the pictures are clear and large, the book can be used by omitting the text that is too difficult and paraphrasing information contained in those sections. It is recommended, however, that age-appropriate books be used whenever possible.

The Importance of Prereading

Prereading the story allows the teacher to know where emotional support may be needed, especially with young children. Tomie dePaola's *Nana Upstairs and Nana Downstairs* has a very sad part in the middle of the story. Knowing this ahead of time, the teacher can anticipate the need for support if or when the children seem upset. This depends on the class. During the story, one might ask such questions as, "How do you think Tommy feels? . . . Would you feel this way? . . . There are more pages in the book; would you like to see what happens?" It is a healthy sign when a book such as this can arouse empathy for a character.

Many books can arouse children's emotions, and one must be sensitive to this potential. The teacher must anticipate reactions when using books that deal with death, divorce, new babies, and so forth. A reading can be a wonderful support for children coping with a similar situation in real life. It can also cause a disruption as children deal with the surfacing of their feelings. When planning to use such books to help a child, have that child sit next to an adult in the room. Be ready to provide support to the child. Allow time at the end of such stories to discuss all the children's feelings. Let them know at the beginning of a book that there will be time to talk after the story. This minimizes disruptions. Allow all the children to respond to the story when it is finished.

TIPS FOR TEACHERS

Listen to recordings of yourself reading a story in order to evaluate your presentation.

- Is your voice is appropriately dramatic from beginning to end?
- Do you use appropriate volume, pitch, and pauses?
- Are there spots in the reading where a pause for comments, questions, or predictions would be appropriate?

Children's Interests

The key to successful story sharing is to select books that are of true interest to children. The interests of adults may or may not be the interests of children. Although it is fine to expose children to new interests, it is important also to satisfy their current interests. If the children are fascinated with dinosaurs, be sure to include books that relate to prehistoric times. If they are interested in superheroes, share storybooks that include such heroes. Be wary of books that seem particularly "cute." Such books are often designed to attract adults by their appearance rather than their interest to children. Flowery language and ornate illustrations will probably not attract most infants, toddlers, and preschoolers.

Although children often have special interests, things such as home, mother, family, pets, and favorite toys have universal interest. Children are also interested in themselves. A variety of appealing interests are portrayed in

© Cengage Learning

Children's activities and interests can be used as a guide to selecting books.

thirteen brief stories in *You Read to Me, I'll Read to You: Very Short Stories to Read Together* by Mary Ann Hoberman. The undying love between mother and child is beautifully shared with rhythmic joy in *Tickle Tum!* by Nancy Van Laan, with gentleness in *Felix Feels Better* by Rosemary Wells, with warmth in books such as *I Can Help* by David Costello and *My Mother Is Mine* by Marion Bauer, with humor in *Mom Pie* by Lynne Jonell, with realism in *Little Ones Do!* by Jana Hunter, and with weary patience in *Grump* by Janet Wong. The concept of one's surroundings is explored in Ann Turner's *In the Heart.* Other stories along this line are Charlotte Middleton's *Tabitha's Terrifically Tough Tooth* about a loose tooth, Sharon McCullough's *Bunbun, the Middle One* about being average,

Steve Henry's *Nobody Asked Me!* about a new baby, and Tony Johnston's *My Best Friend Bear* about a favorite toy that is falling apart. A child with a parent deployed in the military may have a particular empathy for Jerome in *Sometimes We Were Brave* by Pat Brisson. Playing is what children do, and what better way to recall a wonderful time of sand and water play than reading *Maisy at the Beach* by Lucy Cousins.

SMOOTH TRANSITIONS

Transitions are sometimes challenging for both teachers and children. Some children find it difficult to leave an activity in which they are truly involved. Although stories are usually viewed as enjoyable, certain children react with acting-out behavior when story time is mentioned. They equate story time with negative thoughts about having to sit perfectly still, something these children find very difficult. A good transition makes it easier for them to shift gears and approach story time with less anxiety.

Storytellers have found that songs, poems, and fingerplays are effective transitional activities. Children naturally respond to their rhythms. Many short forms of rhymes fit nicely into a transition time frame. Anyone who has ever heard a young child repeating a jingle knows that they are particularly responsive to rhyming words set to music. For this reason, they also pay attention to the songlike quality of fingerplays and other such transitional activities. An effective transition turns the child's attention to the next activity. Indeed, through being involved in the transition activity, the child already is involved in the shift to the next activity.

Transition Ideas

Teachers may choose to either make up their own transition activities or borrow them from books such *101 Learning and Transition Activities* by Bradley Smith and Adam Smith. Chanting messages or singing the message to a familiar tune are other ways to establish a pattern for change. For example, moving from art time to story time may be accomplished while singing the following rhyme to the melody of "O Tannenbaum":

It's story time! It's story time!
Can we get ready for story time?

Some other ways to facilitate transitions are to use unusual objects. Find a gaudy rhinestone ring, the bigger and more colorful the better. Tell the children that this is a magic ring given to you by a sorcerer. Hold up the ring for all to see. Make a special wish for the children. Adding a couple of phrases like "Abracadabra" will help put a feeling of magic into the children's desire to hear the story.

Magic wands can be great aids to transitions. One can use a water-filled or glitter-filled wand, a tinsel-filled wand, a glow-in-the-dark wand, or a light-up wand. Children love to see the wand waved in the air over their heads while the teacher chants magical words and phrases. The children realize that the wand is not really magic, but they love the fun of pretending. A wand draws their attention and that makes it work as a transitional tool.

It is comforting for children to know what will come next. For this reason, many storytellers use the same transitional song or poem at the beginning of each storytelling or reading session. A second song or poem may be added, but the story time always begins with the familiar one.

Wriggle songs, poems, and fingerplays are also useful before a story begins. They allow movement prior to the reading and that helps to keep the children from needing to wriggle so much during the story. The best wriggle activities proceed from active wriggling to nose twitching or eye blinking, which ready the children for a quieter time. Active participation by children is a key factor in any transition.

Several good choices exist for de-wriggling children. An excellent source for blending music with activity and transitions is *Easy Songs for Smooth Transitions in the Classroom* by Nina Araujo and Carol Aghayan. Singing is an energy-consuming activity that also stresses the need for cooperation with others. It is an excellent tool to guide children into an attentive listening attitude.

The use of a transition is part of the planning. It eliminates many behavior problems by avoiding the conflicts caused by an abrupt change in routine. The child who tends to act out has more of an opportunity to choose acceptable behaviors when transition activities are provided.

Sometimes a storybook is just the right thing for a transition. To get ready for play time, Virginia Miller's *In a Minute!* is just right. The mood for a quiet transition to nap time can be set with *Countdown to Bedtime: A Lift-the-Flap Book* by Mike Haines, *What Do Ducks Dream?* by Harriet Ziefert, or the wonderful classic *Can't You Sleep Little Bear?* by Martin Waddell. Children love their family pets, so books about familiar pets capture children's interest and can be used for teaching important ideas. In *Goodnight Dog* by Ed Heck, the silly dog shows both the right and wrong way to get ready for bed.

A HEALTHY ENVIRONMENT

There are many strategies available to promote an enjoyable reading situation. Experience can be a valuable teacher, as it allows one to try different procedures over time. One can also learn from the experience that others have gained. No procedure, however, is effective every time with every child or group. Children and classes have distinct personalities. A procedure that works one time for one group may be ineffective at another time or with another group. The fact that there is no blueprint or plan that one can always follow is part of the challenge of working with children over time. Be willing to approach problems in new and creative ways.

Certain problems tend to occur more frequently than others. Children sit too close, cause disruptions during the reading, act out, and demonstrate inappropriate peer relationships. One must be aware of which behaviors can be accepted as normal, how to regain the attention of the group after a disruption, and how to avoid using inappropriate procedures for dealing with problems.

Children Sitting Too Close

Youngsters need enough space to accommodate their normal movements. One common approach is to place hearts, stars, stickers, or markers at the places where children are to sit. Encourage independence by asking children to find their own spaces. The seating arrangement may be in the form of a circle, semi-circle, or a random pattern. Each child might be assigned a permanent spot, or children could choose an available spot. If permanent spots are assigned to children, names can be added to reinforce name recognition.

Another approach might be to have the children stand up and hold hands in a circle. After expanding the circle so children are separated by a full arm's length, they could let go of each other's hands and sit down where they are

Children come to enjoy each other's company in a shared activity.

standing. This yields a good space between children. One might also tape a circle on the floor or carpet. A cross tape can be placed at each point where a child is expected to sit. Or, using clear contact paper, tape each child's picture to the spot on the floor where that child is to sit. This works well for toddlers and younger children who cannot yet read their own names.

Disruptions during Reading

Disruptions can occur for a variety of reasons that may or may not be related to the story. The most obvious solution to this problem is to establish eye contact with the child and send a brief nonverbal message, such as telling the story directly to that child for a moment. The teacher might also nod to the child and mouth the word "after." If this is not effective, the teacher might verbally acknowledge the child but ask that he or she wait until the end to speak. If the interruption is pursuant to the story, the teacher might wish to allow the child to briefly share the information. The reading could then be continued. The best approach remains preventing the situation in the first place. Consistently reinforcing appropriate behavior identified in the section on listening skills earlier in the chapter is a most effective strategy.

Consider the possibility that the children need to stretch. Use a wriggle or giggle fingerplay, then continue the story. Make the story a serial story by continuing it later in the day or the next day. Engage the children in the story. Ask what might come next, what the giant did, or how the bunny found her way home. Teachers must use their instinct, judgment, and knowledge of the group to decide which course of action to follow.

Acting-Out Children

Every class seems to have one or two children who might be described as overly active or mischievous. Their disruptive behavior is often termed "acting out." These children should be seated near the teacher before the reading begins. Children who are known to have difficulty sitting near each other should be seated apart. Using the illustrations to facilitate discussion and focus attention can be very effective.

Involving these children in the storytelling is effective. Give them the motivational items to hold during the reading. If they are made to feel that they have an important role during story time, they will have less need for attention. But in dealing with these children, remember that literature is its own reward. One doesn't grow to appreciate it by having one's silence "bought" for sitting quietly through it.

A good approach for engaging the attention of especially active children is to have them create a special book to take home. They should draw something on the page that represents the story read that day. The book title and author can be written on the page as well. This will allow children to talk about the story later, and parents can reinforce the story. By doing this, children learn that they are expected to attend to the reading so they can share it with their parents. Praise the whole group for listening and learning. All children should feel that they are part of a social group with certain responsibilities.

TIPS FOR TEACHERS

Plan in advance what you will do to help a child who acts out.

- Give all the children something to do during the reading, such as hand motions and oral responses to parts of the story, and make sure they know what they should be doing.
- Have the active child become a helper in the telling of the story.
- Use great stories so acting out won't become a problem in the first place.
- Keep a basket of stress balls near the reading area.
- Be interesting. You are competing with mass media.

Peer Relations

Children do bump and nudge each other, often unintentionally but sometimes on purpose. When it appears that a safety problem exists or that a behavior is interfering with the reading, an adult must take some type of action. Because the goal is to have everyone engaged in the story, the first course of action might be to simply motion for the acting-out child to come and sit next to the teacher or an aide. The story can then be immediately continued. A reader who is standing can move near the child and involve the child in the story. Involving the child with the reader's presence and the story line will often eliminate the inappropriate behavior. Read some of the words directly to the child: "The wolf huffed and he puffed, Michael." Ask the child to show how the wolf huffed and puffed. It's difficult for a child to ignore the story when brought back into it in this way.

Sometimes children ignore these signals. Discussion about positive and appropriate behavior can be done on a regular basis using books such as *Being a Good Citizen* by Adrian Vigliano as a stepping off point. This book is a nonfiction read-aloud concerning the meaning of what constitutes being a good citizen at home, at school, and with friends. Another choice is *Thanks a LOT, Emily Post*

Coriander the Contrary Hen by Dori Chaconas with illustrations by Marsha Gray Carrington. Illustrations copyright ©2007 by Marsha Gray Carrington. Reprinted by permission of Carolrhoda Books, Inc., a division of Lerner Publishing Group, Inc. All rights reserved. No part of this excerpt may be used or reproduced in any manner whatsoever without the prior written permission of Lerner Publishing Group, Inc.

by Jennifer Huget, which takes a hilarious look at good and bad behavior. As a last resort, disruptive children should be removed from the group as quietly as possible, without conversation. They can be moved to sit at a table. The teacher should return to the group and continue the story for the others. The less attention given to the situation, the less it disturbs the flow of the story. If several stories are being read, or if there are appropriate points to pause in the story, the child can be asked to return to the group later. Positive reinforcement of the appropriate normal behaviors can help them continue. An occasional poem from *Good for You! Toddler Rhymes for Toddler Time* by Stephanie Calmenson is a good source. It includes such amusing titles as "Hello Soap" and "I'm a Very Noisy Person." A storybook that can be used to remind us of how to be aware of our behaviors is *Meet the Barkers: Morgan and Moffat Go to School* by Tomie dePaola. The concept of watching out for your friends is explored by Dori Chaconas in *Coriander the Contrary Hen.* Coriander is a stubborn hen who places herself in a dangerous situation. All of her friends fail to get her to safety except one little girl who uses reverse psychology. The book, which uses a catchy repeating line throughout, helps young readers to recognize and contemplate danger, pride, stubbornness, and the need to listen to others who are trying to help.

Ignoring Normal Behaviors

Children stretch and wriggle. Children react verbally to various parts of a story. Children twist their hair around their fingers. Many times, these are unconscious behaviors that harm no one and actually show that children are listening. Adults sometimes mistakenly try to eliminate all motion from the listening child. Since it is normal for children to act in these ways, they should not be penalized.

If a child exhibits a behavior that the teacher feels must be addressed, it should be done quietly. "No problem" situations can become real problems for both the reader and the child if one attempts to eliminate all movement.

Author Dori Chaconas. Courtesy Dori Chaconas. Photo credit: Maria Story.

Regaining Attention

It can be difficult to regain a group's attention after a distraction. A dog walking into a room or a call on the intercom can disrupt the momentum of a story. It is best to handle the situation by using intuition and common sense. If it appears to be too late to continue the story, it is best not to attempt it. The children can be told that the story will be concluded later or during the next day. Rushing through the end of a book can be most unsatisfactory for all. It can cause the story to lose its charm. If there is enough time to continue, the children can be regrouped with a quiet fingerplay or song. The reader should repeat some of the past action and resume the story. Better yet, involve the children in the retelling of what has happened in the story prior to continuing the reading.

How Not to Handle Disruptions

At some time in life, everyone has seen the unacceptable way to handle a situation. The "wrong way" refers to a procedure that ultimately does more harm than good. Humiliating youngsters in front of their peers may quiet them down, but it is also likely to bring years of mistrust, resentment, and lowered self-esteem. A variety of other negative, yet common, methods for handling problems at story time do more harm than good and should be avoided.

Several of the methods to be avoided merely reveal the adult's frustration. Rolling one's eyes while saying, "Oh, no, not you again," is a good example. Yelling and accusing a child of ruining the reading group or removing a child with visible annoyance fall into this category.

Threatening actions that will not be taken is foolish. For example, warning, "If you don't settle down, there will be no more stories," is a mistake. It may work for the moment, but it has a better chance of backfiring. In making such a statement, the teacher has surrendered control to the disruptive children, who may enjoy their newly discovered role of deciding the day's schedule—if indeed the stories are discontinued. But children know that there will always be more stories. It is a grave mistake to link literature and punishment together in such a way. Threatening to tell a child's parents about a behavior is also ineffective. This admits to a child that the teacher cannot handle the problem and the child is likely to cause more serious problems in the future.

Negative comments, in general, are usually ineffective. It is far better to use positive comments, praising those students who are acting appropriately and offering an alternate activity to those who are not. Positive comments provide attention, build self-esteem, and are effective in managing behavior. Let children hear phrases such as, "I like the way Juan is listening," "I see Beth and Isaac are ready," "I just love the way you look at me with that smile when it is time to read a story." In addition, engage children in clapping, stomping, waving, and naming activities that can be a part of the story.

SUMMARY

Much of the success of reading a story depends on engaging the interest of the children. Armed with a good sense of humor, common sense, and a knowledge of child development, adults can successfully bring magic into story times. Creative and whimsical methods of motivation enhance the enjoyment of literature for both the teacher and the children. When adults are motivated to make books an integral and enjoyable part of life, children will respond with delight and a sense of wonder at the world of literature opening before them.

The choice of books and their presentation are critical in enhancing children's interest. The atmosphere created in the classroom is important to listening and learning. To create an effective atmosphere, teachers must be responsive to children and their needs. Magic boxes, stuffed animals, puppets, and interesting objects do more than just motivate children to listen to a particular book. The special ways that adults use them can help children develop an interest in literature in general. A formative and summative evaluation plan is a helpful tool for determining the success of sharing a story with children.

Helping children learn how to adjust to change, interact with literature, and develop listening skills is an important part of the teacher's role. These skills will make children more productive and responsive social beings. But this process does not occur simply by reading a book to children. Carefully plan the readings, taking into account both how literature can be exciting and how problems can occur. Careful planning will prevent many problems. When students do exhibit inappropriate behaviors during story time, a set of sensitive and effective strategies for dealing with them is indispensable to the teacher.

QUESTIONS FOR THOUGHT AND DISCUSSION

1. What are some of the things a storyteller can do to prevent or minimize disruptive interactions between children?

2. How can a storyteller help children increase their listening time spans?

3. Why should teachers develop lesson plans?

4. Why is a motivational procedure important in a lesson plan?

5. Choose a story, and give some examples of motivations that might be used for it.

6. Defend or refute this statement: Children should never be read books that are above their age-appropriate level.

7. Why is it beneficial for children if the teacher prereads a book?

8. Why should the children's interests be part of the choice of books?

9. Describe a transitional activity a teacher might use in a classroom.

10. What is meant by the term "wriggle song"?

11. How might a teacher deal with the problem of children sitting too close together during story time?

12. What steps could one take with a child who disrupts the reading time?

13. What can the teacher do with children who act out during story time?

14. Defend or refute this statement: The aggressive child who starts fighting with another child during story time should never be removed from the group as it makes him or her feel left out.

15. Describe formative and summative evaluation in regard to a specific children's book.

 For additional resources, access the *Growing Up with Literature* companion website through www.cengagebrain.com <http://www.cengagebrain.com/>.

CHILDREN'S BOOKS CITED

Bauer, Marion. (2001). *My mother is mine.* New York: Simon and Schuster.

Berenstain, Stan and Berenstain, Jan. (1978). *The Berenstain Bears and the spooky old tree.* New York: Random House.

Bloom, Suzanne. (2010). *What about Bear?* Honesdale, PA: Boyds Mills Press.

Boynton, Sandra. (2009). *Hippos go berserk.* Boston: Little Simon.

Brisson, Pat. (2010). *Sometimes we were brave.* Honesdale, PA: Boyds Mills Press.

Chaconas, Dori. (2007). *Coriander the contrary hen.* Minneapolis, MN: Carolrhoda/Lerner.

Costello, David. (2010). *I can help.* New York: Farrar, Straus & Giroux.

Cousins, Lucy. (2001). *Maisy at the beach.* Cambridge, MA: Candlewick.

dePaola, Tomie. (1992). *Nana upstairs and Nana downstairs.* New York: Dutton.

dePaola, Tomie. (2001). *Meet the Barkers: Morgan and Moffat go to school.* New York: Putnam.

Ericsson, Jennifer. (1996). *The most beautiful kid in the world.* New York: Tambourine.

Fierstein, Harvey. (2002). *The sissy duckling.* New York: Simon & Schuster.

Fox, Mem. (1994). *Tough Boris.* San Diego, CA: Harcourt.

Fox, Mem. (2006). *The magic hat.* New York: Voyager.

Gag, Wanda. (1996). *Millions of cats.* New York: Putnam.

Gliori, Debi. (1997). *Mr. Bear says peek-a-boo.* New York: Little Simon.

Haines, Mike. (2001). *Countdown to bedtime: A lift-the-flap book.* New York: Hyperion.

Harris, Richard. (2005). *I'm walking, I'm running, I'm jumping, I'm hopping.* Newburyport, MA: Hampton Roads Publishing.

Heck, Ed. (2010). *Goodnight dog.* New York: Penguin.

Henry, Steve. (2001). *Nobody asked me!* New York: HarperCollins.

Hindley, Judy. (2001). *The perfect little monster.* Cambridge, MA: Candlewick.

Hoberman, Mary Ann. (2001). *You read to me, I'll read to you: Very short stories to read together*. Boston: Little, Brown.

Huget, Jennifer. (2009). *Thanks a LOT, Emily Post*. New York: Schwartz & Wade.

Hunter, Jana. (2001). *Little ones do!* New York: Dutton.

Hutchins, Hazel. (2001). *One dark night*. New York: Viking.

Jandl, Ernst. (2003). *Next please*. New York: Putnam.

Johnston, Tony. (2001). *My best friend bear*. Flagstaff, AZ: Rising Moon.

Jonell, Lynne. (2001). *Mom pie*. New York: Putnam.

Kimmel, Eric. (2001). *Anansi and the magic stick*. New York: Holiday House.

Kindersley, Dorling. (2005). Farm animals: Watch me grow. New York: DK Publishing.

Kopper, Lisa. (2001). *Good dog, Daisy!* New York: Dutton.

Lester, Helen. (1996). *Listen Buddy*. Boston: Houghton Mifflin.

McCullough, Sharon. (2001). *Bunbun, the middle one*. New York: Barefoot.

McNaughton, Colin. (2001). *Little oops!* San Diego, CA: Harcourt.

Middleton, Charlotte. (2001). *Tabitha's terrifically tough tooth*. New York: Penguin Putnam.

Miller, Virginia. (2001). *In a minute!* Cambridge, MA: Candlewick.

Pilkey, Dav. (2005). *The dumb bunnies*. New York: Scholastic.

Potter, Beatrix. (1902). *The tale of Peter Rabbit*. New York: Warne.

Schroeder, Binette. (2009). *Sir Lofty and Sir Tubb*. New York: North-South.

Seuss, Dr. (pseud. for Theodor Geisel) (1960). *Green eggs and ham*. New York: Random House.

Slobodkina, Esphyr. (2004). *Circus caps for sale*. New York: Harper Trophy.

Steig, William. (1970). *Sylvester and the magic pebble*. New York: Simon and Schuster.

Tripathi, Namrata. (2003). *Peter Pan: The adventure begins*. New York: Harper-Festival.

Turner, Ann. (2001). *In the heart*. New York: HarperCollins.

Van Allsburg, Chris. (1991). *The wretched stone*. Boston: Houghton Mifflin.

Van Laan, Nancy. (2001). *Tickle tum!* New York: Simon and Schuster.

Vigliano, Adrian. (2010). *Being a good citizen*. Portsmouth, NH: Heineman/Raintree.

Waddell, Martin. (2002). *Can't you sleep little bear?* Cambridge, MA: Candlewick.

Wells, Rosemary. (2001). *Felix feels better*. Cambridge, MA: Candlewick.

Wong, Janet. (2001). *Grump*. New York: Simon and Schuster.

Yelchin, Eugene. (2009). *Heart of a snowman*. New York: Harper Collins.

Yorinks, Arthur. (2001). *Hey, Al*. New York: Farrar, Straus, Giroux/Spoken Arts.

Ziefert, Harriet. (2001). *What do ducks dream?* New York: Putnam.

SELECTED REFERENCES AND RESOURCES

Araujo, N., and Aghayan, C. (2006). *Easy songs for smooth transitions in the classroom.* St. Paul, MN: Redleaf.

Borgenicht, J., and Rosen, L. (2006). *The baby owner's games and activities book.* Philadelphia, PA: Quirk Books.

Calmenson, S. (2001). *Good for you! Toddler rhymes for toddler time.* New York: HarperCollins.

Church, E. (2001). *Terrific transitions.* New York: Instructor Books/Scholastic.

Essa, E. L. (2003). *A practical guide to solving preschool behavior problems* (5th ed.). Clifton Park, NY: Delmar Learning.

Feldman, J. (2000). *Transition tips and tricks for teachers.* Beltsville, MD: Gryphon House.

Fried, R. L. (2001). *The passionate learner: How teachers and parents can help children reclaim the joy of learning.* Boston: Beacon.

Hayes, K., and Creange, R. (2001). *Classroom routines that really work for pre-K and kindergarten.* New York: Scholastic.

Hendrick, J., and Weissman, P. (2010). *The whole child: Developmental education for the early years.* Upper Saddle River, NJ: Merrill.

Kimmel, G. (2002). *No biting.* St. Paul, MN: Redleaf.

Perry, N. J., and Fides, D. M. (2010). *Constructive guidance and discipline: Preschool and primary education.* Upper Saddle River, NJ: Merrill.

Robinson, M. and Fields, M. V. (2010). *Understanding behavior and development in early childhood.* New York: Routledge.

Shub, J., and DeWeerd, A. *Ready to learn.* Portsmouth, NH: Heineman.

Silberg, J., Schiller, P., and Berry, M. (2006). *The complete book and CD set of rhymes, songs, poems, fingerplays and chants.* Silver Spring, MD: Gryphon House.

Smith, B., and Smith, A. (2006). *101 learning and transition activities.* Clifton Park, NY: Delmar Learning.

Stipek, D., Seal, K. and Stipek, D. J. (2001). *Motivated minds: Raising children to love learning.* New York: Owl/Henry Holt.

Trelease, J. (2006). *The read-aloud handbook.* New York: Penguin.

Watson, C. (2001). *Father Fox's pennyrhymes.* Madison, WI: DEMCO.

INTERNET REFERENCES
AND HELPFUL WEBSITES

Gayle's Preschool Rainbow site. Preschool nursery rhymes for transition times. Retrieved February 17, 2010, from www.preschoolrainbow.org/transition-rhymes.htm

National Center for Infants, Toddlers, and Families. Zero to three. Retrieved February 17, 2010, from http://www.zerotothree.org/

PBS Parents site. "Parents and teachers activities." Retrieved February 17, 2010, from http://www.pbs.org/parents/arthur/activities

Reading Is Fundamental. Motivating kids to read. Retrieved February 17, 2010, from http://www.rif.org/

Searchwarp Writer's Community site. "Transition songs to keep preschool classrooms moving." Retrieved February 17, 2010, from http://www.searchwarp.com

CHAPTER 6

How Many Ways Can a Story Be Told?

A daily structure provides an important security and reassurance to children. Yet variations in routine can provide interest and excitement to the day. No matter how enjoyable a routine might be, sameness can create boredom over time. Thus, good literature can be enhanced with a variety of presentation methods. This chapter introduces a number of unique ways in which stories can be told, and better yet, retold in ways involving children as participants. In addition to reading stories aloud to a group, the chapter explores oral storytelling, flannel boards as a device for telling stories, and a variety of theatrical storytelling methods. Finally, the topic of children as storytellers and illustrators is explored. Also included are discussions on storytelling by storytellers Doug Lipman and Aili Paal Singer and an interview with author/illustrator Charlotte Agell.

Some may be intimidated by the idea of changing the way a story is shared. Others welcome the opportunity to experiment with a variety of presentations. Those who do try a variety of approaches often find the changes refreshing for both the children and themselves. The changes can range from subtle shifts within a familiar presentation style to experimenting with totally new sharing methods. By starting with

"No story is the same to us after a lapse of time."

—George Eliot

177

less obvious changes and proceeding to totally different styles, one can develop a confidence in one's abilities. This chapter explores the possibilities of using such diverse methods as oral storytelling, reading aloud, flannelboard stories, theatrical story presentations, and children as authors. Each of these methods has a number of possibilities within it. One may also choose to combine the various presentation methods, making endless the possible ways of sharing stories.

READING ALOUD

Reading aloud to children should begin when they are infants. The close contact, the sounds of a caring voice, and the rhythms of the language provide reassurance. The child who is read to grows up with the idea that reading is a normal part of life. As language becomes meaningful, children can see new worlds constantly opening up before them. Reading stimulates imagination and provides a foundation upon which to build new knowledge.

The terms "reading readiness" and "reading readiness skills" give a false impression of what learning to read entails. Learning to read is a long, ongoing process beginning with being read to as an infant. It culminates in an ability and desire to engage in reading as an enjoyable part of life.

Reading aloud to children is a part of helping them to read. According to Jim Trelease, author of *The Read-Aloud Handbook* (2006), the child who follows the reader's finger across the page will make a natural connection between the sounds of the words and the letters on the page. It is important that this learning not be pushed upon the child. Children will make this connection naturally and, in so doing, will experience reading as something that possesses joy, mystery, and excitement.

Jim Trelease compares the planting of a desire to read in a child with the kind of advertising done by McDonald's restaurants. McDonald's has achieved success by advertising so frequently that people become familiar with both the commercials and the characters within the commercials. Commercials, stop signs, billboards, newspapers, and other printed messages in the environment expose children to language. In themselves, these do not necessarily motivate children to want to learn to read. Trelease is concerned that the "commercials" for reading—frequently reading aloud to children—do not continue during the school years. Reading aloud should be a part of the everyday routine of children throughout their school lives. Yet, the frequency of reading books aloud to children decreases dramatically as children move up through the grades. By the time children graduate from high school, reading aloud has usually ceased to exist as a regular part of the school day.

Using Read-Aloud Books

In planning the read-aloud experience for children, consider how one can make the reading a fascinating and exciting experience. One need not be a professional storyteller to read aloud effectively. This skill can be achieved by attention and practice using voice, pace, and a flexible approach.

To begin, one can practice using different voice inflections, pitches, and volume levels. Knowing the story helps to determine when one should vary these elements. For example, one can lower the voice to a whisper at an exciting part of the action. One might even stop reading completely to allow the children to think about what is happening for a moment. Reading slowly helps the children use their imaginations to keep up with the story. Speeding up during certain parts where the action picks up can have them sitting on the edge of their seats.

TIPS FOR TEACHERS

Invite active or retired police officers, doctors, athletes, and firefighters to read stories aloud to children.

- A weaver could read *Abuela's Weave.*
- A farmer could read *Barnyard Banter.*
- A police officer could read *Tough Boris.*
- A health-care worker could read *Ten Little Babies.*
- Older students, program directors, and parents could read any book.

When the reader is excited about the story, the feeling is usually contagious. An enthusiastic reader provides a good role model for experiencing the fun of literature. Such enthusiasm can be achieved by carefully choosing the books to be read aloud. There is no substitute for selecting books that both the reader and the children like. Humorous books are good beginning choices because humor provides a built-in motivation. As reading aloud becomes a practice, varying story themes and plots will provide children with the opportunity to experience all types of literature including riddle books, poetry, and more serious stories.

Use the language of the read-aloud books to promote good language and language growth. Talk about some of the phrases and sentences the author uses. This encourages children to use language provided by good models. While good books can usually be read in their entirety, one should not be afraid to summarize or paraphrase some parts of the story so as to adjust a more difficult book to the audience, to recapture the children's interest, or to better assist the children in understanding a story.

Good Choices for Read-Alouds

Most children's picture books were meant to be read aloud. This does not mean, of course, that every picture book can be read aloud successfully. In addition to the usual criteria for selecting books for children, some additional elements might be considered for books to be read aloud.

The choice of a good read-aloud book will depend somewhat on the age of the children. Infants benefit from books with clear, colorful illustrations and little text. They also enjoy short, simple rhymes and poems. Large pictures and pictures of familiar scenes are enjoyed after the reading. Books that encourage the naming of objects, letters, and numbers are good selections because they often contain familiar sights and sounds.

Toddlers are ready for more sophisticated rhymes and stories. They especially like books with predictable repeated lines. They enjoy the feeling of mastery in joining in and saying the lines after the first couple of repetitions. For example, consider the story of "The Farmer in the Dell." As both a story and a song, its familiar lines are quickly mastered by the young child. *Fast Food! Gulp! Gulp!* by Bernard Waber provides a lively rhyming text that should appeal to toddlers. The story reflects the frantic pace of modern life in a fast-food metaphor. Patricia Hubbell's rhyming text in *Sea, Sand, Me!* depicts the happiness of a mother and a young girl out for a day at the beach. Rhyming stories about cats that will appeal to toddlers are *Come Here, Cleo!* by Caroline Mockford and *Cats, Cats, Cats!* by Leslea Newman. On the theme of making noise, toddlers will enjoy *Nora's Room* by Jessica Harper. Finally, toddlers will easily relate to all of the everyday activities portrayed in *Everywhere Babies* by Susan Meyers.

Toddlers also like books that describe mischievous antics of characters to whom they can relate. A sense of the absurd is found in many Dr. Seuss books. This type of humor is often an effective device for involving the independent two-year-old. Lois Lenski and Mercer Mayer have written several small books that toddlers feel are just their size. Many of their books are about cowboys and firefighters and other toddler favorites. Toddlers will relate to the concepts of being too small in Joyce Dunbar's *Tell Me What It's Like to Be Big,* of being ill in Teresa Bateman's *Farm Flu,* and having simple fun in Margaret Wild's *Midnight Babies.*

Preschoolers and kindergartners are ready for more involved plots and a wider range of themes. Humor is still a good choice. Arnold Lobel's *Frog and Toad Are Friends* creates a world where the humor is more subtle and where human nature shines through. Adventure stories become an area of interest at this age. An adventure story with a twist is Eugene Trivizas's *The Three Little Wolves and the Big Bad Pig,* an upside-down retelling of the traditional folktale. The humorous updating includes sledgehammers, pneumatic drills, and steel-reinforced concrete. Using repeated lines and phrases from the original,

Cover from *One Fine Trade* by Bobbi Miller. Jacket art copyright © 2009 by Will Hillenbrand. Reprinted by permission of Holiday House. All rights reserved.

the tale comes to a harmonious conclusion. *Tough Boris* by Mem Fox is an absolute treasure. It is an easy-to-read tale of Boris, a scruffy pirate who is tender enough to weep when his parrot dies. The book is filled with the pirate lore of buried treasure, thievery, and pirate adventures. Young children will identify with the story development through the illustrations. *One Fine Trade* by Bobbi Miller is based on an old folktale from the American South that young children will understand. Georgy trades one thing after another trying to get a silver dollar to buy his daughter a wedding dress. As the tale goes on, children will recognize the repeating line and join in with the reader before too long.

TIPS FOR TEACHERS

Plan how masks might be made from cereal boxes, paper plates, and plastic milk jugs.

- Have children design and decorate masks of their own design.
- Ask children to create a scene from the related story using masks and dialogue.
- Invite parents to come in to assist children with the creations.

Absurd and ridiculous humor will appeal to preschoolers and kindergartners in William Steig's *Toby, What Are You?* The story begins with Toby's father returning home to find Toby pretending to be a doormat, a banana sandwich, and other silly items. Translated from the French, *I Don't Want to go to School* by Stephanie Black has a great repeating phrase that will spark the involvement of the readers. In the story, little bunny Simon is fearful about going to school for the first time and shouts a repeating refrain throughout the book: "No Way!" He eventually does get to school, but when it is time to go home he has the last word when he shouts "No Way!" *Where's My Sock* by Joyce Dunbar also focuses on something lost. When Pippin the mouse and Tog the cat abandon their search for Pippin's lost sock, they both agree to wear mismatched socks for the day. A silly surprise ending is in store for the reader. *The Adventures of Bert* by Allan Ahlberg shares another side of silliness in stories about the home. The surprising and the absurd come to life when a young child's toy animals stretch to life size in Jane Cowen-Fletcher's *Farmer Will.* Often, the illustrations depicting the absurd activities of the story are critical. Two such stories for this age group are *Rattletrap Car* by Phyllis Root and *Fribbity Ribbit!* by Suzanne Johnson.

In *Fooling the Tooth Fairy* by Martin Burton, little Marty embarks on an adventurous plot to fool the tooth fairy with a fake tooth made from paper.

In this beautiful paper-cut book, Marty gets a surprise himself. In *Turkey Surprise* by Peggy Archer, two Pilgrim brothers set out on a hunting adventure to capture a turkey for the Thanksgiving feast. They return successfully with a live turkey, but one little pilgrim boy worries about what will happen to this turkey and cleverly saves the day. Readers will be laughing at the witty and charming watercolor illustrations by Thor Wickstrom in this Thanksgiving story for vegetarians. A nighttime adventure of the imagination is in store for readers in *Tiger Can't Sleep* by S. J. Fore. A boy cannot go to sleep at night out of fear that there is a tiger hiding in his closet . . . eating potato chips. Upon discovering that this imaginary tiger cannot get to sleep, the boy takes on the role of a comforting parent. There are many opportunities for voice modulation and sound effects here. The expressive comic illustration by R. W. Alley will keep everyone laughing throughout the telling. Other adventure stories running from the mild to the fantastic include *Alphabet Adventure* by Audrey Wood, *One Day, Daddy* by Frances Thomas, *The Dirty Little Boy* by Margaret Wise Brown, and *Full Moon* by Brian Wilcox and Lawrence David.

Identifying good read-aloud books is not a difficult task. Knowing the children is the first priority. The next is to use the criteria for good literature in selecting appropriate books. After identifying which books will best lend themselves to an exciting and enjoyable read-aloud experience, the reader must review them

Author Illustrator Thor Wickstrom. Photo credit Walter Sawyer.

to determine just how the story will be read. If this is not done, the reading will not be as effective as it could be and a good deal of potential will be wasted.

Becoming familiar with a large number of books is the best way to prepare oneself for read-aloud experiences. Having this knowledge of books will enable the reader to choose the right book at the right time for a read-aloud activity. The reader should always have a set of well-planned read-aloud books to use when the need arises. The special sharing that will occur as a result will be an effective "commercial" for reading. Read-alouds that do not possess an air of excitement run the risk of losing children to some other activity that may seem more interesting. Once their interest is lost, it may be difficult to bring these children back.

STORYTELLING

In most cultures throughout time, the **storyteller** was a valuable member of the community. In the preliterary world, storytellers were the keepers of the culture. They were both the newspaper of the present and the link to the people's past. They were often the honored guests of kings and queens. As literacy increased, storytellers lost some of their importance. In regions of the world with high illiteracy rates, storytellers continue to hold a position of esteem.

Good storytellers will always hold the power to enchant. They help us to reflect upon our lives, make us laugh, and make us cry. A professional storyteller

Storytelling connects the generations in a comfortable yet powerful manner.

is both a performing artist and a careful student of literature. Some specialize in a certain type of presentation, using a dialect, songs, or costumes from a particular region. Others focus on certain subject matter such as African tales, humor, or stories of the sea. They may combine some of these elements to create a new style unique to themselves.

How to Be a Storyteller

The skill and talent of professional storytellers are wonderful to see and hear. However, their services usually cannot be scheduled very frequently. Because almost anyone can become at least an amateur storyteller—the oral sharing of stories is an old tradition—it makes sense to learn some storytelling methods.

A story can be a shared activity.

One of the best ways to learn the craft of the storyteller is to hear how practicing storytellers go about their work. Aili Paal Singer, a New England storyteller, has a background in teaching, writing, and performing. Along with storytelling, she also works in theater and television. Her presentations include the use of puppetry, mime, and acting. She provides activities and materials designed to involve children in the stories.

Doug Lipman, another New England storyteller, also has a background in teaching, writing, and performing. In addition, he has been involved in music and working with children with disabilities. His presentations include a good deal of active participation and singing. The stories he presents often deal with the themes of African tales, Hasidism, equality of the sexes, and superheroes. He believes that stories should have real content and say something to us as human beings.

Aili Paal Singer, Storyteller

I like to tell stories that allow students to join me in acting out the characters and events. Children have often asked me to tell a story in which everyone in the class can participate.

Aili Paal Singer sets the scene for her African story with props such as a drum. Courtesy Diana Comer.

It isn't easy to find a ready made story that could offer parts for fifty-three people (two classes of twenty-five children, two teachers, and a storyteller). That is what I was looking for. Fortunately, I found one when I read the African folklore "The King's Drum" in *A Treasury of African Folklore by Harold Courlander* (Crown Publishers, 1975). Though I would retell it and adapt it, I knew it would work well with younger children. I proceeded to design and construct fifty-three masks out of colored construction paper of various weights: a lion, a monkey, a spider, leopards, giraffes, porcupines, elephants, and antelopes. I wanted the children to be able to watch everything without obstruction, so I chose to make the mask surround an opening for the face.

These designs were then adapted to more practical sized masks, for 8 1/2" by 11" paper, which I could give out as a follow-up art activity for students.

"What good is it to make a mask if you can't use it?" I asked myself. So, I sat down to write some little stories that could be read and acted out. They contained only the animal characters for which I had masks. These stories were included in my Program Guide for teachers as follow-up material.

Reprinted with permission from NOTES: THE KING'S DRUM © 1988, Aili Paal Singer.

Aili Paal Singer uses children with masks as an integral part of her stories. This participation can help the shy child take a more active role in a class. Courtesy Diana Comer.

Aili Paal Singer and the children become the story. Courtesy Diana Comer.

Characters: LIONS LEOPARDS PORCUPINES ANTELOPES GIRAFFES

The neighborhood was quiet and all the animals were asleep.

But the Lions began snoring with sounds loud and deep.

The Leopards woke up and began to complain.

The Porcupines called out, "You sound like a train!"

The Antelopes screamed, "Quiet down, please!"

The Giraffes jumped up startled, and ran to the trees.

They galloped with hooves pounding hard on the ground.

The Lions slept on without hearing a sound.

In the morning, they yawned, smiled and said.

"How nice it is to get a good night's sleep in one's bed."

When the families of Leopard, Porcupine, Antelope and Giraffe

Heard what the Lions said, they had a good laugh.

Reprinted with permission from THE QUIET NIGHT © 1988, Aili Paal Singer.

Characters: ANTELOPE FAMILY GIRAFFE

The Antelope family was taking a walk.

Giraffe was standing tall, eating the top leaves of a tree.

Antelope's children pointed to Giraffe.

They giggled and said.

"What a funny long neck and such skinny legs!"

Giraffe looked down and said,

"I see Lion coming down the path behind the tree."

He then ran away as fast as the wind.

Antelope's family leaped all the way home.

The next day, the Antelope family again took a walk.

Giraffe was eating the top leaves of a tree.

Antelope's children pointed to Giraffe.

They said, "What a fine long neck, and a great pair of legs!"

Reprinted with permission from ANTELOPE'S CHILDREN, © 1988, Aili Paal Singer.

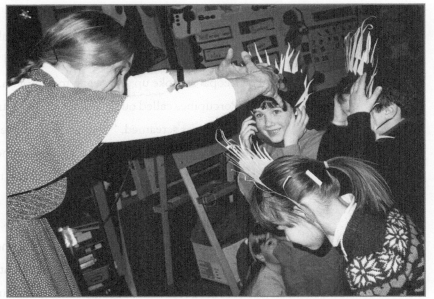

Aili Paal Singer demonstrates how to be a tree in a story by using the entire body to play the role. Courtesy Diana Comer.

Doug Lipman tells a story using voice, movement, and props.

Doug Lipman, Storyteller

Any story can be made into a participation story. In general, the audience may participate by joining in with their voices or with their bodies or by making suggestions.

Join in with the Voice

In the riddle story "In Summer I Die," the audience joins in verbally by repeating rhythmic, chant-like speech (e.g., "Mama, Mama, wake up, we're bored"). This is the easiest way to join in with the voice, because rhythmic speech has simpler, more predictable rhythms than normal speech. One step beyond rhythmic speech is singing; the only difference between rhythmic speech and song is the presence of melody. If teller and audience can be induced to sing, it adds to the fun and the mood. If one or the other is too shy, though, or the words are too minor to warrant melody, we may be better to chant than to give up on all rhythm.

Once the audience has heard a story or a phrase several times, listeners can join in by filling in missing words. To cue an audience for this, we can start a sentence they have heard before but stop before the end. Our gestures and face indicate that they are to continue. For example, the storyteller begins: *In summer I* . . . and stops, mouth open, gesture stopped midair, with an expression of expectancy; the audience chimes in: . . . die.

The position of the body can communicate feelings.

A special case of filling in words is filling in sound effects. For example, "we rang the doorbell, and it went . . . All these forms of verbal participation can be varied or intensified by saying them in different tones of voice, repeating them, or repeating them with additions, as in a cumulative story.

Join in with the Body

Younger children often find it less threatening to join in with movements than with words; older children and adults often find movements more threatening. Depending on the age of our audience, therefore, movements may become a tool for winning our audience or a sign that we have already succeeded in gaining their attention and trust.

Rhythmic movements, such as those to accompany the refrain "Mama, Mama, wake up, I'm bored," or the rhyme "In summer I die . . .," are a natural accompaniment to rhythmic speech. Simple miming of a motion, such as knocking on a door or shaking a sleeping person, can be added almost anywhere to snag the wandering attention of preschoolers. These actions become central to the story if they are repeated

Doug Lipman brings a story to a dramatic conclusion. Courtesy Diana Comer.

at different points with different feeling or with a sense of growing urgency or silliness.

Body participation can also include postures. For example, we could ask our audience to "show me how you'd sit if you were bored." Or: "How would you stand if you had just figured out the answer to Grandmother's riddle?" When we say things in a particular posture, by the way, it often affects our tone of voice.

The furthest extreme of body participation is to actually enact a part of the story. Enactment can be done by a whole group at once, all acting out one part after another, or by small groups or individuals taking on separate roles.

Make Suggestions

Up until now, we, the teller, have made all the choices, and the audience has been invited only to follow along. We can invite the audience to participate by adding their own point of view and giving suggestions. From the teller's perspective, the easiest suggestions to manage are "advisory only" suggestions that are not incorporated into the story. For example, we could ask, "What would you do if you were bored and no one else was awake?" After listening to a few answers, our story continues as planned all along. This allows audience members to express their thoughts and involves them internally in the situation the character faces. It encourages spontaneity from the audience and yet it allows the teller to preserve the carefully learned and rehearsed sequence of the story.

At the opposite extreme, we can throw open the gate of the story for the audience to find its own way through. A round-robin story is the result. The teller, of course, can still retain the role of shepherd:

"And what do you suppose we did, since we were so bored?"

Audience: watched TV.

"So we turned on the TV. What was on?"

Audience: Batman!

"Seeing Batman made us think of something in our backyard. What was it?"

Audience: our toy Batmobile.

"So we went outside to play in our toy Batmobile. But suddenly we saw something very useful. What do you think it was? . . ."

Between the extremes of no audience control and complete audience control, of course, there are still more middle positions. To give the audience some influence over the story, we can incorporate their suggestions into minor details. For example, we can ask what kind of a house we lived in. Were there steps leading up to the front door? What did we have to cross to get to our friend's house? These details can then be incorporated into the story immediately: "So we climbed down the steps, crossed the playground, waited for a green light, looked both ways, and then crossed the street." We must remember these details if they are relevant later: "Then we ran back with the icicles, waited for the green light, looked both ways, crossed the street, ran across the playground, and climbed back up the steps of our house."

The audience suggestions in "In Summer I Die" influence more of the plot than simple details would, but are still contained in a predictable framework. The choice of whom to wake up next stimulates a whole new cycle of waking, chanting, and reacting, but it loops us right back to the same point in the plot: "So we went to find someone else. . . ." The teller decides when to break out of that loop and go on to Grandmother.

A similar loop is repeated later, when the audience suggests what we saw next, and the teller helps compare it to the riddle: "A carrot! What a great idea. So we opened the refrigerator, pulled open the bottom drawer, and took out a carrot. Maybe this is it! Does it die in the summer? . . ." Again, the teller decides when to break out of that loop by taking us outdoors to play with the snow—and when to enter it again to guess outdoor things or the icicle itself.

A Balance of Participation

Any story can be made participatory simply by including some of the techniques described above. The teller's biggest job, though, is to find the right balance: too little participation, and a younger audience loses attention or we lose an opportunity for fun and feedback; too much, or the wrong kind of participation, and the story itself suffers. A story with too much participation feels "gimicky" and its central triumph becomes obscured. As adapters or creators of stories, we strive to choose the techniques of participation—and the places to use them—that will clarify a story's structure and events and heighten its emotional impact.

To choose well, we must be aware of all of our options. Voice, body, suggestions: these three words can remind us of the many choices we have.

Reprinted with permission from General Hints for Making Stories Participatory, © 1985, Doug Lipman.

Good Choices for Oral Storytelling

Almost any story that meets the criteria for good literature is a possibility for **oral storytelling**. It is important to be aware of the fact that this method of sharing is more difficult than reading aloud. In reading aloud, the readers can rely on the book to provide the language. In oral storytelling, readers must put some of themselves and their language into the presentation. The story must be a part of the storyteller's imagination. It would not be effective for one to forget the story at midpoint and to begin reading from the book. The spell of the storyteller would be broken.

It is best to select stories with clear, strong characters. This is especially true if one wishes the children to participate. The setting should be fairly simple in order for children to picture it in their imaginations. Stories with interesting narratives and lines for choral responses are good choices. When children

David Novak, "A Telling Experience." Courtesy David Novak, storyteller.

Reprinted with the permission of Simon & Schuster Books for Young Readers, an imprint of Simon & Schuster Children's Publishing Division from ANOTHER MOUSE TO FEED by Robert Kraus, pictures by Jose Aruego and Ariane Dewey. Illustrations copyright © 1980 Jose Aruego and Ariane Dewey.

are involved, they are more likely to continue following the story. Finally, the story should be fascinating to the storyteller so that it will generate a natural enthusiasm.

Most storytellers interpret a work before using it. This means that they make some decisions about what the story means, what it is useful for, and how this can be brought out in the telling. They make decisions concerning each character, such as the costumes, voice, and actions to be used. They make decisions about the length of time needed for the story, the portions of the story to be summarized or lengthened, and ways to increase the interest and value of the story. They also make decisions about the audience: the appropriateness of the story for the expected audience, the degree of audience participation planned, and the needs of the audience.

A number of storybooks can be learned and shared using oral storytelling. A good choice for toddlers and preschoolers is *Good Morning, Little Fox* by Marilyn Janovitz, in which Little Fox and Father Fox have fun doing chores while waiting for Mother Fox to return. Other choices on the theme of family relations are *Cat and Fish* by Joan Grant, *Big Pig and Little Pig* by David McPhail, *Another Mouse to Feed* by Robert Kraus, and *"Wait for Me!" Said Maggie McGee* by Jean Van Leeuwen.

Slightly older children will enjoy the telling of *Where the Big Fish Are* by Jonathan London and *Mr. Putter and Tabby Feed the Fish* by Cynthia Rylant. An excellent choice for using emotions in an oral storytelling voice is *Grunt* by

Children respond to stories through writing and pictures.

John Richardson. In this story, a skinny little pig is not like the others but learns that it is how you feel inside that's important.

TIPS FOR TEACHERS

Invite members of a community theater group to demonstrate oral storytelling.

- Show how different animal characters might move and talk.
- Combine actors and children in the telling of a story.
- Have actors involve children in demonstrating different uses of the voice in telling a story.
- Have actors demonstrate the use of facial expressions and hand gestures.

FLANNEL BOARD STORIES

A variation of storytelling is the **flannel board** story. A flannel board is a piece of wood or other rigid material covered with felt or flannel. Characters and objects cut from felt are placed on the flannel board to portray the visual action of the story as it is being told. Although the story may be read from a book, the additional task of manipulating pieces on the flannel board suggests that an oral presentation would be easier.

Flannel board stories can be easy and fun to make. A small group of adults can cut the necessary pieces for several stories in a short work session. Once made, they are available for years. The story can be adapted to different age groups by simplifying or elaborating on the plot. New pieces can be added for new plot twists. An alternative to a flannel board is a Velcro storyboard. It can be used like a flannel board, but uses Velcro strips for adhesion. Real objects or props created for the story can be adhered to the board when Velcro dots are attached to them.

Making Flannel Board Materials

The basic components for flannel board stories are the flannel board itself and the pictures of the characters and other objects involved in the story that are to be placed on the flannel board.

Flannel board. Although they can be purchased commercially, flannel boards are relatively easy to make in a variety of sizes and shapes. First, the backing is cut from thick cardboard, plywood, masonite, acrylic plastic, or any other flat, rigid material. It is then covered with either flannel or felt. In addition to a square flannel board shape, one might consider a teepee or tent design.

Two separate boards can be joined at the top or a single board can be folded over. This design provides two flannel board surfaces, allowing a story scene to remain in place over time if desired. A three-sided design provides even more flexibility. If space is limited, one might wish to consider a window-shade flannel board. The shade is covered with the flannel and mounted with brackets on a wall. The wall provides the rigid surface. Animal-shaped flannel boards lend a whimsical touch. They might be used for units involving a variety of animal books.

Characters and Objects. The pictures used on the flannel board can come from a variety of sources. Sets of flannel board objects, characters, letters, and numbers can be purchased commercially. Such a set may be a good basis upon which to build a collection of additional characters and objects. The most common material from which to make the pieces is felt. It is thicker and sturdier than flannel, though the latter is often used. Other materials such as clothes dryer softener sheets, sandpaper, Velcro, and double-faced carpet tape can also be used. Pictures that are hand colored, painted, or cut from magazines and other pieces of felt can be glued to flannel or felt pieces as well. Children are very forgiving of our less-than-professional artistic skills, so do not be afraid to create your own materials.

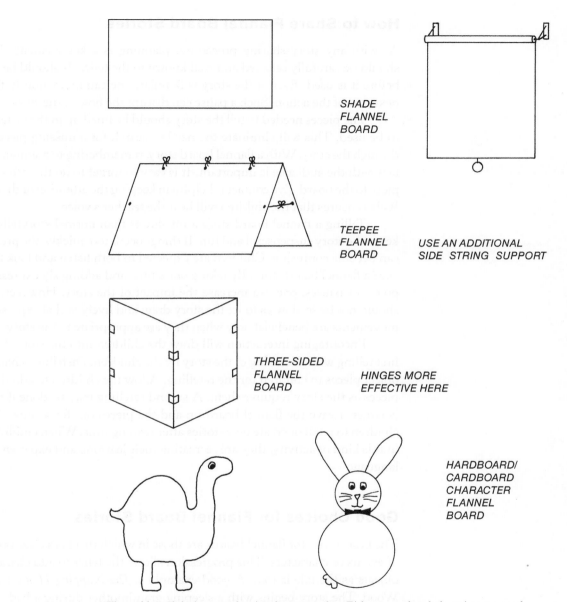

SHADE
FLANNEL
BOARD

TEEPEE
FLANNEL
BOARD

USE AN ADDITIONAL
SIDE STRING SUPPORT

THREE-SIDED
FLANNEL
BOARD

HINGES MORE
EFFECTIVE HERE

HARDBOARD/
CARDBOARD
CHARACTER
FLANNEL
BOARD

Flannel board designs can be simple or complex. Either way, they belong in every early childhood classroom. Courtesy Diana Comer.

A flannel board story library will eventually emerge. The pieces required for a particular book and a copy of the book can be stored together in a plastic storage bag or a heavy envelope. In this way, flannel board stories can be used without the need to collect or make the necessary pieces each time the story is shared.

How to Share Flannel Board Stories

As with any story-sharing procedure, planning is a key element. The story should be carefully selected and well known to the teller. It should be reviewed before it is used. Even if the story is familiar, one can momentarily forget the next part of the action. Such a pause can disrupt the flow of the story.

The pieces needed to tell the story should be lined up in the order they are to be used. This will eliminate the need to search for a missing piece halfway through the story. With a flannel board story, remembering to maintain eye contact with the audience is important. It is easy to forget to do this after adding a piece to the board. Eye contact is helpful in keeping the attention of the children. It also ensures that the children will hear the teacher's voice.

Telling a flannel board story a bit slower than normal storytelling speed keeps the story suspenseful and fun. If things occur too quickly, the presentation can become confusing. Children are expected to both listen and look to experience a flannel board story. By taking one's time and adding sly expressions and poignant pauses, one can increase the impact of the story. However, the pace should not be so slow as to let the story drag; and lively verbal expressions and movements are beneficial only when they are appropriate to the story.

Encouraging interaction will draw the children into the story. Follow the first telling with a retelling of the story by the children. Distribute character and object pieces to children for the retelling. Allow the children to add the correct pieces as the story requires them. A second retelling may be done if the group is larger. Leave the flannel board up and the pieces out for a time. Allow the children to retell or create new stories after reading time. When children engage in this kind of activity, they are recreating their learning and experiencing their language.

Good Choices for Flannel Board Stories

The best stories for flannel boards are those in which there is a clear progression of events or characters. This progression allows the teller to add characters and objects as the tale is told. A good example is *The Napping House* by Audrey Wood. The story begins with a sleeping grandmother during a bad storm. As the action progresses, she is joined in the cozy bed by an assortment of other characters. The beautifully illustrated book contains a wonderful surprise ending. One might wish to follow up the reading of the book with an oral retelling using a flannel board. Children delight in the hands-on fun of adding characters to the bed.

If You Take a Mouse to the Movies by Laura Numeroff lends itself to a flannel board retelling because each page builds humorously on the preceding

Late for School! By
Stephanie Calmenson with
illustrations by Sachiko
Yoshikawa. Illustrations
copyright © 2008 by Sachiko
Yoshikawa. Reprinted with
the permission of Carolrhoda
Books, a division of Lerner
Publishing Group, Inc. All
rights reserved. No part of
this excerpt may be used or
reproduced in any manner
whatsoever without the prior
written permission of Lerner
Publishing Group, Inc.

Author Stephanie
Calmenson. Courtesy
Stephanie Calmenson.

page. The absurdity of the situation maintains the humor and interest of children. The sequence of getting dirtier and dirtier while playing outside with a human playmate is almost made for a flannel board in *Mucky Ducky* by Sally Grindley. The repeating refrain of "Oh, you Mucky Ducky!" is great fun for all to jump in and participate in the storytelling. Readers will enjoy participating in the repeating refrains of Leslie Helakoski's farm story *Big Chickens Go to Town.* When the chickens jump into the back of the farmer's truck to get at a bag of feed, they are startled when the truck starts and they are whisked off to town. A whacky adventure ensues, with some scary close calls, but they get back to the farm safely. Other stories in this series include the original *Big Chickens* and *Big Chickens Fly the Coop.* With Eric Carle's *10 Little Rubber Ducks,* a flannel board can be used to tell the story while teaching directional words, numbers, and colors. The tale is based on an actual event in which a large number of toy rubber ducks fell from a ship and drifted for miles. Continuing with the duck character, *Quack!* by Phyllis Root can be used with even younger children. Using simple cutouts of flannel, the story depicts ducklings from egg to hatching to swimming using sweet pictures and a catchy rhythm.

Usually it is kids who are late for school. In *Late for School* by Stephanie Calmenson, it is Mr. Bungles the teacher who is late. As the story progresses, the reader follows the riotous adventure as Mr. Bungles goes from one form of transportation to another in his attempt to get to school, all of which can be added to the flannel board at the right time. Using an old rhyme, Ted Arnold creates a familiar-sounding story well suited to flannel board retelling in *No More Jumping on the Bed.* The tale follows a jumper going from apartment to apartment in a series of humorous situations. Turning the flannel board so that the longer side is vertical for the retelling would add to the foolishness of the situation. The concepts of nutrition, overeating, and self-control can all be explored in *More Pies* by Robert Munsch, which lends itself well to a flannel board. Samuel is a hungry little boy who enters a pie eating contest after eating a huge breakfast. When he queasily returns home his mother tells him that she has made him pies for lunch. At that point, he realizes his mistake and that leads to a mischievous surprise ending.

Strega Nona by Tomie dePaola can make a hilarious flannel board story. In this book, Big Anthony attempts to use Strega Nona's magic pasta pot. Not knowing how to control the magic, he quickly lets things get out of hand. Pasta ends up everywhere. White felt pieces with white yarn "spaghetti" glued on should provide a good picture of the problem on a flannel board. Animal figures can be used to illustrate each attempt to get the baby to stop crying in Cressida Cowell's *What Shall We Do with the Boo-hoo Baby?* Cutouts of a paper bag, a teacup, and different family members can be used to illustrate different

solutions to the problem in *Hiccup Snickup* by Melinda Long. The construction of a building from the basement up can be depicted using the story *The Lot at the End of My Block* by Kevin Lewis. Alphabet letters can be used to tell the story of *Waffle* by Chris Raschka.

Usually one can tell on a first reading whether a book will make a good flannel board story. The best stories are those in which characters and objects are added gradually. Their addition should be closely related to the problem the plot is exploring. If nothing is added or removed as the story goes along, the flannel board is little more than a still picture.

THEATRICAL STORYTELLING

Everyone likes to see a show performed onstage. The excitement surrounding a performance creates a magic of its own. Even if done on a very small scale, it is a special event. Using a theatrical performance also provides an opportunity to teach children the schema, or procedure, for going to the theater. Before a performance begins, the children can practice the roles of ticket sellers, ushers, announcers, concession stand clerks, and audience.

There are several possible avenues for telling a story using a theatrical framework. The two explored here are puppetry and creative dramatics. Each has strengths and drawbacks. Each works best with a different type of story.

Puppetry

Most children love **puppets**. They are an enjoyable and easy way to enhance or interpret a story for children. Infants, of course, may not quite know what to make of a puppet the first time they see one. If presented with slow, deliberate movements and a soft voice, however, puppets are usually welcome additions to a young child's surroundings.

Puppets can be safe imaginary friends. Most adults and children seem to respond instinctively to them. Shy children will often speak to a puppet before they will speak to an unknown person. Children know that the puppet is not real. They know that it is the person holding the puppet who is actually speaking. Yet the puppet has a reality of its own. Children speak to the puppet without reservation. They don't have to talk as though they are talking to the adult holding the puppet.

Puppets are allowed to be all of the things that people might like to be at times. They can be naughty, silly, brave, and mean. Perhaps that is why children speak to puppets so freely; they feel that puppets will accept them because they understand about not being perfect.

TIPS FOR TEACHERS

Ask parents to donate any puppets they are no longer using at home.

- Use a puppet to tell a story with you.
- Have students talk to each other through the puppets.
- Provide puppets during free play to encourage language play and the re-creation of stories.

Because puppets make such good friends, it makes sense to use them in a variety of story-sharing activities. Purple monster puppets can help teach the color purple. A monkey puppet can motivate, comment, and ask questions when H. A. and Margaret Rey's books about Curious George the monkey are used. If it seems appropriate, puppets can tell some stories. This is especially true for fables, since they usually have only two or three characters.

How to Use Puppets. There are no specific rules for using puppets. They can be used to motivate, tell the story, or take part in the story. It is mostly a matter of the teacher trying a variety of procedures and learning what is comfortable. One of the best ways to continue enthusiasm for puppets is to use a variety of puppet types. Although puppets can always be purchased commercially, some of the most interesting ones are homemade.

Finger puppets are easily constructed from the cut-off fingers of a glove. Facial features can be painted or glued on. Stick puppets are simple and easy to make as well. The puppet can be a photograph or drawing of a character glued onto a stick. Even a story with several characters can be converted to puppets by using child-created pictures or pictures made with a photocopier. The sticks used can be tongue depressors, craft sticks, straws, rulers, or sticks found in the yard.

String puppets are usually made by older children, but even younger ones enjoy making simple versions of these puppets. They are two-dimensional or three-dimensional puppets connected with two or more strings to crossed sticks. For more sophisticated designs, the sticks are held above the puppet. The sticks and strings control the puppet's body parts. Rag dolls can be used as well.

Effectively using puppets requires a knowledge of things one should not do with puppets. Do not try to be a ventriloquist. When not done expertly, ventriloquism is distracting. Do not use too much body movement. Enthusiasm is important, but too much hand waving detracts from the words of the puppet.

SOCK PUPPETS
*Old socks find new life
as puppets!*

BAG PUPPETS
*Brown or colored bags
are fine.*

PAPER ROLL PUPPETS
*Paint or decorate with colored
paper and crayon. Plastic wiggle
eyes and bits of trim look good!*

STICK PUPPETS
*Use straws, sticks, rulers,
and more. Fun is in store.*

GLOVE PUPPETS
*Five Little Pumpkins or any story
looks good on a hand.*

FINGER PUPPETS
*Cut-off gloves, paper rings,
foam balls . . .*

Puppet designs need not be complicated. A simple puppet can make a story memorable.
Courtesy Diana Comer.

Do not distribute puppets to children without planning and guidance. The puppets will simply become toys to fight over. Do not expect puppets to do it all. Most stories require a combination of puppets and a narrator. Do not be afraid to take risks with new and different kinds of puppets. Children tend to be uncritical of puppets, even when one doesn't work out as well as expected. The audience usually loves the show before it begins.

Beginning Puppetry. Trying anything new can make one anxious. Becoming accustomed to using puppets is no exception. Start small, build confidence in your ability, and then expand. Encourage children to explore the range of possibilities for using puppets, too.

Begin by seating the children in front of a mirror so that they can see both the puppet and themselves. Practice emotions by having the puppet look sad while saying, "I lost my favorite teddy bear." Make the puppet look angry while saying, "I'll NEVER go to bed until I'm 200 years old!" Get used to the idea of puppets handling dialogue by using two play telephones.

Give one to the puppet and have the children take turns using the other. Allow the script to emerge spontaneously. Have a puppet on one phone and a child on the other. Another way to become comfortable with puppet dialogue is to have the puppet lead a game such as Simon Says. Use motions at first and then follow up with lines such as "Simon says, 'Say meatball' . . . Simon says, 'Say curly caterpillar.'"

The children will expand the possibilities with the right coaching. For example, have several children each hold a puppet at snack time. Explain that each puppet must take a turn commenting on the snack and answering questions asked by the other puppets. Experiment with other scenarios: discussions about playground behaviors, getting in line, and so on. When all are comfortable with their skills, it is time to use puppets to tell and re-create stories.

Good Choices for Puppetry. The best kinds of stories for puppet presentations are those with a simple plot and only a few main characters. Because stage settings can be difficult, a few simple props must make the story a reality for the children. *The Carrot Seed* by Ruth Krauss makes a good puppet show. The boy, the sun, the rain, and the ever-growing carrot are all that are needed. Any boy puppet would do. A paper-plate sun, a hand-drawn rain cloud, and a real carrot would complete the primary roles. The real carrot can be pushed up from behind the stage as the story unfolds. Cutout shapes of the sun and the cloud, with mouths and eyes drawn on, can become starring characters.

In Gerald McDermott's *Raven: A Trickster Tale from the Pacific Northwest,* the main character steals the sun from the sky chief so that it can be given to the earth people. This Native American myth from the Northwest can be told with puppets of the raven, the sky chief, and the sun chief's daughter. Props such as a bright red ball for the sun could also be used. As a related project, children could make stick puppets and retell the story at home. The theme of stubbornness can be explored using a series of puppets to depict the main character in *Ella Kazoo Will Not Brush her Hair* by Lee Fox. A new puppet can be used to depict the ever longer disheveled hair of Ella and colors can be changed to depict the

© Cengage Learning

The natural world can be a source of possible puppet characters.

changing moods. The story reaches a satisfying conclusion when Ella recognizes and solves her problem on her own.

In *The Great Kapok Tree* by Lynne Cherry, a variety of tropical rainforest animals can be created for a group retelling with puppets. One by one the animals appear, pleading with the ax-man to spare their rainforest home. The tale ends on an environmentally appropriate note. Since the rainforest is full of animals, each child can have a part in a whole group retelling.

Tomie dePaola's *Charlie Needs a Cloak* is a superb story for a puppet presentation. It is the story of a shepherd who finds that his old faithful cloak is too tattered and worn to keep him warm in the winter anymore. He spends the following spring and summer shearing, spinning, weaving, dyeing, and sewing wool into a new cloak. By the following autumn he is ready to face the winter in a new warm red cloak. The story can be told with a boy puppet, one or two sheep puppets, and a few scraps of yarn and fabric. A story that presents similar themes of weaving and making cloth, *Weaving the Rainbow* by George Ella Lyon, can also be told through puppetry. In this tale, a young woman goes through the process of shearing, dyeing, spinning, and weaving to create a piece of artwork.

Denise Fleming's book, *Barnyard Banter,* will delight your children as an interactive puppet story. In the story, all the farm animals make their unique sounds from the appropriate locations. Cows moo in the barn and crows caw in the cornfield. Wolf puppets and a couple of simple props can be used to portray the humorous career decisions in *Max, the Stubborn Little Wolf* by Marie-Odile Judes.

Finger puppets help to tell a story. Courtesy Diana Comer.

Another animal book for puppetry is *Hunwick's Egg* by Mem Fox. Hunwick, the unusual main character of this story, is an old Australian bandicoot, a ratlike animal that carries its young in a pouch and eats insects and vegetables. The plot involves Hunwick finding a curious egg, not knowing what kind of egg it is, and waiting until it hatches to find out. Simple stick puppets could be used to depict the flustered sets of parents and their little ones in *Nighty Night!* by Margaret Wild. The story involves the age-old problem of settling excited children down for the night.

Creative Dramatics

According to Sawyer and Leff (1982), **creative dramatics** is only a bit more structured than puppetry. This type of drama is not designed for the production of a play for an audience. Rather, it is a more spontaneous process aimed at communicating some message, emotion, or story using dramatic techniques. It seeks to increase sensitivity to the feelings of others, to build positive self-concepts, to increase confidence and concentration, to provide new relationships, and to build an appreciation of the arts. Creative dramatics includes pantomime, mime, and acting to create and re-create ideas and stories.

Why is drama such a powerful tool? Why is it so effective for helping children develop language and an understanding of themselves? Drama is a natural activity for most children. Their play is often a suspension of reality that allows them to explore the possibilities of their environments. When children delve into dramatic play, they cross the line between reality and fantasy. Yet they are still aware of reality. This allows children to become astronauts, dinosaur hunters, parents, and buildings. Because it is play, children can easily move among

© Cengage Learning

Masks can play a role in creative dramatics.

the roles of cowboy, firefighter, and medical doctor. They possess a total belief in their roles at the moment they are in those roles. Such an emotional commitment is achieved because of the child's attention and focus when involved in dramatic play.

How to Use Creative Dramatics. The guiding rule for using creative dramatics is to keep things simple. This rule applies to dialogue, characters, setting, and plot. In contrast to puppetry, a creative dramatics format can include everyone.

Each child is not a main character, but each can be included as a fourth little pig, another stepsister, or as one of the sheep in a story. Everyone can help move furniture props, paint a chimney for a Santa Claus story, and bring in old clothes for costumes. If everyone is emotionally involved, the effort and enthusiasm will be contagious.

The **dialogue** may be created or spontaneous. If a chorus line is to be repeated several times, have a group of children do it rather than just a single child. The group will provide security for its members. Use a narrator if needed to help the dialogue flow more smoothly.

Costumes can give a feeling of importance to children taking part in the drama. Costumes can be real clothing, old Halloween outfits, yard sale leftovers, and old uniforms. They are relatively easy to collect, and any classroom can quickly accumulate an adequate variety. Help children use their imaginations in using costumes. They need not find the entire outfit to play the role. An old army hat and a dark jacket make an airline pilot. A hat with ears attached, brown mittens, and a piece of rope can make a cat. A white shirt and a headband with a round silver foil disc create a doctor's outfit. With just these bits and pieces of costumes, imagination will do the rest.

Settings should be simple. If scenery is absolutely essential, a single sheet can be painted or drawn on with markers for a backdrop. Small setting pieces can be cut out of cardboard and painted. They may be freestanding or simply leaned against a chair or a wall.

Props are objects needed to help tell the story. They may be pails, brooms, chairs, crowns, and food items. Props should be minimal and need not be real objects. Play telephones or bananas cut from yellow construction paper work just as well as the real thing. Follow the lead of the children. They will spontaneously engage in dramatic play with the barest of props.

Good Choices for Creative Dramatics. Mother Goose stories and nursery rhymes make a great introduction to creative dramatics. They can be portrayed quite easily with a minimum of costumes and props. Poems and songs can be dramatized with a minimum amount of preparation.

Good possibilities for dramatization include stories with many parts or groups of characters, enabling varying numbers of children to be involved in the experience. Humorous stories and stories with action and suspense make good choices. *Corduroy* by Don Freeman is a wonderful story about a bear searching for a friend. The book has roles that are expandable, since the setting is a department store. It has a great ending and makes a good play. The classic *Another Mouse to Feed* by Robert Kraus is another fine choice.

Cloudy with a Chance of Meatballs by Judi Barrett is a funny book that could become a great play. The story takes place in a land where it rains various kinds of food. Naturally, something goes wrong and a solution to the problem must be found. In one part of the land, it rains meatballs as big as basketballs.

Quick and easy stage settings can be created using a sheet placed over a pole (top) or attached to a rope with clothespins (bottom). Courtesy Diana Comer.

"Book Cover" from GIANT MEATBALL, copyright © 2008 by Robert Weinstock, reproduced by permission of Houghton Mifflin Harcourt Publishing Company.

Staying with the meatball theme is *Giant Meatball* by Robert Weinstock. This offbeat humorous story introduces readers to a somewhat unlikable meatball bully who fails to see what's coming. He finally gets his comeuppance when the townspeople invite him to a . . . spaghetti dinner.

Make-believe meatballs, dropping out of a net from the ceiling, could be made from balloons covered with brown paper. The story would not soon be forgotten.

Legends, fairy tales, and folktales make good plays because they combine magic, mystery, and action. A contemporary story for dramatization, which has the feel of a light folktale, is *One More Egg* by Sarah Burg. In this tale, a bespectacled bunny approaches a very young chicken and asks for an egg. Responding that she cannot provide an egg, she does take the bunny on a tour of the farmyard.

They meet many other animals who also cannot provide an egg, but they tell what they can do. Finally they meet another chicken who can give the bunny an egg but demands to know what it is for. Young readers will be proud of solving this mystery.

Current children's literature has much to offer as well. Many stories meet the requirements for creative dramatics: appropriate numbers of characters, simple plots, memorable dialogue, and few prop requirements. *Little Quack's New Friend* by Lauren Thomson can be dramatized indoors by five or six children. Little Quack wants to play with a frog he meets, but his four siblings are wary. One by one, the others join in. Repetitive phrasing and silly sound effects keep everybody involved. The youngest children will enjoy acting out all or parts *of My Steps* by Sally Derby both individually and in a small group with only a few props needed (blanket, paper, crayons). This story features an African American child going through the tiny events that make up a day of make believe. Another story for dramatizing that also features an African American child is *Glo Goes Shopping* by Cheryl Hudson, in which a child shops for just the right birthday gift for a friend. Younger children will also be enthralled by *Wiggle Giggle Tickle Train* by Nora Hilb and Sharon Jennings. In thirteen stunning spreads by artist Nora Hilb, readers see how the world around them can inspire their creative play. The book features rhythmic poetry, play, and imagination. Only three characters are needed to act out the story of *The Grandmother Doll* by Alice Bartels. A few toy props will help to make this a fun playtime activity. A warm story that slightly older children might enjoy portraying is *Feeding the Sheep* by Leda Schubert. Day to day, season to season, Mom tends, feeds, and shears the sheep. Her little girl watches, and finally inquires "What are you doing?" That's when they make the tasks their joint enterprise while growing closer together.

Content can be easily incorporated into the dramatization. Many tales set in other cultures provide a natural base to learn about those cultures. The Native American Passamaquoddy culture of northern New England is the setting for *Thanks to the Animals* by Allen Sockabasin. As the cold weather arrives, a Passamaquoddy family migrates north to their winter home on a bobsled. On the way, Zoo Sap the baby falls out of the sled. The baby's cries alert the animals and they form a warm protective nest until Zoo Sap's father comes back for him. Information about the Passamaquoddy culture and the names of the animals are included. Another book concerning animals that can involve younger children in the dramatization is *What We Do* by Reg Cartwright. As children learn about animals creeping, leaping, and playing, they can repeat the rhyming sentences that introduce them.

TIPS FOR TEACHERS

Respond positively to children's attempts to re-create favorite stories through drama.

- Watch and listen attentively as children re-create a scene from a story for you.
- Say, "What a wonderful story you just told. I really enjoyed the story all over again."
- Say, "That was a very scary bear you created."

Dramatic play is spontaneous. Creative dramatics takes some planning, but it can be done more spontaneously than putting on a play. The line between the two can be wide and hazy. This type of drama is supportive of children's efforts and is a memorable experience for them. The positive results of a dramatic experience are well worth the effort. Children learn much about life from the pretend situations found in books and made real through creative dramatics. They get to act out their feelings and experiment with their reactions to situations. Creative dramatics gives a shy child the opportunity to safely take some risks, while allowing the aggressive child to take on the role of a shy character. By seeing themselves in new roles, children ultimately learn more about themselves.

CHILDREN AS AUTHORS, STORYTELLERS, AND ILLUSTRATORS

Children are beginning to write as soon as they begin to draw. They are attempting to make sense of their world through some type of visual process. Some children seem to have more to say than others. Some children seem to be more creative than others. All children, however, have something to say and have a variety of ways of saying it. Their expression is to be encouraged. Adults must be accepting of children's attempts at writing. If willingness to take risks is destroyed, growth as authors and storytellers will be damaged as well.

Children's creativity is often overlooked. The goal of writing has long seemed to be to have children spell, punctuate, and print correctly. Unfortunately, focusing on the mechanics of writing has had negative results. Children whose papers are returned full of red correction marks are most likely to write shorter, less interesting pieces in the future. Focusing on mechanics also obscures the more important aspects of writing such as clarity, organization, and a freshness of thinking. Some of this is changing as language research and literature-based approaches

Authorship can be both an individual or shared activity.

to literacy emerge. They reinforce the underlying principle that meaning and communication are the driving forces behind children's efforts to use language.

Stimulating experiences are beneficial to children as authors and storytellers. Exposure to quality art, either through books or in museums and galleries, provides new ideas to think about and talk about. As these opportunities are increased, the potential for intellectual growth is increased as well. Writing and storytelling are thinking activities. The ability to engage in them depends upon one's ability to analyze, question, organize, generate, and reorganize facts and reality. Yet no two people see things in exactly the same way. The following child-dictated stories illustrate how children can take a single topic and come up with several different stories about it.

JUNGLE STORY by Marissa and Megan (Becker Day-Care Center) One day there was an alligator and he was getting a suntan. He got a purple suntan and he put apples on it. His mother got a crab and pinched him. He put a bandaid on it. He laid in bed for a nap. The end.

JUNGLE STORY by Dania and Mellissa (Becker Day-Care Center) One day we went to the jungle. We saw an elephant. He was eating grass. His mommy said to eat snacks and juice and junk. We also saw a hippo and a lion and they were fighting each other. They scratched and they were licking each other. The end.

JUNGLE STORY by Elizabeth and Bryan (Becker Day-Care Center) One day we saw a leopard and a snake. They were eating grass. The leopard was jumping and he saw something and he started to roar. It was a bumblebee who stung him and he bit the bumblebee and he ate the bumblebee up. The snake did go in the water to get a drink of water. The end.

How to Encourage Children as Authors

Children usually have something to say that they feel is important, although sometimes they are reluctant to say it. Providing rich experiences will help keep children's minds active and will help them to construct new meanings and new stories. Because many young children are able to use more language than they can write, an adult can serve as transcriber and facilitator for their stories. These stories can take a variety of forms. Children tell, expand, respond, and create with paint, clay, puppets, and toys well before they encounter writing.

Encourage children to join the community of authors by helping them to know the authors of the books they enjoy. Invite local children's authors to come in to read their work and talk about ideas for stories. Many children's book authors have Websites with information and answers to questions. Libraries have reference books with short biographies about authors. Professional education literature in the field of literacy often includes interviews with children's book authors. Sharing information about an author can be done in conjunction with the reading of that author's books. The following interview provides an example of the information that can make the concept of creating a story approachable:

Charlotte Agell, Author and Illustrator

Author/Illustrator Interview

Author/illustrator Charlotte Agell. Photo credit: Walter Sawyer.

WS: Can you tell me a little bit about how you became an author and illustrator of books for young children?

CA: When I was three years old, my family emigrated from Sweden to Canada. I did not speak any English at the time, so my mother helped me to learn English by reading books and going to the library all the time. I remember telling my mother at a very young age that I wanted to live in the country, have horses, and write and illustrate children's books when I grew up. The horses part never came true. I grew up in Canada and Hong Kong, but we always went back to an island in Sweden in the summer. There were no kids or television around, so I filled my time by making up stories. I often used my impression of the places and countries I had been in my stories.

WS: Where do you get the ideas you use to write your stories?

Book cover from *Dancing Feet*. Text and illustrations copyright © 1994 by Charlotte Agell. Used with the permission of the author.

Book cover from *I Swam with the Seals*. Text and illustrations copyright © 1995 by Charlotte Agell. Used with the permission of the author.

CA: From everywhere, even from something little. There is an old Swedish adage that says, "Find a button, sew a coat." Take *Dancing Feet* for example. A friend had painted a picture of feet. It suggested more than just feet to me. Later I got a rhythm stuck in my head. You know how you sometimes get a song in your head and you can't get rid of it? I decided to put that incessant rhythm to use. As a result, when you read the story, you should get a sense of the rhythm in the language. *I Swam with a Seal* is based on a personal experience. I actually did swim with a very large seal once, though not intentionally. I was in the ocean, and noticed the seal nearby. It stayed nearby and I had the feeling that it was observing me. It gave me the idea to write a story about how we might look to animals.

WS: What are your thoughts about the words, the rhythms, and the language that you use in your books?

CA: It has to be fun to hear and it has to be engaging. It doesn't have to rhyme, but it has to sound good when it is read aloud. I always read my work out loud to myself as I am writing. I think I read aloud in my head. It's like having a personal editor who tells me if it is working or not working. When dealing with just a few words, like you do in a picture book, each word has to be exactly right.

WS: What do you see as the key relationships between the language and the illustrations in a book for young children?

CA: The pictures have their own life, but they have to tell the same story. I think Barbara Cooney once said that the story is like the strand and the pictures are like the pearls. Many of my ideas come from pictures, but ultimately the words have to tell the story. I feel lucky to be able to illustrate my work because I have a picture of the story in my mind and I can work toward that.

WS: What are the challenges a writer faces when writing a story that will appeal to young children?

CA: People who write for children are often writing for themselves. Still, eavesdropping on children is critical. You can't write down to them and you can't be condescending. Kids will catch you. There is nothing worse than preaching. Kids learn language by playing with it. The author has to do this as well. You can't be trite. You have to go out there and risk something.

WS: Do you spend time with young children, or do you try to observe them in order to get a sense of their world?

CA: Yes. I have kids and I'm fortunate to have a local niece and nephew. Also, I teach middle school kids.

WS: Which of your books do you particularly like? Do you have a favorite one?

CA: Kids ask me that all the time. It is always the one I am working on at the moment. It is the one that I am active in the process of writing. I am fond of the product, the books that are published, but it's the process of writing that I really like.

Classroom Books. A **classroom book** is a good beginning activity. It is particularly appropriate after the class has shared a common experience. The experience could be a walk to the firehouse, a visit from a pet rabbit, or a simple science demonstration. Each child draws a picture depicting the experience. After the picture is completed, the child tells about the picture. The teacher writes, at the bottom of the picture, a brief sentence or key phrase that the child has stated. All of the illustrations and the writing are bound, glued, or stapled together to form a book. The book can be shared over the next few days. This activity conveys the message that children have something important to say and are authors who write books.

A related activity involves the previously described language–experience approach (LEA). The LEA uses the child's own language to teach beginning reading and writing. Using the LEA, the adult encourages the children to generate their own stories, which the adult writes for them. The basis for the story might be an experience the class has shared, a story they have heard, or their imaginations. The story usually has a time frame and possesses many of the characteristics of literature.

Frequently LEA stories are written on large sheets of poster paper so that they can be made into "Big Books." Children draw the illustrations for the various pages. They also illustrate their book by pasting pictures on the pages. The story is then shared. The teacher points to each word as it is read. Often the story has a repeated line. When this occurs, children begin to recognize or anticipate the line and join in the reading.

The mechanics of constructing these classroom books are important. The books should be sturdy, so that children will be able to handle them repeatedly. Oaktag or cardboard covers can be used to protect the pages. Clear contact paper on each of the pages protects them over a long period of time. The pages are best bound with yarn or cord to keep them together. Finally, the printing should be done in large manuscript lettering. Typing the words on a computer with a large font can produce good lettering. Photo albums with clear magnetic pages are a commercial alternative to having the children construct their own books.

Good Choices for Child-Created Stories

Making books builds self-confidence and a sense of mastery over language. It may be done using the LEA. It may also be done on an individual or small-group basis. Children often have many things to tell about, and adults can suggest various themes as well. For example, ABC books, counting books, and concept books can be created by individual youngsters or groups of children. The following stories were created, illustrated, and acted out by small groups of children on the concept of spring.

Theme: What Happens in Spring? Charles, David, Jackie, and Marci: "Daffodils grow. It starts to rain. The bees come out and sting you. An elephant at the zoo jumps on you. The Easter Bunny brings eggs and toys. He brings you rabbit candy and chocolate eggs."

Eli, Justin, Erica, and Elizabeth: "In spring, wear spring jackets. Or wear an eagle shirt that says something about a motorcycle. Or wear a Minnie Mouse shirt. Bunnies are funny. I like birds. My favorite is a blue bird. There are blue and white flowers by some trees. I had a dream last night about some yellow flowers that are supposed to grow in spring."

Ryan, Danielle, Ben, and Stacie: "Birds eat worms. They love worms. Bunnies and chickies come out. Easter bunnies hide baskets on tables and behind couches. Sometimes you write on paper when it's spring. Yellow flowers grow in sunshine. Sometimes flowers talk. Sometimes birds take care of worms. Trees begin to get food because they're hungry. Leaves grow."

Reprinted with permission by Judy Brown-DuPaul's class.

Creating books that involve the senses can be very successful. For example, a Christmas holiday book might use the senses of sight, smell, and touch. If an activity for the day is baking cookies, cinnamon and other spices can be sprinkled on a spot of glue in the book. If decorating with pine boughs is part of

© Cengage Learning

Creating their own stories through words, play, and art allows children to have the experience of authorship.

the story, a twig can be pressed and glued into the book. Sawdust can be added to the page that pictures the tree being cut down. The pictures and stories about the holiday will be greatly enhanced by these additions.

The creation of books can be basic and simple. The goal is not to produce professional-looking books, but to validate the children's thoughts and encourage their creativity and self-expression. If adults are accepting of children's literary attempts, children will begin to see themselves as authors. The correct use of mechanics will come as children become more familiar with language and books. At this early stage, making sense of language is the most important part of the process.

SUMMARY

There are literally hundreds of fascinating ways to share stories. Taking a new look at some commonsense approaches is helpful. Reading aloud is a most effective way to share stories if it is done with planning and a little bit of acting. Oral storytelling has a long tradition, though it is practiced less today. Certainly it is more difficult than reading aloud, but it is a skill worth mastering. People of all ages can be mesmerized by the spell a good storyteller can cast over an audience.

With practice, amateur storytellers can capture some of that magic. Various materials can be added to the sharing of stories to create diversity and artistic effects. Flannel boards are effective tools for sharing stories. They provide an avenue for both oral and hands-on involvement. Theatrical storytelling takes this one step further. By using puppetry and dramatics, children are given the power to suspend reality and enter a magical world created exclusively for and by them.

The more involved the children are in the storytelling process, the greater their creative and intellectual growth can be. The ultimate goal is, of course, helping children to attain literacy. Involving them early as authors by guiding them in the construction of their own classroom books can be a critical step in this journey. The positive self-concepts they gain by creating stories provide them with confidence to continue on the road to greater literacy.

QUESTIONS FOR THOUGHT AND DISCUSSION

1. Why is it important to use a variety of approaches for sharing stories?
2. Which method of sharing stories is easiest to begin with?
3. What can one do to prepare to read a story aloud?
4. Why should a teacher read a story aloud to the children every day?

5. What should one consider when choosing a book to read aloud?

6. Why is child involvement important in oral storytelling?

7. What are the characteristics of a good story for oral storytelling?

8. What materials are needed for a flannel board story?

9. What are some things a teacher telling a flannel board story should be aware of?

10. What are the characteristics of a good flannel board story?

11. Why should one use flannel board stories with children?

12. Why are puppets effective as storytelling tools?

13. Defend or refute this statement: A teacher who uses puppets must learn to be a ventriloquist.

14. What kinds of stories are best to use with puppets?

15. Why is drama a useful tool for telling stories to young children?

16. What should be considered when planning a creative dramatic experience with children?

17. Why should young children use costumes and props when involved in dramatics?

18. Defend or refute this statement: Young children are unable to write stories.

19. What is a classroom book?

20. Is the language–experience approach (LEA) useful for preschool children? Why?

 For additional resources, access the *Growing Up with Literature* companion website through www.cengagebrain.com <http://www.cengagebrain.com/>.

CHILDREN'S BOOKS CITED

Agell, Charlotte. (1994). *Dancing feet*. San Diego, CA: Gulliver/Harcourt.

Agell, Charlotte. (1995). *I swam with a seal*. San Diego, CA: Gulliver/Harcourt.

Ahlberg, Allan. (2001). *The adventures of Bert*. New York: Farrar.

Archer, Peggy. (2005). *Turkey surprise*. New York: Dial.

Arnold, Ted. (1994). *No more jumping on the bed*. New York: Dial.

Barrett, Judi. (1978). *Cloudy with a chance of meatballs*. New York: Atheneum.

Bartels, Alice. (2001). *The grandmother doll*. Toronto, Ontario, Canada: Annick.

Bateman, Teresa. (2001). *Farm flu*. Morton Grove, IL: Albert Whitman.

Blake, Stephanie. (2009). *I don't want to go to school*. New York: Random House.

Brown, Margaret Wise. (2001). *The dirty little boy*. Toronto, Ontario, Canada: Winslow.

Burg, Sarah. (2006). *One more egg*. New York: North-South.

Burton, Martin. (2005). *Fooling the tooth fairy*. Montrose, CA: London Town Press.

Calmenson, Stephanie. (2008). *Late for school*. Minneapolis, MN: Carolrhoda/ Lerner.

Carle, Eric. (2005). *10 little rubber ducks*. New York: HarperCollins.

Cartwright, Reg. (2005). *What we do*. New York: Holt.

Cherry, Lynne. (2000). *The great kapok tree*. New York: Voyager.

Cowell, Cressida. (2001). *What shall we do with the boo-hoo baby?* New York: Scholastic.

Cowen-Fletcher, Jane. (2001). *Farmer Will*. Cambridge, MA: Candlewick.

dePaola, Tomie. (1973). *Charlie needs a cloak*. Englewood Cliffs, NJ: Prentice Hall.

dePaola, Tomie. (1975). *Strega Nona*. Englewood Cliffs, NJ: Prentice Hall.

Derby, Sally. (1999). *My steps*. New York: Lee & Low.

Dunbar, Joyce. (2001). *Tell me what it's like to be big*. San Diego, CA: Harcourt.

Dunbar, Joyce. (2006). *Where's my sock*. New York: Scholastic.

Fleming, Denise. (1994). *Barnyard banter*. New York: Henry Holt.

Fore, S. J. (2006). *Tiger can't sleep*. New York: Viking.

Fox, Lee. (2010). *Ella Kazoo will not brush her hair*. New York: Walker.

Fox, Mem. (1994). *Tough Boris*. San Diego, CA: Harcourt Brace Jovanovich.

Fox, Mem. (2005). *Hunwick's egg*. Orlando, FL: Harcourt.

Freeman, Don. (1976). *Corduroy*. New York: Puffin.

Grindley, Sally. (2003). *Mucky ducky*. New York: Bloomsbury.

Harper, Jessica. (2001). *Nora's room*. New York: HarperCollins.

Helakoski, Leslie. (2005). *Big chickens*. New York: Dutton.

Helakoski, Leslie. (2008). *Big chickens fly the coop*. New York: Dutton.

Helakoski, Leslie. (2010). *Big chickens go to town*. New York: Dutton.

Hilb, Nora, and Jennings, Sharon. (2009). *Wiggle Giggle Tickle Train*. Toronto: Annick.

Hubbell, Patricia. (2001). *Sea, sand, me!* New York: HarperCollins.

Hudson, Cheryl. (1999). *Glo goes shopping*. East Orange, NJ: Just Us Books.

Janovitz, Marilyn. (2001). *Good morning, Little Fox*. New York: North-South.

Johnson, Suzanne. (2001). *Fribbity ribbit!* New York: Knopf.

Judes, Marie-Odile. (2001). *Max, the stubborn little wolf*. New York: Harper-Collins.

Kraus, Robert. (1980). *Another mouse to feed*. New York: Simon & Schuster.

Krauss, Ruth. (1945). *The carrot seed*. New York: Harper and Row.

Lewis, Kevin. (2001). *The lot at the end of my block*. New York: Hyperion.

Lobel, Arnold. (1979). *Frog and Toad are friends*. New York: Harper and Row.

London, Jonathan. (2002). *Where the big fish are*. Cambridge, MA: Candlewick.

Long, Melinda. (2001). *Hiccup Snickup*. New York: Simon and Schuster.

Lyon, George Ella. (2004). *Weaving the rainbow*. New York: Atheneum.

McDermott, Gerald. (2001). *Raven: A trickster tale from the Pacific Northwest*. New York: Voyager/HarperCollins.

McPhail, David. (2001). *Big Pig and Little Pig*. San Diego, CA: Harcourt.

Meyers, Susan. (2001). *Everywhere babies*. San Diego, CA: Harcourt.

Miller, Bobbi. *One fine trade*. New York: Holiday House.

Mockford, Caroline. (2001). *Come here, Cleo!* New York: Barefoot.

Munsch, Robert. (2002). *More pies*. New York: Scholastic.

Newman, Leslea. (2001). *Cats, cats, cats!* New York: Simon and Schuster.

Numeroff, Laura. (2003). *If you take a mouse to the movies*. New York: HarperCollins.

Raschka, Chris. (2001). *Waffle*. New York: Simon and Schuster.

Richardson, John. (2002). *Grunt*. New York: Clarion.

Root, Phyllis. (2001). *Rattletrap car*. Cambridge, MA: Candlewick.

Root, Phyllis. (2005). *Quack!* Cambridge, MA: Candlewick.

Rylant, Cynthia. (2001). *Mr. Putter and Tabby feed the fish*. San Diego, CA: Harcourt.

Schubert, Leda. (2010). *Feeding the sheep*. New York: Farrar, Straus & Giroux.

Sockabasin, Allen. (2005). *Thanks to the animals*. Gardiner, ME: Tilbury House.

Steig, William. (2001). *Toby, what are you?* New York: HarperCollins.

Thomas, Frances. (2001). *One day, Daddy*. New York: Hyperion.

Thomson, Lauren. (2006). *Little Quack's new friend*. New York: Simon & Schuster.

Trivizas, Eugene. (2004). *The three little wolves and the big bad pig*. London: Egmont.

Van Leeuwen, Jean. (2001). *"Wait for me!" said Maggie McGee*. New York: Penguin Putnam.

Waber, Bernard. (2001). *Fast food! Gulp! Gulp!* Boston: Houghton Mifflin.

Weinstock, Robert. (2008). *Giant meatball*. Orlando, FL: Harcourt.

Wilcox, Brian, and David, Lawrence. (2001). *Full moon*. New York: Doubleday.

Wild, Margaret. (2001). *Midnight babies*. New York: Clarion.

Wild, Margaret. (2001). *Nighty night!* Atlanta, GA: Peachtree.

Wood, Audrey. (1984). *The napping house*. New York: Harcourt.

Wood, Audrey. (2001). *Alphabet adventure*. New York: Scholastic.

SELECTED REFERENCES AND RESOURCES

Bernier, M., and O'Hare, J. (2005). *Puppetry in education and theory: Unlocking doors to the mind and heart*. Bloomington, IN: Authorhouse.

Bird, E. (2009). *Children's literature gems: Choosing and using them in your library career*. Chicago, IL: American Library Association.

Carlson, A., and Carlson, M. (2005). *Flannel board stories for infants and toddlers*. Chicago, IL: American Library Association.

Carlson, M. A. (1999). *Flannel board stories for infants and toddlers*. Chicago, IL: American Library Association.

Casey, T. (2010). *Inclusive play*. Newbury Park, CA: SAGE.

Faurot, K. K. (2003). *Books in bloom: Creative patterns and props that bring stories to life*. Chicago, IL: American Library Association.

Johnson, D. (2008). *The joy of children's literature*. Florence, KY: Wadsworth.

Macmillan, K., and Kirker, C. (2009). *Storytime magic: 400 fingerplays, flannel boards, and other activities*. Chicago, IL: American Library Association.

McCaslin, N. (2006). *Creative dramatics in the classroom*. Boston: Allyn & Bacon. McConnon, D., Thornton, S. & Williams, Y. (2008). *The encyclopedia of writing and illustrating children's books*. Philadelphia, PA: Running Press/Perseus.

Mellen, N., and Moore, T. (2001). *Storytelling with children*. Gloucestershire, England: Hawthorne.

Reid, R. (2009). *Reid's read-alouds: Selections for children and teens*. Chicago, IL: American Library Association.

Sawyer, W., and Leff, A. (1982). *Elementary school creative dramatics: Coming to your senses*. In Nancy Brizendine & James Thomas (Eds.), Learning through dramatics: Ideas for teachers and librarians (pp. 29–32). Phoenix, AZ:Oryx.

Saxton, M. (2010). *Child language*. Newbury Park, CA: SAGE.

Trelease, J. (2006). *The read-aloud handbook* (5th ed.). New York: Penguin.

INTERNET REFERENCES AND HELPFUL WEBSITES

City of San Jose site. *Why flannel board stories*. Retrieved February 17, 2010, from www.sjlibrary.org/services/early_care

Creation Company. *Storyteller.net*. Retrieved February 17, 2010, from www.storyteller.net

Instructional Technology Development Consortium. *The world of puppets*. Retrieved February 17, 2010, from http://score.rims.K12.ca.us/activity/Puppets/

Tim Sheppards Storytelling Resources for Storytellers site.. *The storytelling FAQ*. Retrieved February 17, 2010, from www.timsheppard.co.uk/story

Pratt's Educational Resources site. *Flannel board stories & instructions, songs, and rhymes for children*. Retrieved February 17, 2010, from www.amug.org/~/ jbpratt/education/mypages/flannelstories.html

The Puppetry Homepage site. Retrieved February 17, 2010, from http://www .sagecraft.com/puppetry

CHAPTER 7

INTEGRATING LITERATURE INTO THE CURRICULUM

Early childhood programs must include a wide range of topics and activities. This variety is needed to address the total development of each child. Literature is only one of the things that should be provided to children in their formative years. Age-appropriate academics, art, music, free play, nutrition, and other parts of the program must all be addressed as well. One might easily feel overwhelmed by the number of topics and activities that should be provided.

How can all of these parts be provided? Should some be dropped from the program? If so, how can one decide which things to drop? Can anything be combined with something else? These questions can be puzzling. Obviously, one must plan carefully in order to avoid leaving out parts of a program that have a truly legitimate purpose. This chapter discusses an innovative webbing strategy for planning activities for young children for each of the important aspects of the program. Descriptions are provided for organizing subject area themes, facilitating integration, and choosing related books.

"Remember always that you have the right to be an individual."

—ELEANOR ROOSEVELT

WEBS AS ORGANIZATIONAL TOOLS

Much time has been spent over the past two decades studying how the human brain works. Scientists have examined this field by trying to make computers behave in the same way as a human brain. Because the computer is a machine and a human being possesses natural intelligence, this concept is known as **artificial intelligence**. From these experiments, it has been concluded that people understand new ideas by relating the new to the known (Weaver, 2009). In other words, they see how the new idea fits with what is already comprehended. The process is likened to fitting new information into a **web** of information already possessed.

This idea of a **web of knowledge** can be applied to planning the various components of an early childhood program. Rather than looking at each part of the program as an isolated activity, visualize each as a piece of the whole. In order to do this, one must understand how each part fits in with the other parts. As new parts of the program are considered and selected, they can be integrated.

This chapter focuses on the use of webbing as an organizational tool due to its ease of expansion and contraction, its flexibility, and its adaptability. Other tools and techniques can be used to organize the same material found in the webs presented here. For example, a table or chart can be constructed on a computer or with pencil and paper. Examples of this technique for the initial knowledge web on dogs and the single book (*Houses and Homes* by Ann Morris) cross-curriculum web described later in the chapter can be found on the companion website. In addition, card files using three-inch by five-inch or four-inch by six-inch index cards can be created to organize the information found in both webs and tables. Each technique has advantages and disadvantages. It is simply a matter of finding the organizational tool one is most comfortable using.

A Web for Understanding

Perhaps the best way to explain how a web might work is to use an example. Consider a young child who sees a man walking a dog on a leash down the street. The child might not be familiar with that particular breed of dog, but even so might point at the animal and proudly exclaim, "Doggy!" How the child knows it is a dog is explained by understanding how the child takes the new information (i.e., an animal being walked) and fit it in with the known (i.e., what the child already knows about dogs).

Although the child might not be able to explain everything, the child already knows some things about dogs: barking, Lassie, a wagging tail, and chasing cats.

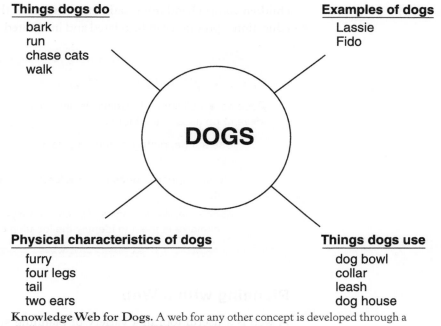

Things dogs do
bark
run
chase cats
walk

Examples of dogs
Lassie
Fido

DOGS

Physical characteristics of dogs
furry
four legs
tail
two ears

Things dogs use
dog bowl
collar
leash
dog house

Knowledge Web for Dogs. A web for any other concept is developed through a similar procedure. Courtesy Walter Sawyer.

It is reasonable to believe that a young child possesses most of the information contained in the **Knowledge Web for Dogs**, with information organized under four subheadings. With this web of knowledge, a child can identify several things about an unfamiliar animal that fit in with what is already known about dogs—for example: leash, collar, four legs, a tail, walking, and perhaps a bark. Based on these characteristics, a child would likely conclude that the unfamiliar animal is a dog even though it does not look like any dog the child has seen previously. Of course, this process doesn't always work out so neatly, which is why children are often heard making errors. The child might just as easily have seen a horse and called it a dog, a false conclusion reached because the child doesn't have enough information about horses to clearly identify one.

In any case, it is seen in the web that the information is organized. It is believed that the human mind organizes knowledge in a similar way. That is why one doesn't constantly mistake cats for dogs and vice versa. Upon meeting the new dog, the child could learn its name and add that new name to examples of dog names that are already known. The process the child goes through is an example of relating the new to the known. It is done by all human beings throughout life.

The lines that make up the knowledge web are similar to the lines that form the web constructed by a spider. The web is helpful in understanding how children comprehend information and thus how the various components of an educational program can be related and integrated with one another.

TIPS FOR TEACHERS

Become a collector of poems, fingerplays, songs, riddles, pictures, and ideas to be used in the future.

- Use songs, pictures, and fingerplays to connect one activity to the next.
- Identify specific poems or pictures to use in themed activities or units.
- Keep several anthologies of poems readily available, and place labeled bookmarks in them to identify the location of poems to be used.

Planning with a Web

A web is a useful tool in a variety of planning situations. It may be used to visualize or organize a total program or just aspects of a program. To construct a web, begin with a central theme. Using a free-flowing brainstorming approach, list a variety of aspects related to that central theme. The next step might be to select relevant items from the list and organize them under subheadings. The final step is to create a web that visually represents the total picture. The figure **Creating a Web for Toys** illustrates the steps one might follow. Notice that some items appear under more than one subheading. Dotted lines are used to point out this relationship in the actual web. As new ideas and new knowledge are gained, the web grows outward and the lines showing relationship may increase.

This same process can be used to plan a unit. The central idea might be art, music, literature, science, social studies, nutrition, or math. The teacher might then generate related ideas such as activities or books to use with the theme. The ideas could be organized under subheadings, creating a web.

Literature Web

A web might be constructed for a literature theme as follows. After a topic has been identified, focus mainly on related literature. In this case, subheadings might include poems, fingerplays, and stories related to a particular literature theme. Under each subheading list examples that might be used in the unit.

Step 1: Brainstorm a list of related terms:

blocks	cars	trucks	stuffed animals
rattles	pots	pans	teddy bears
clay	crayons	paints	board games
balls	bats	markers	rubber duck

Step 2: Select items and organize under subheadings:

Soft Toys	**Bed Toys**	**Group Toys**	**Art Toys**
stuffed animals	stuffed animals	balls	crayons
teddy bears	teddy bears	board games	clay
clay	rubber duck		paint
balls			markers
rubber duck			

Step 3: Create a web and show relationships:

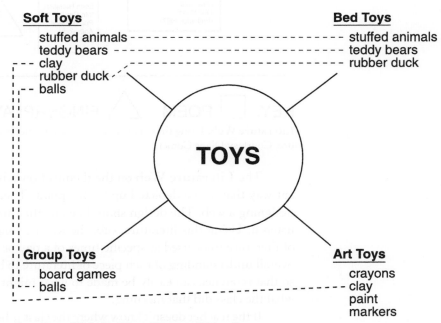

Creating a Web for Toys. Courtesy Walter Sawyer.

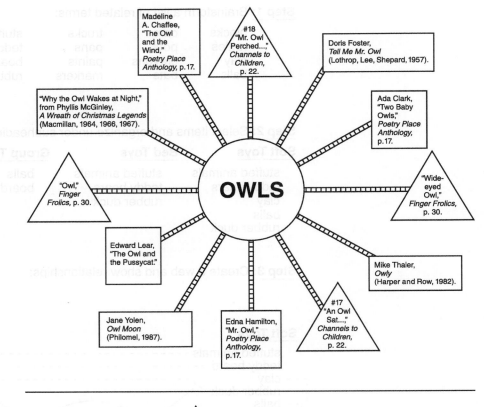

KEY: ☐ POEM   △ FINGERPLAY   ▭ STORY

Literature Web. Using the concept of owls, various pieces of literature are identified for use. Courtesy Diane Comer.

The **Literature Web** on the theme of owls is drawn in a slightly different way than those depicted up to this point. There is no specific method for designing a web. The design should be one that makes sense to the individual using it. Using this literature web, the teacher might designate certain pieces of literature to be used at specific times of a day or week. The web requires an overall understanding of each piece of literature to be used throughout the unit so that reference can easily be made to what might be coming in the future or what the class did that morning.

If the teacher doesn't know where the class is heading, chances are the program is lost. Used as a roadmap for the day or week, the web can be a tremendous help in preventing such a situation. Webs can be revised each year. They can be added to or modified as needed. Keeping the web on file helps reduce planning time in subsequent years.

THEMES FOR DEVELOPING WEBS

Teachers need not think of each theme or book around which to develop a curriculum or literature web. Borrowing and learning from others is a teaching tradition that can and should be relied on. Resources such as *Thematic Units for Kindergarten* (1999) by Kristin Schlosser contain a wealth of ideas to integrate many of the books commonly used in early childhood education.

Webs can be used to plan around one book or a theme using several books. They may be used to plan for a single day or a longer period of time such as a one-week unit. An important use of webs is planning the integration of subject areas around a common theme.

Subject Area Themes

Develop themes around topics and areas of interest to children. Consider combining science, social studies, mathematics, arts, basic concepts, language, movement, celebrations, and other areas through related elements or books.

Science. The most common topic within this area is the study of ourselves. Children are curious about their bodies. Themes might include the body, teeth, foods we eat, illness, good health, and accident prevention. Consider the study

Scary stories book display. Courtesy Walter Sawyer.

© Cengage Learning

Science and social studies activities can be used before, during, and after stories.

of other living things and include pets and pet care, plants and animals, ocean and pond life, insects, sex differences, and babies. Children are also interested in natural phenomena such as magnetism, bubbles, weather, how things grow, electricity, stars, planets, and simple machines such as pulleys and wheels.

Social Studies. In social studies, the focus is often on the community and neighborhood helpers. Many teachers investigate themes of personal safety, emotions, and families. They then expand the focus to include other communities as well, in units such as the farm, the city, the desert, the mountains, lifestyles, outer space, and climates. A theme related to a sense of time could be developed in units on history, dinosaurs, and historical figures. The world community can come alive with themes on the differences and similarities of people, cultural heritage, holidays around the world, climates, ethnic celebrations, and geography.

Mathematics. Mathematics in early childhood education includes more than just learning numbers. Themes can be developed on building principles using shapes and blocks. Early computation skills include the concepts of estimating, counting, and adding and subtracting by using concrete objects. Other mathematics themes might include predicting, measuring, graphing, and charting.

Science and social studies activities can be used before, during, and after stories.

Stories can be extended through the arts.

The Arts. The arts include music, drama, and the visual arts. Music themes might include songs, fingerplays, instruments, and choral singing. Drama themes include plays, puppetry, fingerplays, costuming, skits, and role-playing. Themes in the visual arts could include color, design, collage, painting, markers, clay, 3-D art, junk art, easel art, and ecology art. Book illustrations are a natural springboard for integrating literature and the children's art activities.

Basic Concepts. The term **basic concepts** includes all of the taken-for-granted aspects of life that explain such things as size, proximity, and action. They include spatial concepts such as near, far, in front of, on top of, behind, and so on; actions such as push, pull, open, and close; size and weight concepts such as big, small, heavy, and light; sensory concepts such as color, sound, taste, feel, sweet, soft, and bright. Each can be studied as a separate concept. However, it makes sense to integrate their study. One seldom sees just "red" or experiences the concept of "near" in isolation. One sees red crayons, red fire engines, and red mittens. One is near a cat, or near a mommy, or near a friend. Each of these concepts is integrated in life. It makes sense to integrate them with other components of a program.

Language. Language, of course, can be easily integrated with any of the other theme areas. Language is used to describe and deal with all of them. When considering language, one is concerned with ABCs, color words, word patterns, sequencing, solving puzzles, rebus writing, labeling, name learning, literature, picture dictionaries, listening, and so on. It is often helpful to see language as a device that can be used to link and integrate two or more of the other themes together.

Movement. During the early years, children acquire control over their bodies. This aspect of a program can easily be integrated with other themes. Included in a movement theme are such concepts as growth and development, muscle control, body fluidity, coordination, challenging oneself, and group cooperation. After reading a book about colors, one can easily construct a game in which children are asked to take turns placing a number of objects of various colors at different locations around the room. This activity integrates colors and listening (language and art), spatial awareness (basic concepts), and muscle control (movement) with literature (reading of the book).

Nontraditional Celebrations. The category of nontraditional celebrations covers virtually everything else. Nontraditional refers to times other than holidays or the changing seasons. In a classroom, the teacher and children are in charge of celebrations. They can create unique celebrations using professional resources, imagination, and a sense of adventure. Weeks that do not encompass Thanksgiving, Valentine's Day, or Halloween are ripe for a new celebration. The class could also give their own twist to weeklong celebrations for common themes. "Pets in Our World" week might include books on pets, a trip to a veterinarian or pet shop, making pet rocks, and a contest for drawings of favorite pets. A "Teddy Bear Celebration" might include books about teddy bears, a teddy bear picnic, a teddy dance, bring-a-teddy-bear-to-school day, and snacks made with honey. These celebrations can easily be molded to include activities and content from other theme areas.

© Cengage Learning

Children enjoy sharing both nonfiction and fictional stories.

TIPS FOR TEACHERS

Make an aerobic movement game of "Simon Says" to integrate language and motor skills.

- Simon says to wave and say, "I'm happy!" three times.
- Simon says to hop three times and say, "1 - 2 - 3!"
- Simon says to wiggle your fingers and say, "I have two hands!"
- Simon says to march in a circle and say, "I'm on a merry-go-round!"

Stories, art and science can be combined.

The more that concepts can be integrated into the curriculum, the better the learning will be. If children have had an enjoyable experience, the memories they re-create from that experience will reinforce the concepts learned. Children usually enjoy a multisensory, hands-on approach to learning. Planning that includes this approach will result in more effective instruction. Literature that provides interest, motivation, and language can be used to integrate many parts of the curriculum.

Projects. A **project approach** involves strategies that help to guide children through a study of real-world topics that interest them. Lillian Katz and Sylvia Chard (2000) provide a comprehensive understanding of this approach. They describe how a project can involve children with a wide range of capabilities in play, art, mathematics, language, and construction focused on the project topic. The topic integrates both the activities and different aspects of the world of children. A more in-depth approach and examples of projects for preschool and the early grades can be found at the project approach website identified in the resources found at the end of this chapter.

The early childhood programs of Reggio Emilia, a municipality in Italy, provide exemplary models of the project approach. Nancy Hertzog (2001, 2005) describes the six themes that underpin the program:

- teacher respect for the child
- using relationships to support higher-level thinking

- art as a medium to represent the children's thinking
- communicating the children's learning to others
- children and adults are not hurried
- teachers have a variety of roles

Ongoing projects form the predominant learning activity, and art is the predominant media for communicating what the children have learned. Tess Bennett (2001) notes that the project approach used in the centers in Reggio Emilia enable the program to include all children, and with little or no discipline problems.

Books That Don't Fit Themes

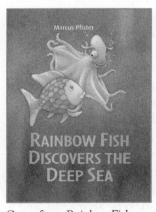

Cover from *Rainbow Fish Discovers the Deep Sea* by Marcus Pfister. Jacket art copyright ©2009 by Marcus Pfister. Reprinted by permission of North-South Books. All rights reserved.

Sometimes one plans a unit for which there doesn't seem to be a good book. At other times, one discovers a particularly good book that doesn't seem to fit any of the units being planned. This doesn't mean that either the unit being planned or the wonderful book should not be used. A unit that provides stimulating learning should always be used even if literature cannot be integrated with it. A good book can be read simply for the enjoyment of the story. In fact, many good books can and should be read solely for that reason.

One might discover a book such as Robert McCloskey's *Time of Wonder* and, knowing that a unit on the sea is planned for a later time, put that book aside until the sea unit is begun. This could be paired with *Rainbow Fish Discovers the Deep Sea* by Marcus Pfister. Based on contemporary research on the discovery of new species on the ocean floor, Rainbow Fish dives deep to find his last sparkling scale and discovers new friends who live in the ocean's depth.

It's also possible to adjust a book or poem to fit a particular purpose when an exact match between a book and a theme cannot be found. In telling a story, one can always add characters, change settings, or lengthen the plot. Take, for example, the kindergarten class that wished to do a Christmas play. Because it was difficult to find a story or play with twenty-two parts, the children adapted one using Dr. Seuss's *How the Grinch Stole Christmas*. The play included a group of really rotten rats (five children) with one lead rat (dressed as a ragged Santa) who burst through a cardboard chimney to steal Christmas. The play also included four other children, the real Santa, the nine reindeer, and a mother and father. All twenty-two children had important roles. Reading the Dr. Seuss story helped the children understand the idea that would be created in the play. The Grinch was a superb model for the behavior of the rotten rats. All children had a speaking role through the use of a choral line that was repeated at key points in the play. One of the best parts of the experience was that no child had to play an "added on" part such as a tree or a bush.

FACILITATING INTEGRATION

Webs can be an immense help in developing **integrated lessons**. They allow one to step back and plan the big picture of a lesson prior to actually using it with children. In addition to planning, other steps can be taken within the lesson to further facilitate integration. Some of these ideas require the acquisition of materials; others take advantage of things that happen within the lesson.

Re-creating the Experience

Providing opportunities for children to **re-create the learning** enhances their understanding of the lesson. Providing inexpensive or no-cost materials can ensure that the learning or the story will be experienced again. Good health care as illustrated in *Dr. Dog* provides an excellent example. Written and illustrated by Babette Cole, Dr. Dog's unorthodox methods are hilarious but right on target in terms of good hygiene and health care. Throughout the book, Dr. Dog strives to reform the unhealthy habits of his human owners. Class books can be used here to re-create the experience as well. The common phrase, "If you want to be healthy, be sure to . . ." can be used by all children to form pages for the class book. Each child creates an ending for the phrase and a picture to illustrate the idea. The repetitive phrasing will encourage children to read the class book.

Another example might be Debi Gliori's *Penguin Post*. This story tells how Milo, a young penguin postal carrier, delivers baby items to others while unknowingly keeping an egg warm in his postal pouch. After the reading, children could be provided with a pile of old envelopes, stickers, an inkpad, and a rubber stamp. Milk cartons could be made into mailboxes, enabling the children to re-create the story. One of the purposes of free play is to allow children to try out the world from a safe harbor. It may be beneficial to allow children to engage in this activity prior to a field trip to a real post office.

Using Children's Interest

Use the motivation of the children to lead into another activity, even if it isn't the next activity originally planned. A high interest level should be a deciding factor in shifting the order of the day's activities. Suppose the motivating factor is the reading of Donald Crews's book, *Freight Train*. If interest is high, the time is ripe to make colored train cars as an expansion of the reading. Teaching shapes (of the cars) or counting (the number of cars) are additional expansions of the initial motivation. A variety of fine motor activities could also be included in the construction of the paper train. This can be a jumping-off point to other books about trains. Good choices include *Trouble on the Tracks* by Kathy Mallat,

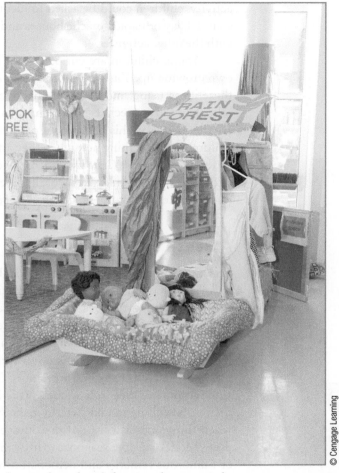

A story about the rainforest can be re-created.

Two Little Trains by Margaret Wise Brown, and *William and the Night Train* by Mij Kelly.

Eric Carle's *My Very First Book of Animal Homes* will provide inspiration for follow-up matching activities of animals with their homes. This board book has split pages that can be used to match the animal with the correct home. The focus can then move to other books about animal homes in the wild such as *Castles, Caves, and Honeycombs* by Linda Ashman and *Robin's Home* by Jeannine Atkins. One might also wish to compare the homes of wild animals with those of domestic animals as depicted in books such as *The Rickety Barn* by Jemma Beeke or *A Cat and a Dog* by Claire Masurel. For a related listening activity, children could be asked to identify the animals that make a particular sound. Clay or papier-mâché houses and animals might be used to integrate art with the other activities.

Young children are curious about such things as new siblings and their own growing up. *You and Me* and *Look at Me,* both by Rachel Fuller, explore these ideas using multicultural characters in a format that toddlers and pre-schoolers will appreciate. Young children involved in new accomplishments will see themselves in this book about momentous changes in young lives. Monster children try something new when they attempt to make a cake for their mother's birthday in *Monster Cake* by Rebecca Dickinson. Even animals sometimes have to do new things. An example of this occurs when a young dog must stay over-night in a kennel for the first time in *Spike in the Kennel* by Paulette Bogan.

A Sense of Flexibility

It is important to keep a sense of **flexibility**. Even carefully made plans do not always work out as expected. Being flexible and being willing to capitalize on unexpected opportunities for further learning is an advantage when working with children. Without these skills, one misses the possibilities that present themselves. Keep the original plan in mind, but don't be a slave to it. A frus-trated reaction to a plan that's not working is detrimental. Children are quite forgiving when things don't work out. They also notice the reactions of adults, since adults are their role models. It is important that both teacher and chil-dren to be willing to take healthy risks. Seeing the negative reactions of adults when things don't work out discourages this risk taking on the part of chil-dren. Model a proper response to life's minor disappointments by making calm or humorous remarks and demonstrating that one can always try again or do something else.

From JOURNEY CAKE, HO! by Ruth Sawyer, illustrated by Robert McCloskey, copyright 1953 by Ruth Sawyer and Robert McCloskey, renewed © 1981 by David Durand and Robert McCloskey. Used by permis-sion of Viking Penguin, A Division of Penguin Young Readers Group, A Member of Penguin Group (USA) Inc., 345 Hudson Street, New York, NY 10014. All rights reserved.

LITERATURE USE IN INTEGRATED UNITS

Integrated units are often taught around a general theme or a key idea. These themes include the content for the lesson or unit. One may wish to develop a theme around a specific book. For example, the **Single Book Extension-Curriculum Web** illustrates a single-book curriculum web developed around the theme of Ruth Sawyer's classic story *Journey Cake, Ho!* The focus may also be in a content area such as science, social studies, basic concepts, or holidays. Selecting both fiction and nonfiction literature to support these content areas will be discussed. In addition to these, other units might be developed around literature, unique classroom projects, or nontraditional topics.

make many-sized (small, smaller, smallest) cakes—magnet fish for them

dramatic play—bake shop

stamp circle journey cakes—tempera paint designs

do story sequence cards

make clay journey cakes and decorate with faces

make real journey cakes or pancakes

dramatize the story; assign parts for all; use picture labels

flannelboard retelling

paper bag puppet of favorite character

visit a bakery or pancake restaurant

play flip the pancake (round potholder) in the frying pan, count times

set up clay corner (rolling pins, pans, etc.)

make a cardboard journey cake; paint or color; cut into a puzzle

make journey cake paper plate masks

run with stick pushing hula hoops—have faces

"Farm Sounds," p. 80; *More Piggyback Songs*

read and compare "The Gingerbread Boy"

Summer "slip 'n slide chase"; roll Frisbee and child tries to slide and catch journey cake

"The Farmer in the Dell" song

play "floppy Frisbee" where it is the journey cake; if miss, sit down until next turn

maze—oven to house

obstacle course—oven to house

Ruth Sawyer,
Journey Cake, Ho!
(New York: Viking, 1953).

Single Book Extension-Curriculum Web. This web was developed around the theme of Ruth Sawyer's classic story *Journey Cake, Ho!* Courtesy Diana Comer.

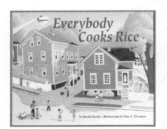

Book cover from *Everybody Cooks Rice* by Norah Dooley, illustrated by Peter Thornton, © 1991. Reprinted by permission of Carolrhoda Books.

While Ruth Sawyer's classic story is used in this example, the same web could be revised for use with a number of contemporary titles related to the theme of food. A story featuring multicultural characters is *Everybody Cooks Rice* by Norah Dooley.

Preschoolers will howl with delight at the antics of the animal characters in *Elephant Pie,* written and illustrated by Hilda Offen and *Once Upon a Banana* by Jennifer Armstrong. Two nonfiction titles about food include the bilingual *My Food* in English and Spanish by Rebecca Emberley and *Food for Thought* by Joost Elffers and Saxton Freyman. The latter title can be used to learn about color, shapes, and numbers as well as food. Almost everybody likes spaghetti, the food and the song. Children will thoroughly enjoy *On Top of Spaghetti* by Paul Brett Johnson. In this song-based story with hilarious illustrations, a hound dog named Yodeler Jones serves nothing by spaghetti and meatballs in his restaurant. This could be paired with a reading of Tomie dePaola's classic story *Strega Nona*. Humor and food create some fast-paced but delectable reading in *Froggy Eats Out* by Jonathan London and *The Lima Bean Monster* by Dan Yaccarino.

The **Single Book Cross-Curriculum Web** provides a curriculum web for the book: *Houses and Homes* by Ann Morris. This nonfiction book presents a wide variety of houses and cultures from around the world. Ken Heyman's crisp clear photographs aid in establishing the similarities and differences of the structures. In addition to the web activities, children can expand on the unit by creating gingerbread houses, designing houses using recycled materials, and learning about houses used in previous centuries.

Single Book Cross-Curriculum Web. Courtesy Diana Comer.

Science Units

While background research should be done on any theme or unit, it is of particular importance to possess current information when developing one on science. This need for up-to-date information should be included as a specific criterion when selecting books for use in the unit. The teacher should read each of the books to be used ahead of time. Anticipating the questions that might be asked by children will help the teacher provide better responses. Careful planning will help to make a content area theme a success. Webs can be particularly helpful. The **Integrated Curriculum Web:** illustrates an example web used to plan a unit on the ocean which will integrate literature with science, social studies, nutrition, the arts, language, and mathematics.

Various authors and some commercial publishing companies specialize in science-related books. The books should, and usually do, contain an abundance of age-appropriate photographs and illustrations. Certain field guides, if they are written at an appropriate level, can be useful as well. A *field guide* is a book used to identify things such as plants, birds, insects, trees, animals, and clouds. It contains clear pictures and brief, descriptive paragraphs of information. Although not a field guide, *Flip the Flap Jungle Animals* by Jinny Johnson describes a wide array of bugs, fish, birds, and reptiles with a short fact about each. It is not a single sitting book, but one that can be gone back to as the need arises.

Aeronautics and space travel have long been an interest of young children. *The Daring Miss Quimby* by Suzanne Whitaker presents the compelling biography of Harriet Quimby, the first woman in America to get a pilot's license and fly across the English Channel. While everyone around her said it would be too dangerous, Harriet believed in herself and did much to make others question their beliefs about bravery, equality, and stereotyping. In Mac Barnett's *Guess Again Moon Shot,* each page has a quatrain wetting up

Cover from *The Daring Miss Quimby* by Suzanne Whitaker. Jacket art copyright © 2009 by Catherine Stock. Reprinted by permission of Holiday House. All rights reserved.

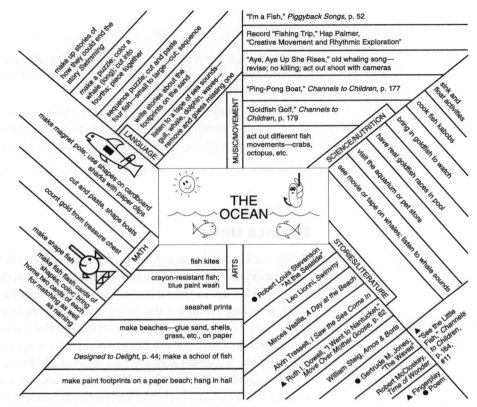

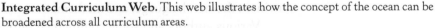

Integrated Curriculum Web. This web illustrates how the concept of the ocean can be broadened across all curriculum areas.

clues and a hole in the page to show part of the illustrated answer on the next page. The final verse and the sometimes outrageous solution is found of the following page.

Books about the seasons include *Spring Song* by Barbara Seuling and *Sun Dance Water Dance* by Jonathan London. In Pat Hutchins's *Shrinking Mouse*, science and math combine to help children learn about both animal behavior and the mathematical concept of spatial perspective. Children will be captivated by the story line; they come to discover that the animals are becoming smaller because they are moving away rather than shrinking. A follow up to this could be the concept of subtraction combined with the growth of plants in *Ten Seeds* by Ruth Brown. A rhythmic prose-poem of the water cycle is combined with lustrous oil paintings in Thomas Locker's *Waterdance.* Other stories related to water and the water cycle are *This Is the Rain* by Lola Schaefer and *Sky, Sea, the Jetty, and Me* by Leonard Fisher. The fictional *The Inside Tree* by Linda Smith deals with the idea of protecting things from the weather. In this story, kindhearted Mr. Potter starts to bring dogs and trees into his home to protect them from a storm. In this ill-advised scenario, the house collapses and he is forced to move to the barn. Another physical science book, exploring rock collecting, is *Rocks in His Head* by Carol Hurst.

Cats, dogs, and other animals are familiar as pets to many children. As such, they represent a good starting point for exploring the animal world. Stories about dogs include *Harry the Dirty Dog,* a board book for babies and toddlers, by Gene Zion and *Clifford the Big Red Dog,* a classic story for preschoolers by Norman Bridwell. Although most of these selections are fictional stories, the dogs and cats portrayed are true to their nature, enabling young readers to develop an

© Cengage Learning

Hands-on science activities go well with books connected with that science.

"Book Cover" from
TADPOLE REX copyright
© 2008 by Kurt Cyrus,
reproduced by permission of
Houghton Mifflin Harcourt
Publishing Company.

understanding of these animals. Twenty years after his death, an all new collection of frog and toad stories by Arnold Lobel has appeared in *Frogs and Toads All Sing*. It is a playful, mischievous, and warmhearted treat not to be missed.

Finding animals and other natural objects has never been as fascinating as in Dee Dee Duffy's *Forest Tracks*, a visual treat for the readers of this book, as they use the words and Janet Marshall's cut-paper illustrations to help them name the animals making different tracks in the landscape. Additional stories about animals include *Sockeye's Journey Home: The Story of a Pacific Salmon* by Barbara Winkelman, *Bilby Moon* by Margaret Spurling, *Bats!* By Laurence Pringle, and *Just Like You* by Jan Fearnley. Little Rex is overwhelmed by the size of the prehistoric dinosaurs in his environment in *Tadpole Rex* by author/illustrator Kurt Cyrus. As the tale unfolds, Rex learns that his personality is more important than his size. The book includes accurate depictions of scientific metamorphosis and the life cycle of frogs. Great close-ups using digitally colored scratchboard illustrations greatly enhance the text. A book that is related to this is *Big Night for Salamanders* by Sarah Lamstein.

Dinosaurs are a perennial favorite of children. A wonderful introduction to these prehistoric creatures is found in *My Big Dinosaur Book* by Roger Priddy. Appropriate even for toddlers, this twelve page board book will spark much interest. A variety of different dinosaurs are depicted in Jane Yolen's *How Do Dinosaurs Say I Love You*. In this fictional approach, naughty young dinosaurs act more like humans as they remind us how and why people love their children.

Commercial publishers often provide a variety of books in science-related areas. Usborne Publishing includes a nature series in its offerings. Topics addressed by its books include birds, butterflies, moths, flowers, and trees. Other publishers that specifically address science-related topics include Scholastic Publishing and the "Read and Wonder" series by Walker Books. They typically offer features that enable a teacher to explore the topic more easily. Care is taken to provide excellent photographs and clear illustrations on important points.

Social Studies Units

In selecting books related to social studies, one must consider other criteria than those discussed so far. Social studies at the early childhood level generally consists of developing an understanding of self, family, community, health/nutrition, and social skills. These are all critical areas that demand that authors be perceptive and sensitive observers of humanity. It may be unwise to use a series of books on one of these sensitive topics without examining each book in the series individually. Books in a series are often written by a number of authors. As a result, each book is only as good as the author who wrote it. Since the literature about early

Hush Harbor by Freddi Williams Evans with illustrations by Erin Bennett Banks. Illustrations copyright © 2008 by Erin Bennett Banks. Reprinted with the permission of Carolrhoda Books, a division of Lerner Publishing Group, Inc. Packaged by Design Press, a division of the Savannah College of Arts and Design. All rights reserved. No part of this excerpt may be used or reproduced in any manner whatsoever without the prior written permission of Lerner Publishing Group, Inc.

childhood social studies concepts is often fictional, the writer becomes the critical component. Identifying authors who write with empathy and understanding on these issues becomes helpful in selecting these books.

Some writers seem to gravitate toward the concepts of family, relationships, and the community in most of their books. Among the writers with multiple titles in these areas are Martha Alexander, Stan and Jan Berenstain, Nancy Carlson, Barbara Cooney, Russell Hoban, Angela Johnson, Mercer Mayer, Helen Oxenbury, and Rosemary Wells. Helen Buckley also explores these areas and includes some excellent work on grandparents in her writings.

Norman Bridwell's Clifford books explore the nature of love, even in the face of imperfections. Michael Bond uses an animal, Paddington Bear, to portray social concepts. Children enjoy exploring the mishaps Paddington encounters in doing things in an individualistic manner.

There are, of course, many other authors and books that can be used to address these areas. Some books are designed to portray a specific or ongoing period of history such as *Century Farm* by Chris Peterson. Some are intended to address a specific problem, while others are not. Many books can be used simply to make a point or to begin a discussion about a social problem. *Hush Harbor: Praying in Secret* by Freddy Williams Evans presents the wrenching story of early nineteenth century enslaved Africans who were not allowed to. In order to pray, they had to gather in secret while Simmy stood watch so they would not get caught. The book is a powerful point to begin discussions on the concepts of slavery, religious freedom, respect for the religion of others, and history. Selecting such books is facilitated by a clear sense of the purpose of the overall unit. Still other books, such as *Gaspard on Vacation* by Anne Gutman, can introduce children to far-off places such as the sights and sounds of Venice, Italy.

Basic Concept Units

Basic concept units address some aspect of mathematics, language, the alphabet, and so forth. The purpose of literature in these units is to **reinforce the learning** of the concept, whether it be counting, spatial relationships, or a letter of the alphabet. Many of the books that would be effective for such a unit might not appear to have been written for that purpose. For this reason, it is important to have a wide knowledge of books and authors.

Tana Hoban is an author who uses photographs to illustrate her texts. Her books have long been used to reinforce such concepts as pushing, pulling, and counting. Eric Carle's books are each imaginatively different. They are also quite effective in reinforcing concept learning with children. *My Very First Book of Colors* and *1, 2, 3 to the Zoo* are two of his books that have been used by early childhood educators for years. Motor skills and movement are topics of some enjoyable and interactive books. *Marie in Fourth Position: The Story of Degas' "The Little Dancer,"* by Amy Littlesugar takes a unique perspective. Marie is a "rat" in the Paris Opera. Her mother agrees to let Marie model for Degas, the famous artist with a frightening reputation. Under Degas's magical guidance, however, Marie is transformed from a clumsy, unattractive dancer to a model of inspired grace. Ian Schoenherr's impressionist illustrations recall the well-known work of Degas. Triangle, circle, and square point out the attributes of shapes in playful rhymes and also point out common objects where those shapes are found in *Shapes That Roll* by Karen Nagel. The rhyming text of *Together* by Hazel Hutchins explores the concept of things that go together like shoelaces with shoes and buttons with shirts. *I Ain't Gonna Paint No More* by Karen Beaumont provides a rollicking good time for learning colors, body parts, styles of painting and a sense of rhythm as the reader watches the little boy get into a pile of mischief with his paints. The bold expressive illustrations by David Catrow lend themselves to careful inspection.

More sophisticated concepts can also be addressed through storybooks. Mary Murphy explores the concept of change on a number of levels in *Some Things Change*. Concepts such as big/small, high/low, and fast/slow are featured in *Too Big, Too Small, Just Right* by Frances Minters. Margaret Wild uses the concepts of left/right and lost/found in *The Pocket Dogs*. The biggest mathematical mystery in nature is addressed in *Growing Patterns* by Sarah Campbell. She presents an easily understood description of Fibonacci numbers, named after the mathematician. The Fibonacci pattern (1, 1, 2, 3, 5, 8, 13 . . .) is comprised of a series of numbers in which the next number is found by adding the two numbers just before it. It is readily identified in the designs of sunflowers, pineapples, daisies, and pinecones. The concept of personal responsibility is explored in *Harley* by Star Livingstone.

Donald Crews has made a substantial contribution to children's concepts with his books about buses, trains, and transportation. Mitsumasa Anno, Arnold Lobel, Tana Hoban, Gail Gibbons, Brian Wildsmith, Richard Scarry, Tomie dePaola, Ed Emberley, and Dr. Seuss are all authors who have made innumerable contributions to this area of children's learning. Their books cover topics such as ABCs, planting a garden, shapes, numbers, seasons, and categorizing.

Cross-Cultural Units

Most cultures identify special days or seasons as times for a celebration of life, traditions, or important values. They bring with them a sense of warmth, cultural values, cohesion, and history. Each has the potential to increase understanding of our mutual humanity. Learning that our culture is increasingly **multiethnic** and **multireligious** is important. Few issues in early childhood education can be as controversial as the celebration of a religious holiday.

A decision can be made to ignore all holidays and seasons, but that is not always a realistic approach. Therefore, careful and thoughtful planning is warranted. From the very beginning, it is best to focus on the meaning and purpose of any holiday in our lives and in the lives of the children. Louise Derman-Sparks (2010) provides helpful guidance in this area based on the anti-bias curriculum approach informed by the developmentally appropriate principles identified by the National Association for the Education of Young Children (Copple & Bredekamp, 2009). She suggests that the approach should be consistent, set and adhere to ground rules, make provisions for reluctant families, and have a clear vision of why we do what we are doing. Rather than focus on the religious aspects, the events should celebrate culture, traditions, and social aspects. In addition, if a program is connected to a government entity, constitutional issues are involved. The focus should be on learning, respecting all cultures and religions, refraining from using religious symbols, acknowledging cultural pride, seeing how our differences give us strength, and not by teaching or advocating any specific religion. It is best to combine a number of holidays around a themed celebration:

- **Liberation theme** – Fourth of July, Passover, Dr. Martin Luther King, Jr. birthday, Cinco de mayo.
- **Festival of Lights theme** – Christmas, Chanukah, Kwanzaa, Diwali.

There is much to learn about all of the cultures of the world. For example, in *Lin Yi's Lantern: A Moon Festival Tale* by Brenda Williams, readers follow Lin Yi as he shops in the market for the needed items for the upcoming Moon Festival. It provides the reader with a deeper understanding of Chinese culture while presenting universal values admired in all cultures. Using Anna McQuinn's *My Friend Mei Jing*, the discussion can broaden from cultural understanding to the issues of cultural differences, immigration issues, and tolerance.

Parental involvement is essential for cultural celebrations. Parents, families, and the community can provide explanations to children from their cultural knowledge. This will help to integrate all in the educational process. It will strengthen the parent–child bond in each involved family as well.

It makes sense to become aware, early in the year, of the cultural diversity of pupils in a class. This will enable the teacher to plan the **themed units** to be recognized throughout the year. Parents can be requested to explain the customs and traditions of particular cultural traditions early in the year to the class so that children unfamiliar with them can gain an understanding of them and perhaps participate in some aspects of the traditional recognition.

December is a major season in many cultures. Instead of a celebration of light, one might choose to combine Christmas, Kwanzaa, Hanukkah, New Year's Day, Ramadan, and Las Posadas into a single-unit "friendship" celebration. The activities can include decorating a friendship tree, playing with a dreidel, making candles and gifts, breaking a piñata, cooking demonstrations, food sharing and perhaps a social activity. The social activity could be a gift to the community. Visiting a nursing home to sing songs or collecting donations for a food pantry would be appropriate.

TIPS FOR TEACHERS

Invite parents in to share a tradition from their cultural ancestry.

- Ask parents to go back several generations if necessary to identify specific countries in their heritage.
- Show children that there are many different countries in Africa, Asia, and the Hispanic world, and that their individual cultures can differ.
- Share traditions that appeal to the senses, such as foods, songs, dances, and decorations.
- Collaborate with families and the community to schedule a culture day from time to time to share pictures, food, and songs from another culture.

Literature for children tends to focus on a specific holiday. While the books suggested here are grouped in this manner, it is recommended that they be shared in a sensitive respectful manner in a themed unit rather than as a celebration of a holiday specific to any one religion.

Tomie dePaola has written several books about Christmas including *An Early American Christmas; Baby's First Christmas; Christmas Pageant; Strega Nona;* and *Tomie dePaola's Book of Christmas Carols.* Margaret Wise Brown's *Christmas in the Barn* is a title that would complement the stories by Tomie dePaola. Some stories can often be used to develop important themes across cultures. In Cyndy Szekeres's *Yes, Virginia, There Is a Santa Claus,* a darling kitten assumes the role of Virginia in a retelling of Virginia O'Hanlon's story. Clement Moore's classic story is recreated in the clever *The Night Before Christmas Popup* with extraordinary pop-up illustrations created by Robert Sabuda. Important seasonal messages about generosity and environmental awareness are brought out in Robert Barry's *Mr. Willowby's Christmas Tree.* A father and son search for a Christmas tree in William George's *Christmas at Long Pond* while the reader is treated to a spectacular celebration of the natural environment. Mary Pope

Book cover from *The Christmas Star* by Marcus Pfister. Copyright © 1993 by Nord-Sud Verlag AG, Gossau Zurich, Switzerland. Used by permission of North-South Books.

Osborne, in *Rocking Horse Christmas,* follows the lives of a boy and his rocking horse as they move through adventures together, grow older, and part company. Ned Bittinger's rich oil paintings enhance the message of longing, hope, and the wonder of childhood.

Several contemporary titles reflect the values that might emerge in a celebration of lights. *The Christmas Star* by Marcus Pfister re-creates the story of the star that guided shepherds, kings, and animals. The author illustrates the book with intriguing holographic foils. *Good King Wenceslas* by John Neale takes the reader beyond the story told in the popular carol, the words of which are included in the book. Christopher Manson's exquisite hand-painted woodcuts of medieval scenes give a powerful dramatic feeling to the story. Joan Oppenheim creates a new story based on a Mexican tale in *The Miracle of the First Poinsettia.* Alan Benjamin provides the perfect way to acquaint young children with the festival of lights in *Hanukkah Chubby Board Book and Dreidels.* The package comes with everything needed to play "Spin the Dreidel." Related to this is the story *Is it Shabbos Yet? by* Ellen Emerman, which provides an easy to understand introduction to the Jewish Sabbath.

Easter and Passover might be combined in a celebration of spring and rebirth. Activities might include creating mosaics with colored eggshells, sharing a meal, hatching baby chicks, and art activities. Easter books include the bible based *The Story of Easter* by Patricia Pingry and the secular *Happy Easter Maisy* by Lucy Cousins. Books about bunnies include James Stevenson's *The Great*

The active involvement of children is the key to helping them understand new information.

Big Especially Beautiful Easter Egg, The Bunny Who Found Easter by Charlotte Zolotow, *The Runaway Bunny* by Margaret Wise Brown, *Zomo the Rabbit* by Gerald McDermott, *Clifford's Happy Easter* by Norman Bridwell, *The Easter Bunny's Baby* by Udo Weigelt, and *Teddy's Easter Secret,* by Gerlinde Wiencirz. Passover stories include *Matzo Ball Moon* by Leslea Newman, *Had Gadya* by Seymour Chwast, and *Matzo Ball: A Passover Story* by Mindy Portnoy.

A Mardi Gras festival might be just the thing to liven up a program toward the end of a long winter. A costume parade and samples of Cajun cooking could be included. Other dates and times to consider for themed celebrations include:

- St. Patrick's Day–March 17
- April Fools Day–April 1
- Arbor Day–April 28
- May Day–May 1
- Rosh Hashanah (Jewish New Year)–September/October
- Harvest Festival (Jewish, Chinese, Asian)–fall
- Halloween–October 31
- Thanksgiving–November
- Purim (Jewish Festival of Happiness)–
- Hinamatsuri (Japanese Doll Festival)–March 3
- Now-ruz (Iranian New Days)–March 21–23
- Holi (Hindu Spring Festival)–Spring
- Songkran (Thai New Year)–mid-April
- Tango no sekku (Japanese Children's Day Festival)–May 5
- Ramadan–ninth month of Islamic calendar
- St. Lucia Day (Candles and Lights)–December 13
- Kwanzaa (African Harvest Festival)–last week of December
- Universal Children's Day (International togetherness)–November 20

Other festivals and celebrations may include such themes as Groundhog Day, Dental Health Week, and Fire Safety Week. Resources from the references at the end of this chapter can be used to provide ideas for celebrating festivals and holidays. Valentine's Day can be celebrated with *Comic Valentine* by Stan and Jan Berenstain, while Thanksgiving can be the occasion for Eileen Spinelli's hilarious food preparation descriptions in *Thanksgiving at the Tappletons',* or Bethany Roberts's *Thanksgiving Mice!* While not actual holidays, birthday parties and weddings are common celebration days that can occur throughout the year. Birthday stories include the Spanish/English *F Is for Fiesta* alphabet book by Susan Elya, *A Birthday Cake Is No Ordinary Cake* by Debra Fraser, *Kipper and Roly* by Mick Inkpen and *When Elephant Goes to a Party* by Sonia Levitin.

Cover from *A Birthday for Bear* by Bonny Becker. Jacket art copyright © 2009 by Katy MacDonald Denton. Reprinted by permission of Candlewick Press. All rights reserved.

A Birthday for Bear by Bonny Becker provides a look at both sides of a birthday celebration. Mouse is determined to celebrate big old Bear's birthday, but Bear doesn't like birthdays or parties of any kind. Mouse learns the valuable lesson that friendship doesn't depend on having identical views of the world. *Don't Spill the Beans* by Ian Schoenherr presents a humorous rhyming birthday story in which a young bear cannot keep a secret. Young children should be able to relate to the wedding story *The Reluctant Flower Girl* by Lynne Barasch.

Halloween books, like Christmas books, abound. They include counting books, scary books, and stories that can be used to deal realistically with fears. Top choices include *Maisy's Halloween* by Lucy Cousins, Deborah Lattimore's hilarious *Cinderhazel, On Halloween Night* by Ferida Wolff and Dolores Kozielski, *By the Light of the Halloween Moon* by Caroline Stutson, *Old Devil Wind* by Bill Martin, Jr., *Halloween Night* by Arden Druce, *Pumpkin Eye* by Denise Fleming, *Monster Mischief* by Pamela Jane, *The Problem with Pumpkins: A Hip & Hop Story* by Barney Saltzberg, *Plumply, Dumply Pumpkin* by Mary Serfozo, *What Will You Be for Halloween?* by Mark Todd, *We're Going on a Ghost Hunt* by Marcia Vaughan, *Teddy's Halloween Secret* by Gerlinde Wiencirz, and *On Halloween Night* by Harriet Ziefert. Nearly all of these books make for a great read-aloud on the days leading up to this favorite holiday.

While not celebrated like Christmas and Easter, other days of importance can also be recognized with a story, an explanation, and an activity. Lloyd Douglas provides a focus on the true importance of the day in *Let's Get Ready for Martin Luther King Jr. Day*. The historical significance of MLK-Jr. Day can be further understood through a reading of *Lucky Beans* by Becky Birtha. In this story, set during the Great Depression, Marshall learns the deeper meaning

Halloween book display. Courtesy Walter Sawyer.

of segregation when a young white girl suggests that his African-American mother could not participate equally in a local bean counting contest. The story has a happy ending, but the meanings are powerfully portrayed. Finally, stories about the meaning and traditions of the Islamic holidays are provided by Jonny Zucker in *Fasting and Dates: A Ramadan and Eid-ul-Fitr Story*.

SUMMARY

Starting with literature and then expanding on its themes will enhance the whole curriculum. Literature can serve as a solid foundation that permits the teacher to have flexibility with planning while lending stability, an important component of early childhood education. Integrating each of the content areas with literature brings cohesiveness to the program and the classroom, yet still allows wonderful things to happen in the classroom.

To achieve integration in the program requires careful planning. A planning process using webs helps the teacher choose the best activities for teaching various concepts, allows the consideration of many choices, and affords time to gather the materials and ideas needed for creative and effective learning activities. Planning webs can be used in a variety of ways. Three types of planning webs discussed in this chapter were the literature web, the single-book web, and the integrated-curriculum web.

Both beginning and experienced teachers should frequently visit a children's library and spend substantial time reading the books. Keeping notes of those books that are enjoyable and helpful is a good way to be organized for upcoming units.

Watch children interact with the books and the library. This is the most effective way to remember a child's level of thinking about literature, which will aid in planning creative lessons for children. Simply browsing through books can generate ideas, thoughts, and memories as the illustrations, words, and characters pass by. Old friends jump out from some books, and delightful new ones draw the reader into others. Planning and integrating a program using webs can be a fascinating process.

QUESTIONS FOR THOUGHT AND DISCUSSION

1. Explain the term *web* as it is used in program planning.
2. What is the difference between a literature web, a single-book web, and an integrated-curriculum web?

3. Defend or refute the following: It is better to create your own ideas for units than to rely on someone else's.

4. What are the reasons for using an integrated curriculum with children?

5. Are there times when a teacher should not use an integrated approach with literature? Explain your reasons.

6. When might a teacher change or adapt a poem or rhyme for class use?

7. How can a teacher facilitate the integration of the curriculum?

8. Defend or refute the following: The use of a book series is never an appropriate approach because the quality is poor.

9. How might a field guide be helpful in early childhood education?

10. Which writers have written several books dealing with either family life or peer relations?

11. Identify a general theme and create an integrated-curriculum web for that topic. Identify the level of the children for whom the unit is being planned.

12. Choose a topic and develop a literature web for it.

13. Develop a single-book web for the preschool or kindergarten level.

14. What is the proper role of holiday-themed books?

For additional resources, access the *Growing Up with Literature* companion website through www.cengagebrain.com <http://www.cengagebrain.com/>.

CHILDREN'S BOOKS CITED

Armstrong, Jennifer. (2006). *Once upon a banana.* New York: Simon & Schuster.

Ashman, Linda. (2001). *Castles, caves, and honeycombs.* San Diego, CA: Harcourt.

Atkins, Jeannine. (2001). *Robin's home.* New York: Farrar.

Barasch, Lynne. (2001). *The reluctant flower girl.* New York: HarperCollins.

Barnett, Mac. (2009). *Guess again moon shot.* New York: Simon & Schuster.

Barry, Robert (ill.). (2000). *Mr. Willowby's Christmas tree.* New York: Penquin.

Beaumont, Karen. (2005). *I ain't gonna paint no more.* Orlando, FL: Harcourt.

Becker, Bonny. (2009). *A birthday cake for Bear.* Somerville, MA: Candlewick.

Beeke, Jemma. (2001). *The rickety barn.* New York: Doubleday.

Berenstain, Stan, & Berenstain, Jan. (1997). *Comic valentine.* New York: Cartwheel Books.

Benjamin, Alan. (1997). *Hanukkah chubby board book and dreidels.* New York: Little Simon.

Birtha, Becky. (2010). *Lucky bears.* Chicago, IL: Albert Whitman.

Bogan, Paulette. (2001). *Spike in the kennel.* New York: Putnam.

Bridwell, Norman. (1994). *Clifford's happy Easter.* New York: Scholastic.

Bridwell, Norman. (2005). *Clifford the big red dog.* New York: Cartwheel/Scholastic.

Brown, Margaret Wise. (1949). *Christmas in the barn.* New York: Crowell.

Brown, Margaret Wise. (1977). *The runaway bunny.* New York: Harper.

Brown, Margaret Wise. (2001). *Two little trains.* New York: HarperCollins.

Brown, Ruth. (2001). *Ten seeds.* New York: Knopf/Borzoi.

Campbell, Sarah. (2010). *Growing patterns.* Honesdale, PA: Boyds Mills Press.

Carle, Eric. (1969). *1, 2, 3 to the zoo.* New York: Collins World.

Carle, Eric. (1985). *My very first book of colors.* New York: Crowell.

Carle, Eric. (2007). *My very first book of animal homes.* New York: Philomel.

Chwast, Seymour. (2005). *Had Gadya.* New York: Roaring Brook.

Cole, Babette. (1997). *Dr. Dog.* New York: Alfred A. Knopf.

Cousins, Lucy. (2004). *Maisy's Halloween.* New York: Walker.

Cousins, Lucy. (2007). *Happy Easter Maisy.* Cambridge, MA: Candlewick.

Crews, Donald. (1985). *Freight train.* New York: Penguin.

Cyrus, Kurt. (2008). *Tadpole Rex.* Orlando, FL: Harcourt.

dePaola, Tomie. (1986). *Strega Nona.* New York: Harcourt Brace Jovanovich.

dePaola, Tomie. (1987). *An early American Christmas.* New York: Holiday House.

dePaola, Tomie. (1987). *Tomie dePaola's book of Christmas carols.* New York: Putnam.

Dickinson, Rebecca. (2001). *Monster cake.* New York: Scholastic/Cartwheel.

Dooley, Norah. (1991). *Everybody cooks rice.* Minneapolis, MN: Carolrhoda.

Douglas, Lloyd. (2003). *Let's get ready for Martin Luther King Jr. day.* New York: Children's Press/Scholastic.

Druce, Arden. (2001). *Halloween night.* Flagstaff, AZ: Rising Moon.

Duffy, Dee Dee. (1996). *Forest tracks.* Honesdale, PA: Boyds Mills Press.

Elffers, Joost, & Freyman, Saxton. (2005). *Food for Thought.* New York: Arthur A. Levine/Scholastic.

Elya, Susan. (2006). *F is for fiesta.* New York: Putnam.

Emberley, Rebecca. (2002). *My food.* New York: Little Brown.

Emerman, Ellen. (2001). *Is it Shabbos yet?* Brooklyn, NY: Hachai.

Fearnley, Jan. (2001). *Just like you.* Cambridge, MA: Candlewick.

Fisher, Leonard. (2001). *Sky, sea, the jetty, and me.* Tarrytown, NY: Marshall Cavendish.

Fleming, Denise. (2001). *Pumpkin eye.* New York: Holt.

Fraser, Debra. (2006). *A birthday cake is no ordinary cake.* Orlando, FL: Harcourt.

Fuller, Rachel. (2010). *Look at me.* Belrose, NSW, Australia: Child's Play.

Fuller, Rachel. (2010). *You and me.* Belrose, NSW, Australia: Child's Play.

George, Suzanne. (2009). *The daring Miss Quimby.* New York: Holiday House.

George, William. (1996). *Christmas as Long pond.* New York: Mulberry Books.

Gliori, Debi. (2002). *Penguin post.* Orlando, FL: Harcourt.

Gutman, Anne. (2001). *Gaspard on vacation.* New York: Knopf/Borzoi.

Hurst, Carol. (2001). *Rocks in his head.* Cambridge, MA: Greenwillow.

Hutchins, Hazel. (2009). *Together.* Toronto, Ontario: Annick.

Hutchins, Pat. (1997). *Shrinking mouse.* New York: Greenwillow.

Inkpen, Mick. (2001). *Kipper and Roly.* San Diego, CA: Harcourt/Red Wagon.

Jane, Pamela. (2001). *Monster mischief.* New York: Simon & Schuster/Atheneum.

Johnson, Jinny. (2009). *Flip the flap jungle animals.* New York: Macmillan/Kingfisher.

Johnson, Paul Brett. (2006). *On top of spaghetti.* New York: Scholastic.

Kelly, Mij. (2001). *William and the night train.* New York: Farrar.

Lamstein, Sarah. (2010). *Big night for salamanders.* Honesdale, PA: Boyds Mills Press.

Lattimore, Deborah. (1997). *Cinderhazel.* New York: Blue Sky.

Levitin, Sonia. (2001). *When elephant goes to a party.* Flagstaff, AZ: Rising Moon.

Littlesugar, Amy. (1996). *Marie in fourth position: The story of Degas' "The Little Dancer."* New York: Philomel.

Livingstone, Star. (2001). *Harley.* New York: North-South/Sea Star.

Lobel, Arnold. (2009). *Frogs and toads all sing.* New York: Harper Collins.

Locker, Thomas. (1997). *Waterdance.* San Diego, CA: Harcourt Brace.

London, Jonathan. (2001). *Froggy eats out.* New York: Viking.

London, Jonathan. (2001). *Sun dance water dance.* New York: Viking.

Mallat, Kathy. (2001). *Trouble on the tracks.* New York: Walker.

Martin, Bill, Jr. (1993). *Old devil wind.* San Diego, CA: Harcourt Brace Jovanovich.

Masurel, Claire. (2001). *A cat and a dog.* New York: North-South.

McCloskey, Robert. (1957). *Time of wonder.* New York: Viking.

McDermott, Gerald. (1992). *Zomo the rabbit.* San Diego, CA: Harcourt Brace Jovanovich.

McQuinn, Anna (2009). *My friend Mei Jing.* Toronto, Ontario: Annick.

Minters, Frances. (2001). Too *big, too small, just right.* San Diego, CA: Harcourt.

Morris, Ann. (1992). *Houses and homes.* New York: Lothrop, Lee and Shepard.

Moore, Clement. (2002). *The night before Christmas pop-up.* Boston: Little Simon.

Murphy, Mary. (2001). *Some things change.* Boston: Houghton Mifflin.

Nagel, Karen. (2009). *Shapes that roll.* Maplewood, NJ: Blue Apple.

Neale, John. (1994). *Good King Wenceslas.* New York: North South.

Newman, Leslea. (1998). *Matzo ball soup.* New York: Clarion.

Oppenheim, Joan. (2003). *The miracle of the first poinsettia.* Cambridge, MA: Barefoot.

Osbourne, Mary P. (1997). *Rocking horse Christmas.* New York: Scholastic.

Peterson, Chris. (2010). *Century farm.* Honesdale, PA: Boyds Mills Press.

Pfister, Marcus. (1993). *The Christmas star.* New York: North-South.

Pfister, Marcus. (2009). *Rainbow fish discovers the deep sea.* New York: North-South.

Pingry, Patricia. (2006). *The story of Easter.* Nashville, TN: Candy Cane.

Portnoy, Mindy. (1994). *Matzo ball: A Passover story.* Rockville, MD: Kar-Ben.

Priddy, Roger. (2004). *My big dinosaur book.* New York: Macmillan/Priddybooks.

Pringle, Laurence. (2010). *Bats!* Honesdale, PA: Boyds Mills Press.

Roberts, Bethany. (2001). *Thanksgiving mice!* New York: Clarion.

Saltzberg, Barney. (2001). *The problem with pumpkins: A hip & hop story.* San Diego, CA: Harcourt/Gulliver.

Sawyer, Ruth. (1953). *Journey cake, ho!* New York: Viking.

Schaefer, Lola. (2001). *This is the rain.* New York: Greenwillow.

Schoenherr, Ian. (2010). *Don't spill the beans!* New York: Harper Collins/Greenwillow.

Serfozo, Mary. (2001). *Plumply, dumply pumpkin.* New York: Simon & Schuster/Margaret K. McElderry.

Seuling, Barbara. (2001). *Spring song.* San Diego, CA: Harcourt.

Seuss, Dr. (pseud, for Theodor Geisel) (1957). *How the Grinch stole Christmas.* New York: Random.

Smith, Linda. (2010). *The inside tree.* New York: Harper Collins.

Spinelli, Eileen. (2004). *Thanksgiving at the Tappletons.* New York: Harper Trophy.

Spurling, Margaret. (2001). *Bilby moon.* Brooklyn, NY: Kane/Miller.

Stevenson, James. (1996). *The great big especially beautiful Easter egg.* New York: Mulberry Books.

Stutson, Caroline. (1996). *By the light of the Halloween moon.* New York: Puffin.

Szekeres, Cyndy. (1997). *Yes, Virginia, there is a Santa Claus.* New York: Cartwheel Books.

Todd, Mark. (2001). *What will you be for Halloween?* Boston: Houghton Mifflin.

Vaughan, Marcia. (2001). *We're going on a ghost hunt.* San Diego, CA: Harcourt.

Weigelt, Udo. (2001). *The Easter Bunny's baby.* New York: North South.

Whitaker, Suzanne George. (2009). *The daring Miss Quimby.* New York: Holiday House.

Wiencirz, Gerlinde. (2001). *Teddy's Easter secret.* New York: North South.

Wiencirz, Gerlinde. (2001). *Teddy's Halloween secret.* New York: North-South.

Wild, Margaret. (2001). *The pocket dogs.* New York: Scholastic.

Williams, Brenda. (2009). *Lin Yi's lantern: A moon festival tale.* Cambridge, MA: Barefoot.

Williams, Freddy. (2008). *Hush Harbor: Praying in secret.* Minneapolis, MN: Lerner/Carolrhoda.

Winkelman, Barbara. (2001). *Sockeye's journey home: The story of a Pacific salmon.* Norwalk, CT: Soundprints.

Wolff, Ferida, and Kozielski, Dolores. (1994). *On Halloween night.* New York: Tambourine.

Yaccarino, Dan. (2001). *The lima bean monster.* New York: Walker.

Yolen, Jane. (2009). *How do dinosaurs say I love you.* New York: Blue Sky.

Ziefert, Harriet. (2001). *On Halloween night.* New York: Puffin.

Zion, Gene. (2006). *Harry the dirty dog.* New York: Harper/Festival.

Zolotow, Charlotte. (1998). *The bunny who found Easter.* Boston: Houghton Mifflin.

Zucker, Jonny. (2004). *Fasting and dates: A Ramadan and Eid-ul-Fitr story.* Hauppauge, New York: Barron's Educational Series.

SELECTED REFERENCES AND RESOURCES

Anderson, N. A. (2009). Elementary children's literature. Infancy through age 13. Upper Saddle River, NJ: Allyn & Bacon/Pearson.

Bromley, K. D. (1995). Webbing with literature. Boston: Allyn and Bacon.

Butzow, C. M., & Butzow, J. W. (2000). Science through children's literature. Portsmouth, NH: Teacher Ideas Press.

Chalufour, I & Worth, K. (2005). Exploring water with young children. Minneapolis, MN: Redleaf.

Copple, C. & Bredekam, S. (Eds.) (2009). Developmentally appropriate practices in early childhood programs serving children from birth through age 8, (3rd ed.). Washington, DC: NAEYC.

Curtis, D. & Carter, M. (2007). Learning together with young children: A curriculum framework for reflective teachers. Minneapolis, MN: Redleaf.

Derman-Sparks, L. (2010). Anti-bias curriculum: Tools for empowering young children. Washington, DC: NAEYC.

Ellery, Valerie. (2009). Creating strategic readers. Newark, DE: International Reading Association.

Goouch, K. (2010). Towards excellence in early years education. New York: Routledge.

Grollman, S., & Worth, K. (2003). Worms, shadows, and whirlpools. Portsmouth, NH: Heinemann.

Herr, J., & Libby Larson, Y. (2004). Creative resources for the early childhood classroom. (4th ed.) Clifton Park, NY: Delmar Learning.

Hertzog, N. B. (2005). Young gifted children, the project approach, and Reggio Emilia. Presented at the 16th World Congress on Gifted and Talented Education. New Orleans, LA.

Jalongo, M. R. (2007). Early childhood language arts. Boston: Allyn & Bacon.

Katz, L. G., & Chard, S. C. (2000). Engaging children's minds: The project approach. Norwood, NJ: Ablex.

Mayesky, M. E. (2002). Creative activities for young children. (7th ed.) Clifton Park, NY: Delmar Learning.

Menard, V., & Marin, C. (2004). The Latino holiday book. New York: Marlowe.

Moehn, H. (2000). World holidays: A Watts guide for children. New York: Franklin-Watts.

Pica, R. (2000). Experiences in movement with music, activities and theory. (2nd ed.) Clifton Park, NY: Delmar Learning.

Rand, D. & Parker, T. (2001). Black books galore. Hoboken, NJ: John Wiley.

Weaver, C. (2009). Reading process and practice. Portsmouth, NH: Heinemann.

Whitehead, M. R. (2010). Language and literacy in the early years 0–7. Newbury Park, CA: SAGE.

Whitin, D., & Wilde, S. (1995). It's the story that counts. Portsmouth, NH: Heinemann.

INTERNET REFERENCES AND HELPFUL WEBSITES

A place of our own. Community Teaching of Southern California. Retrieved March 3, 2010, from http://www.aplaceofourown.org/question_detail.php?id=635

Bennett, T. Reactions to visiting the infant-toddler and preschool centers in Reggio Emilia, Italy. Early Childhood Research and Practice (spring 2001). Retrieved March 3, 2010, from http://www.ecrp.uiuc.edu

Chard, S. The project approach. Project Approach in Early Childhood and Elementary Children's Literature Website. University of Calgary. Retrieved March 3, 2010, from http://www.acs.ucalgary.ca/dkbrown/index.html

Education. Retrieved March 3, 2010, from http://www.projectapproach.com

Hertzog, N. B. Reflections and impressions from Reggio Emilia: It's not about art! Early Childhood Research and Practice (spring 2001). Retrieved March 3, 2010, from http://www.ecrp.uiuc.edu

Hurst, C. *Curriculum areas.* Retrieved January 5, 2007, from http://www.carolhurst.com

Studio Melizo. *Holidays on the Net.* Retrieved March 3, 2010, from http://www.holidays.net

University of California at Berkeley. *Lawrence Hall of Science: Kid's Corner.* Retrieved March 3, 2010, from http://www.lawrencehallofscience.org/

© Cengage Learning

CHAPTER 8

BIBLIOTHERAPY: USING BOOKS TO HEAL

The first part of the term **bibliotherapy** is **biblio**, a derivation of a Greek word referring to books. The second part, **therapy**, is a derivation of a Greek word referring to procedures used to treat bodily disorders. Thus, literally, bibliotherapy means the treatment of bodily disorders using books. The term has come to mean the use of books, and subsequent discussions about those books, to address a variety of psychological concerns. In order to make full use of bibliotherapy, it is necessary to have an understanding of the concerns possessed by young children and an awareness of some of the books that may be helpful in addressing those concerns. This chapter provides the reader with an understanding of the benefits and processes of using bibliotherapy. In addition, it addresses the use of bibliotherapy in the context of self, family, friends, other people, illness, death, fears, and world problems.

"I seldom think about my limitations, and they never make me sad."

—HELEN KELLER

UNDERSTANDING BIBLIOTHERAPY

The use of bibliotherapy as a tool for teachers and librarians was recognized over a half-century ago by educators David Russell and Caroline Shrodes (1950). They described bibliotherapy as a process in which the reader and the literature interacted. Taking a clinical approach, they felt bibliotherapy was a promising tool for assessing personality and monitoring adjustment and growth in individuals.

Years later Patricia Cianciolo (1965) published her beliefs using a less clinical perspective on how books can help the child. She identified six areas in which books could provide positive help to children. Two of these areas addressed education and learning issues. Books could help children acquire information about human behavior, including areas that were a current concern to them. Books could also help children understand the phrase "heal thyself." That is, children could learn that the answer to some problems must come from within. Two of the areas identified focused on the need to extend oneself. Through books, one can find interests outside oneself. Also, stories can be used to relieve stress in a controlled manner. The last two areas focused on the use of books as problem-solving tools. Books provide individuals with an opportunity to identify and compensate for personal problems. That is, it is often easier to talk about a problem if it is someone else's problem. Finally, stories can illuminate personal difficulties and help one acquire insight into personal behavior. That is, a problem can be clarified by seeing it described by another person in a story.

Books as Therapy and Didacticism

Didacticism is an artistic philosophy that focuses primarily on the inherent instructional possibilities and content information in literature or other art forms. There is much less consideration of the artistic merits of style or genre in the art or literature being considered. For example, although the Bible may contain some enduring and fascinating stories, it is seen primarily as a didactic work in which the primary purpose is to provide guidance and lessons on moral and religious issues. Modern poetry, on the other hand, frequently strives to test the limits and conventions of the poetic form in order to challenge the reader. Although there is the possibility of an instructional lesson in the poem, it's often intended to stretch the reader's mind in an entertaining manner.

When creating a book that is meant to be primarily didactic, there is always the danger that the writing will fall into the trap of becoming dull, wordy, and preachy rather than graceful and pleasing. This does not mean that a book that is didactic cannot be entertaining and vice versa. Nearly all literature is didactic to some extent, since nearly all works comment on the human condition. As a result, there are many books written to entertain children that can be used for didactic purposes. The key is to find and use books that grab the attention of the child, provide a developmentally appropriate text, and appeal to the interests and motivations of the audience. Without those things, there is no chance that the book will have any didactic value, for the attention of the audience is lost at the outset. Therefore, a good story is always more of an issue than any potential lesson included. If it is a good story, the reader can guide the children through activities and discussion to some awareness of the important lesson.

Charlotte S. Huck and Barbara Kiefer (2003) provide a picture of how bibliotherapy can be used with children experiencing a variety of fears, anxieties, and worries associated with everyday life. They identify the three processes of psychotherapy and suggest that they can parallel three stages of bibliotherapy. The first process is *identification,* in which there is an association of oneself with an individual found in literature. Second, there is *catharsis,* meaning the releasing of emotion. It is believed that by observing and identifying with a character in a story with a similar problem, one can gain some degree of relief from the stress and emotion caused by the same problem in one's own life. The third process is *insight,* in which one develops an emotional awareness of one's own motivations in dealing with a problem. That is, by observing and understanding how a character in a story deals with an emotion, one can better deal with the same emotion in real life.

This view can be helpful, since it provides a step-by-step procedure for using bibliotherapy with children. Teachers, parents, and others attempting to use bibliotherapy should use some caution, however. It is an appropriate tool for helping children approach minor anxieties associated with everyday life. But when children have deeper psychological problems, they should be referred to other professionals who possess the appropriate training to deal with those difficulties.

The Chronically Ill Child

Bibliotherapy is an effective tool to use with children who are physically ill. Hospitals, clinics, and treatment centers throughout the country frequently use such an approach with their young patients. Regina Houston describes the special considerations that one must have in using bibliotherapy with chronically ill children. At one point, she was the "Story Lady" in the pediatrics ward at the University of Massachusetts Hospital. She shares these thoughts:

> Stories give readers experiences they haven't had in life. Books also acquaint the reader with different ways of looking at life. Watty Piper's *The Little Engine That Could* has inspired many young listeners to try their very best. It has given confidence to children even during the most difficult of times and in the face of the most adverse situations. The stories can help release tension and develop values. They can show one how to evaluate situations and how to solve problems. They do so by allowing us to observe the solutions reached by the characters in both ordinary and unusual situations. In so doing, books extend both a child's experience and world.

All people share the basic needs for food, clothing, shelter, and safety. Other needs that everyone has include the need for love, being part of a group, a positive self-concept, and an understanding of what makes each of us special. Many of these needs can be partially met in books. Stories nurture the hopes and dreams of the child. They reinforce each child's uniqueness and provide courage and friendship.

Hospital-confined children have a special need for bibliotherapy. Children struggling with long-term illnesses find peace and solace in stories. Stories are comforting to the chronically ill child. The association lessens some of the trauma they are dealing with. Justin, a three-year-old, found a safe refuge in stories after his painful weekly injection. Another child, Benjamin, has used stories to come to an understanding that life has a beginning, a middle, and an end. Part of his regular outpatient visits to the hospital include a visit to the Story Lady. It is an enjoyable and nonthreatening part of his visit. The story sessions are not an escape from pain for Benjamin. Rather, they are an important part of Benjamin's total medical program as explained to him by his doctor and his mother.

Pediatric physicians have observed children as being more relaxed during examinations after they have shared and experienced a story. The stories provide a therapeutic vehicle through which the child can deal with fears and doubts. They can both educate the child and facilitate the procedures that the child must endure. One of the greatest benefits, however, comes from the human interaction of the child and the reader. Through voice and body language, the reader can communicate a calmness and a warmth. This acceptance of children and their fears is invaluable to both the pediatric patient and the well child.

Parents, teachers, and others who share stories with the chronically ill child must have certain understandings. Such children have special needs that go beyond that of well children. Medications, phases of an illness, and healing processes can all affect behavior. One should take care not to misread or misunderstand these changes in behavior. Knowledge of a child's physical needs and problems is necessary for anyone using bibliotherapy with a chronically ill child. It requires interest and caring on the part of the reader. That is true for all children, of course. With the chronically ill child, it is critical.

BENEFITS OF BIBLIOTHERAPY

Bibliotherapy can address a number of different needs a child may have in dealing with a difficulty. Obviously, some needs can be addressed better than others. The success of bibliotherapy depends on the child, the problem, and the situation in which bibliotherapy is used. The benefits discussed here include information, mutuality, empathy, options for action, and reaffirmation of life.

Information

The first benefit of bibliotherapy is the providing of **information**. Using books that address a particular problem often enables the child to gather accurate and reliable information in a subtle, unthreatening manner. Educating children to the realities of the world and its problems provides a base of knowledge that they can rely on. Many times children develop anxiety over a problem because they do not see the problem in its proper perspective. Education and the gaining of the truth that can come from books is helpful in destroying myths, misconceptions, and untruths. Problems often become much more solvable when they are seen.

Mutuality

Mutuality refers to the experience of sharing. When children are confronted with a problem that is affecting them deeply, they often feel alone. They are frightened by the sense of isolation they feel. Discovering, through books, that others share the same problem reduces this sense of isolation. Realizing that one isn't the only person in the world with a particular problem is helpful in coping with that problem.

Empathy

Empathy refers to the ability to share the feelings of another individual. Children are not necessarily born with empathy. A visit to most school yards will support the fact that children can be both cruel and thoughtless toward those

Comfort can be found in sharing a book with a friend.

they perceive to be different. Often this cruelty is based on ignorance or fear. It may be that the other child dresses, looks, or acts differently. The development of empathy is one of the most important things children can achieve. It places them firmly within the highest circle of humanity.

Books share the thoughts and feelings of others with their readers. Through books, children learn of their own worth and of the worth of others, even others who may not be like themselves. One might question whether this is truly the role of the educator. It cannot, of course, be otherwise. Achievement in academics without the development of character is of limited worth.

The caregiver is in a unique position to address both character development and academic achievement. As a matter of fact, how can one ignore the importance of each within a classroom? One cannot meaningfully teach a group of children while some in the group are shunned and hurting. Group cooperation is impossible if some children avoid the child with cerebral palsy for fear of "catching it."

The social relationships within a class have a direct influence on the productivity of the class. Addressing or ignoring these issues determines whether or not the group will have a heart and a soul. Bibliotherapy is most effective when used by an adult who is committed to addressing the whole child. Building empathy begins with seeing others as human beings with needs similar to our own.

TIPS FOR TEACHERS

Ask librarians and bookstore employees whether they have new titles that address children's fears and concerns.

- Let these people know the age group you are interested in.
- Mention specific issues of interest.
- Communicate with librarians and bookstore employees on a regular basis.

Options for Action

When faced with a difficult problem, adults can often feel in a bind with no solution. Children are no different. They may be so focused on the problem that they are incapable of stepping back and seeing the situation in a larger framework.

Books provide opportunities to observe how others view a problem. They explore various attempts by characters to resolve that problem. Through books, children come to realize that there are alternative ways for dealing with a problem. In discussing a story with an adult, children can learn that choices can be made in regard to most things in life. It is an important and healthy life skill to be able to cultivate options in problem solving.

Reaffirmation of Life

When a person is faced with what appears to be a tremendous problem, the world can seem a cold and frightening place. It is true that some bad things do happen in life. The world will never be perfect. Yet, there are many wonderful and beautiful things about life. There are some truly caring and loving people on this earth. There are flowers, birds, songs, and gorgeous sunsets. Children need to understand this when faced with problems. They need to be able to affirm that there are some truly beautiful things about life. This does not eliminate the problem; it merely helps put it in perspective.

Children are exposed to many of life's grim realities through television and the media. Children learn about job loss, lack of health insurance, war, and natural disasters. Unfortunately, the good things aren't deemed as newsworthy as the more sordid aspects of life. Children need to talk about the fears they have regarding some of the things they have seen. They often look to adults to help them affirm the positive aspects of their existence as people.

The attack on America that occurred on September 11, 2001, news stories about violent confrontations between people, and even everyday observations of road rage can suggest that violent behavior is a life option. It is important, therefore, to promote nonviolent behavior in children. Bruce D. Perry (2001) suggests six core strengths to foster nonviolent behavior:

- being a friend
- thinking before acting
- joining and contributing to a group
- thinking about the needs of others
- accepting the differences of others
- respecting yourself and others

These core values can be addressed and reinforced through many of the books used in bibliotherapy and in regular story sharing times.

USING BIBLIOTHERAPY

Bibliotherapy can be a powerful and effective tool for addressing the problems and concerns of young children. As with any activity or lesson to be used with children, planning will increase the effectiveness of bibliotherapy. In order to plan effectively, one must be aware of several factors surrounding the use of bibliotherapy: (a) developmental appropriateness, (b) accuracy of content and effectiveness of style, (c) strategies for presentation, and (d) awareness of the limitations of bibliotherapy.

Developmental Appropriateness

The criteria for choosing **developmentally appropriate** books for bibliotherapy are similar to those used for choosing books for other purposes. Be aware of the understanding children have at different developmental levels. Be aware also of the types of concerns they have at different ages. These can vary, of course, but one can reasonably expect three-year-olds to have night fears, for example. Adults must *realize* that the fears children experience are very real to them. The best way to respond is with honesty and empathy. Children's fears must be addressed without ridicule. Although children's fears may not be totally overcome, coping skills and management of the fears can be established. A powerful aid to overcoming fear is an adult who is consistently accessible to the child and reinforces the concept that things are under control. This is true whether the child's fears are real or imaginary.

There are a variety of possible sources of concern for the young child. Some things such as parental separation, divorce, adoption, death, AIDS, pregnancy, or the birth of a new sibling are centered in the family. Other concerns are more closely related to the child's ability to deal with the immediate environment. These include friendship, illness, death, bullies, school, animals, moving, foster care, and self-worth. Still other fears may focus on world events such as nuclear war, crime, terrorism, and drugs. If the child initiates a discussion about one of these fears, chances are it is very real in the mind of that child.

In determining whether a book or an activity is developmentally appropriate, the National Association for the Education of Young Children (NAEYC) (Copple and Bredekamp (Eds.), 2009) warns against seeing the concept as a polarizing "yes/no" issue. That is, there is no single characteristic that makes something developmentally appropriate or not. NAEYC illustrates the complexity of the concept through a set of statements that can be used as a guide to making decisions concerning the developmental appropriateness. Some NAEYC comments that are particularly relevant to book selection observe that children:

- develop their own individual understanding of the world and profit from teaching by peers and adults.
- benefit from knowing their boundaries and from opportunities to make choices within those boundaries.
- grow through practicing new skills and knowledge in realistically challenging situations.

- develop a sense of competence by being treated as individuals and by having opportunities to collaborate with their peers.
- need to develop a sense of respect for themselves and for others who may be different from themselves.

Choice of Books

There are many good books for meeting needs within most problem areas. The illustrations and text must be analyzed with the same criteria used to select books for any use. Particular attention should be paid to the accuracy of the content and the style of delivery. A book that trivializes the problem or solves it in an oversimplified manner might not help a child to deal with reality. In bibliotherapy, the concept of reality is extremely important even though the books may be fictional.

Books that use either animals or people can be appropriate. Even though children know that bears don't talk, the books by Stan and Jan Berenstain are effective in dealing with problems because the issues are realistic. The use of talking bears simply allows the child to look at a problem through another's eyes.

Using books with animal characters can be especially appropriate when dealing with topics that are embarrassing to children. It is easier to talk about an embarrassing problem in the context of an animal character.

To be effective, a book must communicate with children on their level. Children, like adults, do not like to be talked down to. They often react in anger to such an approach or at least end the communication. The story should also have a clear appeal. At an early point in the book the child must be able to relate to the character and the solution. A good message or theme is worthless if the story is not captivating.

Strategies for Presentation

Planning ahead will make bibliotherapy a more powerful tool. Using effective strategies for presentation will help as well. The most helpful strategies deal with such things as (a) informing parents, (b) making decisions about when and how to use bibliotherapy, and (c) planning how to share the experience with children.

Research the Facts. It is important to have a good grasp of the information to be used. Only facts and real information should be used. Half-truths and lies will only destroy credibility, no matter how well-intended they are. This is true whether the information comes from the literature or other sources. If the information is known ahead of time, it can be better tailored to the audience. Review books and articles on the topic for ideas on the best ways to introduce the subject and for how much to introduce at each level.

Be Sensitive. When using bibliotherapy, one is providing help to both the child and the family. A child with a problem does not exist in a vacuum; such a child exists within a family, and the family is most likely aware of the problem as well. Therefore, it makes good sense to let parents know how the problem is being addressed. This can be done through meetings, telephone calls, or newsletters. The method of communication will depend on the type of problem. When working with children, it is helpful to anticipate all of the possible reactions children could have prior to beginning the lesson. By doing this, one can plan responses to these reactions. Such planning can help ensure that bibliotherapy will be carried on in a nonthreatening and supportive manner. As a result, children will be more likely to feel empowered by the experience.

Use Good Timing. Introducing bibliotherapy before children are ready for it can mean failure. Make certain that trust has been established. Trust is something that builds up over time. It is inadvisable, therefore, to discuss anything more than minor concerns during the first week of school. Another aspect of good timing is to ensure an adequate amount of time for fully exploring the issue. It is inappropriate to begin a session on new babies or racial issues at the end of the day or in the middle of a free-play period. A time must be chosen when the classroom is quiet and there will be enough time to talk, to listen, and to internalize.

Integrate the Topic. No problem exists all by itself. Likewise, no solution exists in isolation. All the various parts of our existence are integrated in our life. It is both logical and efficient to integrate the use of bibliotherapy with other parts of the curriculum.

Many of the books one would use in a bibliotherapy session would be appropriate for other aspects of the curriculum as well. By integrating the understandings and issues, the learning is reinforced for children.

Plan for the Long Term. In planning a long-term integrated curriculum, it makes sense to plan bibliotherapy in a logical progression of steps. For example, one might begin with self-concept, followed by family concerns, school concerns, and personal safety. Each topic builds on the previous one. A child's understanding increases when a logical order such as this is followed.

Remember the Role. There will always be the temptation to deal with issues that should be left to others. In *Books to Grow with: A Guide to Using the Best Children's Fiction for Everyday Issues and Tough Challenges* (2004), Cheryl Coon provides a manageable four-step approach to sharing a story for a bibliotherapy-related purpose.

- Set the stage: Describe the time and place of the story.
- Read the book together: This may mean more than one reading.
- Reflect together: When discussing the story, ask open-ended questions such as: What do you think he means? Why doesn't she...? Does he do something different when...? Why do you think she says...?
- Personalize the story: Seek the children's personal involvement with questions such as: Have you ever...? Did you ever find out that...? How would you feel if...? How could we show that...?

The teacher using bibliotherapy should keep in mind that the purpose is to shed light and understanding on some of the normal problems and fears children encounter as they are growing up. Serious mental and psychological problems should be *referred* to others with the appropriate training as soon as they are discovered. If a child is observed reacting with agitation or acting-out behavior when a topic is discussed, the child should be talked to privately.

A calm and supportive manner in posing gentle, nonthreatening questions is the most productive way to deal with a frightened child. If the child is not able to participate and continues to exhibit reactions that are noticeably different from those of other children, a parent conference is suggested. In meeting with the parents, it is important to listen to their understanding of the problem. When a mutual understanding of the problem is achieved, the best decision for the child can be made.

Maintain Flexibility. When working with young children it is important to be flexible. With bibliotherapy, it is particularly important. Be ready to shift gears, take an unexpected turn, or back up as the situation demands. While discussing a problem in a bibliotherapy session, it is a good idea to restate any questions a child might ask. This restating makes sure that everyone understands what is being asked. Then provide just enough information to answer the question. Too detailed an answer could lose the children's interest. One should always respond to a question, however. Choosing to ignore a question that was honestly asked is a poor response. If an appropriate answer cannot be given, one must say so rather than fail to respond. Be aware, too, that children often ask simple and general questions prior to asking the real question that addresses a current problem or difficulty. Allow children time to build up to discussing their real concerns.

ADDRESSING THE CONCERNS OF CHILDREN

Young children often have different concerns than those of older children, adolescents, and adults. Sometimes what adults perceive to be the concerns of children actually cause them little difficulty. The best way to learn of children's concerns is to ask them or listen to their general conversation. Sometimes adults forget to do this, but it is a technique that really does work. Indirect means such as reading a book and discussing it can also bring out the true concerns children possess. There is no one best way to learn of a child's concern. Each individual sees things differently. Each child will use different approaches and coping strategies for dealing with problems.

In general, however, there are certain themes that address the concerns and problems of children: self, family, friends, other people, illness and death, and the world. This is not the only way of grouping these areas, of course. It is used here because it serves as an easily understood frame of reference.

Self

Am I as pretty as Jane? Does my ball bounce as well as the ball that Joe has? Will I always be short? Will Mom have time for me when the new baby arrives? These are only a few of the possible concerns of young children. While adults may see some issues as foolish, they are quite real to the child who wants to fit in with the rest of the world. The problems can be increased if other children learn about them and taunt the child. Such teasing can be the beginning lesson on the dark side of human nature.

Children need adults to bring light to this dark side of life. Sharing a book related to the situation can enable everyone to think about their actions and the effect they have on others. Such a book can help to bring out the importance of feeling good about oneself.

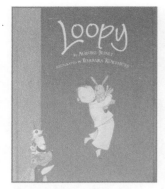

A variety of books can be used to explore this topic. Tomie dePaola's *Oliver Button Is a Sissy,* Claire Alexander's *Small Florence, Piggy Pop Star!,* Jacqueline Jules' *Zapato Power: Freddie Ramos Takes Off,* Karen Beaumont's *I Like Myself,* Aliki's (Brandenburg) *All By Myself,* and Kathi Appelt's *Incredible Me* explore the idea of being true to yourself and trying to do your best in your areas of interest. In *The Name Jar* by Yangsook Choi, a young Korean girl is self conscious about her Korean name until an act of friendship and caring allow her and others to connect through cultural understanding. Vashti, a young artist, finds the answer to her doubts within her own self in *The Dot* by Peter Reynolds. In a hilarious tale, a young pig shows courage in the face of criticism as he gets the whole barnyard dancing in *Dumpy LaRue* by Elizabeth Winthrop. The emotion of personal fear is examined in such favorites as Chris Wormell's *Ferocious Wild Beasts!* and Tony Johnston's *The Chizzywink and the Alamagoozlum.*

Perhaps the most important aspect of bibliotherapy is to help children deal with their fears. Human beings who have fears can relate to characters in stories that have fears, even if the fears are different. Loopy, a much loved stuffed bunny, is left behind at the doctor's office and it is too late to go back in Aurore Jesset's *Loopy.* While this story deals with the loss of a beloved toy with gentleness and wit, it makes a good starting point to deal with the concept of loss of other precious things in a child's life. In *Little Baa,* Kim Lewis shares the story of a little lamb that wakes up alone in a field after taking a nap. In *Can Anybody Hear Me?* By Jessica Meserve, Jack must find his voice when he gets lost. Jack is quiet and his family is loud. When he tells them he is going up the mountain, nobody hears him. When he becomes lost, he realizes that he must overcome his quiet nature in order to save himself. Using animals as the central characters, Martin Waddell deals with the fears of being lost in *Tom Rabbit* and *A Kitten Called Moonlight.* Also using animal characters, Karma Wilson addresses fear and anxiety in *Bears Feel Scared* and *Bears Want More.* A little boy wakes up in fear in total darkness in *Eli's Night Light* by Liz Rosenberg. In *Chicken Chickens* by Valeri Gorbachev, the characters are afraid to go down the playground slide, while in *Iris and Walter, True Friends* by Elissa Guest, the character is fearful of riding a horse. In *Don't Go!* by Jane Zalben, a young boy expresses fear of being left on the first day of preschool. In *Max's Starry Night* by Ken Wilson, Max, an African American boy, shows respect for the fears of others.

An individual's **sense of self** and becoming a competent person are critically important factors in development. This gives us a feeling of confidence in being who we are. Lisa learns to feel comfortable with being alone in Anne Gutman's *Lisa's Airplane Trip.* The power of books to help overcome a sense of being alone is shared in *A Story for Bear* by Dennis Hasely. A similar lesson is learned in *Small World of Binky Braverman* by Rosemary Wells. In an updated republication of a 1945 book, Bill Martin, Jr. and Michael Sampson

© Cengage Learning

Children often see a bit of themselves in the characters they meet in a story.

Reprinted with the permission of Simon and Schuster Books for Young Readers an imprint of Simon & Schuster Children's Publishing Division from ALISTAIR UNDERWATER by Marilyn Sadler, illustrated by Roger Bollen. Illustrations copyright © 1988 Roger Bollen.

share a story of identity and purpose in *The Little Squeegy Bug*. The conflicting feelings associated with growing up and the loss of childhood are explored by Kathy Stinson in a newly released shorter version of *Big or Little*. Dealing with shyness is addressed in a sensitive manner by Cari Best in *Shrinking Violet*. Rejection is dealt with through a sensitive story and breathtaking illustrations by author-illustrator Peter Catalanotto in *Emily's Art*. Anna Alter cleverly presents a story of how to get over a feeling of grumpiness in *Francine's Day*.

Common childhood fears can come to light at bedtime. Ken Baker reverses the issue in *Brave Little Monster* where a little monster is afraid of imaginary little girls and boys hiding in his closet. Still another monster is presented in *Alistair Underwater* by Marilyn Sadler. In Alison Ritchie's *I Don't Want to Sleep Alone*, Joey's parents try to deal with his wanting company in his bedroom with a supply of happy stuffed animals. On the other hand, a Mexican American child is delighted to have her own room in *My Very Own Room* by Amada Perez. *My Monster Mama Loves Me So* by Laura Leuck is so soft and lovable it would even make a good bedtime story. Libba Moore Gray tells the story of how a nearsighted frog overcomes a fear of jumping to the next lily pad in *Fenton's Leap*. Using fewer than forty words, Chris Raschka presents a powerful lesson on fear in *Yo! Yes?* A child's fear for a lost pet is touchingly shared by Uli Waas in *Where's Molly?*

Concerns about being a competent person both at home and at school are addressed in Robert Kraus's *Leo the Late Bloomer* and *Herman the Helper*,

Reprinted with the permission of Simon and Schuster Books for Young Readers an imprint of Simon & Schuster Children's Publishing Division from HERMAN THE HELPER by Robert Kraus, illustrated by Jose Aruego and Ariane Dewey. Illustrations copyright © 1974 Jose Aruego and Ariane Dewey.

Alma Flor Ada's *Let Me Help!*, Maryann Cocca-Leffler's *Bravery Soup*, Tomie dePaola's *Andy, That's My Name*, Peter Reynolds's *So Few of Me*, Mike Thaler's *Hippo Lemonade*, Watty Piper's *The Little Engine That Could*, and Mick Inkpen's *Nothing*. Learning to be a responsible member of society and the world is the focus of Marcus Pfister's *Milo and the Magic Stones*. Milo discovers a marvelous stone with magical properties and must decide what to do. In a unique lesson about environmental costs, Marcus Pfister includes two endings to the story that will lead to different outcomes depending on what Milo decides to do. Finally, Jane Yolen's wonderful book, *Sleeping Ugly*, does an exceptional job of dealing with the concept of physical attractiveness.

Family

The family continues to be seen as the basic social unit of society, but the twentieth century has brought many changes to it. Families are smaller and tend to be more spread out geographically. Separation, divorce, single parenthood, and extended families are more and more common. Children sometimes do not understand these changes, and this causes them to develop fears. Children wonder whether they caused the divorce, whether Dad will ever come back, and whether they will be divorced by their families. They also worry about the mortality of parents, grandparents, and themselves.

The traditional causes of stress in families have never left. New babies, deaths, illness, sibling rivalry, unemployment, poverty, and homelessness continue to create pressures on the young child. These aspects of family life put pressure on the entire family with a variety of results. The young child is the least able member of the family to deal with the fears these changes bring. These fears overwhelm the verbal and coping skills of the very young. Bibliotherapy can help. It will not solve all of the problems, but it will provide both a framework and some of the language necessary for children to understand the stresses.

TIPS FOR TEACHERS

Listen to the concerns and worries of children and their families in a non-judgmental manner.

- Know in advance and use judgment about which issues you should refer to a professional.
- Listen to the whole story the child is telling you.
- Don't invade or usurp the parents' authority.

Cover from *Milo and the Magical Stones* by Marcus Pfister. Jacket art copyright © 2009 by Marcus Pfister. Reprinted by permission of North-South Books. All rights reserved.

The concept of a family being a happy suburban group consisting of mother, father, and two children has long past. A more appropriate idea of a family might focus on the connections, values, commitments, and goals shared among whoever makes up the family group. Using whimsical illustrations, Todd Parr introduces readers to nuclear, interracial, step, extended, gay, divorced, and single-parent families in *The Family Book*. In *Ish* by Peter Reynolds, the reader sees that disagreements happen in any family. In this story, Ramon is sad and hurt when his older brother criticizes his artwork, saying that it does not look real. Ramon crumples and discards his pictures only to have them retrieved, flattened, and displayed by his little sister in her bedroom. She likes them because they are tree-ish and silly-ish. Ramon realizes that the value of art is how it makes someone feel. Adele Sansone addresses the issue of adoption in *The Little Green Goose*. Mr. Goose finds and cares for an abandoned egg and has visions of being a good father to the newborn gosling. When the egg finally hatches with a surprising result, he loves his new baby like any new parent. Other books dealing with family issues include Cynthia Rylant's *When I Was Young in the Mountains*, Natalie Kinsey-Warnock's *A Farm of Her Own*, Steve Henry's *Nobody Asked Me!*, Anne Bowen's *I Loved You Before You Were Born*, Chinlun Lee's *The Very Kind Rich Lady and Her One Hundred Dogs*, Martha Alexander's *Nobody Asked Me if I Wanted a Baby Sister*, and Tom Birdseye's *A Regular Flood of Mishap*.

Numerous books deal with specific family members. Fathers are the focus of Robert Munsch's *50 Below Zero* and Will Smith's *Just the Two of Us*. Clever young Emily Green creates a game of hide and seek when her father calls her to lunch in Norma Fox Mazer's *Has Anyone Seen My Emily Green?* Good humor, warmth, and parent-child love are felt throughout this whimsical adventure that will have young readers searching for Emily Green on every page. Mothers are the focus of Anne Bowen's *How Did You Grow So Big, So Soon?*, Carol Carrick's *Mothers Are Like That*, and Lennie Goodings's *When You Grow Up*. Joan Goodman in *Bernard Goes to School* and Harriet Ziefert in *Grandma, It's for You* demonstrate the special relationships that can develop between children and their grandmothers. The special connection between children and grandfathers is established in *Can You Hear the Sea?* by Judy Cumberbatch. The continuing value of individuals even as they grow older and weaker is beautifully portrayed in Jim Arnosky's *Grandfather Buffalo*. In another vein, a young Chinese girl is upset about having to give up her room when her grandfather comes to live with the family until she discovers the joy of mutual learning in *Grandfather Counts* by Andrea Cheng.

Other issues, some controversial, can be explored through literature if it seems appropriate. The issue of illiteracy in the family is addressed in Eve Bunting's *The Wednesday Surprise*. Children have concerns about gender, sex, and where babies come from. The best answers to questions children raise are, of course,

Book cover from *A Regular Flood of Mishap* by Tom Birdseye, illustrated by Megan Lloyd, copyright © 1994. Reprinted by permission of the Holiday House, New York.

Book cover from *Two Places to Sleep* by Joan Schuchman, illustrated by Jim LaMarche. Copyright © 1979. Reprinted by permission of Carolrhoda Books.

honest explanations. Explain the use of books to address these issues and discuss possible topics with parents at a parents' meeting. There are several books to help address some of the issues and provide information as well. Human reproduction is addressed in *It's Perfectly Normal* by Robie Harris. Siblings and sibling rivalry are the issue in books such as *Matty Takes Off* and *Matty Is a Mess,* both by Miriam Moss, *What Brothers Do Best, What Sisters Do Best* by Laura Numeroff, Wolfram Hanel's *Little Elephant Runs Away,* and Audrey Penn's *A Pocket Full of Kisses.*

Issues affecting the family can be explored in books as well. Poverty is the focus in the Depression-era stories *Potato* by Kate Lied and *Leah's Pony* by Elizabeth Friedrich as well as in Helen Ketteman's *Mama's Way.* A touching story with a thoughtful ending, *The Teddy Bear* by David McPhail touches on the issue of homelessness. An excellent book on grandparents suffering from Alzheimer's disease is Jonah Schein's *Forget Me Not.* Selling a home and moving into a nursing home or assisted-living facility is the theme of *Miss Opal's Auction* by Susan Vizurrga. The stresses and worries of a child whose parents are divorced are addressed in Eve Bunting's *The Days of Summer,* Claire Masurel's *Two Homes,* Barbara Santucci's *Loon Summer,* and *Two Places to Sleep* by Joan Schuchman. *The Princess and the Castle* by Caroline Binch addresses the issue of the death of a parent. In this story, Genevieve lives in an English fishing village with her mother and younger brother after her father's death at sea. Though she hates the ocean now, she is intrigued by the old castle she sees across the bay. When another sailor comes into her and her mother's life, she learns to confront her fears. Single-parent households and unmarried-couple families are the topic in *Porky and Bess* by Ellen Weiss and Mel Friedman. In this story, sloppy bachelor pig Porky moves in with single mother cat Bess, who is a neatnik. The beginning chapter book shows how the two must evolve in their relationship and make compromises in sharing household duties much like members of every other family.

As more families are created through gay marriages and civil unions, children become aware of the joys and pressures involved. Books that can lead to a more inclusive understanding include *Emma and Meesha My Boy,* by Kaitlyn Considine, *ABC: A Family Alphabet* and *Molly's Family* by Nancy Garden. Though great care should be taken, the issue of child abuse is addressed in *One of the Problems of Everett Anderson* by Lucille Clifton. Finally, imaginary fears are expertly dealt with in *My Mama Says There Aren't Any Zombies, Ghosts, Vampires, Creatures, Demons, Monsters, Fiends, Goblins, or Things* by Judith Viorst.

Friends

As children grow, they move from a focus on themselves to the need to be a part of a group. They want to extend their social interactions beyond their families. They seek friendships. This is a long process along a path that can have many obstacles and pitfalls. Since humans are social beings by nature, it is a path that all must somehow travel.

Adults wince at what young children sometimes say and do to their friends. They can be alternatively very loving and very hostile. Toddlers may hug each other one minute and bite each other the next. Preschoolers change best friends as though they are participating in a card game. Kindergartners announce the beginnings and endings of best friendships as publicly as political campaigns announce endorsements. As a result, childhood friendships possess a combination of happiness, pain, and chaos. One can deal with these issues through discussion, understanding, and the use of bibliotherapy. It is through the reading of a story that sounds familiar to the real situation that the best and most sensitive discussions will emerge.

It is not always easy for children to make a meaningful connection between their lives and the lives of characters in a story. Caregivers can guide the discussion with questions:

- *Why did this happen?* This will help children probe the character's motives.
- *How did this make the character feel?* This can help children see how one character's actions can influence the feelings of another character.
- *What does this remind you of in your own life?* This will help children link the story to their own experience.

Books that can be used to generate bibliotherapy discussions include Karen Beaumont's *Being Friends* and Simms Tayback's *Where Is My Friend*. Two superb books on the subject of sleeping over at a friend's house are Jacqueline Rogers's *Best Friends Sleep Over* and Bernard Waber's *Ira Sleeps Over*. The joys of friendship are celebrated in *Forever Friends* by Carin Berger, *Play Ball, Corduroy* by B. G. Hennessey, and *You and Me* by Salley Mavor.

The sadness of moving away is explored in *Faraway Drums* by Virginia Kroll. In this touching story about an urban African American family, Jamila is very unhappy in the new apartment her family has moved to. Having to come home right after school to baby-sit her little sister Zakiya makes things even worse. Zakiya is even more unhappy, because the new nighttime sounds frighten her. Floyd Cooper's gritty but striking illustrations lend an air of realism to the story. This book will help stimulate young people to talk about the difference between a building and a home. Other stories about friends moving away include *Big Ernie's New Home* by Teresa and Whitney Martin, *Friends for All Seasons* by Geraldine Elschner, and *My Best Friend Moved Away* by Nancy Carlson. Carlson's book also explores the idea of what makes a friendship. Continuing this idea on the concept of friendship is *Widget* by Lyn McFarland. The ups and downs of friendship are addressed in Arnold Lobel's *Frog and Toad Are*

Friends, Megan McDonald's *Reptiles Are My Life,* Lisa Jahn-Clough's *Simon and Molly Plus Hester,* Tony Johnston's *Alien and Possum: Friends No Matter What,* Jonathan London's *Froggy Plays in the Band,* Mary Wormell's *Bernard the Angry Rooster,* and Judith Caseley's *Bully.*

Other People

Children and adults try to make sense of the world. When things don't fit neatly into place in the child's mind, fear can arise. **Other people** is a grouping, used here in a no-pejorative way, that refers to people who may be different from ourselves in some way. While it is not always clear why this is so, the difference may cause stress and fear. Any unfamiliar person may fall into this category. A perfectly silly book to introduce this idea is *Squarehead* by Harriet Ziefert. Animal characters dealing with tolerance and acceptance are portrayed in the touching *Sophie's Masterpiece: A Spider's Tale* by Eileen Spinelli. The stress and fear are usually caused by ignorance on the part of the child. Children with disabilities and children of different ethnicity who appear to be different can cause anxiety. Children often exhibit fear toward people with disabilities because they are afraid that they will "catch it." Skin color, dress, and language that are not familiar can cause anxiety for both minority and non-minority children. Continuing research is examining the assumptions that have been accepted concerning when in a child's life racial bias emerges. By analyzing a wide range of recent studies, Bronson and Merryman conclude that very young children may establish beliefs in this area through ongoing observations regarding developing in-group identification and preferences. They suggest that honest and thoughtful discussions about race and bias should begin well before children make comments in reference to this subject. Through bibliotherapy, children can learn that despite the differences, people are all human beings. Bibliotherapy can help decrease ignorance and focus discussions on the common humanity of all people.

There are many books that explore the concept of other people. Physical disabilities are clarified and explained in stories such as Eveline Hasler's *A Tale of Two Brothers.* Visual disabilities are dealt with in Colleen Adams's *The Courage of Helen Keller,* Ezra Jack Keats's *Apartment Three* and Patricia MacLachlan's *Through Grandpa's Eyes.* Hearing disabilities are the focus of such books as Elana's *Ears* by Gloria Lowell. This story has the added advantage of demonstrating a special sibling relationship. Isabelle and Charlie share a friendship and appreciate all the similarities and differences about themselves in *My Friend Isabelle by Eliza Woloson.* The fact that one of them has a disability is just one part of the many differences that they note but do not focus upon. Other disabilities and differences are addressed in Tomie dePaola's *Oliver Button Is a Sissy,* Charlotte Zolotow's *William's Doll,* Janet Rickert's *Russ and the Almost Perfect Day,* and Daniel Pinkwater's *Uncle Melvin.*

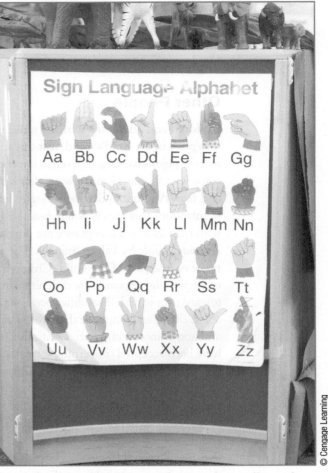

© Cengage Learning

Knowledge about disabilities can foster understanding and acceptance.

TIPS FOR TEACHERS

Use books about many cultures and about characters with a disability so that children will know that these differences are a natural part of life.

- Use multicultural books throughout all aspects of the day.
- Treat characters in books with disabilities matter-of-factly, making the disability only a single aspect of the character.
- Invite people with disabilities to read books with children, not to discuss their disabilities, enabling children to focus on the reader as a person.

Cover from *Shades of People* by Shelley Rotner and Sheila Kelly. Jacket art copyright © 2009 by Shelley Rotner. Reprinted by permission of Holiday House. All rights reserved.

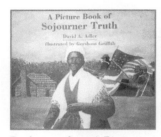

Book cover from *A Picture Book of Sojourner Truth* by David Adler, illustrated by Gershom Griffith, copyright ©1994. Reprinted by permission of Holiday House.

Author Isabell Monk. Photo used by permission of Lerner Publishing Group/ Carolrhoda.

Books are available that can help educate children to the concept that regardless of various religious, ethnic, and national origins, we are all more similar than different as members of the human family. Good choices to explore this issue are *Black Is Brown Is Tan* by Arnold Adoff, *Tan to Tamarind* by Malathi Michelle Iyengar, and *We All Sing with the Same Voice* by J. Philip Miller and Shepard Greene. *Shades of People* by Shelley Rotner and Sheila Kelly addresses the fact that people within families can often have just as many differences as between families. The story helps young readers to look beyond the obvious differences with sensitivity and vibrant illustrative photographs. African Americans are the focus of books such as Debbi Chocolate's magical and musical *The Piano Man*, Angela Johnson's *Daddy Calls Me Man*, Ezra Jack Keats's *The Snowy Day*, David Adler's *A Picture Book of Sojourner Truth*, and Patricia McKissack's *A Million Fish . . . More or Less*.

Three delightful books by Angela Johnson featuring African American families are *Joshua by the Sea*, *One of Three*, and *When I Am Old with You*. Books involving Hispanic Americans include *F Is for Fiesta* by Susan Elya. Other multicultural stories include *Family* by Isabell Monk, *Dim Sum for Everyone* by Grace Lin, *Jin Woo* by Eve Bunting, and *Henry's First-Moon Birthday* by Lenore Look. Stories from other places in the world can introduce children to those who may be different from themselves. Jeanette Winter transports the reader to Mali in *My Baby*, while Barbara Goldin explores a biblical tale from Mount Sinai in an updated version titled *A Mountain of Blintzes*. All of these stories are superb tales that transcend cultures.

Illness and Death

Illness and death are a part of life that most people fear to some extent. For children, who have less understanding of these events than adults, the anxiety may be greater. The topics of illness and death can trigger powerful emotions, particularly in a child who is close to someone who is seriously ill or who has just died. For this reason, it is important to be particularly sensitive when dealing with these topics. The death of a classroom pet may provide an opportunity to explore this concept on a less emotional level. On the other hand, the fears associated with medical and dental visits can be addressed quite readily with bibliotherapy.

The topic of illness and death are addressed in Tomie dePaola's *Now One Foot, Now the Other*, Rebecca Rissman's *People Who Help Us*, and H. A. and Margaret Rey's *Curious George Goes to the Hospital*. Traumatic brain injury (TBI), an increasing occurrence in military deployment and auto accidents, is addressed in a supportive sensitive manner in *I Know You Won't Forget* by

Book cover from *Family* by Isabell Monk, illustrations Janice Lee Porter, text copyright © 2001 by Isabell Monk, Illustrations copyright © 2001 by Janice Lee Porter. Reprinted by permission of the publisher Lerner Publishing Group/ Carolrhoda. All rights reserved.

Reprinted by Diana Comer

Children can bring personal knowledge and experience to story time.

Book cover from *The Snow Goose*, written and illustrated by Pirkko Vainio. Copyright © 1993 by Nord-Sud Verlag AG, Gossau Zurich, Switzerland. Reprinted by permission of North-South Books.

Truly Blessed Ink, a collaboration of authors with TBI. Medical visits and illnesses are dealt with in Tomie dePaola's *Strega Nona Meets Her Match* and Sabine Kraushaar's *Say Ahh!* The topic of death is explored in a sensitive manner in Amy Ehrlich's *Maggie and Silky and Joe*, Mem Fox's *Tough Boris*, Oliver Jeffers's *The Heart and the Bottle*, Nan Gregory's *Wild Girl and Gran*, Elizabeth Warfel's *The Blue Pearls*, Robert Munsch's *Love You Forever*, Eleanor Schick's *Mama*, and Pirkko Vainio's *The Snow Goose*. The death of a beloved pet is sensitively portrayed in Robie Harris's *Goodbye Mousie*, Maggie Smith's *Desser the Best Ever Cat*, Pat Thomas's *I Miss You*, Judith Viorst's *The Tenth Good Thing about Barney*, and Udo Weight's *Bear's Last Journey*. Tomie dePaola deals with

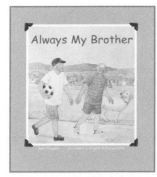

Cover from *Always My Brother* by Jean Reagan. Jacket art copyright Phyllis Pollema-Cahill. Jacket art copyright © 2009 by Phyllis Pollema-Cahill. Reprinted by permission of Tilbury House. All rights reserved.

the death of a grandparent in an honest and straightforward manner in *Nana Upstairs, Nana Downstairs*.

The deaths of other children can be particularly troubling. Caution should be used when reading books about the death of friends and acquaintances such as Sebastian Lath's *Remembering Crystal* and Audrey Penn's *Chester Raccoon and the Acorn Full of Memories*. One of the most difficult points in the life of a child, as well as the child's family, is the death of a sibling. In *Always My Brother* by Jean Reagan, readers share Becky's grief as she struggles to overcome her guilt and sadness over the death of her brother. She and John were best friends and did everything together. Accompanied by Phyllis Pollema-Cahill's beautiful illustrations, the story is told with great sensitivity as Becky deals with grief, acceptance, and recovery.

A fine contemporary book for young children on the topic of HIV/AIDS is *Too Far Away to Touch* by Leslea Newman. In this story, Zoe's Uncle Leonard is dying from AIDS. With touching sensitivity, Uncle Leonard provides reassurance to Zoe that he will always live in her memories. Catherine Stock's watercolor illustrations support the compassionate focus of this significant book.

The World

The world of children is technically the same as the world of adults, but children often perceive it differently. They have lived a shorter time, have not had the opportunity to study our world, and have not developed the mental capacities to comprehend the intricacies of modern life. However, children watch the news, listen to adults as they express their fears, and observe such things as pollution, crime, school shootings, and homelessness in many neighborhoods.

Childhood Fears. Children have reason to have fears. In fact, some fear can be a healthy thing. Fear keeps one from engaging in dangerous activities and reminds one to use common sense. On the other hand, fear can be overwhelming if it produces stress beyond the point that children can effectively cope. Many children develop fears about the great unknowns of the world. Adult explanations of the problems of the world are very often too complex and sophisticated for young children to comprehend. When children are without satisfactory understandings of a major societal problem, they may turn to the solutions offered in the media. The media of their childhood world, particularly television, often stress a violent solution to problems. In addition, many of the toys aimed at children encourage violent and warlike play. Such play often makes adults uncomfortable, but there is a reluctance to interfere because it is just play.

TIPS FOR TEACHERS

Accept the fears of children as genuine and real to those children.

- Ask children why they have a certain fear.
- Agree that something can be scary when it is a legitimate fear, and beware of ridiculing a fear that seems foolish.

Doug Lipman, a New England storyteller, has studied the issue of violent play modeled after the superheroes children observe on television. He conducts workshops on this topic for parents and teachers. He contends that one should look at the issue from the child's point of view in terms of the needs that the play is meeting. As those needs are met in other ways, the superhero play will diminish. It is not necessarily desirable to totally eliminate this type of play. After all, there are many admirable heroes in life, song, and literature.

Causes of Pressure. According to Doug Lipman, there are six underlying emotional causes to superhero play. Since the play is usually a result of stress or pressure, children are affected in different degrees. The first stress is the fact that children sometimes feel powerless. Children need to possess a certain amount of power to feel competent. Adults can avoid power struggles and use the need for power to build independence skills. A second cause is a feeling of incompetence. Children need to constantly be made aware of the fact that they are loved and have much worth. Boys especially feel the expectation to be "super competent." Children need to be told that they can do many things well. The third cause of pressure applies to boys: it is the subtle societal understanding placed on boys that they may have to take command at any time. They often feel that they might not be able to meet the challenge. The fourth cause also applies mostly to boys, who quickly learn that they, more often than girls, will be the agents and objects of violence. While there has been some enlightenment in society's attitude toward sex roles over the past decades, boys are aware that they are more likely than girls to kill and be killed in wars and that they will be involved in most of the violent crimes. The fifth cause is again applicable to boys, who are discouraged from dealing with their feelings. They are aware of the expectation that they "must be strong" and "not show that they are afraid." It is a tremendous burden, and one that is both unhealthy and unfair. The sixth and final cause relates to girls. Girls learn that they are often expected to remain dependent on males and that they will be treated as objects by males. Part of this message is given by the superhero play of boys. Girls learn that such play is

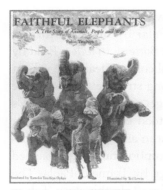

Cover from FAITHFUL
ELEPHANTS by Yukio
Tsuchiya, illustrated by Ted
Lewin. Jacketillustration
copyright © 1988 by Ted
Lewin. Reprinted by
permission of Houghton
Mifflin Harcourt Publishing
Company. All rights
reserved.

the proper role for boys. The role of girls is different. Each of these pressures is unhealthy. Unfortunately, society has not yet succeeded in eliminating violence and sexist attitudes.

Books on World Stresses. The world can be a highly complex and frightening place. Even very young children are sometimes aware of the acts and effects of terrorism that have become a real but unwelcome part of life. While they may not comprehend the complexity of the causes, they can be aware of the concern felt by those who care for them. To address some of the needs of children in trying to understand the world's complexity and danger, bibliotherapy can again be a powerful tool. Through books, children can learn facts and begin to deal with those facts through discussions with caring and sensitive adults. Books that address the issues of war include Jane Cutler's *The Cello of Mr. O*, Tres Seymour's *We Played Marbles,* and Dr. Seuss's *The Butter Battle Book.* Another powerful book on the subject of war is the newly reissued *Faithful Elephants* by Yukio Tsuchiya. It is a somber reminder of the inhumanity and irrationality of war. Children and adults will both be moved by its message.

Several books for children relate directly or indirectly to the 9/11 attack on America. Two books based on historical fact that can be used in a sensitive approach with four- to eight-year-old children are *Fireboat* by Maira Kalman and *New York's Bravest* by Mary Pope Osborne. *Fireboat* tells the true story of a 1931 New York City fireboat that had been retired prior to the attack on the World Trade Center. Because city utilities were disrupted in the attack, the fireboat was pressed back into service to provide water pressure to fight the fires that occurred. Although not directly about the attack, *New York's Bravest* shares a parallel story from the nineteenth century. It tells of legendary New York City firefighter Mose Humphreys who exhibited the same brave, unselfish, and deadly heroism to save others as was exhibited by the firefighters who perished in the collapse of the World Trade Center towers. Terrorism and other violent world events in the news are addressed in *Jenny Is Scared! When Sad Things Happen in the World* by Carol Shuman.

The long-term effects of war, often horrifying, are dealt with in some books. In *The Lily Cupboard,* Shulamith Oppenheim tells the story of a Dutch family whose members risked their lives to save a young Jewish girl from Hitler's madness. *Anna's Goat* by Janice Keefer expresses the ravages of war from a refugee child's point of view. While no specific country is mentioned in the story, it is based on a true story from the Second World War. Uri Shulevitz describes the challenging life that awaits war refugee families as they struggle to find a place where they can live and be safe in *How I Learned Geography.*

A wide range of other troubling issues can be addressed through literature. Books on pollution include Dr. Seuss's *The Lorax* and Jonah Winter's *Here*

Cover from *Alert!* by Etienne Delessert. Jacket art copyright © 2007 by Etienne Delessert. Reprinted by permission of Houghton Mifflin Harcourt Publishing Company. All rights reserved.

Cover from *S Is for Save the Planet* by Brad Herzog. Cover art copyright © 2009 by Linda Ayriss. Reprinted by permission of Sleeping Bear Press. All rights reserved.

Comes the Garbage Barge. The need to care for the environment is shown in *The Last Polar Bear* by Jean Craighead George, *Baby Polar* by Yannick Murphy, *Where Do Polar Bears Live?* by Sarah Thomson, and *Butternut Hollow Pond* by Brian Heinz. In *Rachel* by Amy Ehrlich, readers will come to learn the valiant and inspiring story of Rachel Carson and her lifelong struggle to protect the endangered eagle from the pesticide DDT. For younger readers, Brad Herzog's *S Is for Save the Planet* provides an easily understood blueprint for getting everyone involved in taking care of our environment in an alphabet book format. Catastrophic natural events such as a volcano eruption can be approached through a story such as *Little Grunt and the Big Egg* by Tomie dePaola. The issue of crime is confronted in *Alert!* by Etienne Delessert. In this story, Tobias collects beautiful pebbles and then hides them to keep them safe. As the tale unfolds, he learns lessons about crime, trust, and unwarranted fears.

SUMMARY

Bibliotherapy is a powerful tool to be used with children at all ages and grade levels. It can be effective with even very young children. Educators must not ignore the emotions and feelings of children as they attempt to be a part of their environment. The understandings of children must be clarified and expanded. It is only through that process that children will decrease their ignorance and gain confidence in their ability to deal with the world.

There are many benefits to using bibliotherapy. The use of books to clarify misconceptions and to encourage discussion can lead the way to understanding and self-confidence. When children feel safe and competent, achievement in academics will be enhanced. The benefits of bibliotherapy are likely to be long term. Caution should, of course, be exercised when dealing with highly emotional topics and with children who have severe psychological needs.

A variety of childhood concerns can be addressed with bibliotherapy, including those related to self, family, friends, other people, illness, death, and problems of the world in general. There are many books that can be used for bibliotherapy. In addition to the regular criteria for choosing books, particular care should be taken with the content and presentation of books used in this way.

QUESTIONS FOR THOUGHT AND DISCUSSION

1. What is bibliotherapy?
2. How does one know whether or not a book is age appropriate for a child?
3. Why is it important that a book dealing with an issue be first and foremost a good story?

4. Briefly describe some of the emotional causes of superhero play.

5. If superhero play is not all bad, what is the role of the educator regarding this type of play?

6. Why should a teacher use caution with bibliotherapy?

7. What are some of the benefits of bibliotherapy?

8. What are some of the concerns of young children?

9. Fear can be both a benefit and a liability. When does it become a liability? When is it a benefit?

10. Briefly explain some of the strategies one should utilize with bibliotherapy.

11. List three different books for young children that deal with any of the following topics: divorce, poverty, war, sibling rivalry, death, illness, minority groups, and people with special needs.

12. Is parental notification and involvement important when using bibliotherapy? Why or why not?

13. Why expose a child to a book that deals with war?

14. Why and how can didacticism limit the effectiveness of bibliotherapy?

For additional resources, access the *Growing Up with Literature* companion website through www.cengagebrain.com <http://www.cengagebrain.com/>.

CHILDREN'S BOOKS CITED

Ada, Alma Flor. (2010). *Let me help!* San Francisco, CA: Children's Book Press.

Adams, Colleen. (2003). *The courage of Helen Keller.* New York: Rosen.

Adler, David. (1994). *A Picture book of Sojourner Truth.* New York: Holiday House.

Adoff, Arnold. (2004). *Black is brown is tan.* New York: Amistad/HarperCollins.

Alexander, Claire. (2010). *Small Florence, piggy pop star!* Park Ridge, IL: Albert Whitman.

Alexander, Martha. (1971). *Nobody asked me if I wanted a baby sister.* New York: Dial.

Aliki (Brandenburg). (2000). *All by myself.* New York: HarperCollins.

Alter, Anna. (2003). *Francine's day.* New York: HarperCollins.

Appelt, Kathi. (2003). *Incredible me.* New York: HarperCollins.

Arnosky, Jim. (2006). *Grandfather Buffalo.* New York: Putnam.

Baker, Ken. (2001). *Brave little monster.* New York: HarperCollins.

Beaumont, Karen. (2002). *Being friends.* New York: Dial.

Beaumont, Karen. (2004). *I like myself.* Orlando, FL: Harcourt.

Berger, Carin. (2010). *Forever friends.* New York: Greenwillow.

Best, Cari. (2001). *Shrinking Violet.* New York: Farrar.

Binch, Caroline. (2006). *The princess and the castle.* Melbourne, Australia: Red Fox/Random House.

Birdseye, Tom. (1994). *A regular flood of mishap.* New York: Holiday House.

Bowen, Anne. (2001). *I loved you before you were born.* New York: HarperCollins.

Bowen, Anne. (2003). *How did you grow so big, so soon?* Minneapolis, MN: Carolrhoda.

Bunting, Eve. (1989). *The Wednesday surprise.* New York: Clarion.

Bunting, Eve. (2001). *Jin Woo.* New York: Clarion.

Bunting, Eve. (2001). *The days of summer.* San Diego, CA: Harcourt.

Carlson, Nancy. (2001). *My best friend moved away.* New York: Viking.

Carrick, Carol. (2000). *Mothers are like that.* New York: Clarion.

Caseley, Judith. (2001). *Bully.* New York: Greenwillow.

Catalanotto, Peter. (2001). *Emily's art.* New York: Simon and Schuster.

Cheng, Andrea. (2003). *Grandfather counts.* New York: Lee & Low.

Chocolate, Debbi. (1998). *The piano man.* New York: Walker.

Choi, Yangsook. (2003). *The name jar.* New York: Dragonfly/Dell.

Clifton, Lucille. (2001). *One of the problems of Everett Anderson.* New York: Henry Holt.

Cocca-Leffler, Maryann. (2005). *Bravery soup.* New York: Albert Whitman.

Considine, Kaitlyn. (2005). *Emma and Meesha my boy.* Merrick, NY: Twomoms.

Cumberbatch, Judy. (2006). *Can you hear the sea?* London: Bloomsbury.

Cutler, Jane. (2004). *The cello of Mr. O.* New York: Puffin.

Delessert, Etienne. (2007). *Alert!* New York: Houghton Mifflin (Walter Lorraine Books).

dePaola, Tomie. (1973). *Andy, that's my name.* New York: Simon and Schuster.

dePaola, Tomie. (1973). *Nana upstairs, Nana downstairs.* New York: Simon and Schuster.

dePaola, Tomie. (1979). *Oliver Button is a sissy.* New York: Harcourt Brace Jovanovich.

dePaola, Tomie. (1981). *Now one foot, now the other.* New York: G. P. Putnam.

dePaola, Tomie. (1993). *Strega Nona meets her match.* New York: Putnam.

dePaola, Tomie. (2006). *Little Grunt and the big egg.* New York: Putnam.

Ehrlich, Amy. (1994). *Maggie and Silky and Joe.* New York: Viking.

Ehrlich, Amy. (2003). *Rachel.* New York: Silver Whistle/Harcourt.

Elschner, Geraldine. (2006). *Friends for all seasons.* New York: North-South/Chronicle.

Elya, Susan. (2006). *F is for fiesta.* New York: Putnam.

Fox, Mem. (1994). *Tough Boris.* San Diego, CA: Harcourt Brace Jovanovich.

Friedrich, Elizabeth. (1999). *Leah's Pony.* Honesdale, PA: Boyds Mills.

Garden, Nancy. (2004). *Molly's family*. New York: Farrar, Straus, & Giroux.

George, Jean Craighead. (2009). *The last polar bear*. New York: Harper Collins.

Goldin, Barbara. (2001). *A mountain of blintzes*. San Diego, CA: Harcourt/Gulliver.

Goodings, Lennie. (2001). *When you grow up*. New York: Penguin Putnam.

Goodman, Joan. (2001). *Bernard goes to school*. Honesdale, PA: Boyds Mills.

Gorbachev, Valeri. (2001). *Chicken chickens*. New York: North-South.

Gray, Libba Moore. (1994). *Fenton's leap*. New York: Simon and Schuster.

Gregory, Nan. (2001). *Wild girl and Gran*. Red Deer, Alberta, Canada: Red Deer.

Guest, Elissa. (2001). *Iris and Walter, true friends*. San Diego, CA: Harcourt.

Gutman, Anne. (2001). *Lisa's airplane trip*. New York: Knopf/Borzoi.

Hanel, Wolfram. (2001). *Little Elephant runs away*. New York: North-South.

Harris, Robie. (1994). *It's perfectly normal*. Cambridge, MA: Candlewick.

Harris, Robie. (2001). *Goodbye Mousie*. New York: Simon and Schuster.

Hasely, Dennis. (2002). *A story for bear*. Orlando, FL: Harcourt.

Hasler, Eveline. (2006). *A tale of two brothers*. New York: North-South/ Chronicle.

Heinz, Brian. (2000). *Butternut Hollow Pond*. Wallingford, CT: Millbrook.

Hennessey, B. G. (2010). *Play ball, Corduroy*. New York: Viking.

Henry, Steve. (2001). *Nobody asked me!* New York: HarperCollins.

Herzog, Brad. (2009). *S is for save the planet*. Ann Arbor, MI: Sleeping Bear Press.

Inkpen, Mick. (1998). *Nothing*. New York: Orchard.

Iyengar, Malathi Michelle. (2010). *Tan to tamarind*. San Francisco, CA: Children's Book Press.

Jahn-Clough, Lisa. (2001). *Simon and Molly plus Hester*. Boston: Houghton Mifflin.

Jeffers, Oliver. (2010). *The heart and the bottle*. New York: Philomel.

Jesset, Aurore. (2009). *Loopy*. New York: North-South.

Johnson, Angela. (1990). *When I am old with you*. New York: Orchard.

Johnson, Angela. (1991). *One of three*. New York: Orchard.

Johnson, Angela. (1994). *Joshua by the sea*. New York: Orchard.

Johnson, Angela. (1997). *Daddy calls me Man*. New York: Orchard.

Johnston, Tony. (1998). *The chizzywink and the alamagoozlum*. New York: Holiday House.

Johnston, Tony. (2001). *Alien and Possum: Friends no matter what*. New York: Simon & Schuster.

Jules, Jacqueline. (2010). *Zapato power: Freddie Ramos takes off*. Park Ridge, IL: Albert Whitman.

Kalman, Maira. (2002). *Fireboat*. New York: Putnam.

Keats, Ezra Jack. (1962). *The snowy day*. New York: Vanguard.

Keats, Ezra Jack. (1983). *Apartment three.* New York: Macmillan.

Keefer, Janice. (2000). *Anna's Goat.* Custer, WA: Orca.

Ketteman, Helen. (2001). *Mama's way.* New York: Dial.

Kinsey-Warnock, Natalie. (2001). *A farm of her own.* New York: Dutton.

Kraus, Robert. (1971). *Leo the late bloomer.* New York: Simon and Schuster.

Kraushaar, Sabine. (2006). *Say ahh!* New York: North-South/Chronicle.

Kroll, Virginia. (1998). *Faraway drums.* Boston: Little, Brown.

Lath, Sebastian. (2010). *Remembering Crystal.* New York: North-South.

Lee, Chinlun. (2001). *The very kind rich lady and her one hundred dogs.* Cambridge, MA: Candlewick.

Leuck, Laura. (2002). *My monster mama loves me so.* New York: Harper Trophy.

Lewis, Kim. (2001). *Little Baa.* Cambridge, MA: Candlewick.

Lied, Kate. (2002). *Potato.* Washington, DC: National Geographic.

Lin, Grace. (2001). *Dim sum for everyone.* New York: Knopf/Borzoi.

Lobel, Arnold. (1970). *Frog and Toad are friends.* New York: Scholastic.

London, Jonathan. (2002). *Froggy plays in the band.* New York: Viking.

Look, Lenore. (2001). *Henry's first-moon birthday.* New York: Simon and Schuster.

Lowell, Gloria. (2000). *Elana's ears.* Washington, DC: Magination.

MacLachlan, Patricia. (1980). *Through Grandpa's eyes.* New York: Harper and Row.

Martin, Bill, Jr., and Sampson, Michael. (2001). *The little squeegy bug.* Toronto, Ontario, Canada: Winslow.

Martin, Teresa, and Martin, Whitney. (2006). *Big Ernie's new home.* Washington, DC: Magination.

Masurel, Claire. (2001). *Two homes.* Cambridge, MA: Candlewick.

Mavor, Salley. (1997). *You and me.* New York: Orchard.

Mazer, Norma Fox. (2007). *Has anyone seen my Emily Green?* Cambridge, MA: Candlewick.

McDonald, Megan. (2001). *Reptiles are my life.* New York: Scholastic/Orchard.

McFarland, Lyn. (2001). *Widget.* New York: Farrar.

McKissack, Patricia. (1992). *A million fish … more or less.* New York: Knopf.

McPhail, David. (2002). *The teddy bear.* New York: Henry Holt.

Meserve, Jessica. (2008). *Can anybody here me?* New York: Houghton Mifflin Harcourt (Clarion).

Miller, J. Philip, and Greene, Shepard. (2001). *We all sing with the same voice.* New York: HarperCollins.

Monk, Isabell. (2001). *Family.* Minneapolis, MN: Carolrhoda.

Moss, Miriam. (2010). *Matty is a mess.* London: Anderson.

Moss, Miriam. (2010). *Matty takes off.* London: Anderson.

Munsch, Robert. (1986). *50 below zero.* Toronto, Ontario, Canada: Annick.

Munsch, Robert. (1988). *Love you forever.* Scarborough, Ontario, Canada: Firefly.

Murphy, Yannick. (2007). *Baby polar.* New York: Clarion.

Newman, Leslea. (1998). *Too far away to touch.* New York: Clarion.

Numeroff, Laura. (2009). *What brothers do best, What sisters do best.* New York: Chronicle.

Oppenheim, Shulamith. (1992). *The lily cupboard.* New York: HarperCollins.

Osborne, Mary Pope. (2002). *New York's bravest.* New York: Knopf.

Parr, Todd. (2003). *The family book.* Boston: Little Simon.

Penn, Audrey. (2004). *A pocketful of kisses.* Edison, NJ: Child and Family.

Penn, Audrey. (2009). *Chester Raccoon and the acorn full of memories.* Terre Haute, IN: Tanglewood.

Perez, Amada. (2000). *My very own room.* San Francisco, CA: Children's Book.

Pfister, Marcus. (2009). *Milo and the magical stones.* New York: North-South.

Pinkwater, Daniel. (1989). *Uncle Melvin.* New York: Macmillan.

Piper, Watty. (1954). *The little engine that could.* Eau Claire, WI: Hale.

Raschka, Chris. (1993). *Yo! Yes?* New York: Orchard.

Reagan, Jean. (2009). *Always my brother.* Gardiner, ME: Tilbury House.

Rey, H. A., and Rey, Margaret. (1966). *Curious George goes to the hospital.* Boston: Houghton Mifflin.

Reynolds, Peter. (2003). *The dot.* Cambridge, MA: Candlewick.

Reynolds, Peter. (2004). *Ish.* Cambridge, MA: Candlewick.

Reynolds, Peter. (2006). *So few of me.* Cambridge, MA: Candlewick.

Rickert, Janet. (2001). *Russ and the almost perfect day.* Rockville, MD: Woodbine House.

Rissman, Rebecca. (2010). *People who help us.* Portsmouth, NH: Heineman-Raintree.

Ritchie, Alison. (2002). *I don't want to sleep alone.* Wilton, CT: Tiger Tales.

Rosenberg, Liz. (2001). *Eli's night light.* New York: Scholastic/Orchard.

Rotner, Shelley. (2009). *Shades of people.* New York: Holiday House.

Rylant, Cynthia. (1982). *When I was young in the mountains.* New York: E. P. Dutton.

Sadler, Marilyn. (1988). *Alistair underwater.* New York: Prentice Hall.

Sansone, Adele. (2010). *The little green goose.* New York: North-South.

Santucci, Barbara. (2001). *Loon summer.* Grand Rapids, MI: Eerdmans.

Schein, Jonah. (1988). *Forget me not.* Toronto, Ontario, Canada: Annick.

Schick, Eleanor. (2000). *Mama.* London: Marshall Cavendish.

Schuchman, Joan. (1979). *Two places to sleep.* Minneapolis, MN: Carolrhoda.

Seuss, Dr. (pseud. for Theodor Geisel). (1984). *The butter battle book.* New York: Random House.

Seuss, Dr. (pseud. for Theodor Geisel). (1971). *The Lorax*. New York: Random House.

Shulevitz, Uri. (2008). *How I learned geography*. New York: Farrar, Straus & Giroux.

Shuman, Carol. (2003). *Jenny is scared! When sad things happen in the world*. Washington, DC: Magination.

Smith, Maggie. (2001). *Desser the best ever cat*. New York: Knopf/Borzoi.

Smith, Will. (2001). *Just the two of us*. New York: Scholastic.

Spinelli, Eileen. (2001). *Sophie's masterpiece: A spider's tale*. New York: Simon and Schuster.

Stinson, Kathy. (2009). *Big or little*. Tronto, Ontario: Annick.

Tayback, Simms. (2006). *Where is my friend*. New York: Blue Apple/Chronicle.

Thaler, Mike. (1986). *Hippo lemonade*. New York: Harper.

Thomas, Pat. (2001). *I miss you*. Hauppauge, NY: Barron's Educational.

Thomson, Sarah. (2010). *Where do polar bears live?* New York: Collins.

Tsuchiya, Yukio. (1988). *Faithful elephants*. New York: Houghton Mifflin.

Truly Blessed Ink. (2007). *I know you won't forget*. Voorheesville, NY: Square Circle.

Vainio, Pirkko. (1993). *The snow goose*. New York: North-South.

Viorst, Judith. (1971). *The tenth good thing about Barney*. New York: Atheneum.

Viorst, Judith. (1977). *My mama says there aren't any zombies, ghosts, vampires, creatures, demons, monsters, fiends, goblins, or things*. New York: Atheneum.

Vizurrga, Susan. (2000). *Miss Opal's auction*. New York: Henry Holt.

Waas, Uli. (1993). *Where's Molly?* New York: North-South.

Waber, Bernard. (1972). *Ira sleeps over*. Boston: Houghton Mifflin.

Waddell, Martin. (2000). *Tom Rabbit*. Cambridge, MA: Candlewick.

Waddell, Martin. (2001). *A kitten called Midnight*. Cambridge, MA: Candlewick.

Warfel, Elizabeth. (2001). *The blue pearls*. New York: Barefoot.

Weight, Udo. (2003). *Bear's last journey*. New York: North-South.

Weiss, Ellen, and Friedman, Mel. (2010). *Porky and Bess*. New York: Random House.

Wells, Rosemary. (2003). *Small world of Binky Braverman*. New York: Viking.

Wilson, Karma. (2003). *Bears want more*. New York: Margaret K. McElderry.

Wilson, Karma. (2008). *Bears feel scared*. New York: Margaret K. McElderry.

Wilson-Max, Ken. (2001). *Max's starry night*. New York: Hyperion.

Winter, Jonah. (2010). *Here comes the garbage barge*. New York: Random/Schwartz & Wade.

Winter, Jeanette. (2001). *My baby*. New York: Farrar.

Winthrop, Elizabeth. (2001). *Dumpy LaRue*. New York: Henry Holt.

Woloson, Elza. (2003). *My friend Isabelle*. Bethesda, MD: Woodbine.

Wormell, Mary. (2001). *Bernard the angry rooster*. New York: Farrar.

Wormell, Chris. (2009). *Ferocious wild beasts!* New York: Knopf.

Yolen, Jane. (1981). *Sleeping Ugly.* New York: Coward McCann.

Zalben, Jane. (2001). *Don't go!* New York: Clarion.

Ziefert, Harriet. (2001). *Squarehead.* Boston: Houghton Mifflin.

Ziefert, Harriet. (2006). *Grandma, it's for you.* New York: Blue Apple/Chronicle.

Zolotow, Charlotte. (1972). *William's doll.* New York: Harper and Row.

SELECTED REFERENCES AND RESOURCES

Bronson, P. and Merryman, A. (2009). *Nurtureshock.* New York: Hachette.

Campbell, L. A. and Campbell, L. K. (1999). *Storybooks for tough times.* New York: Fulcrum.

Carle, E. et al. (2007). *Artist to artist: 23 major illustrators talk to children about their art.* New York: Philomel.

Casper, V. and Steven, B. S. (1999). *Gay parents/Straight schools: Building communities and trust.* New York: Teachers College Press.

Cianciolo, P. (1965). Children's literature can affect coping behaviors. *Personnel and Guidance Journal 43,* 897–901.

Cloud, N., Genessee, F., and Hamayan, E. (2009). *Literacy instruction for English language learners.* Portsmouth, NH: Heineman.

Coon, C. (2004). *Books to grow with: A guide to using the best children's fiction for everyday issues and tough challenges.* Portland, OR: Lutra.

Copple, C. and Bredekamp, S. (Eds.). (2009). *Developmentally appropriate practices in early childhood programs serving children from birth through age 8.* Washington, DC: NAEYC.

Golding, J. M. (2006). *Healing stories: Picture books for the big and small changes in a child's life.* New York: M. Evans.

Grace, C. and Shores, E. (2010). *After the crisis: Using storybooks to help children cope.* Silver Spring, MD: Gryphon House.

Howard, V. F., Williams, B., and Lepper, C. E. (2010). *Very young children with special needs: A foundation for educators, families and service providers.* Upper Saddle River, NJ: Merrill.

Huck, C. and Kiefer, B. (2003). *Children's literature in the elementary school.* New York: McGraw-Hill.

Jacobson, T. (2003). *Confronting our discomfort.* Portsmouth, NH: Heineman.

Malchiodi, C. A. (Ed.). (2008). *Creative interventions with traumatized children.* New York: Guilford Press.

Perry, B. D. (2001). Promoting nonviolent behavior in children. *Scholastic Early Childhood Today 16*(1) 26–29.

Robb, L. (2003). *Literacy links*. Portsmouth, NH: Heineman.

Russell, D. and Schrodes, C. (1950). Contributions of research in bibliotherapy to the language arts program. *School Review 58*, 335–392.

Sclafani, J. D. (2004). *The educated parent: Recent trends in raising children*. Westport, CT: Praeger.

Tolson, N. (2008). *Black children's literature got de blues*. New York: Peter Lang Publishing.

Trelease, J. (2006). *The read-aloud handbook*. New York: Penguin.

INTERNET REFERENCES AND HELPFUL WEBSITES

Bibliotherapy and realistic fiction. Library Book Lists site. Retrieved March 3, 2010, from http://librarybooklists.org/fiction/children/jbibliotherapy.htm

Bibliotherapy: Good books, happier kids? Best children's books. Retrieved March 3, 2010, from http://www.best-childrens-books.com/bibliotherapy.html

Bibliotherapy–Elementary. Indiana University site. Retrieved March 3, 2010, from http://www.indiana.edu/~reading/ieo/bibs/biblele.html

Books to help young children cope in today's world. Carnegie Library–Pittsburgh site. Retrieved January 8, 2007, from http://www.clpgh.org/kids/booknook/bibliotherapy

Helping your child deal with death. The Nemours Foundation site. Retrieved March 3, 2010, from http://kidshealth.org/parent/emotions/feelings/death.html

© Cengage Learning

CHAPTER 9

USING COMMERCIAL AND EDUCATIONAL MEDIA

There have been many debates and arguments concerning the relationship of children with **television, computers**, videos, electronic games, cell phones, and other media. Since these media are here to stay, some of the arguments are moot. American families usually own at least one television set. Many of the programs depict violence, greed, and unrealistic pictures of life. Most households, and the number is increasing daily, also own DVD players, iPods, Mp3 players, high definition video screens, computers with high speed internet, and compact disc (CD) players. Families receive newspapers and magazines in the home, go to movies, watch movies on DVD in the automobile, conduct Internet communication and watch television on cell phones, and see billboards along the highways. Because much of the media is presented for the purpose of earning revenue for advertisers, the quality is not always appropriate for children. The role of teachers and parents is to use the media effectively and to help children begin to make critical choices. It is important to keep in mind that participation in the viewing of media is always a choice. In life and in early childhood education programs, media need not be used simply because it is available. This chapter discusses the

The press, like fire, is an excellent servant but a terrible master.

—JAMES FENIMORE COOPER

benefits of various media and the criteria for the selection in each medium within the context of the development of children's literacy.

MEDIA AND LITERATURE

There are two relationships between the **media** and literature, one friendly and the other adversarial. The friendly relationship is the blending of literature and media to provide more powerful learning experiences for children. Literature can give depth to the superficial aspects of media presentations by allowing children to learn more about a concept or an event. Media can be used to enhance a child's involvement with literature, for example, and to expand on the experience of reading a book. Media can also be used as a springboard for further discussion of a book or to instill a desire to read a certain book or books about a particular subject.

The adversarial relationship occurs when the media overwhelm and take the place of literature in the lives of children. Media will always be present in children's lives. It is up to parents and educators to control the media rather than letting the media control their children and themselves. If it is to be a positive force in children's lives, the use of media must be planned to tap the best qualities of each medium. Media can be valuable as experiences in their own right, but care should be taken to see that they do not replace literature, play, adult supervision, or the development of friendships.

Categories of media seem to be increasing rapidly. Hardly a day goes by without a new interactive video, cell phone application, laser disc, or innovative digital device being used. However, the predominant media used with young children are television shows, DVDs, magazines, newspapers, and computer programs. Criteria for selecting these materials will be suggested. The focus will be on effectively using each medium in conjunction with literature for the purpose of enhancing the experience of a story.

TELEVISION: SEEING THE WORLD FROM A CHAIR

There is no doubt about it: television can be a fantastic medium. From the comfort of an easy chair one can go on an African safari, explore the oceanic coral reefs of Australia, take a shuttle into space, or participate in a bloody military skirmish in a third-world country. The seemingly endless variety of experiences available through television is part of the problem. We simply watch too much television.

Negative Aspects of Television

By the time children enter kindergarten, they have watched more than 5,000 hours of television. Between the ages of three and seventeen, the average American child watches 15,000 hours. This is 2,000 hours more than that same child will spend in a classroom during those years. Prior to age seventeen, that child will watch 350,000 commercials and 18,000 acts of violence on television. Research portrays a worrisome trend among even very young children in the United States. In a study reported by the American Medical Association, it was found that 90 percent of children under the age of three months spend up to one hour per day watching television and videos. By the time these children reach two years of age the daily viewing time averages one and one-half hours (Zimmerman, Christakis, and Meltzoff, 2007).

Television viewing is a **passive activity**. Little thought or mental activity is required by viewers as they are bombarded by a steady stream of sounds and images. This fact is particularly important in regard to young children, who expand their language and thinking skills through active interaction with stories and books as well as with their environment.

TIPS FOR TEACHERS

Increase awareness by having parents keep a log of every minute of technology viewing for a period of one week, including:

- Television viewing
- Time spent in an area with a television on, but not actively viewing it
- Computer, DVD, and videogame viewing

The shows offered and the commercials embedded within these shows are another problem area. The quality of television shows seems to have decreased as the advertised offerings of toys, clothes, fast food, and beauty products related to children's television programming has increased. Lyn Mikel Brown and Sharon Lamb (2007) provide strong evidence concerning marketers' television advertising that portrays stereotyped images of girls and women that can produce negative self images. Our society appears to be more and more drawn to the flashy and the violent. Many good-quality shows have been removed and replaced with violent fare, mostly because of rating points and advertising dollars.

During the past few years, a new low has been reached in which those advertising dollars have become the controlling factor in much of children's programming. Previously, children's toys and other products related to characters from a television show were created and marketed after a show had become popular. Currently, new shows are being programmed based upon the successful marketing of a child star or related product. These include robots, dolls, clothing lines, cosmetics, and action toys. In effect, children who watch the shows are merely watching an ongoing half-hour advertisement based on greed and violence.

Controlling Television Viewing

Most adults know that children watch far too much television. For that matter, most adults spend too much time watching television. There is a need to be aware of this problem and consider its effects. Following awareness and understanding, an appropriate response can be launched.

Awareness. To become aware of the seriousness of the problem requires closer study. Literature from groups such as the National Education Association (NEA) and the International Reading Association (IRA) is helpful. So is collecting information on children's television viewing. Distribute to parents television-viewing recording charts with boxes for half-hour time slots and days of the week. By blackening a box for each half-hour time slot a child watches television, parents can document a weekly picture of their child's television viewing. A chart with large areas of blackened time slots representing time spent in front of a television set will have far more impact on parents than anything that might be said. In a statement on their Web site, the American Academy of Pediatrics recommends that children aged birth through two years not watch any television. For children older than two years of age, they recommend no more than one to two hours per week of educational nonviolent programming *(American Pediatric Association, 2010)*.

Understanding. Young children need to develop an understanding of some of the basic facts about television in order to make decisions about it. An effective approach to this is the use of a DVD recorder, memory-based recording device, or digital video recorder (DVR) to record and store various commercials and television shows. The recording can be played and stopped at various critical points for discussion of what is happening. For example, advertising uses a wide variety of propaganda tricks to get consumers to buy certain products. By stopping to discuss the commercial, you can help children to understand this advertising ploy. Such an understanding will not lessen their trust in people. Rather, it will increase their trust in people who care about them. The understanding will also make them more aware of their own intelligence and their ability to make decisions. In addition, using language to discuss a problem will enhance their command of language.

Children can usually understand the concept of excess. What would happen if it rained all the time? What would it be like if we ate only apples? The comparison can be made with television. What would it be like if we watched television all of our waking hours? What would it be like if there were no television? Children can learn that watching television, like any other activity, can be a part of life without being the sole focus. Television can help us learn to cook, to draw, and to understand many things. It can be a wonderful machine or it can be frightening. If children are subjected to news channels throughout the day, their perceptions of the often violent images can become disproportionate to reality. While television is a part of life, there are many other important parts as well.

Response. Awareness accomplishes nothing without a response. One response is to simply eliminate or drastically reduce television viewing, but this will only partially solve the problem. When one activity is decreased, it is important to offer healthy alternatives. Otherwise, the replacement activity will probably be children pleading to return to their original television habits.

More than anything else, parental involvement and modeling are the most effective means for teaching children the skills needed to develop reasonable television viewing habits. Parental involvement would include helping children to understand what they are doing with their lives when they spend excessive amounts of time watching television. However, it may be unrealistic to eliminate all television viewing for young people. It may not accomplish all of the things one might hope for anyway. For example, most people are aware of the violence exhibited on television and the reports of its effect on young children. Yet eliminating all television violence will not eliminate all the fears, nightmares, and aggression children might experience.

This does not mean, of course, that unmonitored and indiscriminate viewing of television is acceptable. Rather, one's response should be to talk to and listen to children more. By attempting to understand the perspective of children, one can help them come to a better understanding of themselves. Better understanding leads to better control. This is true whether the topic is a story being read or a television program being viewed. Empowered this way, children become more able to make critical choices, including what and how much television programming they will watch. In addition, they will be better able to make choices about alternatives to television viewing.

Positive Aspects of Television

There have always been good-quality television programs for children, and there are still some wonderful programs. In the past, such shows as *Ding Dong School, The Howdy Doody Show, Captain Kangaroo,* and *Kukla, Fran and Ollie* were favorites. Later came *Mister Rogers' Neighborhood,* which celebrates the joys of children learning about the world. Fred Rogers, the show's main character, used language, humor, and stories as integral parts of the program. He also published a series of books for sharing between child and parent. These informative books, which do not talk down to children, cover such topics as child care, doctors, and new babies.

Sesame Street evolved when the Children's Television Workshop turned market research into productive children's programming. Using Jim Henson's Muppet characters and a diverse cast, *Sesame Street* provides learning experiences through a series of short segments that take into account the attention span of young children. This was one of the first programs for children to feature a multiethnic cast. Women, minorities, and individuals with disabilities are all featured with realism and dignity.

TIPS FOR TEACHERS

Encourage decision making by involving children in selecting the one program to watch during the day. Assist them by asking them:

- What type of program do you like best and why?
- If you had to pick one or two programs, which would they be and why?

Public television has continued to expand its programs related to literacy for young children with shows based upon actual children's literature or shows related to literacy. *Arthur* is based on the Arthur character created by author Marc Brown. *Clifford* provides shows based on the numerous books written by Norman Bridwell about the big red dog. *The Berenstain Bears* provides a similar show based on the books of Stan and Jan Berenstain. *Share a Story* provides activities such as acting, drawing, and writing that expand the concept of a story. *Between the Lions* provides stories, songs, and parent-teacher activities. Other literacy related shows include *Dragon Tales, Mister Rogers* (in syndication), *Sid the Science Kid,* and *Word World.* Most of the children's programming has an accompanying Web site that can be reached through http://www.pbskids.org.

Commercial networks have also adapted several well-known children's books for television. The quality of the presentations is uneven; some ring remarkably true to the original story, whereas others have been disturbingly altered. Cable television, through outlets such as the Disney channel, has tied several of its programs to literature. Again, the quality of the adaptations varies and the range of choices is confined to only those books that have had wide commercial success.

Using Elements of Television

Because television can be a vehicle for learning, parents and educators can harness its power. By using selected television programs, parents and educators can reinforce basic concept skills, socialization skills, and self-esteem. Some of the thousands of commercials children watch can be used to teach about nutrition and critical decision making. By critically analyzing food commercials, children can learn about alternative snacks and nutrition. By analyzing toy commercials, children can make better decisions about whether they really need a particular toy.

The concept of developing their own programs can be appealing to children. A large cardboard box can become a television set on which children broadcast their own shows and commercials. The spontaneous acting that will result during free-play periods can reinforce language development. Brief skits and commercials, some based on stories they have read, will help children to recreate the experience of the story. The emphasis should not be on the excellence of the production. The main focus should be on the use of language within the experience.

AUDIOVISUAL MATERIALS

Audiovisual materials include recorded media, photographs, files stored on computers, iPods, and Mp3s, DVDs, CDs, slides, films, online videos, and the equipment needed to use them. Each can be used effectively to enhance the curriculum. A wide range of literature related to them is available as well. As a result, audiovisual materials can be used to extend and enhance the literature used in the curriculum.

When using any audiovisual material to enhance a story, more planning time is needed to organize the presentation. Because the teacher will be less involved in the presentation, the children may need more help in understanding what is happening than was apparent in the reading of the book. The machine may set the pace. Of course, a machine cannot detect a puzzled look on a child's face. Audiovisual materials should never replace the teacher, the parent, or the book. They should be used only as a supplement.

Many sources exist for audiovisual materials. Public libraries and elementary school libraries are both good sources. They usually have a variety of literature-related materials. New materials may be purchased from various commercial sources. Educational supply companies usually have catalogs

© Cengage Learning

Electronic media can be used to re-create the experience of the original reading of a story.

offering their materials. Increasingly, as companies have sought to reduce costs by emphasizing online sales, actual catalogs have decreased in number.

The use of audiovisual materials should be an occasional rather than a regular activity. There are two very important reasons for this. First, nothing can replace the warmth of the live human voice and the caring eye of a sensitive storyteller or reader. Although new devices including cell phones, tablet readers, and digital panels do sometimes provide children's literature content, the loss of the visual impact of the full-size illustrations on the page greatly diminishes the reading experience. As a result, audiovisual materials should be used mainly as a support for a live reading.

Second, the range of audiovisual materials related to children's literature is quite limited. Very few books reach this format. Those that do reach it do so only after they have proved themselves effective in the print market. As a result, production cost considerations dictate that the majority of titles available will be limited to older but popular classics and a few recent titles that have been commercially successful.

Criteria for Selecting Audiovisual Materials

Audiovisual material that brings a book to another medium must be carefully screened. The electronic version of a story should neither diminish nor replace the original story. The illustrations, flow, and feeling of the story should create the same impact as the initial reading of the story. Effective use of an audiovisual presentation should extend the reading and re-create the story for the child.

Disney Studios has successfully produced animated versions of stories for years. The Disney stories, however, are often not faithful to the original texts. As a result, many of them seem to be new stories with lives of their own. It is still important for children to see and hear the original stories. This will add to the magic of the literature and broaden children's understanding of the story.

Infusing a desire to read and nurturing an enjoyment of literature in young children are two very important objectives for parents and educators. Audiovisual materials should be selected with these criteria in mind: The materials should enhance the original version of the story. They should be clear and coherent to the child. They should re-create or extend the magic of the original story and should never be used to replace it.

Using Audiovisual Materials

DVDs, television shows, online videos, and CDs may present stories, music, or stories that include music. Electronic versions contain a visual and sound recreation of a story. The selection of materials should depend mainly on how well they fit into the overall objective for sharing or experiencing a story in the first place. When that is clear, a wide range of possible activities can be used in conjunction with the audiovisual materials.

Compact Discs and Audiotapes. Designating a specific quiet area of the room is helpful for using electronic media. The area can serve for both instructional purposes and free-play listening. Providing additional headsets enables several children to listen to a story at one time without filling the room with sound. Using a copy of the book with the recording is usually beneficial. Recordings often use professionals with dramatic, expressive voices that can make the story special. A good example of this is Thacher Hurd's *Moo Cow Kaboom,* a combination book and CD set read by John Beech. In a book/audio CD version, Gwyneth Paltrow provides a superb narration of the much loved *Brown Bear, Brown Bear, What Do You See?* by Bill Martin, Jr. Most recordings have a signal indicating the need to turn the page. Even if the children cannot read the words, they will become accustomed to the concept of reading words and the idea that language flows by turning the pages as the story proceeds. In addition to using CDs of well-known books such as Stan and Jan Berenstain's *The Berenstain Bears and the Messy Room,* classroom recorded media can be created whenever the teacher reads a book. Children can listen to these recorded media as well. A case can be made for using audio-only presentations over those that provide sound and visual matter on a screen. With audio-only, children must become actively involved in the story, creating the visual aspect in their minds.

Some companies specifically distribute recorded versions of children's books. Some companies also offer take-home packets for parents that include the book, a recording, and a sheet of activities related to the story. These packets can also be created by caregivers as a curriculum project. Through Weston Woods, Scholastic distributes titles such as *Alice the Fairy* by David Shannon, *Noisy Nora* by Rosemary Wells, *One Hungry Monster* by Susan O'Keefe, *Ruby the Copycat* by Margaret Rathmann, and *This Is My House* by Arthur Dorros. Spoken Arts distributes titles such as *Someday* by Alison McGhee. Lion Books offers titles such as *The Lion Book of Five Minute Animal Stories* by John Goodman, which contains lively animal classics such as "The Nightingale" and "The Lion and the Mouse"; the accompanying CD provides music and sound effects.

There is a limited selection of older classic fairy tales and other stories past copyright protection available free for personal listening devices. The Florida Educational Technology Clearinghouse provides files for Mp3 downloading, and the Eastern Washington University Library provides files for iPod downloading. Story recordings of newer books can be played at nap time so children relive the story at a quiet time. Consider making some of these recordings available for parents to sign out. In this way, parents can share the story with their children and enhance the experience with further discussion.

In addition to stories, CDs and other recordings of music can enhance language and literacy. In *Best Friends: Rockin' Music for Kids,* Sue Schnitzer presents eighteen tracks of songs with such titles as "Best Friends," "My Dreams," "The Library Song," and "You Can Be." The Flannery Brothers' *Love Songs for Silly Things* CD includes upbeat energetic songs such as "Dilly Beans," "Rutabaga," and "Best Pillow in the World." Mary Kaye presents songs such as "Bug," "Family," and "Hot Chocolate Fairy" in her CD *Music Box.* Sukey Molloy presents twenty new and traditional songs for circle time on the CD *Circle Songs.* On the CD *Toucan Jam: A World of Music,* Kelly Mulhollan and Donna Stjevna present thirteen multicultural folk songs based on stories and legends from around the world.

DVDs and Videocassettes. DVDs and older VHS videocassettes are similar in function to a film, with the story shown on a television screen or monitor. *Happily Ever After Collection: Fairy Tales for Every Child* by Robert Guillaume and others is a DVD collection based on the award-winning Home Box Office series. It includes "Mother Goose," "The Pied Piper," "Pinocchio," and "The Golden Goose." Some classic and current books are also available in these formats, although DVD is the most common. Random House distributes DVDs of *Bear Wants More* by Karma Wilson, *Diary of a Spider* by Doreen Cronin, and

Knuffle Bunny by Mo Willems. Titles available from Scholastic/Weston Woods include *Hans Christian Andersen Stories, Favorite Fairy Tales* by Paul Zelinsky and Charlote Huck, *Everyone Loves Clifford—Good Friends, Good Times,* by Norman Bridwell, *Crazy Hair Day* by Barry Saltzberg, *Don't Let the Pigeon Drive the Bus* by Mo Willems, *Fletcher and the Falling Leaves* by Julia Rawlinson, *Jigsaw Jones* by James Preller, and *Curious George Goes to the Chocolate Factory* by Margaret and H. A. Rey. DVDs are available from the publishers of *Sesame Street Elmo's Easy as ABC Book* by Carol Monica and *Sleep Tight Little Bear* by Martin Waddell. Other companies with similar offerings include AV Café, Building Block Entertainment, and Live Oak Media.

These presentations should not replace the use of a book for the telling of stories. Rather, the presentation can and should be used to extend and enhance the story. For example, if fairy tales are being used in the classroom, their concepts can be extended with a re-creation of some of the original stories using a camcorder. If a camcorder can be used, children in costume can re-create the stories as well.

Photographs and slides in either traditional or electronic format can be used to create books about any topic. Both original pictures and photographs of pictures from books and magazines can be starting points for original stories. Photographs of children enacting a story could also be used with a language-experience approach (LEA). When creating with audiovisual equipment, it is best to consider a few things prior to the activity. Parents should always be informed. This is particularly true if the pictures will be used by the press. If parents don't wish their child to be included, the request should be honored without comment. Letting parents know ahead of time also gives them the opportunity to have their children look their best. If costumes or props are to be used, it allows parents enough time to create them.

Planning for the unexpected is recommended. Practice with the equipment beforehand so that sufficient skill will have been achieved. Obtain additional lighting and extra extension cords as needed prior to the activity. Finally, a backup plan should always be ready. Equipment malfunctions. Children get sick. An alternate plan can help achieve the goals of the project even when these problems occur.

MAGAZINES AND NEWSPAPERS

Magazines and newspapers abound in our culture. It is challenging, however, to find quality magazines that appeal to the interest of children. Likewise, it requires some creativity to develop appropriate uses for newspapers with young children.

Magazines and newspapers are low cost and filled with superb illustrations. They are also up-to-date and they contain short pieces on a variety of topics that cater to different interests. It makes sense to use them as a resource for developing literacy with young children. To do this in conjunction with a literature program requires two things: First, one must have certain criteria for deciding to include newspapers and magazines. Second, one must develop a set of activities and strategies for effectively using them.

Children's Magazines

Babybug includes brief stories, poems, and rhymes for infants and toddlers. Cobblestone Publishing, 30 Grove Street–Suite C, Peterborough, NH 03458

Ladybug includes stories, read-alouds, songs, and poems for toddlers and preschoolers. Cobblestone Publishing, 30 Grove Street–Suite C, Peterborough, NH 03458

Spider includes stories and poems on all topics for preschoolers and kindergarteners. Cobblestone Publishing, 30 Grove Street–Suite C, Peterborough, NH 03458

Click includes nonfiction for the early elementary grades. Cobblestone Publishing, 30 Grove Street–Suite C, Peterborough, NH 03458

Ranger Rick includes material on nature and ecology for preschoolers through grade two. National Wildlife Federation, 11100 Wildlife Center Road, Reston, VA 20190

Your Big Backyard includes nature stories, activities, photographs, and recipes (toddlers and preschoolers). National Wildlife Federation, 11100 Wildlife Center Road, Reston, VA 20190

Wild Animal Babies includes related stories and pictures for toddlers. National Wildlife Federation, 11100 Wildlife Center Road, Reston, VA 20190

Turtle includes poetry, stories, and games about health (preschoolers). Children's Better Health Institute, 1100 Waterway Boulevard, Indianapolis, IN 46202

Let's Find Out includes activities and games for holidays, seasons, and other topics (preschool to kindergarten). Scholastic, 557 Broadway, New York, NY 10012

National Geographic Little Kids features science-and world-related photographs, activities, and stories. National Geographic Society, 1145–17th Street NW, Washington, DC 20036

Criteria for Selecting Magazines and Newspapers

First, determine whether the magazine, article, story, or illustration supports the objective or purpose of the lesson or activity. Does it fit into the curriculum web for this lesson? Does it reinforce a concept that is being learned? Does it clarify the meaning of something the class is doing? Does it extend the learning in some way? The answers to these questions will help to determine how well the print media will support the purpose of the lesson.

TIPS FOR TEACHERS

Make use of early childhood journals, activities magazines, and computer software for planning activities for children.

- Read the issues of journals at the public library if you are not a subscriber.
- Use library databases to access a wide range of journals.
- File pages of journals and magazines you plan to use.
- Use computer software by yourself before having a child use it in order to identify the places the child may become confused.

Second, determine the suitability of the piece for children. Try to see it through the eyes of a child. What might be a stunning photograph to an adult or even an older child might be too complex and vague to a younger child. A written text that might be fascinating to an adult or older child might be too abstract and confusing to a younger child.

Using Magazines and Newspapers

In addition to magazines specifically designed for children, other magazines might be useful as well. Although the texts might be inappropriate, the titles and photographs from many different magazines might be helpful in reinforcing or extending a story or a concept. For example, sports magazines might contain illustrations and photographs appropriate for a unit on books dealing with sports and motor skills. Family magazines might include pictures of foods mentioned in the stories children are reading. Newspaper advertising headlines may contain words and phrases used in language development and story activities.

A variety of hands-on activities related to a story can be done with pictures and words cut from the pages of magazines and newspapers. Collages can be made from pictures of animals, foods, and shapes. Category charts can be constructed from pictures of houses, trucks, animals, or parts of the body. Sequences of a sports activity, a plant growing, or a cake being made can be cut out and mounted as a project. A series or set of related pictures can be displayed to children so that they can create their own story about the pictures. Games such as "War" and "Old Maid" can be created by mounting various types of pictures on index cards. Laminating any of these projects can protect them for long-term use.

COMPUTERS AND SOFTWARE

There are many arguments for using computers with young children. Computers are a part of the increasingly technological society that children live in. Children will have to know about computers when they enter school. Computers can give them a head start on reading. On the other hand, there are several arguments against the use of computers with young children. They take children away from **social interactions**. The **software,** that is the programs that run on a computer, are often of poor quality. Children aren't ready to use a computer at a very young age. Each of the arguments on both sides of the issue may have some truth. One's decision on computer use might vary depending on the age of the child.

It is important to have a clear idea of the issues involved here in determining the amount of computer use in a literacy development program for young children. The position taken in this chapter is that computers can be an effective tool to supplement and enhance literacy with young children. For example, if a child wishes to read a favorite book that is not available in the classroom, demonstrate how to access a public library's online catalog of books and show the child how to solve the problem and obtain the book. National Geographic now provides free video downloads of such things as fishing trips, animals, and forces of nature for children who are interested in a faraway land. If the equipment and training are available, digital cameras, DVD burners, LCD projectors, plasma and HDTV screens, and podcast creation software create the possibility of downloading and uploading child-created podcasts, e-books, and e-magazines. Technology must be used, however, as part of a carefully thought-out plan that considers the child's development, the purpose for using the computer, and the software that will be used.

Criteria for Computer Use

The criteria for using computers must address child development, the purpose of the computer use, and the software selected for use.

Child Development. The child's development will have an effect on his or her ability to use the computer keyboard and other peripheral devices. Parents and caregivers may be concerned about the possibility of eyestrain in children who look at a computer screen for lengthy periods of time. One might, therefore, question the appropriateness of having children work independently at a computer terminal.

On the other hand, if the teacher manages or guides the use of the keyboard while the children view the screen, there may be ample reason for using certain programs. Teacher management of the keyboard does not mean that children are not allowed to touch it. Opportunities to experiment and manipulate parts of the computer environment can and should be provided. Realistic expectations are necessary, however, when children are given control of a computer, as development takes place over a period of time.

TIPS FOR TEACHERS

Seek family and community assistance to schedule effective use of computers in programs and classrooms.

- Public libraries
- Child related nonprofit organizations
- Local government agencies

Purpose. Use a computer only to satisfy legitimate literacy goals. One might have as a purpose the simple notion of exposing children to a powerful technology. While that may be a valid purpose, it is not necessarily part of a literacy program. If the purpose is to drill young children on letter and number identification, it would be at odds with current thought on developing such skills. Computer drills tend to take children away from the social interactions and the opportunities to re-create stories and events that are important to language development. These drills can also lead to a belief that language and reading are monotonous and boring activities.

Computer use can harmonize with a contemporary view of literacy development when it is used to reinforce and enhance the development of literacy in a social context. This can be done in several ways. As noted earlier, the teacher can control or guide the use of the keyboard while children interact with each other and the program on the screen. The teacher guides the group so that the technology is used as a means to create and re-create language and stories in meaningful ways. The teacher can also provide opportunities in which pairs of students interact with each other as well as the computer in order to accomplish a task. Guidance is a key to providing effective opportunities for computer use with young children.

Software. A great deal of poor-quality software is available, making it more challenging to find the really useful programs. The type of software to avoid is that which tends to require little more than rote responses from children. In effect, it does little more than duplicate a ditto sheet or a workbook page on an electronic screen. One should seriously question using an expensive piece of electronic equipment for a task that can be accomplished just as easily with a pencil and paper.

The software selected might better be used to encourage the development of original stories or to re-create stories the child has experienced. Creative art programs and simplified word processing programs are available for this purpose. They better reflect contemporary thought on literacy development. They also provide an experience for the child that is much more meaningful than the simple recall of rote information. The Northwest Educational Technology Consortium (*Early Connections: Technology in Early Childhood Education,* 2010) provides four key characteristics that researchers cite as important for selecting software for young children:

- Software that invites children to explore, imagine, and solve problems.
- Software that uses and extends what children already know.
- Software that is multi-sensory (sound, voice, visual, musical).
- Software that keeps the child in control of the speed and direction of the program.

Methods of Computer Use

It is best to use the computer as a means rather than an end. Learning about computers is important for nearly everyone, but it is not absolutely essential that children acquire this familiarity in early childhood. The focus in an early childhood education program should be on using the computer as a means to enhance literacy development. While children might be allowed to actually use the computer, it can be a more powerful tool when the teacher guides children in a language-development activity using the computer. For example, a computerized version of a previously read story can be explored through a computer program presentation. Titles available on computer media from The Learning Company include Kevin Henkes's *Sheila Rae the Brave,* Marc Brown's *Arthur's Teacher Trouble* and *Arthur's Birthday,* and Mercer Mayer's *Just Grandma and Me* and *Little Monster at School.*

An LEA story can be created as an original piece on the computer. A previously read story can be re-created on the computer using the words of the children. Scholastic's "Wiggle Works" program includes books in English and Spanish, as well as a word processing program appropriate for young children. This title is also an interactive computer-based program designed to encourage reading, listening, and speaking skills for three levels of emergent literacy development. Sunburst markets a multisensory interactive alphabet program called "A to Zap." The major point with these approaches is that the language and the understanding of the story are the focus rather than the computer. Thus these approaches coincide with the major purposes and objectives of a literacy curriculum for young children.

Online programs have evolved to the point that they are more easily accessed by both children and adults. If the equipment resources are available, they can provide a useful language and literacy resource. *Elmo's Keyboarder-Rama* by Sesame Workshop uses simple games to teach young children the letter keys on a keyboard. Some online programs are also available that provide high-quality presentations of children's literature. At www.grandviewlibrary. org, Sarah Chauncey presents children's picture books along with written and podcast presentations created by young children at the Grandview Library in Monsey, New Jersey. A variety of complete children's picture books can be read free at the Children's Storybook site at www.magickeys.com/books. At www .storyplace.org, the site of the Public Library of Charlotte and Mecklenburg counties in North Carolina, children's picture books are presented in both English and Spanish with online and take-home activities. From London, the Storynory site created by Hugh Fraser and Mathew Lynn is available at www.storynory. com. This site, which creates weekly new podcast stories read by actress Natasha Lee-Lewis, provides free downloadable audio files of children's stories.

Multiple Literacies

Over the last several decades, researchers and educators have studied the links between storybook reading and learning to read. Although the primary goal with young children is to develop a love and enthusiasm for books, the fostering of literacy is of interest as well. Don Holdaway (1984) found that reading to children helped them to develop **self-monitoring** and **predictive reading strategies**. Frank Smith (1999) held that sharing stories fostered an understanding that printed language has meaning. Sulzby and Teale (1991) argued that sharing stories leads children to understand the language and conventions of books.

More recently, Cynthia Church (2001) contends that since reading requires the reader to use a number of literacy skills and since children live in a technological age with a number of ways of knowing, it makes sense to consider the concept of multiple storybook literacies. In her year-long case study research she investigated the effects of multiple storybook shared experiences. These included shared reading, LEA storybooks, and computer (CD-ROM) storybooks. In all cases, an adult shared the storybook experience with the child.

Church found that children can benefit from multiple literacy experiences due to the fact that they seemed to focus on different literacy concepts depending on which type of reading experience they were engaged in. During traditional storybook sharing, the child tended to focus primarily on the text and the illustrations. With an LEA storybook, the child tended to focus mainly on interacting with the print and reading strategies. With a CD-ROM storybook, the focus was on concepts such as the book itself, turning pages, left to right, and nonprint aspects such as the voice of the reader and the songs that went along with the story. Therefore, it seems that when children are drawn to multiple experiences with a favorite storybook, such opportunities can foster the multiple literacies that they will need to use as they progress in their own literacy development.

More recently, the concept of multiple literacies related to language-based literacy has broadened more into technology literacy. As children read books, particularly books that go beyond the traditional mainstream culture, they often seek to go beyond the information presented there. Technology supports that curiosity, but only to the extent that young people have developed their digital literacy skills, particularly with computers and the internet. The digital literacy skills that support young language and literacy learners might include the ability to solve or get help on technical problems, the ability to use the basic parts of a computer (e.g., mouse, keyboard), the ability to use the web to obtain and share information, and the ability to reflect upon their use of technology.

Useful Web Sites

The Internet is fast becoming a useful resource for parents and early childhood caregivers. It is particularly useful in linking children and adults with literacy resources beyond the classroom and community. Useful Web sites for emergent literacy are listed at the end of this chapter.

SUMMARY

The commercial media is a major influence in the lives of young children. It brings forth a constant stream of new ideas and images. Children, however, need to grow at their own pace. They are often not able to discriminate between the important, unimportant, truthful, and deceptive images they find before them. They are exposed to television, audiovisual materials, newspapers, magazines, and computer software. The question isn't whether children should or should not be exposed to this; it will happen anyway. The question for teachers and parents is how to control the amount, the timing, and the use of that media exposure.

Appropriately introduced and used, commercial media can support the development of literacy in young children. Introduced too soon and in inappropriate amounts, they can leave a child confused about many aspects of reality. Teachers and parents must decide how to use the media for their own purposes rather than for the purposes the media may have developed. While television can be a tremendous problem if overused, it can support constructive purposes. The same is true for audiovisual materials, magazines, newspapers, and computers. Adults must develop appropriate structures for their effective use. The key ingredients include understanding the development of the child, developing clear purposes for media use, and carefully selecting the appropriate media for those uses.

QUESTIONS FOR THOUGHT AND DISCUSSION

1. What are some of the dangers of overusing the media?
2. What are some of the positive aspects of television?
3. What are some of the negative aspects of television?
4. Why is it important to have alternative activities available when television viewing is decreased or eliminated?
5. What are the criteria for effectively using television with young children?
6. Describe an activity in which television can be used to support the development of literacy.
7. What are the criteria for effectively using audiovisual materials with young children?
8. Describe an activity in which audiovisual materials can be used to support the development of literacy.
9. What are the criteria for effectively using print media with young children?
10. Describe an activity in which print media can be used to support the development of literacy.
11. What are the criteria for effectively using computers with young children?
12. Describe an activity in which computers can be used to support the development of literacy.
13. Although television viewing is not the sole cause of nightmares and childhood fears, how can violence on television affect a young child?
14. What is the appropriate role of computer technology in the early childhood program?

For additional resources, visit the *Growing Up with Literature* companion website at www.cengage.com/education/sawyer.

CHILDREN'S BOOKS CITED

Andersen, Hans Christian. (2006). *Hans Christian Andersen stories.* New York: Weston Woods/Scholastic.

Berenstain, Stan, and Berenstain, Jan. (2005). *The Berenstain bears and the messy room.* New York: Random House.

Bridwell, Norman. (2006). *Everyone loves Clifford—good friends, good times.* New York: Weston Woods/Scholastic.

Brown, Marc. (1989). *Arthur's teacher trouble.* Boston: Little, Brown.

Brown, Marc. (2005). *Arthur's birthday.* Boston: Little, Brown.

Cronin, Doreen. (2005). *Diary of a spider.* New York: Joanna Cotler/HarperCollins.

Dorros, Arthur. (1998). *This is my house.* New York: Scholastic.

Flannery Brothers. (2009). *Love songs for silly things.* Hampden, ME: Flannery Brothers.

Goodman, John. (2009). *The lion book of five minute animal stories.* Scarsdale, NY: Lion Books.

Henkes, Kevin. (1996). *Sheila Rae the Brave.* New York: Mulberry.

Hurd, Thacher. (2006). *Moo cow kaboom* (CD and book read by John Beech). Pine Plains, NY: Live Oak Media.

Kaye, Mary. (2009). *Music box.* Portland, OR: CDBaby.

Martin, Jr., Bill. (2009). *Brown bear, brown bear, what do you see?* (book/audio CD). New York: Macmillan Young Listeners; Pap/Com Edition.

Mayer, Mercer. (1994). *Little monster at school.* New York: Random House.

Mayer, Mercer. (2001). *Just Grandma and me.* New York: Random House.

McGhee, Alison. (2007). *Someday.* New York: Atheneum.

Molloy, Sukey. (2005). *Circle songs CD.* Portland, OR: CDbaby.com.

Monica, Carol. (2005). *Sesame Street Elmo's easy as ABC book.* Pleasantville, NY: Reader's Digest.

Mulhollan, Kelly, and Donna Stjevma. (2006). *Toucan jam: A world of music CD.* Portland, OR: CDbaby.com.

O'Keefe, Susan. (2001). *One hungry monster.* Boston: Little Brown.

Preller, James. (2007). *Jigsaw Jones.* New York: Scholastic.

Rathmann, Margaret. (2006). *Ruby the copycat.* New York: Scholastic.

Rawlinson, Julia. (2008). *Fletcher and the falling leaves.* New York: Greenwillow.

Rey, Margaret, and Rey, H. A. (2006). *Curious George goes to the chocolate factory.* New York: Weston Woods/Scholastic.

Saltzberg, Barry. (2003). *Crazy hair day.* Cambridge, MA: Candlewick.

Schnitzer, Sue. (2006). *Best friends: Rockin' music for kids CD.* Lincoln, NE: AV Café.

Shannon, David. (2004). *Alice the fairy.* New York: Blue Sky Press.

Waddell, Martin. (2005). *Sleep tight little bear.* Cambridge, MA: Candlewick.

Wells, Rosemary. (1997). *Noisy Nora.* New York: Dial.

Willems, Mo. (2003). *Don't let the pigeon drive the bus.* New York: Hyperion.

Willems, Mo. (2005). *Knuffle bunny.* New York: Walker.

Wilson, Karma. (2004). *Bear wants more.* New York: Simon & Schuster/McElderry.

Zelinsky, Paul, and Huck, Charlotte. (2006). *Favorite fairy tales.* New York: Weston Woods/Scholastic.

SELECTED REFERENCES AND RESOURCES

Brown. L. M., and Lamb, S. (2007). *Packaging girlhood: Rescuing our daughters from Marketers' schemes.* New York: St. Martins Griffin.

Bryant, J. A. (2006). *The children's television community.* Hillsdale, NJ: Lawrence Erlbaum.

Bus, A. G., and Neuman, S. B. (2008). *Multimedia and literacy development.* New York: Routledge.

Church, C. R. (2001). Click and turn the page: An exploration of multiple storybook literacy. *Reading Research Quarterly 36* (2), 152–183.

Holdaway, D. (1984). *The foundations of literacy.* New York: Scholastic.

Norelli, J. (2001). *Easy activities for using KidPix software in the classroom.* Clifton Park, NY: Delmar Learning.

Plowman, L., Stephen, C., and McPake, J. (2010). *Growing up with technology: Young children learning in a digital world.* New York: Routledge.

Smith, F. (1999). *Understanding reading* (3rd ed.). New York: Holt, Rinehart and Winston.

Sulzby, E., and Teale, W. (1991). Children's emergent reading of favorite storybooks: A developmental study. *Reading Research Quarterly 20,* 458–481.

Trelease, J. (2006). *The read-aloud handbook.* New York: Viking Penguin.

Zimmerman, F., Christakis, D., and Meltzoff, A. (2007). Television and DVD/video viewing in children younger that two years. *Archives of Pediatric and Adolescent Medicine 161,* 463–479.

INTERNET REFERENCES
AND HELPFUL WEBSITES

American Academy of Pediatrics. Television and your family. Retrieved March 12, 2010, from http://www.aap.org/publiced/BR_TV.htm

Children's Storybook. Retrieved March 12, 2010, from http://www.magickeys.com/books

Connect for Kids. Technology and young children. Retrieved March 12, 2010, from http://www.connectforkids.org/

Grandview Library, Monsey, NJ. Grandviewlibrary. Retrieved March 12, 2010, from www.grandviewlibrary.org

Eastern Washington University Library site. Retrieved March 15, 2010, from http://www.ewu.edu/x59077.xml

Florida Educational Technology Clearinghouse site. Retrieved March 15, 2010, from http://etc.usf.edu/lit2go/

International Society for Technology in Education. ISTE Teacher resources. Retrieved March 12, 2010, from http://www.iste.org/

Kidsource site. Computers and young children. Retrieved March 12, 2010, from www.kidsource.com/education/computers/children.html

National Institute on Media and the Family. Retrieved March 12, 2010, from http://mediafamily.org/

Northwest Educational Technology Consortium. Early connections: Technology in early childhood education. Retrieved March 12, 2010, from http://www.netc.org/earlyconnections/

Parent Television Council site. Retrieved March 12, 2010, from http://www.parentstv.org/

Public Library of Charlotte and Mecklenburg Counties, North Carolina. Storyplace. Retrieved March 12, 2010, from http://www.storyplace.org

Sesame Workshop. Elmo's Keyboard-O-Rama. Retrieved March 12, 2010, from http:// www.sesameworkshop.org/

Storynory. Retrieved March 12, 2010, from www.storynory.com

USEFUL WEB SITES FOR PARENTS AND CAREGIVERS: EMERGENT LITERACY

Retrieved March 12, 2010.

http://www.amazon.com/—This site identifies itself as "Earth's Biggest Bookstore." If you can't find the titles found in this book at your local bookstore, you will almost always be able to order them through this Web site.

http://pbskids.org/—This is the PBS-linked site focused on children's programming containing information on all programs and local access information.

http://www.cbcbooks.org/—This is the Children's Book Council Web site, containing valuable ideas for teaching with children's books year round.

http://www.ucalgary.ca/~dkbrown/—This University of Calgary site maintained by David K. Brown is one of the best. It contains listings of children's book awards, information about children's literature, teaching ideas, and links to authors, stories, organizations, storytellers, and journals.

http://www.trelease-on-reading.com/—This is Jim Trelease's site. It contains selections from The Read-Aloud Handbook, children's author profiles, book lists, and censorship information.

http://www.carolhurst.com/—This is Carol Hurst's site. It contains hundreds of reviews of children's picture books.

http://www.naeyc.org/resources/—This is the site for the National Association for the Education of Young Children. It has a wealth of information on literacy and other topics.

http://www.ala.org/—This is the site of the American Library Association. It contains information on children's books, book awards, censorship, and literacy-related activities.

http://www.zerotothree.org/—This is the site for the National Center for Infants, Toddlers, and Families. It has excellent information on literacy and developmental activities in plain language.

http://www.projectapproach.org/—The Project Approach site contains an enormous amount of information on projects appropriate for young children. It contains numerous sources and examples of successful projects.

http://www.pilkey.com/—This is author/illustrator Dav Pilkey's Web site.

http://www.janbrett.com/—This is author/illustrator Jan Brett's Web site.

http://www.ericcarle.com/—This is author/illustrator Eric Carle's Web site.

http://www.meganmcdonald.net—This is author Megan McDonald's Web site.

© Cengage Learning

CHAPTER 10

INVOLVING THE COMMUNITY

Every community, large and small, contains a wonderfully rich variety of resources. Young children can and should learn about these resources. From infancy through the kindergarten years, children are fascinated by the world around them. Use this intrinsic motivation to enrich the lives of children by focusing attention on the people and places found in the community. Make a visit to a library, auto repair shop, or bank. Invite a visit from a farmer, a nurse, or a bookstore owner. Whatever the occasion, community involvement can be combined with literature and the educational program for children. Recent reform movements at the national, state, and local levels have made it a point to stress the need for much greater involvement of families and communities in education programs and decision making.

In viewing a community, it may be helpful to see it in more than one way. First of all, a community contains people and places. The people have many different jobs, and the places have many different roles. The buildings have been constructed to serve a variety of purposes. Some buildings are like big empty boxes that can be used for a variety of things such as a store, an office, or a business. Other buildings have specific designs and contain specialized equipment so that they can be

"At the heart of all that civilization has meant and developed is community.

—DR. MARTIN LUTHER KING, JR.

used as a police station, church, or hospital. Another way of viewing the community is to determine how it can best be used to benefit children's education.

Is it best to bring the children to the community? Or should the community be brought to the children? Actually, both approaches can be effective depending on the situation. Both approaches will be explored here.

PLACES TO GO: EXPLORING THE COMMUNITY

A field trip is always exciting for children. Because it can be such a powerful learning experience, it makes good sense to plan a field trip within an integrated program. Literature can easily be correlated with parts of the program. Depending on the community, the possibilities are wide and varied. Each place visited will be important in developing the schemas children will use to continue to make sense of the world. Libraries, museums, parks, zoos, banks, theaters, and municipal service buildings are all appropriate field trip destinations. The concept of what comprises a community can be introduced to children with *What Is a Community* by Rebecca Rissman and Sian Smith. Following this, the idea of a field trip could be established with *Miss Fox's Class Earns a Field Trip,* a board book by Eileen Spinelli. Before attempting such a visit, it's necessary to develop a sound field trip plan.

Although there is nothing that can match the excitement and learning potential of an actual trip, there are times when a trip to a site related to a particular topic is simply not possible. Virtual field trips using the Internet can fill this void. Although there are numerous commercial websites (.com) that provide virtual field trips for a fee, many sites provided by nonprofits (.org) and educational institutions (.edu) provide virtual field trips for free. The Pinellas County Florida site provides virtual field trips to its parks featuring such things as a boardwalk, pond, trail, footbridge, fort, museum, butterfly garden, veteran's memorial, firehouse, log house, church, and aquatic habitat. New York City's Greenwich Village Society for Historic Preservation site provides an urban virtual field trip featuring cityscapes, row houses, tenements, churches, and shops. The American Dairy Farmers site provides a virtual field trip to a dairy farm featuring cropland, calving, milking, and recycling.

Field Trip Planning

In order to have a successful and effective field trip, attend to both the trip details and the learning details. Ignoring either of these can result in an experience that is less meaningful or even unsafe for the children.

Trip Details. When taking a group of children into the community, safety must be a constant thought. If it is planned ahead of time, the trip will go more smoothly. Always make arrangements with the people at the destination, and have an understanding of what the experience will be like for the children. Planning trips for warmer weather eliminates the need to focus on extra clothing, weather-related closings, and driving conditions. Parental permission slips, children's name tags, and car assignments are all details that must be attended to. A walking field trip presents safety concerns for crossing streets and keeping the group together and accounted for. Always make parents feel welcome in the program and on field trips. Parental participation should extend beyond chaperoning duties. Mothers, fathers, and grandparents can participate in the planning, implementing, and extension activities of the field trip.

Learning Details. Question a field trip to the firehouse if the trip is being planned simply because the firehouse is only a block away. If closeness is the main reason for the field trip, it may be more of an entertainment experience than an opportunity for learning. With careful planning of integrated units, it is not difficult to choose both appropriate field trip destinations and appropriate literature to share before, during, and after the trip. Appropriate literature will help children anticipate, enjoy, and re-create the experience, bringing them the greatest benefit.

Libraries

Reprinted with the permission of Aladdin Paperbacks, an imprint of Simon & Schuster Children's Publishing Division from ALISTAIRS ELEPHANT by Marilyn Sadler, illustrated by Roger Bollen. Ilustrations copyright © 1983 Roger Bollen.

In any program that views books and literature as important to child development, visits to libraries quickly come to mind. Nearly all communities have libraries with long visiting hours. Many offer a weekly bookmobile. The children's department of most libraries typically schedules story times and activities for a number of age groups throughout the year. Library visits can have important outcomes. First, children learn that libraries have a major focus on books. Second, they become aware of the enormous variety of books. Finally, children learn that libraries are places of learning that go well beyond books. Good stories to introduce the library to children include Jane Yolen's *Baby Bear's Books*, Suzanne Williams' *Library Lit*, and Joseph Slate's *Miss Bindergarten Takes a Field Trip with Kindergarten*. Marilyn Sadler shares another of Alistair's adventures in *Alistair's Elephant*, this one taking place as he is returning some books to the library.

Learning to Love Books. From late infancy on, it is possible for children to understand the rules of book friendship. The librarian, as an expert in books, can reinforce what children have been taught about books and reinforce the modeling of their parents' and teachers' use of books. Other concepts, such as not writing or coloring in books, can also be reinforced. Children often do not distinguish between coloring books and other books.

TIPS FOR TEACHERS

Invite the local librarian to a parent meeting to issue cards and explain library programs:

- Story hours for infants, toddlers, and preschoolers
- Seasonal and community celebrations held in the library
- Community outreach programs

A World of Books. Libraries are special places within the community. One will see many different kinds of people in the library: young, old, rich, poor, men, women, and children. Those people are there because libraries have books and resources for everyone.

Gone are the days when librarians tried to make the library a place of absolute silence. Today, children talk quietly about a project in the library and even listen to the librarian reading a story out loud. There are programs for toddlers and preschoolers. Libraries sponsor films and puppet shows related to children's books in order to encourage children to use the library. Summer reading programs, craft hours, cooking, singing, and dramatic storytelling are all a part of a modern library program.

© Cengage Learning

Introducing children to the library is an important milestone in the development of literacy.

Adults can model the benefits of using the library and knowing the librarian. Having a library card will allow children to take home wonderful stories to be read during the week. By asking the librarian, children can find out about new books by a favorite author or about a favorite topic.

More Than Just Books. Libraries house more than books. They contain digital media, computers, CDs, magazines, and historical records. Local historical information can be most interesting to children, particularly those whose families have been living in the community for a long time. By using the historical records, one can find answers to many fascinating questions. What was it like to live in the community one hundred years ago? Were there Native Americans? Was it unsettled land or a village? Were there buildings? Was our school here then? Posters, maps, and photographs can often be found in the library to answer many of these questions. This activity can be a springboard to future field trips and for developing LEA stories about this topic.

Heroes sometimes emerge out of a search of historical records. The library can help children learn about the sacrifices and accomplishments of people who lived and worked in the community many years ago. Once this knowledge emerges, it can lead to other activities. The children might be able to visit the childhood home of the individual or have a descendant of the individual visit them. The library is a versatile place. It houses a tremendous variety of resources about nearly any topic. Librarians are willing to assist visitors and groups in locating information and materials. The library is a place that children can use for many purposes.

TIPS FOR TEACHERS

Use a variety of locations for story sharing.

- INDOORS: firehouse, restaurant, clothing store, railroad station, flower shop, pet store, bank, shopping mall, and so on.
- OUTDOORS: pond, farm, park, zoo, playground, college campus, farmer's market, and so on.

Museums, Parks, and Zoos

Museums, parks, and zoos offer opportunities to extend and enrich the lives of children. They are special places that compress much of life into a framework that one can experience in a matter of hours. Each of these places has a character of its own. Some museums focus on art, science, natural history, or technology. Some specialized museums re-create colonial villages. Parks feature terrains, trees, and gardens. Most zoos contain many of the same animals, but some zoos specialize in birds, monkeys, reptiles, or large cats. Planetariums and aquariums are two other places that can be used to create powerful learning experiences for young children. Most of these resources have a designated education coordinator who can help make a field trip a most beneficial experience for young people.

TIPS FOR TEACHERS

Bring a chart with related pictures and name words on field trips to draw attention to the connection between language and the environment:

- Park field trip—trees, benches, pond, flowers, walkway, and animals
- Fire Station trip—fire engine, ladder, hat, building, colors

Literature can be used before, during, and after a field trip. To encourage students to stay together as a group, one might read Laurent de Brunhoff's *Babar's Museum of Art* prior to the trip. In this story, the familiar Babar and his family turn an old railroad station into an art museum for his art collection. A bonus is the recreation of such works as "Mother and Child" by Cassatt, "The Scream" by Munch, and additional works by Whistler, Cezanne, and Pollock. While going through an art museum with a group of children, one may wish to pause for a story about a visit to an art museum. *Museum Trip* by Barbara Lehman is a fascinating wordless picture book about a class field trip in which a boy loses track of his group, blends into part of the exhibits, and eventually finds his way back. Here, too, skillful reproductions of old masters are portrayed. A wild time is had by Hector, the night watchman at the Museum of Natural History, when he awakens to find that all of the dinosaur skeletons have disappeared in Milan Trenc's *The Night at the Museum*. A similar book is *The Mixed Up Museum* by Gail Herman.

The books used need not be set in a museum or a park. Rather, books should be selected with learning in mind. If there are no museums in an area, children can learn about valuable related information and history. The book *Remember Me: Tomah Joseph's Gift to Franklin Roosevelt* by Donald Soctomah and Jean Flahine can be used in this way. It is the story of Elder Tomah, a Passamaquoddy Native American who was an expert basket maker and canoe builder. He formed a friendship with FDR when the latter spent summers in Maine. He taught his culture to the man who would one day become a great

Cover from *Remember Me: Tomah Joseph's Gift to Franklin Roosevelt* by Donald Soctomah and Jean Flahine. Jacket art copyright © 2007 by Mary Beth Owens. Reprinted by permission of the publisher, Tilbury House. All rights reserved.

president and presented him with a beautiful birch bark canoe. To this day, the canoe remains at the Campobello Island FDR historic home site, a symbol of the friendship. The story can be combined with a President's Day event, a unit on friendship, or a celebration of multicultural understanding. As another example, one might simply wish for children to learn about some of the animals, insects, and plants found in the area. A book that could be used for this purpose is *Dinosaurs?!* by Lila Prop, a humorous story in which the chickens are shocked to learn that they are descended from dinosaurs. Two humorous stories also on the topic of parks are *More Pies!* by Robert Munsch and *Shark in the Park* by Nick Sharratt. In this tale, Timothy spots what he believes to be a shark's dorsal fin while trying out his new telescope in the park. It is a good starting point to generate ideas about what we would typically find in a park. Sharing this type of literature during the field trip can greatly enhance the children's learning and understanding. Museum shops often carry related books and artwork that could be used in discussions before and after the museum visit. Large museums usually operate a children's shop that could become part of the field trip experience.

Book Covers from *Mud Makes Me Dance in the Spring, I Wear Long Green Hair in the Summer, Wind Spins Me Around in the Fall,* and *I Slide into the White of Winter.* Text and Illustrations copyright © 1994 by Charlotte Agell. Reprinted by permission of the author.

A visit to a museum need not be a one-time activity. Many museums contain a large number of exhibits, and trying to see everything in a single visit could make the trip too long and too tiring. It would be more productive to tie the books, activities, and specific aspects of a museum to a single theme and then visit only the exhibits related to that theme. If the museum has a re-creation of some type of building or structure, for example, that might be a theme. An extension activity following such a visit would be to involve the children in the creation of their own museum. Activities might include creating buildings with blocks or cardboard. Picking colors for the structure could lead to a discussion about how to make the building blend into its environment or create a certain feeling. If the museum has an art gallery, the theme could be self-expression using an assortment of media such as paint, clay, play dough, and recycled materials. Water, natural resources, sea life, or wetlands might be used as a theme if the museum has an aquarium. Books could include *The Fishy Field Trip* by Brian James, *Oceanarium* by Joanne Oppenheim, and *Curious George's First Words at the Aquarium* by H. A. Rey and Margaret Rey. Activities could include creating a pictorial classroom aquarium or an actual aquarium.

Book cover from *To the Island.* Text and Illustrations copyright © 1994 by Charlotte Agell. Reprinted by permission of the author.

The picture books of Charlotte Agell are a great accompaniment to a field trip to an imaginary place or to just around the block. Although not everyone has an ocean or mountain nearby, hills and small bodies of water are everywhere. Good choices to share before trips include *To the Island* and *Up the Mountain.* Charlotte Agell also has a series about the different seasons; these books can be used with a simple walk around the block. They include *Mud Makes Me Dance in the Spring, I Wear Long Green Hair in the Summer, Wind Spins Me Around in*

Book cover from *Up the Mountain.* Text and Illustrations copyright © 1994 by Charlotte Agell. Reprinted by permission of the author.

Re-creating the experience of a field trip through art transforms children into authors and illustrators of their own experiences.

the Fall, and *I Slide into the White of Winter.* All have a bouncing rhythm and an appeal to the senses.

Places Serving the Community

A community cannot exist without a variety of services. Some services, such as fire and police protection, are an absolute necessity. Others such as stores are more of a convenience. Still others such as movie theaters are there solely to entertain. Each place, however, can add to the quality of life in the community. The people working at these places have a variety of interesting jobs, and their work is important. By understanding this, children can develop a better understanding of the community. The places serving the community can basically be divided into two groups: commercial and public service.

Commercial Locations. Places that exist to earn a profit constitute commercial locations. These include banks, stores, newspaper buildings, theaters, florists, some hospitals, and so forth. Children can understand the importance of these places to the community because they often know people who work in them. Learning more about these places will help children to better comprehend the books they read that are set in commercial locations.

Meeting some of the people who work at commercial locations and hearing them discuss the work they do is helpful. It might be possible to have one of the workers read a related story to the children. Books such as *Curious George's First Words at the Zoo* by H. A. Rey and Margaret Rey are appropriate prior to a trip to the zoo. Other books to share in conjunction with a zoo trip include *1, 2, 3 to the Zoo* by Eric Carle, *If I Ran the Zoo* by Dr. Seuss, *Lift-the-Flap Shadow Book at the Zoo* by Roger Priddy, and *Alistair's Elephant* by Marilyn Sadler. If the opportunity arises to attend a musical concert, Isaac Millman's *Moses Goes to a Concert* is an excellent choice. Moses and his classmates, who are all deaf, attend a concert and meet the percussionist. The book includes sign language illustrations. A humorous book on concerts that should appeal to a wide range of children is *Chicken Dance* by Tammi Sauer. Hens Marge and Lola are determined to enter the barnyard talent contest in order to win the prize, a pair of tickets to the Elvis Poultry concert. Fun abounds as they compete against their arch rivals, a flock of ducks. Books that could be read in conjunction with a field trip to a store include *What Moms Can't Do* by Douglas Wood and *The Storekeeper* by Tracy Campbell Pearson. If there is a green grocer, farm, or farmer's market in the area, a visit might be paired with *Harvest Year* by Chris Peterson, a book about foods that are harvested year round. Before (or after) taking children to visit transportation-related businesses, share books such as *Trains: A Pop-up Railroad Book* by Robert Crowther, *Trains* by Lynn Curlee, *How We Get Around* by Rebecca Rissman, and *Grandma Drove the Garbage Truck* by Katie Clark.

Public Service Locations. In addition to the businesses found in the community, many services are provided through the work of public and private agencies. These services are often aimed at providing protection to residents, maintaining good health, and responding to the religious needs of the population. The places that provide these services are quite varied, making them fascinating field trip destinations. They include water filtration plants, firehouses, police stations, hospitals, clinics, weather stations, courthouses, churches, and so forth. The buildings often contain specialized equipment that performs important jobs related to the safety and health of the community. The people who work in these places are often quite willing to explain the importance of their work.

A wide variety of books can be used in conjunction with a field trip to a public service location. When visiting a firehouse, one might read *The Great Big Fire Engine Book* by Tibor Gergely or *A Very Busy Firehouse* by Alyse Sweeney. *Police Puppies* by Christopher Hart might be appropriate for use during a visit to the police station. A visit to a church or synagogue might include a reading of *Cathedral Mouse* by Kay Chorao. Books to read prior to visits to

© Cengage Learning

Hand-on experiences from field trips can have the power to help children re-create the experiences in words and art.

specific locations include: *The Bus for Us* by Suzanne Bloom; *Curious George's First Words at the Farm* and *Curious George's First Words at the Circus*, both by H. A. Rey and Margaret Rey; *The Little Red Hen Makes a Pizza* by Philemon Sturges; *Penguin Post* by Debi Gliori; *Dentist from the Black Lagoon* by Mike Thaler; and *Mocha, the Real Doctor* by Jane Wood.

Wherever a field trip has been scheduled, it is important to acknowledge and thank the people responsible for making it possible. Sharing a copy of an LEA story developed by the children after the trip is a thoughtful gesture. A thank-you note might be accompanied by photographs or children's drawings of the visit. Inviting radio, television, or newspaper reporters and photographers to accompany the children on these field trips is still another way of demonstrating the importance of the occasion.

PEOPLE TO SEE

It is impossible to arrange field trips to every place one would like children to visit, but many times a visit by a person with an interesting or specialized job may be even more meaningful. People are often flattered and quite willing to devote the time to such an activity. They can explain their jobs, demonstrate a piece or two of the equipment they use in the job, and perhaps read a story about their job to the children.

TIPS FOR TEACHERS

At program registration, survey parents for possible future field trips and visitors:

- Occupations, hobbies, interests, volunteerism
- Places of work, travel, countries of origin

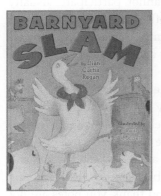

Cover from *Barnyard Slam* by Dian Curtis Regan. Jacket art copyright © 2009 by Paul Meisel. Reprinted by permission of the publisher, Holiday House. All rights reserved.

Parents of children can be recruited for these activities. A meteorologist might demonstrate the use of a weather map and read *Maisy's Wonderful Weather Book* by Lucy Cousins. A boater, sailor, or shipyard worker might show how to make a paper boat and read *Busy Boats* by Tony Mitton. A florist or gardener might show how to display flowers and read *Song of the Flowers* by Takayo Noda. A visitor who works in a grocery market could tell about how food grows and reaches the market and then read *What's in Grandma's Grocery Bag?* by Hui-Mei Pan or *Apple Countdown* by Joan Holub. If there is a farm nearby, a farmer might be persuaded to have some fun by reading Dian Regan's *Barnyard Slam* with the children. In this tale, the barnyard erupts in a commotion as Mama Goose tries to host a poetry reading slam. In the end peace ensues, and things get back to normal. Each of these presentations could be followed by reenactments by the children. Parents may be the most overlooked group of positive contributors to learning within an educational program. Most likely, they will represent a number of different occupations and resources. It is critical to maintain frequent and effective communications with parents concerning the program. In this way, they will be better able to support it and contribute to it. Other classroom visitors might include local artists or illustrators, teenagers, senior citizens, hockey players, and Santa Claus, to name a few possibilities.

Involving Parents

Parents often seek ways in which they can become actively involved in the education of their children. Parental involvement in both the literature and the content parts of the program can benefit parents, children, and the program. Parental inclusion in the program allows children to see various adults model the importance of books, provides children with additional opportunities to learn, and helps them understand how books are related to life. Children are usually delighted and proud of the fact that their parents are visiting the classroom.

The involvement of parents in the education of their children is limited only by the creativity, time, and effort of everyone involved. Among the possible opportunities for this involvement are:

- Making the initial contact, inviting parents to be involved, and providing feedback right away.
- Providing weekly, or monthly newsletters and encouraging parents to suggest ideas.
- Hosting regular parent nights to solicit ideas and information that will make the program more effective.
- Inviting parents to participate in professional workshops with staff.
- Creating and maintaining a regular program of parent involvement including such things as classroom readers, coordinators of regular celebrations and festivals, and membership on decision making panels.

Be sensitive to the fact that some parents cannot participate, usually because their jobs will not permit them to take time off. When this occurs, other family members should be invited. Older siblings, aunts, uncles, and grandparents represent an additional source of people willing and eager to contribute to the education of children.

Careful planning of a parental visit will contribute to the success of the event. Inviting a parent to participate early or late in the day can help them fit the visit around their work schedule more easily. Day of the week, inclement weather, time of the year, and refreshments are all factors that must be considered when planning parental participation. Notices and time schedules can aid the parent, teacher, and program. With careful planning, the program will not be overscheduled. Planning will also help to ensure that such things as notices and thank-you notes are not overlooked. Developing a schedule for parental participation well in advance can help the planning for all involved. Keeping other parents informed about what is happening in advance can also be a benefit. They may be able to attend the program and even, in some cases, offer further discussion on ideas presented.

As with any effective part of the program, literature and books can be integrated with a parental visit. If parents are visiting the program to explain their jobs as bakers, lawyers, plumbers, or auto repair technicians, having them share a related story can enhance the visit. The story may be one selected by the teacher, parent, or child. Resources could be shared with parents beforehand to aid them in selecting an appropriate book. For example, a copy of one of the resource books by Jim Trelease (2006) could be sent home two weeks before a planned visit by parents. In this way, parents could carefully consider a number of stories and choose the one they feel best supports the ideas they will talk about. Parents may also have children's books at home that were purchased because they were related to their employment.

Involving parents in this manner is a positive approach because it integrates them into their children's education. Parental involvement also makes use of a valuable resource: the work lives of the parents. Many parents are willing to help with the usual tasks: baking cookies, supervising field trips, and helping at school parties. By including them in the actual educational program as well, one accords them additional respect.

Communicating with Parents

The key to an effective parental involvement program is communication. Parents must be aware of what is happening in the educational lives of their children. They need to know how they can help in the classroom, and what can

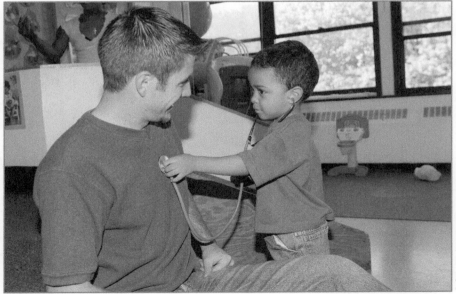

© Cengage Learning

A basic occupational tool used by the classroom visitor can allow children to experience themselves in community helper roles.

be done at home with their children. This information goes beyond the usual notices about the topic being studied this month and the recommendation that parents read with their children. Those kinds of communications, although well intended, are too general to provide much guidance.

This does not mean that a total home instructional program must be prepared to back up what is being done in the classroom. That would put undue pressure on parents and children. But if parents have a better idea of the topics being studied, why they are being studied, and what books they may wish to share at home, they will be in a better position to be involved. The idea is not to place pressure on anyone, parents or children, but to provide parents with enough information to be actively involved in making their children's educational life more meaningful.

© Cengage Learning

Classroom projects can involve many people.

Notes and Newsletters. Formal and informal parental communications are a primary source of information. They can be used to notify parents about more specific topics to be studied, the classroom visitor's schedule, meeting notices, and special projects for which supplies are needed. Newsletters can also be used to suggest books and stories related to the program. They can include home-based activities related to the literature and themes being used. These might include suggestions for repeated readings, museum visits, scavenger hunts, and local sightseeing opportunities. Written communications should always be clear and straightforward. If a multicultural population is being served, notices and newsletters can be provided in the first language of the parents.

TIPS FOR TEACHERS

Involve parents in the literacy development of their children.

- Send home a weekly or monthly newsletter describing topics and activities being planned.
- Send home copies of books to be read with the children again, this time by the parents.
- Provide lists of great children's books and authors.
- Provide weekly suggestions for related activities to be done at home.
- Set up a lending library for parents.

Questionnaires and Surveys. Questionnaires and surveys can be distributed separately, or they can be part of a newsletter. Either way, they help to foster two-way communication. Requesting information and opinions gives parents an opportunity to provide input about their needs and potential contributions, such as classroom visits they would be willing to make, hobbies they could demonstrate, areas of concern, and activities in which they would like to be involved.

Community Representatives

In many cases, representatives of the community may be identified among the parents of children in a program. When this is not the case, businesses, municipal departments, service organizations, and charitable foundations may be contacted as potential resources. The choices of whom to seek should be based upon the educational program and the learning goals for the children.

Cover from *Who Will Plant a Tree?* by Jerry Palotta. Cover art copyright © 2010 by Tom Leonard. Reprinted by permission of Sleeping Bear Press. All rights reserved.

Canadian author Robert Munsch.

Requesting a visit from an individual simply because he or she happens to be available may not be worthwhile. If the ensuing visit presents nothing to do with the program, it will be merely a diversion.

Individuals selected for classroom visits should represent the types of organizations one would visit on a field trip. The key is to include a diversity of visitors who can focus on specific areas of the program. They may be bankers, nurses, musicians, construction workers, office workers, or dentists. The books they choose to share with the children will be equally diverse. Some books could be shared by many different individuals. *Who Will Plant a Tree?* by Jerry Palotta tells of how trees are planted by animals, ocean currents, the wind, and a variety of other natural forces. This book would be a good match for a meteorologist, an arborist, a biologist, a farmer, a pilot, or anyone involved with any of the natural forces. Other possible pairings of books with specific workers includes:

- **Lawyer or elected official**–*Max for President* by Jarrett Krosoczka
- **Nurse or Medical Assistant**–*I Want to Be a Nurse* by Dan Liebman; *The School Nurse from the Black Lagoon* by Mike Thaler
- **Meteorologist**–*The Stars Are Waiting* by Marjorie Murray
- **4-H Representative or Farmer**–*Farmer Duck* by Martin Waddell; *Pumpkin Hill* by Elizabeth Spurr; *Chicken, Pig, Cow—On the Move* by Ruth Ohi; *Duck and Goose Find a Pumpkin* by Tad Hills; *Crash Bang Donkey!* by Jill Newton
- **Health Food or Restaurant Worker**–*What's Cooking, Jamela?* by Niki Daly
- **Baker or Chef**–*More Pies* by Robert Munsch
- **Architect or Construction Worker**–*A Year at a Construction Site* by Nicholas Harris
- **Postal Employee**–*Owney, the Mail Pouch Pooch* by Mona Kerby
- **Musician or Singer**–*Chicken Dance* by Tammi Sauer;
- **Fireman or Police Officer**–*A Very Busy Firehouse* by Alyse Sweeney
- **Train, Bus, or Truck Driver**–*Trains* by Lynn Curlee
- **Anyone**–*Whose Shoes* by Stephen Swinburne

Classroom visits require the same careful planning as a field trip. Making arrangements early helps all involved. A thank-you note accompanied by illustrations or a copy of the LEA story developed by the children after the visit is usually appreciated by the guest. Including announcements in the parents' newsletter before and after a visitation is beneficial. It enables parents to extend the learning through discussion and by listening to their children tell about the experience.

SUMMARY

Most communities have a wealth of resources that can be useful to an early education program. The resources may be somewhat different from place to place, but such things as firehouses and restaurants are usually common to all. Since learning often depends on the development of background knowledge and an understanding of the world, it is beneficial to include the resources of a community in the educational program. Literature can be used to enhance this part of an integrated curriculum.

A community can be seen as including places and people. The places that make up a community are diverse, including everything from libraries to stores to churches. The people of the community reflect that diversity. In most communities one will encounter a variety of workers in such fields as banking, fire protection, music, and dentistry. Whether one takes the children to the place of work or brings the workers to the children, much will be learned. Parents can be an outstanding source of support for field trip coordination and classroom visitations. A key component of tapping this resource is effective two-way communication. Such communication enables both parents and teachers to understand the concerns and needs of the children. Through this sharing, more effective instruction and learning can be planned.

QUESTIONS FOR THOUGHT AND DISCUSSION

1. What are some of the ways in which young children can learn about their community?
2. Why should field trips be planned as part of an integrated educational program? What can be done if an actual field trip is not possible?
3. Why is it important for young children to learn about their communities?
4. What are the two major areas to be considered in field trip planning?
5. When and why should literature be used in conjunction with a field trip?
6. What are some of the things children can learn from a field trip to a public library?
7. How should one select the books to be used in conjunction with a field trip?
8. Why can a class visitor sometimes provide an experience that is just as meaningful as a field trip?
9. How can parents as class visitors contribute to the educational programs of young children?

10. Why is effective communication important to successful parental involvement in the educational program?

11. How can parent/school communication be made more meaningful?

For additional resources, access the *Growing Up with Literature* companion website through www.cengagebrain.com <http://www.cengagebrain.com/>.

CHILDREN'S BOOKS CITED

Agell, Charlotte. (1994). *I slide into the white of winter.* Gardiner, ME: Tilbury House.

Agell, Charlotte. (1994). *I wear long green hair in the summer.* Gardiner, ME: Tilbury House.

Agell, Charlotte. (1994). *Mud makes me dance in the spring.* Gardiner, ME: Tilbury House.

Agell, Charlotte. (1994). *Wind spins me around in the fall.* Gardiner, ME: Tilbury House.

Agell, Charlotte. (1998). *To the island.* New York: Dorling Kindersley.

Agell, Charlotte. (2000). *Up the mountain.* New York: Dorling Kindersley.

Bloom, Suzanne. (2001). *The bus for us.* Honesdale, PA: Boyds Mills.

Carle, Eric. (2007). *1, 2, 3 to the zoo.* New York: Grosset & Dunlap.

Clark, Katie. (2006). *Grandma drove the garbage truck.* Camden, ME: Downeast.

Cousins, Lucy. (2006). *Maisy's wonderful weather book.* Cambridge, MA: Candlewick.

Crowther, Robert. (2006). *Trains: A railroad pop-up book.* Cambridge, MA: Candlewick.

Curlee, Lynn. (2009). *Trains.* New York: Atheneum.

Daly, Niki. (2002). *What's cooking, Jamela?* London: Frances Lincoln.

DeBrunhoff, Laurent. (2003). *Babar's museum of art.* New York: Abrams.

Gergely, Tibor. (2003). *The great big fire engine book.* New York: Random/Golden.

Gliori, Debi. (2002). *Penguin post.* Orlando, FL: Harcourt.

Harris, Nicholas. (2009). *A year at a construction site.* Minneapolis, MN: Millbrook.

Hart, Christopher. (2003). *Police puppies.* New York: Watson-Guptill.

Herman, Gail. (2001). *The mixed up museum.* New York: Cartwheel/Scholastic.

Hills, Tad. (2009). *Duck and Goose find a pumpkin.* New York: Random/Schwartz & Wade.

Holub, Joan. (2009). *Apple countdown.* Morton Grove, IL: Albert Whitman.

James, Brian. (2007). *The fishy field trip.* New York: Scholastic.

Kerby, Mona. (2008). *Owney, the mail pouch pooch.* New York: Farrar Straus and Giroux.

Krosoczka, Jarrett. (2004). *Max for president.* New York: Knopf.

Lehman, Barbara. (2006). *Museum trip.* Boston: Houghton Mifflin.

Liebman, Dan. (2001). *I want to be a nurse.* Richmond Hill, Ontario, Canada: Firefly.

Millman, Isaac. (2002). *Moses goes to a concert.* New York: Farrar, Straus and Giroux.

Mitton, Tony. (2005). *Busy boats.* Boston, MA: Kingfisher/Houghton Mifflin.

Munsch, Robert. (2002). *More Pies!* New York: Scholastic.

Murray, Marjorie. (1998). *The stars are waiting.* Tarrytown, NY: Marshall Cavendish.

Newton, Jill. (2010). *Crash bang donkey!* Morton Grove, IL: Albert Whitman.

Noda, Takayo. (2006). *Song of the flowers.* New York: Dial.

Ohi, Ruth. (2009). *Chicken, pig, cow—on the move.* Toronto, Ontario: Annick.

Oppenheim, Joanne. (1994). *Oceanarium.* New York: Byron Press.

Palotta, Jerry. (2010). *Who will plant a tree?* Ann Arbor, MI: Sleeping Bear Press.

Pan, Hui-Mei. (2004). *What's in Grandma's grocery bag?* New York: Starbright Books.

Peterson, Chris. (2010). *Harvest year.* Honesdale, PA: Boyds Mills Press.

Priddy, Roger. (2010). *Lift-the-flap shadow book at the zoo.* New York: Macmillan/Priddy Books.

Prop, Lila. (2010). *Dinosaurs?!* New York: North-South.

Regan, Dian. (2009). *Barnyard slam.* New York: Holiday House.

Rey, H. A. and Rey, Margaret. (2006). *Curious George's first words at the aquarium.* Boston: Houghton Mifflin.

Rey, H. A. and Rey, Margaret. (2006). *Curious George's first words at the circus.* Boston: Houghton Mifflin.

Rey, H. A. and Rey, Margaret. (2006). *Curious George's first words at the farm.* Boston: Houghton Mifflin.

Rey, H. A. and Rey, Margaret. (2006). *Curious George's first words at the zoo.* Boston: Houghton Mifflin.

Rissman, Rebecca. (2009). *How we get around.* Portsmouth, NH: Heinemann.

Rissman, Rebecca, and Smith, Sian. (2010). *What is a community?* Portsmouth, NH: Heinemann.

Sadler, Marilyn. (1983). *Alistair's elephant.* New York: Prentice Hall.

Sauer, Tammi. (2009). *Chicken dance.* New York: Sterling.

Seuss, Dr. (pseud. for Theodor Geisel) (2003). *If I ran the zoo.* London: Picture Lions.

Sharratt, Nick. (2007). *Shark in the park*. St. Albans, UK: Corgi Children's.

Slate, Joseph. (2001). *Miss Bindergarten takes a field trip with kindergarten*. New York: Dutton.

Soctomah, Donald and Flahine, Jean. (2009). *Remember me: Tomah Joseph's gift to Franklin Roosevelt*. Gardiner, ME: Tilbury House.

Spinelli, Eileen. (2010). *Miss Fox's class earns a field trip*. Morton Grove, IL: Albert Whitman.

Spurr, Elizabeth. (2006). *Pumpkin hill*. New York: Holiday House.

Sturges, Philemon. (2001). *The little red hen makes a pizza*. New York: Dutton.

Sweeney, Alyse. (2006). *A very busy firehouse*. New York: Scholastic.

Swinburne, Stephen. (2010). *Whose shoes*. Honesdale, PA: Boyds Mills Press.

Thaler, Mike. (2008). *Dentist from the Black Lagoon*. New York: Scholastic.

Thaler, Mike. (2009). *The school nurse from the Black Lagoon*. New York: Scholastic.

Trenc, Milan. (2006). *The night at the museum*. Haupauge, NY: Barron's Education Series.

Waddell, Martin. (2005). *Farmer duck*. New York: Walker.

Williams, Suzanne. (2001). *Library Lil*. New York: Puffin.

Wood, Douglas. (2001). *What moms can't do*. New York: Simon and Schuster.

Wood, Jane. (2004). *Mocha, the real doctor*. Albany, TX: Bright Sky.

Yolen, Jane. (2006). *Baby bear's books*. Orlando, FL: Harcourt.

SELECTED REFERENCES AND RESOURCES

Broadhead, P. (2010). *Play and learning in the early years*. Newbury Park, CA: Sage.

Butler, D. and Clay, M. (2008). *Reading begins at home*. Portsmouth, NH: Heinemann.

Couchenour, D. and Chrisman, K. (2011). *Families, schools, and communities: Together for young children/4E*. Belmont, CA: Wadsworth/Cengage.

Gestwicki, C. (2010). *Home, school, and community relations: A guide to working with parents*. Belmont, CA: Wadsworth/Cengage.

Rockwell, R. E., Andre, L. C., and Hawley, M. K. (2010). *Families and educators as partners: Issues and challenges*. Belmont, CA: Wadsworth/Cengage.

Shockley, B., Michaelson, B., and Allen, J. (1995). *Engaging families: Connecting home and school literacy communities*. Portsmouth, NH: Heinemann.

Trelease, J. (2006). *The new read-aloud handbook*. New York: Viking Penguin.

INTERNET REFERENCES AND HELPFUL WEBSITES

. . . and they lived happily ever after.

American Dairy Farmers site. Retrieved March 15, 2010, from http://www.dairyfarmingtoday.org/DairyFarmingToday/Virtual-Tour.htm

Children's Literature magazine. Children's Literature links page. Retrieved March 12, 2010, from http://www.childrenslit.com/

Greenwich Village Society for Historic Preservation site. Retrieved March 15, 2010, from http://www.gvshp.org/south_villagevirtualtour

Pinellas County, Florida site. Retrieved March 15, 2010, from http://www.pinellascounty.org/park/virtual_tour_menu.htm

Trelease, Jim. Trelease on reading. Retrieved March 12, 2010, from http://www.trelease-on-reading.com

APPENDIX A

PUBLISHERS AND SUPPLIERS

Books for Children

Companies identified with an asterisk (*) have a focus on one or more of the following: multiculturalism, disabilities, gender issues, social justice, and self-esteem.

* Advocacy Press, P.O. Box 236, Santa Barbara, CA 93102
* Africa World Press, 541 West Ingham Avenue – Suite B, Trenton, NJ 08607

Annick Press, 15 Patricia Avenue, Toronto, Ontario, Canada M2M 1H9

Atheneum Books, 1230 Avenue of the Americas, New York, NY 10020

Bantam Doubleday Dell, 1745 Broadway – 19th Floor, New York, NY 10019

Boyds Mills Press, 815 Church Street, Honesdale, PA 18431

Candlewick Press, 99 Dover Street, Somerville, MA 02144

* Carolrhoda/Lerner, 1251 Washington Avenue North, Minneapolis, MN 55401

Children's Book Press, 965 Mission Street, San Francisco, CA 94103

Chronicle Books, 880 Second Street, San Francisco, CA 94107

Clarion Books, 222 Berkeley Street, Boston, MA 02116

Crown Publishers, 1745 Broadway–18th Floor, New York, NY 10019

Dell/Delacorte/Dial/Doubleday, 1745 Broadway– 18th Floor, New York, NY 10019

Dutton Children's Books/Penguin, 375 Hudson Street, New York, NY 10014

Farrar, Straus, Giroux, 175 Fifth Avenue, New York, NY 10010

* Free Spirit Publishing, Suite 200, 217 Fifth Avenue North, Minneapolis, MN 55401

Greenwillow, 10 East 53rd Street, New York, NY 10012

Grolier Publishing/Scholastic, 557 Broadway, New York, NY 10012

Harcourt, 9205 South Park Center Loop, Orlando, FL 32817

HarperCollins, 10 East 53rd Street, New York, NY 10012

Henry Holt, 175 Fifth Avenue, New York, NY 10010

Holiday House, 425 Madison Avenue, New York, NY 10017

Houghton Mifflin Harcourt, 9205 South Park Center Loop, Orlando, FL 32817

* Just Us Books, 356 Glenwood Avenue, East Orange, NJ 07017

* Kar-Ben Publishing, 1251 Washington Avenue North, Minneapolis, MN 55401

Alfred Knopf, 1745 Broadway – 18th Floor, New York, NY 10019

* Lee and Low Books, 95 Madison Avenue – Suite 1205, New York, NY 10016

Little, Brown and Company, 3 Center Plaza, Boston, MA 02108

William Morrow, 10 East 53rd Street, New York, NY 10012

* North-South Books, 350 Seventh Avenue – Room 1400, New York, NY 10001

* Open Hand Publishing, P. O. Box 20207, Greensboro, NC 27420

Orchard Books, 95 Madison Avenue, New York, NY 10016

Price/Stern/Sloan, 375 Hudson Street, New York, NY 10014

Puffin, 375 Hudson Street, New York, NY 10014

G. P. Putnam's Sons, 375 Hudson Street, New York, NY 10014

Random House, 1745 Broadway – 18th Floor, New York, NY 10019

Richard C. Owen Publishers, Box 585, Katonah, NY 10536

Scholastic, 557 Broadway, New York, NY 10012

Simon and Schuster, 1230 Avenue of the Americas, New York, NY 10020

Sleeping Bear Press, 315 East Eisenhower Parkway – Suite 200, Ann Arbor, MI 48108

Steck-Vaughn, 181 Ballardvale Street, Wilmington, MA 01887

* Tilbury House, 103 Brunswick Avenue, Gardiner, ME 04345

Viking Penguin, 375 Hudson Street, New York, NY 10014

Walker & Company, 175 Fifth Avenue, New York, NY 10010

Franklin Watts, 95 Madison Avenue, New York, NY 10016

* Albert Whitman, 250 South Northwest Highway – Suite 320, Park Ridge, IL 60068

Big Books

Carson Dellosa, P. O. Box 35665, Greensboro, NC 27425

Harcourt, 9205 South Park Center Loop, Orlando, FL 32817

Pembroke Publishing, 538 Hood Road, Markham, Ontario, Canada L3R 3K9

Rigby, 9205 South Park Center Loop, Orlando, FL 32817

Scholastic, 557 Broadway, New York, NY 10012

Steck-Vaughn, 181 Ballardvale Street, Wilmington, MA 01887

Stenhouse Publishing, 480 Congress Street, Portland, ME 04101

Walker, 175 Fifth Avenue, New York, NY 10010

Wright Group/McGraw-Hill, 220 East Danieldale Road, DeSoto, TX: 75115

APPENDIX B

CALDECOTT MEDAL WINNERS

Date	Title	Author/Illustrator
1959	*Chanticleer and the Fox*	(Adaptation) Geoffrey Chaucer/Barbara Cooney
1960	*Nine Days to Christmas*	Marie Hall Ets and Aurora Labastida/Marie Hall Ets
1961	*Baboushka and the Three Kings*	Ruth Robbins/Nicolas Sidakov
1962	*Once a Mouse*	Marcia Brown
1963	*The Snowy Day*	Ezra Jack Keats
1964	*Where the Wild Things Are*	Maurice Sendak
1965	*May I Bring a Friend?*	Beatrice Schenk De Regniers/Beni Montresor
1966	*Always Room for One More*	Sorche Nic Leodhas/Nonny Hogrogian
1967	*Sam, Bangs & Moonshine*	Evaline Ness
1968	*Drummer Hoff*	Barbara Emberley/Ed Emberley
1969	*The Fool of the World*	Arthur Ransome/Uri
1970	*Sylvester and the Magic Pebble*	William Steig
1971	*A Story—A Story*	Gail E. Haley
1972	*One Fine Day*	Nonny Hogrogian
1973	*The Funny Little Woman*	(Retold) Arlene Mosel/Blair Lent

Date	Title	Author/Illustrator
1974	*Duffy and the Devil*	Harve Zemach/Margot Zemach
1975	*Arrow to the Sun*	(Adaptation) Gerald McDermott
1976	*Why Mosquitoes Buzz in People's Ears*	(Retold) Verna Aardema/Leo and Diane Dillon
1977	*Ashanti to Zulu: African Traditions*	Margaret Musgrove/Leo and Diane Dillon
1978	*Noah's Ark*	Peter Spier
1979	*The Girl Who Loved Wild Horses*	Paul Goble
1980	*Ox-Cart Man*	Donald Hall/Barbara Cooney
1981	*Fables*	Arnold Lobel
1982	*Jumanji*	Chris Van Allsburg
1983	*Shadow*	(Translation) Blaise Cendrars/Marcia Brown
1984	*The Glorious Flight: Across the Channel with Louis Bieriot*	Alice and Martin Provensen
1985	*St. George and the Dragon*	(Retold) Margaret Hodges/Trina Schart Hyman
1986	*The Polar Express*	Chris Van Allsburg
1987	*Hey Al*	Arthur Yorinks/Richard Egielski
1988	*Owl Moon*	Jane Yolen/John Schoenherr
1989	*Song and Dance Man*	Karen Ackerman/Stephen Gammell
1990	*Lon Po Po/A Red-Riding Hood Story from China*	Ed Young (Illustrator and translator)
1991	*Black and White*	David Macaulay
1992	*Tuesday*	David Wiesner
1993	*Mirette on the High Wire*	Emily Arnold McCully
1994	*Grandfather's Journey*	Allen Say
1995	*Smoky Night*	David Diaz
1996	*Officer Buckle and Gloria*	Peggy Rathman
1997	*Golem*	David Wisniewski
1998	*Rapunzel*	Paul O. Zelinsky
1999	*Snowflake Bentley*	Jacqueline Briggs Martin/Mary Azarian
2000	*Joseph Had a Little Overcoat*	Simms Taback
2001	*So You Want to Be President?*	Judith St. George/David Small
2002	*The Three Pigs*	David Wiesner

Date	Title	Author/Illustrator
2003	*My Friend Rabbit*	Eric Rohmann
2004	*The Man Who Walked Between the Towers*	Mordicai Gerstein
2005	*Kitten's First Full Moon*	Kevin Henkes
2006	*The Hello, Goodbye Window*	Norton Juster/Chris Raschka
2007	*Flotsam*	David Wiesner
2008	*The Invention of Hugo Cabret*	Brian Selznick
2009	*The House in the Night*	Susan Marie Swanson/Beth Krommes
2010	*The Lion and the Mouse*	Jerry Pickney

THEMATIC UNIT
OUTLINE FOR
PRESCHOOLERS: BEARS

The purpose of a unit for three- and four-year-olds is to expand opportunities to use and acquire language. To do this, there should be an increased emphasis on stories with simple plots. Simple plots enable children to develop a sense of story while reinforcing their understanding of the power of language. Stories provide ideas for play. Children frequently re-create scenes from within the stories. Oral language skills grow rapidly during the early childhood years, and children may seek to retell parts of the stories. Encourage them to share some of their own background that is relevant to the story.

This thematic unit is adapted from one originally published in *Integrated Language Arts for Emerging Literacy* by Walter and Jean Sawyer, published by Delmar Learning, Clifton Park, NY, in 1991. The outline presented here includes objectives, activities, poems, songs, and parental activities related to the central theme of "bears." Although one objective is that children will learn information about bears from this unit, there are many more important language goals to be realized in the process.

Objectives

The purpose of the unit is to enable children to
- Develop an understanding of the concept of bears.

- Acquire information about kinds of bears (e.g., grizzly, teddy, polar) and where they might be found.
- Draw, write, or orally tell about a scene from a book about bears.
- Retell or re-create a concept or an idea from a story about bears.
- Function in a developmentally appropriate way as a part of a group being read a story.

Activities

To support the learning of children, adults might
- Lead a discussion about bears. Elicit information from the children to help them see that they already have some knowledge about bears. Possible ideas for the discussion include kinds of bears, homes, habits, hibernation, colors, and size.
- Help children engage in a creative dramatics activity based on the story of "Goldilocks and the Three Bears."
- Read aloud books related to bears on a regular basis during this period.
- Ask children to guess or predict what will happen at different points in the story.

- Count the number of different kinds of bears discovered in the books read.
- Make cookies in the shape of teddy bears. Eat the cookies at snack time.
- Use a snack recipe from the *Teddy Bears' Picnic Cookbook* (Darling and Day, 1991).
- Have children bring in their favorite teddy bear from home. Give the children an opportunity to talk about their bears at circle time.
- Engage children in a cooperative project (e.g., constructing a mobile or a chart) related to bears.

Books

Asch, Frank. (1988). *Happy birthday, moon*. New York: Prentice Hall.

Becker, Bonny. (2009). *A birthday for Bear*. Somerville, MA: Candlewick.

Bedford, David. (2001). *Big bears can*. Wilton, CT: Tiger Tales.

Bedford, David. (2009). *Little Bear's big sweater*. Intercourse, PA: Good Books.

Berenstain, Stan and Berenstain, Jan. (2005). *The Berenstain Bears and the messy room*. New York: Random House.

Berenstain, Stan and Berenstain, Jan. (1988). *The Berenstain Bears: ready, get set, go!* New York: Random House.

Carlstrom, Nancy W. (2005). *Jesse Bear, what will you wear?* New York: Aladdin.

Darling, Abigail and Day, Alexandra. (1991). *Teddy bears' picnic cookbook*. New York: Viking Penguin.

Dyer, Jane. (2003). *Little Brown Bear won't take a nap*. New York: Little Simon.

Freeman, Don. (1976). *Bearymore*. New York: Penguin.

Freeman, Don. (1968). *Corduroy*. New York: Viking.

George, Jean Craighead. (2009). *The last polar bear*. New York: Harper Collins.

Glen, Maggie. (1991). *Ruby*. New York: G. P. Putnam's Sons.

Gorbachev, Valeri. (2001). *Goldilocks and the three bears*. New York: North South.

Haseley, Dennis. (2002). *A story for bear*. Orlando, FL: Harcourt.

Hest, Amy. (2009). *When you meet a bear on Broadway*. New York: Farrar, Straus, and Giroux.

Ichikawa, Satomi. (2001). *The first bear in Africa*. New York: Philomel.

Kennedy, Jimmy. (2001). *The teddy bears' picnic*. Hauppauge, NY: Barron's Educational Series.

London, Jonathan. (2002). *Count the ways, little Brown Bear*. New York: Dutton.

Marshall, James. (1988). *Goldilocks and the three bears*. New York: Dial.

Martin, Bill, Jr. (1967). *Brown Bear, Brown Bear, what do you see?* New York: Holt, Rinehart, and Winston.

McCue, Lisa. (1987). *Corduroy on the go*. New York: Viking-Kestral.

McPhail, David. (2007). *The teddy bear*. New York: Henry Holt.

Minarik, Else H. (1957). *Little Bear*. New York: Harper and Row.

Murphy, Yannick. (2009). *Baby polar*. New York: Clarion.

Parenteau, Shirley. (2009). *Bears on chairs*. Somerville, MA: Candlewick.

Pinkwater, Daniel. (2006). *Bad bears in the city*. Boston: Houghton Mifflin.

Rosen, Michael. (2009). *Bear flies high*. New York: Bloomsbury.

Rosen, Michael. (2009). *We're going on a bear hunt (anniversary edition)*. New York: Margaret K. McElderry.

Ryder, Joanne. (2006). *Bear of my heart*. New York: Simon & Schuster.

Scarry, Richard. (2001). *Goodnight little bear*. New York: Golden.

Schoenherr, Ian. (2010). *Don't spill the beans*. New York: Greenwillow.

Scott, Evelyn. (2005). *The fourteen bears in summer and winter*.

Silsbe, Brenda. (2009). *The bears we know.* Toronto, Ontario: Annick.

Thomson, Sarah. (2010). *Where do polar bears live?* New York: Collins.

Waber, Bernard. (1997). *Bearsie Bear and the surprise sleepover party.* Boston: Houghton Mifflin.

Waddell, Martin. (2002). *Can't you sleep little bear?* Cambridge, MA: Candlewick.

Weight, Udo. (2003). *Bear's last journey.* New York: North South.

Wilson, Karma. (2008). *Bears feel scared.* New York: Margaret K. McElderry.

Wilson, Karma. (2004). *Bear wants more.* New York: Simon & Schuster.

Wright, Maureen. (2009). *Sleep, Big Bear, sleep.* Tarrytown, NY: Marshall Cavendish.

Yolen, Jane. (2006). *Baby bear's books.* Boston: Houghton Mifflin.

Poems

Alexander, Rosemary. (1999). "Bear Weather." In *Poetry place anthology.* New York: Scholastic.

Carlson, Nancy. (1990). *It's about time, Jesse Bear.* New York: Scholastic.

Chute, Marchette. (1986). "My teddy bear." In J. Prelutsky (Ed.), *Read aloud rhymes for the very young.* New York: Knopf.

Goldstein, Bobbye. (1989). *Bear in mind: A book of bear poems.* New York: Viking-Kestral.

Hillert, Margaret. (1986). "Teddy bear." In J. Prelutsky (Ed.), *Read aloud rhymes for the very young.* New York: Knopf.

Johnston, Tony. (1991). *Little Bear sleeping.* New York: G. P. Putnam's Sons.

Kredenser, Gail. (2000). "Polar Bear." In J. Prelutsky (Ed.), *The Random House book of poetry for children.* New York: Random House.

Martin, Bill, Jr. (1983). *Brown Bear, Brown Bear, what do you see?* New York: Henry Holt.

Prelutsky, Jack. (1986). "Grandma Bear." In *Ride a purple pelican.* New York: Greenwillow.

Scott, Steve. (1998). *Teddy Bear, Teddy Bear.* New York: HarperCollins.

Stewart, M. T. (2010). *If you ever; My teddy bear; If you like; Time for sleeping; When a bear;* and *Big brown bear.* Retrieved March 8, 2010, from http://www.edu.pe.ca/mtstewart/Grade1/Poems.htm.

Yolen, Jane and Dyer, Jane. (1995). *The Three Bears holiday rhyme book.* San Diego, CA: Harcourt.

Yolen, Jane. (1983). "Grandma Bear." In J. Prelutsky (Ed.), *The Random House book of poetry for children.* New York: Random House.

Songs

Bailey, Carolyn (2010). *Goldilocks and the three bears.* Retrieved March 8, 2010, from http://www.KIDiddles.com.

Brown, Margaret Wise. (2001). *Love songs of the Little Bear.* New York: Hyperion.

Charette, Rick. (1983). "Baxter the Bear." In *Where do my sneakers go at night?* (record). Windham, ME: Pine Point Records.

Fyleman, Rose. (2010). *Dancing bears.* Retrieved March 8, 2010, from http://www.KIDiddles.com.

Jenkins, John, & Robinson, Marty. (2000). *The teddy bears picnic.* Troy, NY: Dorian Recordings.

Nelson, Esther (1984). "The Bear Song" and "Fuzzy Wuzzy (Was a Bear)." In *The funny song book.* New York: Sterling.

Rosen, Bill, & Shontz, Gary. (1984). "One Shoe Bear" and "House at Pooh Corner." In *Rosenshontz: It's the truth* (record). Brattleboro, VT: RS Records.

Rosen, Bill, & Shontz, Gary. (1986). "Rock 'n Roll Teddy Bear." In *Rosenshontz: Rock n roll teddy bear* (record). Brattleboro, VT: RS Records.

Rosen, Bill, & Shontz, Gary. (1988). "Party Teddy Bears." In *Rosenshontz: Family vacation* (record). Brattleboro, VT: RS Records.

Roth, Kevin. (2006). *Unbearable bears.* Hollywood, FL: Stargazer Productions.

Trapani, Iza. (1999). *Row row row your boat.* Cambridge, MA: Charlesbridge.

Hands-on Activities

- "Bear String Block Printing"—Children create a block print in the shape of a bear. If string is used, thick, flexible string is best for younger children.
- Complete instructions are found in *Storybook Stew* by Suzanne Barchers and Peter Rauen, published in 1996 by Fulcrum Publishing, Golden, CO.
- "Teddy's Refrigerator Cookies"—A smaller group of children can make refrigerator cookies using this recipe. Plastic utensils should be used for slicing. The complete directions are available in the *Storybook Stew* publication.
- Go outdoors for a teddy bear picnic. If the weather permits, do it on October 25, Teddy Roosevelt's birthday.
- Provide flannel board objects (bears, house, trees, car, boat, etc.) and create stories using these objects.

Parent Activities

Teachers should

- Remind parents of the benefits of reading aloud books with bear characters and bear themes during this time.
- Encourage parents to reread, at home, the books that were read aloud at school.

- Suggest that parents listen to the child retell a story that was read in school.
- Help parents to locate a toy store in order to look at the teddy bears on display. Talk about the different teddy bears (e.g., colors, size, attractiveness, and similarities).
- Encourage parents to make up a story about a teddy bear and to come in to share that story.
- Suggest that the family visit a zoo to see live bears.
- Share the benefits of a visit to a library to take out books about bears.
- Share songs about bears and teddy bears.
- Ask parents to visit a museum to view an exhibit about bears.
- Encourage playing with teddy bears with the child. Talk about the play, and encourage the child to talk about what is happening.
- Suggest that families make cookies with a teddy bear cookie cutter.
- Share activities such as making a sculpture of a bear using clay or play dough.
- Suggest that parents invite other children to have a teddy bear picnic in the park. Bring bear-shaped cookies, juice, and teddy bears.

From *Integrated Language Arts for Emerging Literacy 1st edition* by Walter E. Sawyer and Jean C. Sawyer, 1993. Reprinted by permission of Delmar Learning, a division of Thomson Learning: www.thomsonrights. com. FAX 800 730-2215.

APPENDIX D

SUBJECT GROUPS AND MULTICULTURAL AUTHORS

The groupings of books in this section were selected because of their proven value with children. They are seen as truly exceptional pieces of literature containing important concepts and ideas that many young children will find motivating and interesting. The list does not contain every title found in this book. It is intended as a quick reference to be used on a regular basis as a starting point for locating high-quality books for children. Only the titles and authors are listed here. Full bibliographical information can be located using the author index and end-of-chapter references in this book.

Animals and Animal Characters

Clare Beaton, *There's a Cow in the Cabbage Patch*
Betty Birney, *Tyrannosaurus Tex*
Sara Burg, *One More Egg*
Eve Bunting, *Whales Passing*
Eric Carle, *The Grouchy Ladybug*
Eric Carle, *The Very Hungry Caterpillar*
Eileen Christelow, *The Great Pig Search*
Pamela Edwards, *Four Famished Foxes and Fosdyke*
Harvey Fierstein, *The Sissy Duckling*
Wanda Gag, *Millions of Cats*

Maggie Glen, *Ruby*
Sally Grindley, *Mucky Ducky*
Tad Hills, *Duck and Goose Find a Pumpkin*
Bob Kolar, *Stomp, Stomp*
Dorothy Kunhardt, *Pat the Bunny*
Marcus Pfister, *The Rainbow Fish*
Dav Pilkey, *The Dumb Bunnies*
Lila Prop, *Dinosaurs*
H. A. and Margaret Rey, *Curious George*
Lauren Thomson, *Little Quack's New Friend*
Sarah Weeks, *Without You*
David Wiesner, *The Three Pigs*
Margaret Wild, *The Pocket Dogs*

Basic Skills (ABC, Counting)

Keith Baker, *Quack and Count*
Keith Baker, *Potato Joe*
Michael Bond, *Paddington's 123*
Norman Bridwell, *Clifford's ABC*
Eric Carle, *1, 2, 3 to the Zoo*
Doyle Dodds, *The Shape of Things*
Ed Emberley, *First Words: Animals*
Michael Folsom and Mary Elting, *Q Is for Duck, An Alphabet Guessing Game*

Petr Horacek, *Strawberries Are Red*
Shirley Hughes, *Olly and M 1 2 3*
Mick Inkpen, *Kipper's A to Z*
Angela Johnson, *One of Three*
David Kirk, *Miss Spider's ABC*
Leo Lionni, *The Alphabet Tree*
Bill Martin, Jr. and John Archambault, *Chicka Chicka Boom Boom*
Sue McDonald, *Look Whooo's Counting?*
Patricia McKissack, *A Million Fish . . . More or Less*
Frances Minters, *Too Big, Too Small, Just Right*
Peter Pavey, *One Dragon's Dream: A Counting Book*
Andrew Plant, *Could a Dinosaur Play Tennis?*
Audrey Wood, *Alphabet Adventure*

Community

Suzanne Bloom, *The Bus for Us*
Eric Carle, *1, 2, 3 to the Zoo*
Katie Clark, *Grandma Drove the Garbage Truck*
Jan Dobbing, *Driving My Tractor*
Tibor Gergoly, *The Great Big Fire Engine Book*
Christopher Hart, *Police Puppies*
Joan Holub, *Apple Countdown*
Barbara Lehman, *Museum Trip*
Isaac Millman, *Moses Goes to a Concert*
Hui-Mei Pan, *What's in Grandma's Grocery Bag?*
Robert Munsch, *More Pies!*
Nick Sharratt, *Shark in the Park*

Disabilities

David Adler, *Helen Keller*
Maggie Glen, *Ruby*
Sharlee Glen, *Keeping Up with Roo*
Eveline Hasler, *A Tale of Two Brothers*
Ezra Jack Keats, *Apartment Three*
Robert Kraus, *Leo the Late Bloomer*
Gloria Lowell, *Elana's Ears*
Daniel Pinkwater, *Uncle Melvin*
Eileen Spinelli, *Sophie's Masterpiece: A Spider's Tale*
Eliza Woloson, *My Friend Isabelle*
Harriet Ziefert, *Squarehead*

Elderly Persons

Jim Arnosky, *Grandfather Buffalo*
Andrea Cheng, *The Lemon Sisters*
Andrea Cheng, *Grandfather Counts*
Tomie dePaola, *Nana Upstairs and Nana Downstairs*
Berlie Doherty, *Willa and Old Miss Annie*
Barbara Hicks, *Jitterbug Jam*
Gloria Houston, *My Great Aunt Arizona*
Oliver Jeffers, *The Heart and the Bottle*
Sebastian Lath, *Remembering Crystal*
Robert Munsch, *Love You Forever*
Eleanor Schick, *Mama*
Susan Vizurrga, *Miss Opal's Auction*
Harriet Ziefert, *Grandma, It's for You*

Family and Friends

Arnold Adoff, *Black Is Brown Is Tan*
Aliki, *We Are Best Friends*
Tom Birdseye, *Waiting for Baby*
Anne Bowen, *I Loved You Before You Were Born*
Anthony Browne, *Willy and Hugh*
Nancy Carlson, *My Best Friend Moved Away*
Carol Carrick, *Mothers Are Like That*
Peter Catalanotto, *The Painter*
Dorothy Corey, *Will There Be a Lap for Me?*
Lucy Cousins, *Za-za's Baby Brother*
Jennifer Eachurs, *I'm Sorry*
Claire Friedman, *When We're Together*
Susanna Hill, *Not Yet Rose*
Janet Holmes, *Me and You*
James Howe, *Houndsley and Catina and the Quiet Time*
Angela Johnson, *Joshua by the Sea*
Lynne Jonell, *Mom Pie*
Holly Keller, *Lizzy's Invitation*
Jonathan London, *Froggy's Baby Sister*
Diane Low, *Come Out and Play*
George Ella Lyon, *Mama Is a Miner*
Paul Maar, *Gloria the Cow*
James Marshall, *George and Martha*
Claire Masurel, *Two Homes*
Sally Mavor, *You and Me*

Sharon McCullough, *Bunbun, the Middle One*
Susan, Meyers, *Everywhere Babies*
Susan Middleton, *Adios*
Else Holmelund Minarik, *Little Bear's Friend*
Lisa Moser, *Kisses on the Wind*
Audrey Penn, *A Pocketful of Kisses*
Dav Pilkey, *A Friend for Dragon*
Robin Pulver, *Never Say Boo*
Peter Reynolds, *Ish*
Justin Richardson, *And Tango Makes Three*
Eric Rohmann, *My Friend Rabbit*
Chris Soentpiet, *Around Town*
Susan Steggall, *Rattle and Rap*
Frances Thomas, *One Day, Daddy*

Fears and Concerns

Caroline Binch, *The Princess and the Castle* (fear of water)
Sarah Brannen, *Uncle Bobby's Wedding*
Marc Brown, *Arthur Goes to Camp* (imaginary fears)
Nancy Garden, *Molly's Family* (same sex parents)
Linda Garner, *Some Secrets Hurt*
Valeri Gorbachev, *Chicken Chickens*
Libby Hathorn, *Grandma's Shoes* (death of a grandparent)
Judy Hindley, *The Perfect Little Monster*
Hazel Hutchins, *One Dark Night*
Kate Klise, *Little Rabbit and the Night Mare*
Sabine Kraushaar, *Say Ahh!*
Janice Keefer, *Anna's Goat* (poverty/homelessness)
Virginia Kroll, *Faraway Drums* (moving)
Joe Kulka, *Wolf's Coming*
Kate Lied, *Potato* (poverty, homelessness)
Jonathan London, *Gray Fox* (illness)
Sheila MacGill-Callahan, *And Still the Turtle Watched* (pollution)
Teresa and Whitney Martin, *Big Ernie's New Home*
Leslea Newman, *Too Far Away to Touch* (HIV/AIDS)
Shulamith Oppenheim, *The Lily Cupboard* (prejudice)
Audrey Penn, *Chester Raccoon and the Acorn Full of Memories*
Jean Reagan, *Always My Brother*
Marasabina Russo, *A Very Big Bunny*

Barbara Santucci, *Loon Summer*
Dr. Seuss, *The Butter Battle Book* (war)
Carol Shuman, *Jenny Is Scared! When Sad Things Happen in the World*
David Stein, *Pouch!*
Pat Thomas, *I Miss You* (death of a pet)
Yukio Tsuchiya, *Faithful Elephants* (war)
Judith Viorst, *Mama Says There Aren't Any Zombies, Ghosts, Vampires, Creatures, Demons, Monsters, Fiends, Goblins, or Things* (monsters)
Judith Viorst, *The Tenth Good Thing about Barney* (death)
Bernard Waber, *Ira Sleeps Over* (sleeping at a friend's house)
Elizabeth Winthrop, *As the Crow Flies* (divorce/separation)

Holidays and Seasons

Arnold Adoff, *In for Winter, Out for Spring*
Stan and Jan Berenstain, *Comic Valentine*
Jan Carr, *Splish, Splash, Spring*
Seymour Chwasti, *Had Gadya*
Lucy Cousins, *Happy Easter Maisy*
Lloyd Douglas, *Let's Get Ready for Martin Luther King Jr. Day*
Ellen Emerman, *Is It Shabbos Yet?*
Douglas Florian, *Winter Eyes*
Kim Lewis, *First Snow*
Robert Maass, *When Winter Comes*
Bill Martin, Jr., *Old Devil Wind* (Halloween)
Marcus Pfister, *The Christmas Star*
Bethany Roberts, *Thanksgiving Mice*
Phyllis Root, *Grandmother Winter*
Ben Schecter, *When Will the Snow Trees Grow?*
Eileen Spinelli, *Summerbath Winterbath*
Eileen Spinelli, *Thanksgiving at the Tappletons*
Mark Todd, *What Will You Be for Halloween?*
Martin Waddell, *Little Mo* (winter)
Brenda Williams, *Lin Yi's Lantern: A Moon Festival Tale*
Jonny Zucker, *Fasting and Dates: A Ramadan and Eid-ul-Fitr Story*

Multicultural

Eve Bunting, *Jin Woo*
Yangsook Choi, *The Name Jar*
Debbie Chocolate, *The Piano Man*
Susan Elya, *Bebe Goes to the Beach*
Susan Elya, *F Is for Fiesta*
Mem Fox, *Ten Little Fingers and Ten Little Toes*
Nick Giovanni, *Rosa*
Barbara Goldin, *A Mountain of Blintzes*
Sheila Hamanaka, *All the Colors of the Earth*
Yumi Heo, *One Afternoon*
Angela Johnson, *Daddy Calls Me Man*
Angela Johnson, *Joshua by the Sea*
Tony Johnston, *My Abuelita*
Norman Juster, *The Hello, Goodbye Window*
Verla Kay, *Broken Feather*
Ezra Jack Keats, *The Snowy Day*
Grace Lin, *Dim Sum for Everyone*
Maurice Manning, *Kitchen Dance*
Isabel Monk, *Family*
Ann Morris, *Houses and Homes*
Toni Morrison and Slade Morrison, *Peeny Butter Fudge*
John Muth, *Zen Shorts*
Chris Raschka, *Yo! Yes?*
Maxine Rosenberg, *Brothers and Sisters*
Shelley Rotner, *Shades of People*
Judy Sierra, *Silly and Sillier*
Catherine Stock, *Where Are You Going, Manyoni?*
Truong Tran, *Going Home, Coming Home*
Jeanette Winter, *My Baby*
Paula Young, *Child of the Civil Rights Movement*

Nature and Science

Adam Butler, *Those Darn Squirrels*
John Butler, *Bed time in the Jungle*
Catherine Chambers, *Flood*
Elisha Cooper, *Beach*
Mark Darling, *Can I See My House from Space*
Douglas Florian, *Handsprings*
Gail Gibbons, *Tornadoes*
Thacher Hurd, *Bad Frogs*
Peter Linenthal, *Look at the Animals*

Jonathan London, *Sun Dance, Water Dance*
David Macaulay, *The Way Things Work*
Tina Matthews, *Out of the Egg*
Megan McDonald, *Reptiles Are My Life*
Kim Parker, *Counting in the Garden*
Komako Sakai, *Emily's Balloon*
Joyce Sidman, *Song of the Water Boatman and Other Pond Poems*
Joyce Sidman, *Butterfly Eyes and Other Secrets of the Meadow*
Jennifer Ward, *The Busy Tree*
Maureen Wright, *Sleep, Big Bear, Sleep*
Charlotte Zolotow, *The Seashore Book*

Self-Esteem

Kathi Appelt, *Incredible Me*
Cari Best, *Shrinking Violet*
Kimberly Bradley, *Ballerina Nate*
David Costello, *I Can Help*
Kurt Cyrus, *Tadpole Rex*
Tomie dePaola, *Oliver Button Is a Sissy*
Joyce Dunbar, *Tell Me What It's Like to Be Big*
Ruth Galloway, *Clumsy Crab*
Helen Lester, *Three Cheers for Tacky*
Libba Moore Gray, *Fenton's Leap*
Holly Keller, *Lizzy's Invitation*
Lisa McCue, *Quiet Bunny*
Margaret Miller, *Now I'm Big*
Watty Piper, *The Little Engine That Could*
Peter Reynolds, *The Dot*
Elizabeth Winthrop, *Dumpy LaRue*
Jane Yolen, *Sleeping Ugly*

Multicultural Authors

As the world's people migrate and choose new places to live, the opportunities for children to learn about other cultures expand. The authors listed here are some of those who write children's picture books. Sometimes their stories use the culture as a part of the story. At other times, they simply share a good tale that just happens to be set in a different cultural setting or told from a different cultural perspective.

African American Children's Authors

Colin Bootman
Gwendolyn Brooks
Ashley Bryan
Debbi Chocolate
Lucille Clifton
Floyd Cooper
Donald Crews
Pat Cummings
Leo Dillon
Elizabeth Howard
Nicki Giovanni
Eloise Greenfield
Virginia Hamilton
Elizabeth Howard
Angela Johnson
Ezra Jack Keats
Patricia McKissack
Angela Medearis
Isabell Monk
Toni Morrison
Isaac Olaleye
Ifeoma Onyefulu
Andrea Pinkney
Brian Pinkney
Jerry Pinkney
James Ransome
John Steptoe
Mildred Taylor

Hispanic American Children's Authors

Alma Ada
Francisco Alarcon
Linda Altman
Pura Belpre
Carlos Castaneda
Lulu Delacre
Arthur Dorros
Juanita Havil
Alejandro Martinez
Pat Mora

Amada Perez
Enrique Sanchez
Gary Soto

Asian/Pacific American Children's Authors

Andrea Chang
Sook Nyul Choi
Yangsook Choi
Grace Lin
Junko Morimoto
Koko Nishizuka
Soyung Pak
Linda Sue Park
Komako Sakai
Allen Say
Yin Sontpiet
Truong Tran
Yoshiko Uchida
Janet Wong
Gene Luen Yang
Taro Yashima
Laurence Yep
Ed Young

Native American Children's Authors

Joseph Bruchac
Louise Erdich
Joy Harjo
Kathleen Lacapa
Michael Lacapa
Scott Momaday
Esther Sanderson
Allen Sockabasin
Cynthia Leitich Smith
Donald Soctoman
Dovie Thomason
Jan Waboose
Bernelda Wheeler

AUTHOR INDEX

SUBJECT INDEX

A

ABC books, 48–51, 125
    activities for, 127–128
    selecting, 126
Alphabet books, 48–51, 125–128
    activities for, 127–128
    selecting, 126
Alphabetic principles, 19, 125–128
Anti-bias factors, 100–103
Arts, 231, 246
Attending, 152
Attitudes, 7–10
Audio-visual materials, 299–303
    selection criteria for, 300–301
    using, 301–303
Authors, 23–24, 210–216, 352–353
    children as, 210
    classroom books by child, 214–216
    interview of, 212–213
Awards, 141–142

B

Banned books, 87–89
Basic concepts, 123–128, 231–232, 245–246, 349–350
    alphabet, 125–128

counting, 124–125
    units, 245–246
Bias in stories, 100–103
Bibliotherapy, 259–284
    benefits of, 262–265
    books for use in, 260–261, 267, 271–281
    definition of, 259
    developmental ap266propriateness and,
    didacticism and , 260–261
    empathy and, 263–264
    ill children and, 261–262
    information through, 263
    mutuality and, 263
    options discovered through, 264–265
    reaffirmation of life related to, 265
    strategies used in, 267
    understanding and, 259–262
    using, 265–270
Big books, 16, 62
Books, 58–61, 73–103, 111–143, 238–252
    alphabet, 125–128
    child created, 214–216
    choosing, 59–61, 73–74, 180–183, 193–195, 198–200,
        203–205, 207–210
    concept, 123–128, 245–246, 349–350
    controversial, 101, 275